Explore Australia Publishing Pty Ltd
85 High Street
Prahran, Victoria 3181, Australia

Published by Explore Australia Publishing Pty Ltd in association with Australian Geographic Pty Ltd, 2004

ISBN 1 74117 055 9

Printed and bound in China by
SNP Leefung

Publisher's Note: Every effort has been made to ensure that the information in this book is accurate at the time of going to press. The publisher welcomes information and suggestions for correction or improvement. Write to the Publications Manager, Explore Australia Publishing, 85 High Street, Prahran 3181, Australia, or email explore@hardiegrant.com.au

Disclaimers: The publisher cannot accept responsibility for any errors or omissions. The representation on the maps of any road or track is not necessarily evidence of public right of way.

contents

How to Use this Book

*Explore Australia's Coast features activity and attraction highlights,
a state-by-state guide to coastal destinations and a section on safety.*

**BEST OF THE
COAST**

A series of double-page spreads introduce coastal highlights.

A list of the best places to go to experience a particular activity or attraction.

WHERE TO GO

State introduction

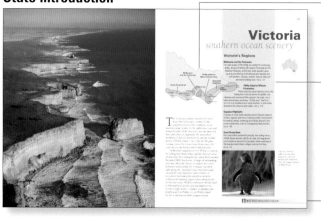

Each state has a map with regions marked.

Each state has a summary of the regions, with page references.

State visitor information contact details for easy reference.

Region introduction

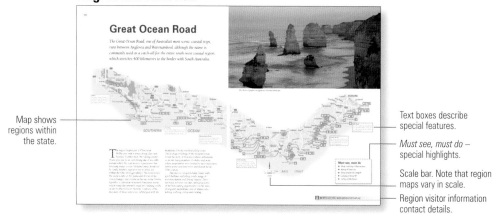

Map shows regions within the state.

Text boxes describe special features.

Must see, must do – special highlights.

Scale bar. Note that region maps vary in scale.

Region visitor information contact details.

MAP SYMBOLS

M20 ⬡**5**	Freeway or motorway with route marker
A1 **1**	Highway with route marker
B140 **11**	Secondary road with route marker
	Minor road
	Vehicle track
	Walking track
	Ferry
◄—— 46 ——►	Distance in kilometres
GEELONG ○	Major city
FOOTSCRAY	Suburb
Cranbourne ○	Major town
Ventnor ○	Small town
Popes Eye Beacon ●	Point of interest
Mt Liptrap + 171	Mountain or hill with height in metres
✈	Airport
Nullarbor Roadhouse ⊞	Roadhouse
Cape Otway Lighthouse ★	Lighthouse
	State border
	River
	Lake

▢	National park, state park, nature reserve, coastal park
▢	Marine park
▢	Built-up area
▢	Aboriginal land
▢	Prohibited area

Information		Horseriding
Patrolled beaches		Camel treks
Sailing		Shipwreck
Kayaking		Lookout
Surfing		Lighthouse
Diving		Camping
Snorkelling		Wildlife
Walking		Penguins
Whales		Marine stingers
Dolphins		Crocodiles
Seals		Turtles
Coastal birds		Sharks
Fishing		Dugongs

Region

Fact File contains top coastal events, climate charts, regulations and safety information.

Contacts box lists visitor information centres, national park offices and other useful information, with phone numbers and websites.

Specialist maps

Special features have a detailed map of an area with additional information on walking tracks and local features.

TAKING CARE

This section contains advice on coastal safety. Additional information on conservation and marine and national parks. A list of useful contacts is included.

INDEX

Extensive index includes all town names in the text, wildlife and coastal activities.

Edge of Paradise
our magnificent coast

The Australian coast, which forms the border of the world's only island continent, is incredibly diverse, environmentally rich, culturally significant and stunningly beautiful in all its parts.

The coastline stretches 35 877 kilometres. Offshore lie 8500 territorial islands, which, when included in the total, bring the length of the Australian coastline to an impressive 60 000 kilometres. What we refer to so simply as 'the coast' incorporates 10 000 mainland beaches and countless coves, inlets, points, peninsulas, estuary openings, harbours, reefs and rock shelves. It includes the sultry mangrove inlets of the far north; the palm-fringed islands of the tropics; the iconically 'Australian' foreshores of the Pacific, with their rolling waves, yellow sands and balmy climes; the wave-battered cliffs fronting the Southern Ocean; and the blue–green water and white-sand coves of the Indian Ocean.

The coast's great beauty competes with – but never overshadows – an extraordinarily rich ecology. On the Great Barrier Reef alone, 1500 species of fish dart across cities of brilliant coral; in the south, huge colonies of plump seals haul-out on rocky islands; and in the west, the world's largest fish cruises the shallows, unfazed by the small bands of curious divers that occasionally drift by.

Beyond its exquisite beauty and natural wonder, the coast is a place of great cultural significance. The bush and outback may be the source of many a myth, but it is the coast that overwhelmingly dominates contemporary life and thought. With the exception of Canberra, all of Australia's capital cities are located on the coast. The bulk of the Australian population, around 95 percent, live within an hour's drive of a beach. Australians holiday on the coast, retire there and engage in fantasies about dropping out of mainstream society and leading a simpler life in Byron Bay, Broadbeach or Barwon Heads. The rest of the world understands what it is to be Australian through the images of beaches that appear in television soaps and films and, enticingly, on travel posters; ask a non-Australian to describe the nation and the phrase 'sun, surf and sand' will figure prominently. For many, the Australian coastline is as much a state of mind as it is a location.

For the holiday-maker, the coastline is a vast and limitless pleasure ground. It caters to every level of fitness, interest, ability, budget and inclination. It offers every possible kind of holiday experience, from a sojourn at an international-style resort, to a week in a tent in a national park campground. It is for children, couples, singles and the elderly. Overseas visitors take to it passionately; locals spend their lives in a constant state of gravitational pull towards it, knowing that for however long they live and far they travel, there will always be another beach to explore, another dune to clamber across, another headland to stand upon.

Land meets sea on the Nullarbor

Best of the Coast

activities and experiences

Best Beaches

from city to outback

Australia is blessed with thousands of magnificent beaches, from suburban pleasure grounds to unspoilt gems in remote locations.

Above The blue waters of Esperance
Opposite Enjoying the waves at famous Bondi Beach
Previous pages Green Island, Great Barrier Reef

Australia's 10 000 or so beaches are among the country's greatest natural resources. They provide extraordinary scenery, and a place to walk and watch, to sunbake and socialise, to marvel at the marine wildlife and to engage in endless sporting endeavours, from swimming and surfing to the ubiquitous beach cricket. Some of our most exquisite beaches are also the least visited, found in remote regions of the country.

Most Australians have a favourite beach, but what makes one beach better than another is strictly a matter of taste. Some like their beaches long and lonely; others prefer teams of lifesavers, foreshore cafes and bustling promenades. The clear aquamarine waters and pure white sands of tropical beaches appeal to many; but for others, the ideal beach embraces the drama of high-energy waves, scudding clouds and weather constantly on the move, features typical of the Southern Ocean coast. The beachgoer's preferred activity also affects the choice: surfers need waves, anglers want rock platforms, walkers like cliff-tops and views, divers look for coral or wrecks or caves, families seek beach patrols and mild currents.

Where to find the best beach

The best beach is as likely to be the cove in a tiny village or an isolated national park as it is the sandy swath fronting a resort of international fame – here are a few favourites.

Whitehaven Beach, Qld
Powdery white sand, clear tropical waters and pristine surrounds make this a perfect example of an Australian tropical island beach – no surf but superb swimming. See *Great Barrier Reef*, p. 50

Bondi Beach, NSW
Australia's most famous beach lies near the heart of the country's biggest city. Constant surf patrols, paved promenades, rock pools, good surf and a lovely, deep crescent shape are among the attractions. See *Sydney and Surrounds*, p. 80

Port Fairy Beach, Vic
A perfect holiday-town beach: in summer there is a bustle of patrols, body surfers, paddling toddlers and beach tents; in winter, surfers, anglers and well-wrapped walkers dot the quiet 6 km stretch. See *Great Ocean Road*, p. 144

Wineglass Bay, Tas
Within Freycinet NP and accessible only to walkers and boaters, this beach is a perfectly formed crescent of sand and water set within a frame of forested mountains. See *The East and North-East*, p. 164

Vivonne Bay, SA
This remote stretch on Kangaroo Island exemplifies the drama of the Southern Ocean coastline: it has rugged headlands, plentiful wildlife, big strong waves,

and it remains free of development. See *Fleurieu Peninsula and Kangaroo Island*, p. 188

Esperance Beaches, WA
Breathtakingly beautiful and completely unspoilt, these beaches of remote south-east Western Australia are known for the intensity of the contrast between the crisp white sand and vivid blue water. See *Esperance and the Nullarbor*, p. 226

Cable Beach, WA
A beach of both the tropics and the outback, Cable borders the remote resort of Broome. Camel trains, pearl luggers bobbing on the horizon and striped beach umbrellas complement the superb natural scenery. See *Broome and Kimberley Coast*, p. 240

World Heritage Areas
rare coastal treasures

Australia's coastal World Heritage areas acknowledge the natural and cultural significance of our littoral landscapes and our remarkably rich and diverse marine environments.

Australia has 15 World Heritage areas, eight of which are to be found on or near the coastline. The list includes the world's largest living form, the Great Barrier Reef; Shark Bay, site of one of the world's largest concentrations of sea mammals; several islands where isolation has helped protect ecosystems of inestimable scientific value; and pristine coastal forests preserving examples of life in its most ancient form.

UNESCO adopted the World Heritage Convention in 1972. Australia's first site to be listed was the Great Barrier Reef, in 1981, with other areas listed progressively since then. Inclusion on the list is a mark of world recognition of the natural and/or cultural value of the nominated area, and a commitment to ensuring its ongoing preservation and protection for generations to come.

Some World Heritage areas are major visitor destinations, including the Great Barrier Reef, the Wet Tropics of Queensland and Lord Howe Island. Others are more remote, but still attract a steady band of sightseers. Then there are a small group of places, principally the subantarctic Heard and McDonald islands and Macquarie Island, which are – for the time being – the preserve of scientists, the occasional sailor and handfuls of adventure tourists. Regardless of the location, visitors to World Heritage areas will get the opportunity to experience some of the richest and most unusual coastal sites on earth.

Left *Macquarie Island*
Opposite *Lord Howe Island*
Following pages *Great Barrier Reef*

Where to visit World Heritage areas

Fraser Island, Qld
This is the largest sand island in the world. Forty dune lakes lie cradled within huge sand dunes, and a 75 km surf beach edges the east coast. See *Sunshine Coast to Fraser Island*, p. 42

Great Barrier Reef, Qld
The reef stretches 2300 km and is one of the richest, most complex ecosystems in the world. It is also known for the sublime tropical beauty of its many islands. See *Great Barrier Reef*, p. 50

Wet Tropics, Qld
The rainforest here contains a near-complete record of the major stages of plant evolution. Running alongside the Great

Barrier Reef, this is the only place on earth where two World Heritage areas meet. See *Cairns, Cape York and the Gulf*, p. 68

Lord Howe Island, east of NSW
A subtropical island valued for its volcanic landscapes, large number of endemic plant and animal species and a rare, primordial beauty. See *Lord Howe Island*, p. 106

Tasmanian Wilderness
Much of this pristine wilderness, with its ancient trees, extends deep into the state's interior; its coastal regions can be explored on foot. See *Hobart and the South*, p. 158

Macquarie Island, south-east of Tas
Unique geological features, huge gatherings of penguins and a cold, bare beauty attract adventure travellers, who join a shifting population of scientists and conservation workers. See *Hobart and the South*, p. 158

Shark Bay, WA
Stunningly beautiful, Shark Bay is home to rare dugongs, whale sharks and dolphins. Boulder-like stromatolites represent the oldest form of life on earth and extensive seagrass meadows thrive. See *Shark Bay and Outback Coast*, p. 232

Islands

the continent's fringe

An astonishing 8200 islands, ranging from mere slivers of rock to the island state of Tasmania, are scattered throughout Australia's extensive territorial waters.

The island continent – the epithet so often given to Australia – conjures images of a solitary landmass in a vast expanse of ocean. In fact, Australia is fringed by islands, though some are tiny and most are unpopulated. These islands include bleak rocky outcrops, coral cays built up of coral and debris, and the world's largest sand island, the fascinating Fraser Island. Islands are often important habitats for sea creatures, including migratory birds, nesting sea turtles, penguins and seals. Some are national park protected and make ideal destinations for anglers, sailors, divers and wildlife-watchers. Some tropical islands, particularly those of the Great Barrier Reef, offer holiday resorts or idyllic camping, perfect beaches, balmy weather and the opportunity to explore thriving marine life in the surrounding warm waters. Islands of the southern climes, such as the Bass Strait islands and Kangaroo Island, might mix wild, scenery with tight-knit communities, shipwreck sites and abundant wildlife.

While most islands fall within the country's 200 km Economic Exclusion Zone, some, such as the tropical Cocos and the subantarctic Heard and McDonald islands, are external territories, lying thousands of kilometres away. Christmas and the Cocos, both Indian Ocean islands, and Norfolk and Lord Howe, Pacific Ocean islands, have various forms of self-government, although their populations retain Australian citizenship.

Opposite Cocos Islands
Below Flinders Island,
Bass Strait

Where to island hop

Moreton Bay Islands, Qld

Some 350 islands fringe the calm expanse of Moreton Bay on the Brisbane coastline; with their swaths of national park they remain largely unspoilt; a handful of them have good holiday facilities. See *Brisbane and Gold Coast*, p. 34

Great Barrier Reef Islands, Qld

The reef has around 900 islands, of which some 22 offer holiday facilities ranging from resort accommodation to national park campsites. See *Great Barrier Reef*, p. 50

Bass Strait Islands, Tas

Buffeted by wild southern weather, King and Flinders islands are for outdoor adventurers, maritime enthusiasts and lovers of unspoilt scenery. See *The East and North-East*, p. 164 and *The West and North-West*, p. 174

Rottnest Island, WA

Tiny Rottnest Island, just offshore from Perth, is a peaceful retreat for mainlanders, with its clear water, sandy coves, rich heritage sites – on land and underwater – and relaxed, easy going environment. See *Perth to Geraldton*, p. 210

Cocos (Keeling) Islands, west of WA

These 27 tropical coral islands form Australia's most westerly external territory. Fishing, diving, walking and wildlife-watching in this truly unspoilt environment are among the attractions. See *Broome and Kimberley Coast*, p. 240

Tiwi Islands, NT

Bathurst and Melville islands (the Tiwi Islands), lying 80 km off the Darwin coast, are the home of the Tiwi people. Short tours operate from Darwin; visitors can experience the rich local culture and explore the beautiful landscapes. See *Darwin and Cobourg Peninsula*, p. 250

Walking and Camping
the coast up close

National parks protect the coastline but also make it accessible to those seeking an intimate experience of our most beautiful places.

Above Walkers take a rest on Hinchinbrook Island Opposite View south from Mt Oberon, Wilsons Promontory

One of the most impressive aspects of Australia's coast is its diversity and by far the best way to experience this is up close. A wealth of national parks, the small population and generally benign – often magnificent – weather mean there are a multitude of places to walk in peace, to camp in comfort and to enjoy the coastline's many and varied treasures.

In Queensland, for example, Hinchinbrook Island's Thorsborne Trail traverses mangrove-lined creeks, crystal-clear streams and dazzling white beaches, with a backdrop of rainforest. In New South Wales' Ben Boyd National Park, walkers can watch for whales as they tour the coast. Tasmania's Freycinet Peninsula offers spellbinding views,

deserted beaches and fragrant silver peppermint gums. Birdwatchers in particular enjoy South Australia's Coorong, where long stretches of marshy sands and water attract masses of birdlife. Western Australia has remote parks with pristine coastline.

The level and length of the walks vary enormously. Experienced walkers might tackle walks such as the 100 km wilderness trek through Victoria's Croajingolong National Park. For others, there are hundreds of short walks introducing visitors to the sights of a particular area. Always check with parks regarding entry and camping fees and bushwalking guidelines (see *Taking Care*, p. 260), and remember: tread lightly, leave nothing but footprints, take nothing but photos.

Where to walk and camp

Hinchinbrook Island, Qld
The challenging 32 km Thorsborne Trail along the east coast is considered one of the world's great wilderness walks. Permits are limited — book well ahead. See *Great Barrier Reef*, p. 50

Ben Boyd NP, NSW
The 30 km Light to Light Walk links the state's most southerly lighthouse and a historic whale-watching tower. Plentiful birdlife, panoramic views and heathland and eucalypt forest are among the attractions. See *South Coast*, p. 90

Wilsons Promontory, Vic
A ranger-led, 2–3 day return trek to the mainland's most southerly tip explores the Prom's wild beauty. Walkers can stay in the lighthouse keeper's quarters. Bookings are essential. See *Phillip Island to Wilsons Promontory*, p. 130

South Coast, Tas
This 85-km, 6–8 day trek makes the ruggedly beautiful World Heritage-listed coastline of the Southwest NP accessible to fit, experienced walkers; seek advice from park staff. See *Hobart and the South*, p. 158

Freycinet Peninsula, Tas
In a state renowned for its world-class walks, this is one of the finest, with spectacular views, deserted beaches, magnificent gums and rich native heathlands. See *The East and North-East*, p. 164

Innes NP, SA
A range of trails within this 9000 ha park enable walkers to experience towering granite coastal cliffs, undulating terrain and some exceptional bird-watching. See *Adelaide and Yorke Peninsula*, p. 182

Kalbarri NP, WA
Dramatic landscape, prolific birdlife and a startling profusion of wildflowers, May–Nov, make this coastal park a favourite with bushwalkers. See *Shark Bay and Outback Coast*, p. 232

Marine Wildlife
birds, fish, reptiles, invertebrates

Australia's marine wildlife is plentiful, varied and fascinating. It is a unique world, with seabirds, rare corals, sharks and manta rays converging in and around the continent's vast oceans.

Around 4200 species of marine fish occupy Australian waters. Some, such as clown fish, are known for their tropical brilliance; others, such as rare sea dragons, for their bizarre shapes; and still others, such as sharks, for their predatory nature. Invertebrates – corals, sponges, sea urchins and many more – create the magical world of the Great Barrier Reef, though many species can be found wallpapering the underwater architecture of caves and tunnels right around the coast, particularly in the far south. Marine reptile species include the six species of turtles that nest and feed along northern shores, around 20 species of sea snakes and the dangerous saltwater crocodiles or 'salties' that inhabit northern Australia's estuaries and coastal waters.

Birds are an intrinsic part of Australia's coastal life, from the oystercatchers and herons of beaches and rocky shores to the shearwaters and gannets of the high seas. About 80 species of seabird migrate annually to Australia's coastline. Little penguins, blue-hued and growing 30 to 40 cm high, can be seen nesting in parts of southern Australia. Magnificent white-breasted sea eagles soar gracefully across the coastal skies, and gulls – the most prominent member of which is the ubiquitous picnic-raider, the silver gull – are a familiar sight along the shores.

Above Flatback turtle hatchlings off the Darwin coast
Opposite A white-breasted sea eagle takes flight

Where to see marine wildlife

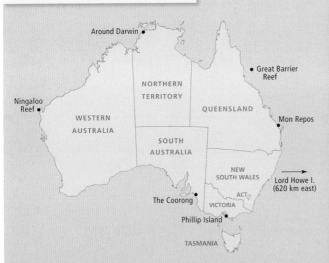

Great Barrier Reef, Qld
The reef shelters 1500 species of fish, over 200 bird species, more than 500 types of mollusc and all six species of marine turtles that frequent Australian waters. See *Great Barrier Reef*, p. 50

Mon Repos, Qld
Australia's most accessible turtle-viewing site lies north of Bundaberg. Marine turtles (mostly loggerhead and green turtles) lay eggs in the sand Nov–Jan; supervised viewing takes place in season. See *Capricorn and the Mid Tropics*, p. 62

Lord Howe Island, east of NSW
Hundreds of thousands of seabirds nest on and around Lord Howe Island. The world's most southern tropical reef is found here, as well as 98 species of coral, a variety of reef fish and marine turtles. See *Lord Howe Island*, p. 106

Phillip Island, Vic
Each evening, hordes of little penguins totter from the water's edge to their beach burrows, heading home after a day's fishing. Visitors can watch the spectacle from special viewing areas. See *Phillip Island to Wilsons Promontory*, p. 130

The Coorong, SA
This chain of dunes and saltwater lakes is an internationally recognised habitat for birdlife, including Northern Hemisphere migratory birds, seabirds, waders, Cape Barren geese and endangered Australian species. The area is wild and remote: suitable for campers, walkers and 4WD adventurers. See *The Coorong and Limestone Coast*, p. 196

Ningaloo Reef, WA
The world's largest fish, the whale shark, is a big attraction in these pristine waters, but sea turtles, dugongs, 500 species of fish and 220 species of coral compete for visitors' attention. See *Shark Bay and Outback Coast*, p. 232

Around Darwin, NT
Seabirds, turtles and saltwater crocodiles inhabit the rivers, mangrove swamps and beaches of one of Australia's least traversed coastal regions. Visit one of the wildlife centres near the capital to see crocs – safely – up close, or take a cruise across the flood plains and be amazed at the sheer number and variety of birds. See *Darwin and Cobourg Peninsula*, p. 250

Marine Mammals
whales, seals, dolphins, dugongs

Sea mammals thrive along remote and well-conserved stretches of coast, providing extraordinary wildlife-watching opportunities.

Whales, at one time slaughtered for their blubber, are now prized for their magnificence and natural wonder. The two most common species in Australian waters are humpback and southern right whales. Humpbacks, known for their crowd-pleasing acrobatic displays, migrate north along Australia's east and west coasts during autumn, returning via the same route in spring; southern rights establish nurseries along the Southern Ocean coast during the winter months.

Around 35 species of dolphin have been identified in Australian waters. Frequenting most parts of the coast, they engage humans with displays of gregariousness and curiosity: they cruise alongside boats, catch waves with surfers, and swim in to be handfed in shallow water. Awkward on land, but remarkably graceful in the water, Australian sea lions and New Zealand fur seals haul-out on the islands and rocky shorelines of the south. Dugongs are more retiring, living in tropical and subtropical waters, feeding on fields of seagrass and emerging only to breathe. They swim in large herds and can be spotted in shallow waters, particularly in calm weather.

Where to see marine mammals

Hervey Bay, Qld
Hundreds of migrating whales visit Hervey Bay, Aug–Oct, on the return leg of their annual migration from the Antarctic to the tropics. An early morning whale cruise provides the best viewing opportunity. See *Sunshine Coast to Fraser Island*, p. 42

South Coast, NSW
The rocky shores of Montague Island are a major haul-out site for Australian fur seals, with numbers peaking Aug–Oct, while whales and dolphins are drawn to the clean, nutrient-rich waters of the general area. See *South Coast*, p. 90

Warrnambool, Vic
Most years, from winter into spring, female southern right whales come to the town's Logans Beach to calve and then nurse their young. Viewing platforms above the beach provide a lookout. See *Great Ocean Road*, p. 144

Eyre Peninsula and the Nullarbor, SA
A large sea lion colony lies near Baird Bay, on Eyre Peninsula's west coast. The mighty Nullarbor cliffs provide a perfect vantage point for viewing nursing southern right whales, sometimes as many as 100 during the winter months. See *Eyre Peninsula and the Nullarbor*, p. 200

Kangaroo Island, SA
Seal Bay is home to around 500 Australian sea lions, while around 6000 fur seals live and breed around Cape du Couedic in Flinders Chase NP. See *Fleurieu Peninsula and Kangaroo Island*, p. 188

Monkey Mia, WA
Ten thousand dugongs (10 percent of the world's population) live here and humpback whales swim by, but top billing goes to the 400 or so resident dolphins, some of which swim into shore daily to be handfed. See *Shark Bay and Outback Coast*, p. 232

Lighthouses
beacons of hope

Australia has over 500 lighthouses. Many attract visitors with tours, museum displays and holiday accommodation.

Above *Cape Nelson,
near Portland*
Opposite *Cape du Couedic,
Kangaroo Island*

For Australia's European settlers in the days of sailing ships, lighthouses on the treacherous coastline were truly beacons of hope. Then, as now, they stood tall on soaring cliffs and barren outposts, tropical islands and wind-blown southern refuges. No longer manned, they still symbolise the safety of the shore, the dedication of the lighthouse keepers and the romance of the past.

The country's first recorded 'lighthouse', a wood-fired beacon lit in 1793 on Sydney's South Head and watched over by convicts, began a proud tradition. Since those early days, whale-oil burners have been replaced by electricity and even solar power and automated lights have finally replaced all manned stations. The keeper's role was to keep the lights burning, though maintaining the equipment, rescuing survivors from shipwrecks and reporting on the weather were other duties in these isolated but strategic locations. Lighthouse keepers and their families often lived in isolation for long periods, their only contact being with those who delivered essential supplies every few months or so. Although all working lighthouses are now automated – the last, Maatsuyker Island Lighthouse, 10 km off Tasmania's south coast, was automated in 1996 – a number of stations have permanent caretakers.

Where to view lighthouses

Macquarie Lighthouse, NSW

Convict architect Francis Greenway designed this, Australia's first official lighthouse, in 1816; poor workmanship meant that the lighthouse had to be rebuilt (to the same design) in 1823. The structure graces the rocky cliffs of South Head. See *Sydney and Surrounds,* p. 80

Cape Byron Lighthouse, NSW

The most easterly lighthouse on the mainland, no longer operational, is now a popular vantage point for whale-watching and a lovely place to walk. It is possible to stay in the original lighthouse keeper's quarters. See *Byron Bay and the Subtropical North,* p. 112

Cape Leveque Lighthouse, WA

Protruding above a mass of greenery on the red soil at the northern tip of Dampier Land is Cape Leveque Lighthouse. Built in 1911, it marks the western entrance to the remote King Sound, some 220 km north of Broome. See *Broome and Kimberley Coast,* p. 240

Cape du Couedic Lighthouse, SA

This distinctive pink-brown lighthouse is made from 2000 pieces of local granite.

The heritage site, with its three keepers' cottages, has hardly changed since the lighthouse was built in 1909. Tours and accommodation are available. See *Fleurieu Peninsula and Kangaroo Island,* p. 188

Cape Leeuwin Lighthouse, WA

Completed in 1896, this lighthouse, near the tiny town of Augusta, marks the meeting point of the Southern and Indian oceans. It was not converted to electricity until 1982, when it was also automated. Tours are available and whales can be seen. See *The South-West,* p. 218

Low Isles Lighthouse, Qld

This picture-book perfect beacon was built in 1878. With its pristine natural setting – it is sited on the Low Isles, two small coral cays 13 km from Port Douglas – it makes a popular daytrip from the mainland. See *Cairns, Cape York and the Gulf,* p. 68

Cape Nelson Lighthouse, Vic

Located in a romantically remote and wind-blown corner of far western Victoria, this stone lighthouse, with its red and white tower, was lit in 1884. Music evenings, accommodation and tours are on offer. See *Great Ocean Road,* p. 144

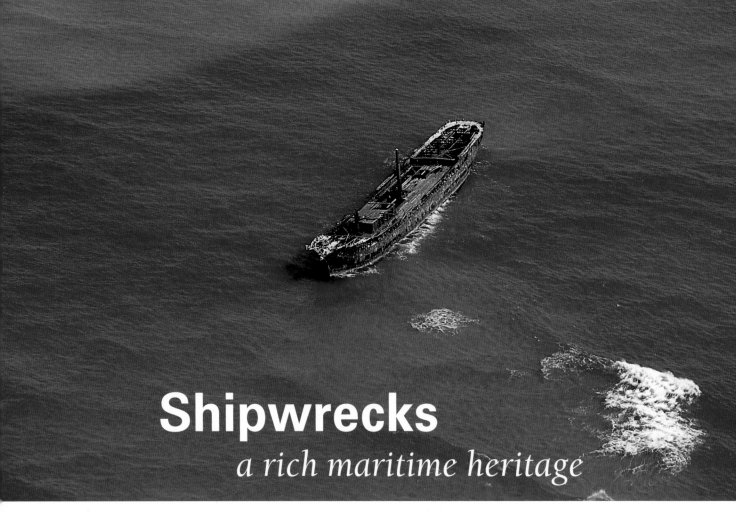

Shipwrecks
a rich maritime heritage

The scattered remains of thousands of shipwrecks around Australia's coast – fragile remnants of the country's maritime history – have many dramatic and mysterious stories to tell.

In the 1600s and 1700s, Dutch merchant ships, headed for the Spice Islands, followed the Roaring Forty winds east from the Cape of Good Hope to the Great South Land, before turning north to Batavia (now Jakarta). The unknown and uncharted waters proved treacherous – and often deadly. The discovery of shipwrecks, in particular the *Batavia*, which foundered on Western Australia's Houtman Abrolhos Islands in 1629, has yielded rich archaeological treasure and provides a rare insight into life at sea hundreds of years ago.

On the continent's east coast, ships have come to grief on the Great Barrier Reef's maze of jagged and intricate coral. Further south, vessels plying their trade – at first, sailing ships carrying convicts and cargo, gold-seekers and settlers and then later, steamships – have met an untimely end. In the cold, turbulent waters of Bass Strait, wild seas, gale force winds and human error have seen hundreds of ships wrecked.

Many of these shipwrecks, scattered across the seabed, are time capsules, but they also provide a significant habitat for marine species, making them even more fascinating to experience. Some hulks can be seen beached or rusting in the shallow surf.

For history buffs, Australia's excellent maritime museums, such as Sydney's Australian National Maritime Musuem, are another way of exploring this part of the nation's history.

Above The Farsund, *wrecked 1912, lies stranded on a sandbar off Flinders Island*
Opposite Wrecks provide a significant habitat for marine species

Where to find shipwrecks

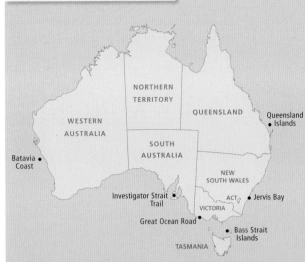

Queensland Islands
The islands and reefs off the Queensland coast have snared many a vessel. Highlights include the beached SS *Maheno*, Fraser Island and the hundreds of wrecks that lie strewn on the Great Barrier Reef. See *Sunshine Coast to Fraser Island*, p. 42, and *Great Barrier Reef*, p. 50

Jervis Bay, NSW
More than 30 ships have been lost in and around Jervis Bay, swept off course by south-easterlies. The SS *Merimbula* is a favourite dive site. See *South Coast*, p. 90

Great Ocean Road, Vic
A fascinating heritage trail traces scores of shipwrecks, and the story of their fate, along this treacherous coast, from Moonlight Head to Nelson. See *Great Ocean Road*, p. 144

Bass Strait Islands, Tas
In Bass Strait, around 60 shipwrecks lie off King Island and another 120 in the rocky maze around Flinders Island. See *The East and North-East*, p. 164, and *The West and North-West*, p. 174

Investigator Strait Trail, SA
Between 1849 and 1982, at least 26 vessels were shipwrecked in Investigator Strait, between Yorke Peninsula and Kangaroo Island. See *Adelaide and Yorke Peninsula*, p. 182

Batavia Coast, WA
Dutch East India Company ships wrecked in the 17th and 18th centuries have yielded remarkable treasure, much of it now displayed at the wonderful WA Maritime Museum in Perth and Geraldton. See *Perth to Geraldton*, p. 210

Diving and Snorkelling
the world below

Magnificent underwater formations, waving meadows of seagrass and kelp, brilliant corals, richly varied marine life and the haunting remains of shipwrecks are waiting to be explored in Australia's waters.

Deep-sea diving over shipwrecks, skimming over brilliant coral, diving with sharks (for an adrenalin rush), pier diving where pylons are encrusted with marine life, snorkelling with playful dolphins – donning a mask offers a whole new perspective on the world below. Australia has fantastic dive sites right around the country, from tropical to temperate waters.

Queensland's Great Barrier Reef, one of the world's top dive sites, is a wonderland of marine life and unique coral formations. At Ningaloo Reef in Western Australia's north, you can literally step off the beach into crystal-clear waters and start swimming over coral. Swimming with whale sharks,

the world's largest fish, watching manta rays glide by, and seeing vast seagrass meadows are other drawcards. In the cold, heaving waters of the Southern Ocean, spectacular landforms, deep caves, sheer drops and hundreds of notable historic shipwrecks are among the myriad underwater sights.

Charter and diving services including scuba diving schools and clubs, make diving and snorkelling accessible to all ages. Strict safety regulations apply; it is possible in some areas (especially the Great Barrier Reef) to sign-up for short courses on-site, enabling newcomers to undertake basic dives with experienced guides.

Above Snorkelling in tropical Indian Ocean waters
Opposite Diving on the Great Barrier Reef

Where to dive and snorkel

Great Barrier Reef, Qld
Breathtakingly beautiful, a kaleidoscope of colours, with hundreds of coral species, 1500 fish species and more than 20 types of marine mammal. See *Great Barrier Reef*, p. 50

Jervis Bay, NSW
Seal colonies, weedy sea dragons, giant cuttlefish, underwater caves, sponge gardens, kelp forests and the wreck of the SS *Merimbula* are located in clear waters. See *South Coast*, p. 90

Port Campbell, Vic
Impressive canyons, arches and cavernous tunnels, as well as historic shipwreck sites (notably the *Loch Ard*), feature in these comparatively cold waters. See *Great Ocean Road*, p. 144

Port Phillip, Vic
The bay offers a range of dive experiences, but diving with seals and dolphins from Queenscliff, Sorrento and Portsea are highlights. See *Melbourne and the Peninsulas*, p. 122

Eaglehawk Neck, Tas
Spectacular underwater landforms, giant kelp forests, the wreck of the SS *Nord* and vast numbers of fish provide a fascinating backdrop for diving. Other great dive spots in Tas include the brilliant underwater landscapes off the East Coast and the wrecks in Bass Strait. See *Hobart and the South*, p. 158, and *The East and North-East*, p. 164

Yorke Peninsula, SA
Many divers come for the shipwreck sites, but there are also outstanding jetty dives with prolific marine life, from colourful sponges and curious leafy sea dragons to eagle rays. See *Adelaide and Yorke Peninsula*, p. 182

Ningaloo Reef, WA
An encounter with whale sharks, manta rays or humpback whales makes for exhilarating diving in these crystal-clear waters. Other attractions include 500 species of fish, marine turtles, humpback whales and dolphins. See *Shark Bay and Outback Coast*, p. 232

Fishing

an angler's paradise

From oceans and bays to broad estuaries and coastal lakes, Australia offers outstanding fishing for everyone, from dedicated anglers to hopeful amateurs.

Thousands of kilometres of coastline, from the tropical north to the cool temperate south, provide an almost endless range of options to indulge in this sport. Australians take ample advantage of the many possibilities – an estimated five million people enjoy recreational fishing as a leisure activity.

For many, the joy lies in tossing in a line from the end of a city pier, often in the company of a group of like-minded anglers. For some, the joy is standing in the rolling surf, waves pounding into the shore. Others prefer to take their chances on ocean-ravaged rocks or cliffs. Land-based anglers need to be well prepared with the right tackle and bait for target species. They should also know how to work the tides so that they are there at the same time as the fish.

All types of boat fishing are also popular, from a 'tinnie' just offshore to a well-equipped, deep-sea charter boat. In northern Australia the challenge is to land Australia's most famous fighting fish, the great barramundi. Further offshore, the sleekly powerful marlin, tuna and other big game fish are prized for the challenge they present.

Whether fishing a calm estuary or tackling the open sea, boating anglers must always observe the safety laws set out by the states and territories. As well, there are regulations that specify bag limits, species bans, use of equipment (such as spearguns) and closed areas. Refer to the *Fact File* in each region for more detail.

Left *Fishing on Fraser Island*
Opposite *Boats at Lakes Entrance, Gippsland*

Where to fish

Fraser Island, Qld
Huge hauls of tailor are the prize for anglers along the wild surf coast of World Heritage-listed Fraser Island (July–Oct); other species bite year-round on both the east and west coasts. See *Sunshine Coast to Fraser Island*, p. 42

The Gulf, Qld
In this remote region, deep-sea, estuary and reef-fishing yield huge hauls from virtually unfished waters. See *Cairns, Cape York and the Gulf*, p. 68

South Coast, NSW
Tathra and Merimbula wharves offer great pier fishing. Offshore from Bermagui, there is exceptional deep-sea fishing, with yellow-fin tuna and marlin two of the prized catches. See *South Coast*, p. 90

Gippsland, Vic
Coastal lakes, rivers, estuaries and Ninety Mile Beach ensure year-round fishing. Australian salmon, bream, garfish, snapper and trevally are a few typical catches. See *Gippsland Highlights*, p. 138

East Coast, Tas
The East Australian Current, via towns like St Helens, attracts professional and recreational anglers in search of tuna, shark and marlin. See *The East and North-East*, p. 164

Eyre Peninsula, SA
Cold, clear waters here offer diverse angling opportunities, with salmon, tuna, monster mulloway and whiting being typical catches. See *Eyre Peninsula and the Nullarbor*, p. 200

Kimberley Coast, WA
One of the country's last fishing frontiers, this isolated coast yields barramundi, red emperor, sailfish, queenfish and trevally in impressive sizes. See *Broome and Kimberley Coast*, p. 240

Gove Peninsula, NT
The fishing here is legendary – the remoteness, the pristine waters, endless horizons, and the size and quality of the fish make it an unforgettable experience. See *Gove Peninsula and the Gulf*, p. 256

Surfing
legendary breaks

Australia can claim some of the world's best surfing beaches.
For many, surfing is as much a way of life as it is a great way
to take time-out, get some exercise and soak up the scenery.

Surfing came to Australia in 1914 with a surfing demonstration by Hawaiian Duke Kahanamoku at Freshwater in Sydney, but it was not until the 1950s that the activity became widely popular. Today an estimated 1.4 million Australians use a surfcraft of some kind each year. The surf industry, which began with the manufacture of boards, 'togs' and 'wetties' in the 1960s, is now worth $400 million annually. Thousands turn up to watch professional surfing events, which began in 1973 with the Bells Beach Surfing Classic (now Rip Curl Pro Classic). Surfing in Australia is for anyone and everyone, from 60-year-old, malibu-riding veterans, to young kids with short boards, frontier surfers looking for remote breaks in impossible places and, of course, the long list of locally bred world champions, such as Peter Drouyn, Nat Young, Midget Farrelly and Wayne 'Rabbit' Bartholomew, who have helped make Australia one of the great surfing nations.

A huge range of surf schools and surf shops can be found at major destinations around Australia. Novice surfers should take advantage of the knowledge of local surf instructors and sign up for lessons ahead of going out. If you are experienced but unfamiliar with an area, talk to locals and get some advice on conditions. Surf with a mate and always check the weather.

Above Competition action at Bells Beach, Victoria
Opposite Indian Ocean rollers on the Western Australian coast

Where to surf

Gold Coast, Qld
Beautiful weather and great waves make this major holiday area an obligatory stop on any surfing safari. Expect big crowds in the water at certain times of the year. See *Brisbane and Gold Coast*, p. 34

Byron Bay, NSW
Surfers come here for the region's legendary big right-hand reef breaks; the subtropical surrounds and tranquil alternative vibe are a bonus. See *Byron Bay and the Subtropical North*, p. 112

Bells Beach, Vic
Powerful, fast waves make this beach Australia's premier surfing destination. The country's top professional surfing event, the Rip Curl Pro Classic, is held here at Easter. See *Great Ocean Road*, p. 144

West Coast, Tas
This region is something of a surfing frontier: remote, wild and rugged. The swell is consistently big, and there is rarely, if ever, a crowd. See *The West and North-West*, p. 174

Around Cactus, SA
Good right-hand reef breaks are on offer here, and the extreme isolation of the place — perched as it is on the edge of the desert — means the crowds are thin. See *Eyre Peninsula and the Nullarbor*, p. 200

Margaret River, WA
From Perth to Augusta, this area is renowned for its large and extremely powerful Indian Ocean waves. Some breaks are hard to access, but there are plenty of options. See *The South-West*, p. 218

Sailing, Windsurfing and Kayaking

adventures on the water

Clear skies, blue water, a flurry as the wind billows in your sail – and off you go. Or perhaps you prefer the more measured pace of kayaking?

Sailing can mean steering a small dinghy with a sail or skippering a sleek ocean cruiser that can power its way around the coast. Whatever the size, the sense of exhilaration when the wind hits the sails and the boat races across the water is similar. For those wanting to get started, contact a yacht club – many offer lessons. Skipper-yourself (bareboat) charters are available in comparatively safe waters, such as Queensland's lovely Whitsunday Islands. Or, if you prefer to let others do the work, there are yacht cruises and charters in many locations.

Windsurfing, another exhilarating watersport, has devotees around the country. Many beaches and resorts have windsurfers for hire and lessons available. Australia has some renowned venues, with Sandy Point in Victoria and the Geraldton/Lancelin area in Western Australia two of the top locations.

Sea-kayaking is an increasingly popular sport, with minimal impact on the environment. Kayaks can be fairly easily transported, do not use fuel, do not disturb flora or fauna, and – unless you hit rough waters – enable kayakers to glide along the surface, enjoying the marine environment at a gentle pace. Of course, if the waves build, it can become considerably more exciting. Kayaking as a means of exploring remote environs, particularly around southern Tasmania, is becoming very popular; joining a tour is recommended.

Left *Sailing in the Cocos Islands*
Opposite *Kayaking in Tasmania*
Following pages *Shark Bay, Western Australia*

Where to sail, windsurf and kayak

Whitsunday Islands, Qld
This chain of tropical islands is rated one of the world's great sailing destinations, with safe harbours and sun-drenched, white-sand beaches. See *Great Barrier Reef*, p. 50

Sydney Harbour, NSW
The harbour's intense natural beauty and its iconic landmarks make being on the water here one of the most pleasurable ways of travelling around a major city. See *Sydney and Surrounds*, p. 80

Port Phillip, Vic
The bay's generous size and consistent sailing conditions have built up

a dedicated fraternity of sailing enthusiasts. See *Melbourne and the Peninsulas*, p. 122

The South-East, Tas
Top-class kayak trips include the Derwent River estuary, Tasman Peninsula, Bruny Island, D'Entrecasteaux Channel and, for the more accomplished, a trip to the remote south coast. See *Hobart and the South*, p. 158

Lancelin, WA
Breezy Lancelin is Australia's windsurfing capital, famous for its annual summer windsurfing event. See *Perth to Geraldton*, p. 210

Fremantle, WA
Fremantle, the site of the America's Cup Challenge in 1987, is home to a sizeable blue-water sailing fleet and an impressive maritime tradition. See *Perth to Geraldton*, p. 210

Cocos (Keeling) Islands, west of WA
Some enthusiasts sail from the mainland to this remote Australian territory, but most are content to arrive by air and then take to the water to explore the myriad reefs and cays of an unsung tropical paradise. See *Broome and Kimberley Coast*, p. 240

Where to Go

coastal destinations

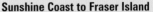

Thursday
Island

**Cairns, Cape York
and the Gulf**

Cape Melville

CAPE YORK
PENINSULA

Cape Tribulation

Cairns

Normanton

Townsville

WHITSUNDAY
ISLANDS

**Capricorn and
the Mid Tropics**

Great Barrier Reef

Rockhampton

Sandy Cape
Fraser Island

**Sunshine Coast
to Fraser Island**

Maryborough

**Brisbane and
Gold Coast**

BRISBANE

Coolangatta

Queensland
the sunshine state

Queensland's Regions

Brisbane and Gold Coast
Brisbane's Moreton Bay has a string of largely undeveloped islands offering bush and beach holidays. South lies the Gold Coast, a long line of glittering developments fronting spectacular surf beaches. *See p. 34*

Sunshine Coast to Fraser Island
Sophisticated holiday towns border areas of undisturbed coastal beauty. Sip lattes on the beachfront at Noosa, or trek and camp along the wild, dune-fringed foreshores of the Cooloola Coast and World Heritage-listed Fraser Island. *See p. 42*

Great Barrier Reef
The world's largest coral reef stretches 2000 km along the Queensland coast, a magnet for divers, snorkellers and sailors. Access to the reef is from the mainland towns between Bundaberg and Cooktown. *See p. 50*

Capricorn and the Mid Tropics
Straddling the state's broad mid-section, this is a region of balmy weather, friendly towns, quiet beaches and coastal national parks. Its proximity to the Great Barrier Reef is an added attraction. *See p. 62*

Cairns, Cape York and the Gulf
This northern Queensland region encompasses the tropical resort areas of Cairns, Port Douglas and Mission Beach as well as the precious World Heritage-listed Daintree rainforest. To the west is the isolated but fascinating coast of the Gulf of Carpentaria, an angler's paradise. *See p. 68*

The Queensland coast is world-famous for its extraordinary natural assets. The coast stretches 6973 km, a figure that doubles when the state's 1955 offshore islands are included. Two-thirds of the state is classified tropical, the remainder subtropical. This translates into warm temperatures year-round and plenty of sunshine.

The south-east, although heavily urbanised, has lovely stretches of untouched coastline, along with wild offshore islands. Despite heavy mining and farming activity, the middle section of the east coast has golden, palm-fringed beaches and pockets of forested foreshore. The tropical north is a tangle of dense rainforest edged by the trackless foreshores and remote waters of Cape York. Running parallel to the constantly varying but singularly beautiful coastline is the Great Barrier Reef, with its brilliant underwater coral cities and 900 tropical islands. The west coast, which is shaped by the waters of the Gulf of Carpentaria, is a remote and ecologically rich frontier territory of mudflats and mangroves, big rivers, huge skies and endless opportunities for fishing.

Several million travellers each year experience these wonders, and the state's outstanding tourist facilities are as famous as the scenery. The best time to visit is during the dry season (April to November). The main arrival points for air travellers are Brisbane, Coolangatta (Gold Coast) and Cairns.

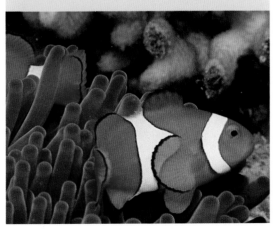

Opposite
Whitsunday Island
Left *Clownfish and coral,
Great Barrier Reef*

Brisbane and Gold Coast

The Gold Coast attracts around three million visitors each year with world-class facilities and plenty of bustle; nearby, off the Brisbane coast, a handful of beautiful Pacific islands offer an antidote of natural beauty and tranquillity.

Surfers Paradise

Brisbane sits on the edge of the protected waters of Moreton Bay. While the foreshore is of more ecological than scenic interest, the offshore islands – and the furthest is only two hours from the mainland by ferry – are spectacular: quiet, partially wild retreats with surf and calm-water beaches, forests and bushland, lakes and dunes, and opportunities for surfing, fishing, swimming, wildlife-watching, walking and boating. South of Brisbane, about an hour by car, the Gold Coast stretches to the state border, an unbroken line of sun-lit, high-rise buildings and shopping plazas, flanked by the blue and gold glories of the 42 km surf coast.

The region has a subtropical climate and is comfortable year-round, although the summer months are humid. School holiday periods are very busy and bookings should be made well in advance of travel. Brisbane and the Gold Coast have domestic and international airports.

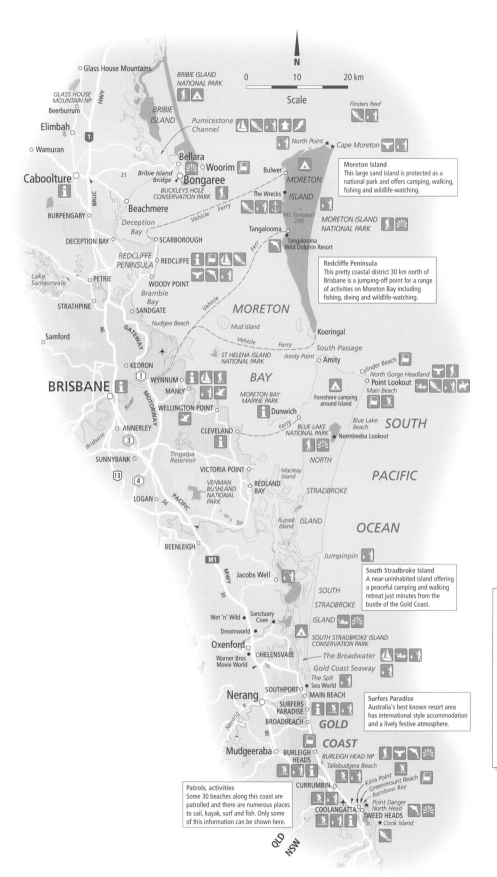

Glass House Mountains

GLASS HOUSE
MOUNTAIN NP
Beerburrum

Elimbah

Wamuran

Caboolture

BURPENGARY

DECEPTION BAY

Samford

STRATHPINE

PETRIE

Lake
Samsonvale

KEDRON

BRISBANE

ANNERLEY

SUNNYBANK

LOGAN

BEENLEIGH

Jacobs Well

Wet 'n' Wild

Sanctuary
Cove

Dreamworld

Oxenford

Warner Bros
Movie World

Nerang

SOUTHPORT

SURFERS
PARADISE

BROADBEACH

Mudgeeraba

BURLEIGH
HEADS

CURRUMBIN

COOLANGATTA

BRIBIE ISLAND
NATIONAL PARK

BRIBIE
ISLAND

Pumicestone
Channel

Bellara

Woorim

Bribie Island
Bridge

Bongaree

BUCKLEYS HOLE
CONSERVATION PARK

Beachmere

Deception
Bay

SCARBOROUGH

DECEPTION BAY

REDCLIFFE
PENINSULA   REDCLIFFE

WOODY POINT

Bramble
Bay

SANDGATE

Nudgee Beach

WYNNUM

MANLY

WELLINGTON POINT

CLEVELAND

VICTORIA POINT

REDLAND
BAY

Tingalpa
Reservoir

VENMAN
BUSHLAND
NATIONAL
PARK

Bulwer

North Point   ★ ★ Cape Moreton

Flinders Reef

MORETON
ISLAND

The Wrecks

Mt Tempest
280

Tangalooma

Tangalooma
Wild Dolphin Resort

MORETON ISLAND
NATIONAL PARK

MORETON

Mud Island

Kooringal

St Helena Island   South Passage
NATIONAL PARK   Amity Point

BAY   Amity

MORETON BAY
MARINE PARK

Dunwich

Ferry

BLUE LAKE
NATIONAL PARK

Macleay
Island

Russell
Island

SOUTH
STRADBROKE

ISLAND

SOUTH STRADBROKE ISLAND
CONSERVATION PARK

HELENSVALE

The Broadwater

Gold Coast Seaway

The Spit
Sea World

MAIN BEACH

GOLD

COAST

BURLEIGH HEAD NP

Tallebudgera Beach

Kirra Point
Greenmount Beach
Rainbow Bay

Point Danger
North Head

TWEED HEADS

★ Cook Island

Cylinder Beach

North Gorge Headland

Point Lookout
Main Beach

SOUTH

Blue Lake
Beach

Neembeeba Lookout

NORTH

STRADBROKE

PACIFIC

ISLAND

OCEAN

Jumpinpin

QLD
NSW

Moreton Island
This large sand island is protected as a
national park and offers camping, walking,
fishing and wildlife-watching.

Redcliffe Peninsula
This pretty coastal district 30 km north of
Brisbane is a jumping-off point for a range
of activities on Moreton Bay including
fishing, diving and wildlife-watching.

South Stradbroke Island
A near-uninhabited island offering
a peaceful camping and walking
retreat just minutes from the
bustle of the Gold Coast.

Surfers Paradise
Australia's best known resort area
has international style accommodation
and a lively festive atmosphere.

Patrols, activities
Some 30 beaches along this coast are
patrolled and there are numerous places
to sail, kayak, surf and fish. Only some
of this information can be shown here.

Must see, must do

► Fish the mangrove-laced
  waters of Jumpinpin

► Sea-kayak to South
  Stradbroke Island

► Surf one of the world's top
  breaks at Kirra Point

► Bathe, bake and people-watch
  on Surfers Paradise Beach

► Watch migrating whales from
  the Cape Moreton Lighthouse

Fact File

When to go
South-east Qld is subtropical and enjoys warm temperatures year-round – the average winter maximum is 21°C. The region catches the edge of the tropical Wet (Oct – Mar), which brings heavy rainfalls and cyclonic winds. For weather updates contact the Bureau of Meteorology (BOM): 1900 955 360; www.bom.gov.au

Top coastal events
Jan   *Australian Beach Volleyball Championships* (Surfers Paradise)
Feb   *Billabong Junior Series* (surfing, Burleigh Heads)
Mar   *Quiksilver Pro* (men's surfing, around Coolangatta)
Quiksilver Roxy Pro (women's surfing, around Coolangatta)
Australian Surf Life Saving Championships (Kurrawa Beach, Broadbeach)
April   *Gold Coast Cup Australian Outrigger Canoe Ultra Marathon*
May   *Sanctuary Cove International Boat Show*
Wintersun Festival (rock 'n' roll, Coolangatta)
Sept   *Brisbane River Festival* (aquatic feats, regattas)

Safety
Swimming Lifesavers patrol around 30 beaches in south-east Qld. Most clubs run patrols on weekends and public holidays Sept – May. For further information contact Surf Life Saving Queensland: (07) 3846 8000; www.lifesaving.org.au

Other water activities South-easterly winds produce large swells in summer. Tropical cyclones are a chance Dec – April but are weak this far south. All entrances in this region, except those inside Moreton Bay, involve crossing a bar. The Gold Coast Seaway, which runs between South Stradbroke Island and the Spit, provides safe, deep-water access in most conditions. For tidal information, boating charts and general safety information contact Maritime Safety Queensland: 13 2380 (within Qld); (07) 3253 4500; www.transport.qld.gov.au For weather reports contact BOM: 1900 926 115 (south-east coastal waters); 1300 360 427 (marine warnings); www.bom.gov.au

Restrictions/regulations
Fishing A recreational fishing licence is not required in Qld but minimum and maximum fish sizes, bag limits, tackle restrictions and seasonal closures apply to certain species. For further information contact Dept of Primary Industries: 13 2523; www.dpi.qld.gov.au/fishweb

Marine parks The Moreton Bay Marine Park protects the tidal lands and tidal waters of Moreton Bay, including Pumicestone Channel. Normal recreational activities are permitted, including fishing, diving and boating. In a small number of protection zones, which preserve underwater environments of high conservation value, all forms of fishing are prohibited; for further information contact the Dept of Environment: (07) 3821 9000; www.env.qld.gov.au

National parks Permits are required for camping in Qld's national parks and a permit is required to take a vehicle onto Moreton Island. For all permit inquiries call 13 1204, or purchase online at www.epa.qld.gov.au

CLIMATE												BRISBANE
	J	F	M	A	M	J	J	A	S	O	N	D
Max °C	29	29	28	27	24	21	21	22	24	26	27	29
Min °C	21	21	20	17	14	11	10	10	13	16	18	20
Rain mm	169	177	152	86	84	82	66	45	34	102	95	123
Raindays	14	14	15	11	10	8	7	7	7	10	10	11

CLIMATE												COOLANGATTA
	J	F	M	A	M	J	J	A	S	O	N	D
Max °C	28	28	27	25	23	21	20	21	22	24	26	26
Min °C	20	20	19	17	13	11	9	10	12	15	17	19
Rain mm	184	181	213	114	122	96	103	49	108	137	166	
Raindays	14	15	16	14	10	9	7	9	9	11	11	13

Brisbane Foreshore

Brisbane turns inland, arranging its city centre around the banks of the Brisbane River and relegating its outer suburbs to the Moreton Bay foreshores. The 'beaches' of Moreton Bay are tidal flats and the water is shallow and often muddy. Nevertheless, there are some lovely places for walking and birdwatching (see *Moreton Bay wildlife*, opposite) and a handful of scenic seaside suburbs offering waterside dining, marinas and access to the Moreton Bay islands and the sensational fishing opportunities in the bay. The Manly–Wynnum area is 15 km east of the CBD and, with its large recreational harbour, is a base for sailing, fishing and cruising activities on Moreton Bay. Further south is the district of Redlands, centred around the suburb of Cleveland, where the signature attraction is the sensational Cleveland Bayside Market, held each Sunday.

Redcliffe Peninsula lies 30 km north of Brisbane. Edged with distinctive red volcanic cliffs, the peninsula's sandy beaches provide for swimming, fishing and sailing.

Moreton Bay Islands

Moreton Bay encircles the mouth of the Brisbane River in a giant arch, its waters protected from the Pacific Ocean by several large islands and a chain of smaller ones, some 365 in all. These islands, the furthest just two hours from the mainland by boat, provide Brisbanites with a series of beautiful, well-preserved coastal environments, perfect for a range of leisure activities including swimming, fishing, camping and walking.

Sailing boats, Bribie Island

Dugong mother and calf

Moreton Bay wildlife

Moreton Bay supports a prolific animal population. The Tangalooma Wild Dolphin Resort on Moreton Island has developed a care and handfeeding program for dolphins, which are also to be seen in the wild in the surrounding waters. Migrating humpback whales appear between June and November, and are best viewed from Cape Moreton Lighthouse and North Gorge Headland on North Stradbroke Island. Pumicestone Channel, between Bribie Island and the mainland, is a protected haven for turtles, dolphins and dugongs; wildlife-watching cruises depart from the mainland. Diving and snorkelling tours, which operate around all three islands, explore the crystal waters and rich underwater life of the bay. Around 400 bird species have been recorded in the Greater Brisbane area. The tidal flats of Moreton Bay are a renowned area for waders, with some 24 migratory species in the area between September and April. Good birdwatching spots include Wellington Point and the mangrove boardwalk at Wynnum.

Bribie Island

Bribie Island forms the north-west perimeter of Moreton Bay. A bridge via Caboolture connects the island to the mainland. The three small towns that lie to the island's south – Woorim, Bellara and Bongaree – offer a range of accommodation, including camping. Buckleys Hole Conservation Park is a good picnicking and walking area, particularly for daytrippers. The north-west coast, which borders Pumicestone Channel, is protected by the Bribie Island National Park, where there are two camping areas with basic facilities (take your own water and firewood) and a number of bush and beach camping spots. A couple of short trails and long stretches of untracked foreshore attract walkers. The waters of Pumicestone Channel are a haven for windsurfers, sailors and anglers, with crabs a popular target for the latter.

Moreton Island

This 38 km long island offers a magnificent coastal wilderness within 35 km of Brisbane (see *Moreton Island highlights*, p. 39). Around 96 percent of the island's 17 000 ha is protected by national park. Many travellers visit as part of a tour. Self-drive visitors must have a 4WD vehicle – a permit is required. Ferries leave from suburban wharves on the Brisbane River. The island has settlements with basic retail facilities, an eco-resort at Tangalooma, midway along the west coast, and five campgrounds with facilities.

North Stradbroke Island

This island and bush paradise shelters Moreton Bay in the south-east. Access is by vehicular ferry from Cleveland to Dunwich, the island's main town and site of a 19th-century quarantine and penal centre.

Most holiday activity takes place in the north around Point Lookout, where holiday homes and resorts nestle into the surrounding bushland. The patrolled Cylinder and Main beaches offer safe swimming, while respectable breaks at the latter keep surfers coming back (newcomers can book a lesson with the local surf school). Fishing and diving charters, trail-rides and sea-kayaking expeditions operate around Point Lookout. The range of coastal treks includes the almost obligatory North Gorge Headland Walk.

Contacts

Visitor information

Brisbane Queen St Mall
(07) 3006 6290

Burleigh Heads 1171 Gold Coast Hwy
(07) 5535 3032

Caboolture (for Bribie Island)
1800 833 100

Cleveland 152 Shore Street West
(07) 3821 0057

Coolangatta cnr Griffith and Warner sts
(07) 5536 7765

North Stradbroke Island Junner St
(07) 3409 9555

Redcliffe Pelican Park Hornibrook Esp
(07) 3284 3500

Surfers Paradise 64 Ferny Ave
(07) 5538 4419

Wynnum 66 Bay Tce
(07) 3893 0589

Parks and reserves

Queensland Parks and Wildlife Service (QPWS)
For information on parks and marine reserves
(07) 3227 8185 (general)
13 1304 (camping and vehicle permits)

Blue Lake NP
(07) 3821 9000

Bribie Island NP
(07) 3408 8451

Burleigh Head NP
See *Burleigh Heads* above

Moreton Bay Marine Park
(07) 3821 9000

Moreton Island NP
(07) 3408 2710

Activities/island ferries

Contact visitor information centres (see above) for details of tours, charter services and mainland-to-island ferries.

Gold Coast **fishing**

Although a heavily urbanised area, the Gold Coast offers sensational fishing opportunities. About 450 km of sheltered canals and tidal rivers crisscross the foreshore; many of these are natural systems that have been enlarged during successive phases of development. The Broadwater and the mangrove-lined, island-dotted area known as Jumpinpin, on the Gold Coast's northern fringes, are great boat-fishing spots, with anglers able to enjoy safe, sheltered conditions; bream, whiting and flathead are target catches. Council-owned fishing platforms run the length of the coast, north from Currumbin. Other good shore-based spots include the breakwaters of the Gold Coast Seaway (a safe entrance between South Stradbroke Island and the Spit); the rocks around Burleigh Head and the bridges over Tallebudgera and Currumbin creeks. Offshore, a string of reefs offer good catches of Spanish mackerel, tuna, bonito and snapper; fishing charter services offer half- and full-day outings.

At the centre of the island, 9 km from Dunwich, is the Blue Lake National Park. The park protects the freshwater Blue Lake and its surrounding fringe of melaleucas, eucalypts and banksias. A walking track leads to sweeping island views from Neembeeba Lookout.

The Gold Coast

It is easy to forget these days, but the Gold Coast developed and flourished by virtue of its natural assets. The region, which stretches south of Brisbane to the New South Wales border, claims more inland waterways than Venice, 42 km of coastline and around 40 beautiful beaches – all wide, liberally carpeted with soft white sand, lapped by the long rolling waves of the Pacific Ocean and bathed in sunshine for a well-advertised 300 days a year.

Today the Gold Coast appears as one long line of apartments, hotels and shops, from Southport to Coolangatta, culminating in the high-rise sprawl of Surfers Paradise. The region offers every kind of accommodation, from backpacker hostels to opulent resorts in the style of European palaces. Shopping and dining are world-class, while activities include everything from dolphin-watching to gondola cruising, fishing – land-based or offshore – joy flights, tall ship charters, golf at any one of 40 courses, scuba diving, and competition quality waves for surfers.

Above Handfeeding the dolphins at Sea World Below Cape Moreton Lighthouse

MORETON ISLAND *highlights*

Surf beaches, dunes, open heathlands and clear, still lagoons make up the fragile ecology of this sparsely settled island. The island is a haven for campers, walkers and 4WD adventurers. Other activities include diving, fishing and wildlife-watching.

Visitor information
See *Contacts*, p. 37

The Wrecks
Old ships, dredges and sunken barges create a boat harbour off the island's west coast. This is a popular diving spot, with depths of between 8 and 13 m. Other dive sites are off the island's north-east, including popular Flinders Reef.

Mt Tempest
The 280 m Mt Tempest is thought to be the world's largest stable sand dune. Superb views await those who make it to the top.

Tangalooma dolphins
This eco-resort runs a handfeeding program for the wild bottlenose dolphins that live in Moreton Bay. Tourists can feed the eight or nine dolphins that show up to the regular sessions; some have been coming since the mid-1990s.

Cape Moreton Lighthouse
Built in 1857, this is the oldest operating lighthouse in Queensland. It is 20 m high and incorporates a complex of detached buildings. The cape is a good vantage point for whale-watching.

Island walks
Dedicated walking trails are few on the island, but vehicle tracks serve the walker well, as do the miles of unmarked foreshore. Much of the walking is across sand, which can take longer and be tiring.

CAMPING GUIDELINES

- There are five campsites with facilities; book well in advance (see *Contacts*, p. 37)
- Camping is permitted along the beach, except where otherwise indicated
- Permits and fees apply to camping; barge operators and rangers stationed on the island can assist
- Use fuel stoves or bring your own firewood
- Take your rubbish with you

Surfing the Gold Coast

Gold Coast **surfing**

The Gold Coast is one of Australia's top surfing destinations. The waves are big and the water is warm, with wetsuits not required for most of the year. The crowds can be large here and newcomers need to watch and learn when it comes to issues of etiquette. The range of surfing 'services' is almost overwhelming, with a hire outlet, surf school or surf shop never far from where you need it. The key break is Kirra Point, a big, barrelling right-hander, offering some exceptional waves — definitely one for the more experienced surfer. Another great right-hander is found at Burleigh Head, along with many a surfing celebrity and the requisite crowd of spectators. There are three very respectable breaks in the vicinity of Coolangatta, another at Currumbin and a variety of beach breaks along Surfers Paradise Beach.

The Broadwater

The Broadwater is a large body of calm water, branching off into a complex network of canals lined with residential properties. The busy town of Southport is the main centre. Further south is Main Beach, which is partially protected from heavy surf by an artificially built reef. Main Beach is the home of Sea World, the first Gold Coast theme park, which has a range of animal exhibits, including a giant aquarium, along with sea lion and dolphin performances. The Gold Coast's other three big theme parks – Movie World, Wet 'n' Wild and Dreamworld – are located to the north, on the Pacific Highway near the settlement of Oxenford.

South Stradbroke Island is just half an hour by boat across the Broadwater but half a century away in terms of development. The island offers a couple of small resorts, but the main attraction is the natural landscape, a 22 km sweep of beaches, rolling dunes and melaleuca wetlands. Four council-run campgrounds sit along the sheltered west coast. The east coast, facing long, wild surf beaches, is virtually undeveloped. Access to the island is by taxi or launch (the resorts provide complimentary transport) from the Runaway Bay Marina near Southport. Sea-kayaking is very popular around the island and the Broadwater generally, as is fishing.

Surfers Paradise

Surfers Paradise is for those who want their holiday on a plate. Every event, recreational pursuit, nightclub experience and child-friendly activity is available. Surfers Paradise Beach, a long, wide sweep of golden sand, is second only to Bondi when it comes to national fame. The beach is chock-a-block with bakers and bathers during the busy season. Volleyball competitions run regularly and, on Fridays, a lively craft market sets up along the foreshore. Shoppers are very well catered for in nearby Cavill Avenue.

Broadbeach to the border

The Australian Surf Life Saving Championships take place annually at Broadbeach's protected Kurrawa Beach. Further south, the township of Burleigh Heads is favoured by surfers (see *Gold Coast surfing*, opposite). Pandanus palms and pines frame the gently curving beach, from where there are views north to Surfers Paradise. Burleigh Head National Park protects 27 ha of mangrove-lined creeks, littoral rainforest, tussock grassland and patches of coastal heath; the coastal walking is good – head for Tumgun Lookout for views of passing whales and dolphins; camping is not permitted within the park.

South of the head there is good surfing and bodysurfing at Tallebudgera Beach and safe swimming at the estuary beaches along Tallebudgera Creek. The beaches of the Currumbin–Palm Beach area have gentle surf and plenty of rock pools for kids to enjoy. Just north of Coolangatta is Kirra Point, a famed board-riding beach. Coolangatta, the most southerly of Queensland's coastal towns, faces its twin town of Tweed Heads across the state border. It has very good surfing, as well as safe swimming for families at Greenmount and Rainbow Bay. Point Danger is a rugged headland with panoramic views and good dolphin-spotting prospects. Diving is popular on the Gold Coast, but most local operators favour the Cook Island Marine Reserve in New South Wales (see *Byron Bay and the Subtropical North,* p. 112).

Greenmount Beach

Sunshine Coast to Fraser Island

Boasting an average seven hours of sunshine a day, the subtropical Sunshine–Fraser Island region is a major resort area with top-of-the-line tourist facilities, as well as a place to experience the natural beauty and environmental wonder of the Queensland coast.

In a state where stunning scenery is the norm, the Sunshine Coast still overwhelms with the beauty of its natural setting. There are golden surf beaches, sandy coves nestled between bush-clad headlands and wide, lazy subtropical rivers. The towns are big but not brash; some of the buildings are high-rise, but modestly so. Sophisticated Noosa Heads, with its five-star hotels and trend-setting restaurants, is the region's resort centrepiece. To the north is Hervey Bay, famous as a centre for Australian whale-watching.

Lying between Noosa and Hervey Bay is the 50 km Cooloola Coast, an undeveloped coastal wilderness and a target destination for outdoor adventurers. Offshore, and sharing many of the same landscape characteristics, lies the 122 km long Fraser Island, where massive 500 000-year-old dunes cradle freshwater lakes, rainforests grow out of the sand, beaches are measured in tens of miles, and where the camping, walking, fishing, surfing and nature-based activities are some of the best in the state.

Must see, must do

► Ride a camel along Noosa's north shore
► Sea-kayak in the Pumicestone Channel via Caloundra
► Take a cruise of the Noosa River headwaters
► Bathe in dune lakes on Fraser Island
► Dive at Wolf Rock near Rainbow Beach

Fishing on Fraser Island

Fraser Island
The world's largest sand island is an unspoilt paradise of massive dunes, rainforest, freshwater lakes and wild surf beaches.

Hervey Bay
Around 400 humpback whales visit these calm waters from late winter to early spring.

Cooloola Coast
Encompassing the headwaters of the Noosa River, this national park protected coastline is a major walking, camping and boating destination.

Noosa National Park
The rocky headlands, coves and pandanus palms of this park provide a perfect counterpoint to the glamour of nearby Noosa Heads.

Noosa Heads
Arguably Australia's most up-market coastal town, Noosa Heads offers resort-style luxury within a superb natural setting.

Scale
0 10 20 30 km

Noosa Heads ☎ (07) 5447 4988; www.sunshinecoast.org
Fraser Coast ☎ (07) 4121 4111; www.frasercoast.org

Fact File

When to go
Qld's south-east is subtropical and has warm temperatures year-round – the winter daily maximum is around 21°C. The region catches the edge of the tropical Wet (Oct–Mar), which can bring heavy rains and cyclonic winds. For weather updates contact the Bureau of Meteorology (BOM): 1900 955 360; www.bom.gov.au

Top coastal events
Jan	*Kellogg's Nutri-Grain Iron Man Series* (various locations)
Feb	*Ma & Pa Bendall Memorial Surfing Contest* (Caloundra)
Mar	*Noosa Longboard Pro Am* (surfing, Noosa Heads) *Mooloolaba Triathlon*
April	*Pier to Pub Ocean Swim* (Hervey Bay) *Quintrex International Saltwater Fly Fishing Expo* (various locations)
May	*Fraser Island Bird Week* *Toyota Fraser Island Fishing Expo* *Wide Bay Water Bay to Bay Yacht Race* (Tin Can Bay to Hervey Bay)
July	*Rainbow Beach Family Fishing Competition*
Sept	*Tin Can Bay Seafood Fun Festival* *Noosa Jazz Festival*
Nov	*Noosa Triathlon Multi Sports Festival*

Safety
Swimming Beaches from Caloundra to Hervey Bay are patrolled by 14 clubs. For details of patrol periods contact Surf Life Saving Queensland: (07) 3846 8000; www.lifesaving.com.au The surf beaches along the Cooloola Coast and the beaches on Fraser Island are not patrolled.

Other water activities South-easterlies produce large swells in summer. Tropical cyclones are a chance Dec – April but are weak this far south. Entrances on the Sunshine Coast at Caloundra, the Maroochy River, the Noosa River and at the southern end of Fraser Island should be approached with caution. For tidal information, boating charts and general safety information contact Maritime Safety Queensland: 13 2380 (within Qld); (07) 3253 4500; www.transport.qld.gov.au For weather reports contact BOM: 1900 926 115 (south-east coastal waters); 1300 360 427 (marine warnings); www.bom.gov.au

Restrictions/regulations
Fishing A recreational fishing licence is not required in Qld but minimum and maximum fish sizes, bag limits, tackle restrictions and seasonal closures apply to certain species. For further information contact Dept of Primary Industries: 13 2523; www.dpi.qld.gov.au/fishweb

CLIMATE												NOOSA HEADS
	J	F	M	A	M	J	J	A	S	O	N	D
Max °C	29	29	27	26	24	22	21	22	24	26	27	28
Min °C	20	20	10	16	13	10	9	9	12	15	17	19
Rain mm	218	234	236	176	152	112	86	53	64	91	117	155
Raindays	12	14	15	12	11	8	7	7	7	8	9	10

Protected marine environments Hervey Bay Marine Park protects the waters of Hervey Bay, from the mainland to the north-west coast of Fraser Island. Beyond normal state restrictions, there are no special fishing restrictions within the park. Queensland Parks and Wildlife Service (QPWS) enforces whale-watching regulations in season (1 Aug – 30 Nov); regulations are displayed along the Hervey Bay waterfront. For further information contact QPWS in Maryborough: (07) 4121 1800; for a copy of the regulations go to www.epa.qld.gov.au

National parks Permits are required for camping in Qld's national parks and a permit is required to take a vehicle onto Fraser Island. For all permit inquiries contact QPWS: 13 1204; or purchase online at www.epa.qld.gov.au

Sunshine Coast
The Sunshine Coast, like its more southerly counterpart the Gold Coast, is a major resort offering holiday-makers world-class facilities. But development is less intense on the Sunshine Coast, the natural landscapes are better preserved and the overall tone is more relaxed. Despite the preponderance of international-style resorts and upmarket restaurants, particularly around Noosa, the Sunshine Coast is still a place where you can go to the shops barefoot without attracting attention.

Caloundra to Maroochydore
The towns here, once a series of quiet holiday villages, have fused in a single chain of development. The beaches, though, have lost none of their natural appeal.

Main Beach, Noosa Heads

An encounter with pelicans,
Noosa River

Caloundra is a jumping-off point for sailing, kayaking and fishing the calm waters of Pumicestone Channel. Golden Beach, just south of Caloundra, is a favoured family swimming spot. Caloundra's Kings Beach is the first true surf beach north of Brisbane and attracts thousands of visitors each weekend.

The entire area offers quality breaks for surfers. Top spots include Dicky and Kings beaches, Caloundra; Port Cartwright, Mooloolaba; and Maroochy Beach, Maroochydore. Many of the surf beaches in the area are patrolled and therefore suitable for swimming. The region's estuary beaches attract families with small children.

Mooloolaba is the centre for diving tours to the area's offshore reefs and underwater sandstone formations, where corals, tropical fish and turtles come together in visually splendid configurations. To dive with sharks, go no further than UnderWater World, a giant oceanarium in the middle of Mooloolaba itself, where other attractions include miniature marine ecosystems, seal performances and a huge tunnel aquarium.

Coolum Beach to Sunshine Beach

This is the quietest section of the Sunshine Coast. All the requisite facilities are available but the pockets of development, which include the odd high-rise, are all but eclipsed by long, wide stretches of untouched foreshore. Coolum, Peregian and Sunshine have patrolled beaches and offer good surfing, with Sunshine Beach said to have the best pipeline waves on the coast. The southern section of Noosa National Park preserves a large pocket of coastal heathland between Coolum and Peregian; there are no marked walking tracks here, but the foreshore walking is sensational.

Contacts

Visitor information

Caloundra 7 Caloundra Rd
(07) 5491 0202
www.caloundratourism.com.au

Hervey Bay
Maryborough—Hervey Bay Rd
(07) 4124 2912
www.herveybaytourism.com.au

Maroochydore cnr Sixth Ave
and Aerodrome Rd
(07) 5479 1566
www.maroochytourism.com.au

Noosa Heads Hastings
St roundabout
(07) 5447 4988
www.tourismnoosa.com.au

Parks and reserves

Queensland Parks and Wildlife Service (QPWS)
For information on parks and marine reserves
(07) 3227 8185 (general)
13 1304 (camping and vehicle permits)
www.epa.qld.gov.au

Great Sandy NP (Cooloola)
(07) 5449 7792

Great Sandy NP (Fraser Island)
(07) 4127 9191 (Central Ranger Base)
(07) 4127 9128 (Eurong)
(07) 4127 9138 (Dundubara)

Hervey Bay Marine Reserve
(07) 4121 1800

Noosa NP
(07) 5447 3243

Activities

Contact visitor information centres (see above) for details of activities, tours and charter services.

Other

Fraser Island ferries

Rainbow Beach (Inskip Point) to Hook Point
(07) 5486 3154

River Heads and Urangan Boat Harbour to Kingfisher Bay
1800 072 555

River Heads to Wanggoolba Creek
(07) 4125 4444

Urangan Boat Harbour to Moon Point
(07) 4125 4444

Noosa Heads

Noosa Heads, a surf haven of the 1960s, now vies with tropical Port Douglas as Queensland's most sophisticated holiday town. Developed to fit in with rather than overwhelm the natural landscape, Noosa occupies the southern shores of Laguna Bay and the estuary banks of the Noosa River. The town's hub is Hastings Street, where restaurants, bars and stylish boutiques line up parallel to the soft sands and blue–green waters of Main Beach. The accommodation is exceptional – much of it five-star; also available are caravan parks, family-style apartments and backpacker hostels.

Noosa is not all shopping, eating and afternoon cocktails, despite appearances to the contrary. The patrolled, mirror-like Main Beach attracts crowds of swimmers. Sailing is popular; experienced surfers flock to the legendary breaks off the headland (see *Noosa National Park*, right), while beginners learn the ropes with local surf instructors. Across the mouth of the Noosa River lies the relatively undisturbed North Shore. The beaches are not patrolled here, but the walking is good, and camel treks and horserides offer an unforgettable sightseeing experience. The protected waters of the Noosa River offer great conditions for sailors, anglers and canoeists, while sightseers make the most of the variety of river cruises available – from gondolas to eco-tours.

Noosa National Park

The headland section of Noosa National Park is an irregular-shaped triangle of bushland, rainforest, rocky headlands and sandy beaches minutes from Noosa Heads. Attractions include the precipitous cliffs of Hells Gate and the glorious sweep of Alexandria Bay, where visitors can expect good surfing along with nude bathing. Walking tracks, ranging in length from 2 to 8 km, lead through heathland, open woodland and along the shoreline to both areas. Non-walkers can take a drive to Laguna Lookout for views across the park to the ocean beyond. The headland's northern frontage, which includes the picturesque Tea-Tree Bay, boasts half-a-dozen or so sensational surfing breaks; these are all accessible via the parking area at the end of Park Street. Camping is not permitted within the park.

The cliffs of Cooloola

Humpback whale

Humpback facts

An adult humpback whale (*Megaptera novaeangliae*) can grow to 14.6 m and weigh 36 000 kg. A humpback female bears a calf every two or three years. At birth, a calf will weigh around 900 kg; it nurses on its mother's milk, which has a fat content of up to 60 percent. Despite their size humpbacks are extraordinary acrobats: they breach (leap full length out of the water), tail and flipper slap, and spy hop (rise partway out of the water and rotate in the manner of a periscope). Humpbacks are found in all the oceans of the world. The slow-moving species was a popular target for whalers for much of the 20th century. In 1966, the International Whaling Commission granted the species protection. Today there is a world-wide population of between 15 000 and 20 000, approximately 20 percent of the 19th-century estimate.

Cooloola Coast

The Cooloola Coast is a 50 km strip of wild beaches, multicoloured cliffs of sand and pristine inland waterways, protected within the Great Sandy National Park. The area is a major walking, camping and boating destination. Access is 4WD-only to most areas. Alternatively, visitors can walk into the park or hire a canoe and spend a few days exploring the Noosa River headwaters. Campsites line the inland waterways, and beach campsites and beach camping (no facilities) are available.

Rainbow Beach provides access to the northern section of the park. Hang-gliding from the surrounding cliffs and diving offshore at Wolf Rock are popular activities here. The nearby town of Tin Can Bay sits at the head of Tin Can Inlet, the fertile waters of which offer good angling opportunities. Dolphins are regular visitors and daily handfeedings take place at the boat ramp at Norman Point. Houseboats are available from the town for extended tours of the Great Sandy Strait, the calm, dugong-rich waters that stretch between Fraser Island and the mainland, and of the Hervey Bay area (see right).

Hervey Bay

The large commercial centre of Hervey Bay lies between Maryborough and Bundaberg, its waters sheltered by the long northern arc of Fraser Island. Family-friendly beaches, plenty of dining and shopping facilities, miles of foreshore caravan parks and good motels, apartments and resorts make it a popular holiday choice. Fishing is a big drawcard (see *Fishing the Sunshine–Fraser coast*, p.48), with many local charter services running trips to the fertile seas off the continental shelf.

Hervey Bay's star attraction is whale-watching. Hundreds of whales (see *Humpback facts*, above) visit the bay each year. Their journey begins in the winter months, as around 2000 whales travel 5000 km north to the waters of the Great Barrier Reef to mate or calve. On their way south again (August to mid-October) many whales stop at Hervey Bay, some say to allow the calves to build up another layer of insulating blubber before they reach Antarctica. The best time to see the whales is early morning aboard a whale-watching cruise; most cruises leave Urangan Boat Harbour between 7 and 8 am; contact visitor information for details (see *Contacts*, p. 45).

Above Lake McKenzie, Fraser Island
Inset Fraser Island dingo

Fraser Island

The 122 km long Fraser Island has been protected as a World Heritage site since 1992. For 5000 years the island was the preserve of the Badtjala people, who called it K'gari, meaning 'paradise'. The English colonists named it Fraser after Eliza Fraser, the survivor of an 1836 shipwreck, who lived among the Badtjala until her rescue seven weeks later. Miners and loggers exploited the island's resources from the mid-1800s on. International conservation battles resulted in the banning of sand mining in the 1970s, and in 1991 the extensive logging program ceased when the whole of the island was declared part of the Great Sandy National Park.

Resort-style accommodation is scattered around a handful of settlements, but visitors come for Fraser's famous natural attractions. Camping is very popular. There are 40 tracks for walkers and endless miles of foreshore to tramp along. Swimmers choose between freshwater lakes and creeks, and the protected ocean waters along the west coast, while surfers rise to the challenge of quality right-handers around Indian Head and Waddy Point. The fishing is some of the best Queensland has to offer.

The island is a 4WD-only destination; vehicles are available for hire on the island or at Hervey Bay. Drivers of private vehicles need to apply for a permit from the Queensland Parks and Wildlife Service (see *Fact File*, p. 44). Vehicular ferries operate between the mainland and the island (see *Contacts*, p. 45).

Fishing the Sunshine–Fraser coast

The Sunshine Coast has great fishing year-round. The mouth of the Mooloolah River is a protected entry giving small-boat anglers safe passage to ocean reefs. Reefs begin 2 km out from the coast and produce catches of snapper, sweetlip, Spanish and spotted mackerel, yellowtail kingfish and cod, among others. Onshore, the estuaries, rocks and beaches offer a great mix of temperate and tropical species. In spring, the estuaries yield some of the biggest flathead in Australia, with fish over 80 cm common. Boat and equipment hire outlets are found in most towns, and offshore charter services are based in Mooloolaba.

Fraser Island's angling drawcard is its northern run of tailor, which occurs July to October. Anglers patrol the eastern shore, particularly the northern half of Seventy Five Mile Beach, in 4WDs, looking for good gutter formations and signs of tailor schools, then stand, shoulder-to-shoulder, reeling them in.

FRASER ISLAND'S *east coast*

The east coast between Hook Point and Waddy Point is a haven for campers, walkers and nature lovers. Campsites dot the foreshores of the island's lakes and beaches and mark the starting point for numerous walks. From the ferry drop-off at Hook Point, there is 4WD access along the beach, although areas may be inaccessible either side of a high tide.

Visitor information
See *Contacts*, p. 45

SS *Maheno*

This trans-Tasman luxury liner, used as a hospital ship during World War I, was being towed to Japan in 1935 when a cyclone struck, snapping the towline and forcing the ship aground. The wreck is now a prominent landmark.

Eli Creek

This freshwater creek runs between palm-lined sandy banks in a rugged gorge. More than 50 creeks, said to contain some of the world's purest water, run through Fraser's dunes.

Lake Wabby

The lucid waters of the island's deepest freshwater lake, Lake Wabby, can be reached via a 45-minute walk from the coast. A large sand blow – a wind-blown dune that buries everything in its path – is slowly filling the lake.

The Cathedrals

Sheer cliffs, comprising layers of multicoloured sand, stretch between Happy Valley and Indian Head. They rise to heights of about 15 m.

Lake Boomanjin

Covering 200 ha, this is the world's largest dune lake (dune lakes are formed by the redistribution of sand by wind). It sits 70 m above sea level and is surrounded by 120 m high dunes. The five-hour-return walk begins at Dilli village.

Middle Rocks

The Badtjala people used the large rock pool at Middle Rocks as a natural fish trap. Prior to colonisation Fraser Island had a permanent population of between 400 and 600. This swelled to around 3000 during winter with the increase in seafood resources.

ACCESS AND SAFETY

- Vehicular ferries run to the island from Rainbow Beach and Hervey Bay
- A 4WD vehicle is required (these can be hired on the mainland or on Fraser Island)
- Vehicle and camping permits are required (apply to Queensland Parks and Wildlife Service, see *Contacts*, p. 45)
- Caravans and 4WDs with low clearance may not be able to access parts of the island
- Beaches may be inaccessible for two hours either side of a high tide
- The dingoes on Fraser Island can be threatening; read the *Dingo-Aware!* brochure that is provided with all vehicle permits

Great Barrier Reef

This dazzling and unique marine environment is the largest reef system in the world. Its islands offer the perfect tropical getaway and superb opportunities for sailing, diving and wildlife-watching.

The reef sweeps north for 2300 km, from Gladstone to Cape York, finally dissipating around the estuary of Papua New Guinea's Fly River. It supports the most diverse ecosystem in the world: more than 3000 individual coral reefs; over 900 islands; and a web of flora and fauna that embraces living coral, micro-marine organisms, seagrass beds, 1500 species of fish, over 200 bird species and more than 500 types of mollusc. Six species of marine turtles and more than 30 types of marine mammal – including giant humpback whales, placid dugongs and dolphins – swim and breed in the warm, tropical waters. Above sea level it is magical, below sea level it is an awe-inspiring world of colour and movement.

Exploring the reef provides endless fascination and it can be done in a number of ways – diving, snorkelling and reef-watching from glass-bottomed boats and semi-submersibles. Sailing, sea-kayaking, windsurfing, swimming, fishing, birdwatching, bushwalking and camping are just some of the other activities on offer. Resorts, eco-friendly lodges and national park islands of near-pristine wilderness provide access to this remarkable destination. Almost the entire reef has World Heritage status and is protected within the Great Barrier Reef Marine Park.

Island getaway on the reef

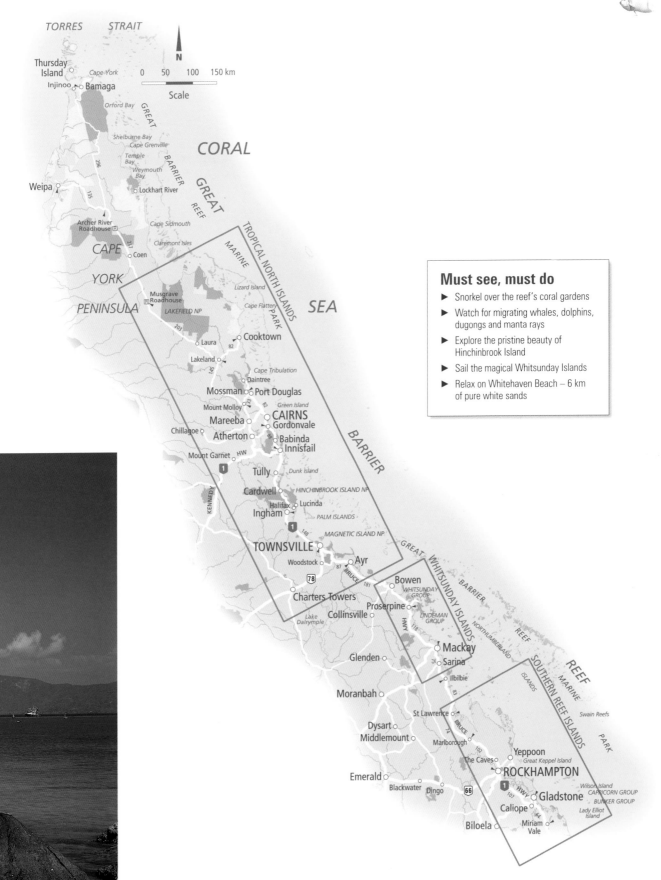

TORRES STRAIT

Thursday Island
Injinoo ○ ○ Bamaga
Cape York

Orford Bay

CORAL

Shelburne Bay
Cape Grenville
Temple Bay
Weymouth Bay

Weipa ○ ○ Lockhart River

GREAT BARRIER REEF

Cape Sidmouth

CAPE

Archer River
Roadhouse

Claremont Isles

○ Coen

YORK

Musgrave
Roadhouse

LAKEFIELD NP

PENINSULA

Lizard Island

SEA

Cape Flattery

○ Laura ○ Cooktown

Lakeland ○
Cape Tribulation
○ Daintree

Mossman ○ ○ Port Douglas

Mount Molloy ○
Green Island

Mareeba ○ **CAIRNS**
Chillagoe ○ ○ Gordonvale

Atherton ○ ○ Babinda
○ Innisfail

Mount Garnet ○

BARRIER

Tully ○
Dunk Island

Cardwell ○
HINCHINBROOK ISLAND NP

Halifax ○ ○ Lucinda
Ingham ○
PALM ISLANDS

MAGNETIC ISLAND NP

TOWNSVILLE ○

Woodstock ○ ○ Ayr

Charters Towers ○

GREAT

Lake Dalrymple

Collinsville ○

Bowen ○
WHITSUNDAY GROUP

Proserpine ○
LINDEMAN GROUP

WHITSUNDAY ISLANDS

BARRIER

NORTHUMBERLAND

Glenden ○ **Mackay** ○
○ Sarina

Moranbah ○ ○ Ilbilbie

REEF

ISLANDS

SOUTHERN REEF ISLANDS

Swain Reefs

St Lawrence ○

Dysart ○
Middlemount ○

Marlborough ○

The Caves ○ ○ Yeppoon
Great Keppel Island

Emerald ○
ROCKHAMPTON ○

Blackwater ○ ○ Dingo

○ Gladstone
Wilson Island CAPRICORN GROUP
BUNKER GROUP

Caliope ○
Lady Elliot Island

Biloela ○ ○ Miriam Vale

Scale
0 50 100 150 km

Must see, must do

► Snorkel over the reef's coral gardens
► Watch for migrating whales, dolphins, dugongs and manta rays
► Explore the pristine beauty of Hinchinbrook Island
► Sail the magical Whitsunday Islands
► Relax on Whitehaven Beach – 6 km of pure white sands

☎ (07) 3876 4644; www.Great-Barrier-Reef.com

Fact File

When to go

The Great Barrier Reef has year-round tropical (warm) temperatures. The southern region (as far north as Rockhampton) can get cool in mid-winter and very hot in summer. Mar–May and Sept–Nov are the best months. From Rockhampton heading north, May–Nov is usually best. From Townsville to Cape York, summer is hot and humid with tropical downpours (the further north, the heavier the summer rain, with Jan–Mar usually the peak). The reef islands are in the summer cyclone belt. Best diving months, when waters are clearest, are Aug–Nov. For weather updates contact the Bureau of Meteorology (BOM): 1900 955 369 (general); 1900 969 925 (northern); 1900 969 926 (central); www.bom.gov.au

Top coastal events

Aug *Hamilton Island Race Week*
Nov *Coral spawning on the reef*
Whitsunday Food and Wine Festival

Safety

Swimming and water sports Potentially deadly marine stingers (tropical jellyfish) inhabit shallow tropical coastal waters north of Agnes Water, Oct–April. Some species have been found near islands close to the coast, at sea and on the outer reef. Look for and observe warning signs (see *Taking Care*, p. 260). The beach at Picnic Bay (Magnetic Island) is usually patrolled Sat, Sun and public hols Sept–May, and longer hours Dec–late Jan. For details contact Surf Life Saving Queensland: (07) 3846 8000; www.lifesaving.com.au

Boating Reefs are hazardous; use reliable navigation charts and seek local advice about conditions. Fragile coral beds can be damaged by anchoring gear – take extra care. For tidal information, boating charts and general safety information contact Maritime Safety Queensland: 13 2380 (within Qld); (07) 3253 4500 (interstate callers); www.transport.qld.gov.au For weather reports contact BOM: 1900 969 923 (coastal waters); 1300 360 427 (marine warnings); www.bom.gov.au

Restrictions/regulations

Fishing A recreational fishing licence is not required in Qld but minimum and maximum fish sizes, bag limits, tackle restrictions and seasonal closures apply to certain species. For further information contact Dept of Primary Industries: 13 2523; www.dpi.qld.gov.au/fishweb Fishing is prohibited in certain zones in the Great Barrier Reef Marine Park (GBRMP). Commercial spearfishing and spearfishing with underwater apparatus are prohibited in all of the GBRMP.

Protected marine environments The GBRMP is divided into zones; these specify permitted activities, regulate commercial and recreational use and protect scientific and preservation areas; contact the GBRMP Authority for further information: (07) 4750 0700; www.gbrmpa.gov.au Information is also available from regional park offices and visitor centres (see *Contacts*, opposite) and from resort staff on the islands.

CLIMATE				LADY ELLIOT ISLAND									
	J	F	M	A	M	J	J	A	S	O	N	D
Max °C	29	29	28	26	24	22	21	22	24	25	27	28
Min °C	24	24	23	22	20	18	17	17	19	20	22	23
Rain mm	124	171	130	107	116	92	94	61	37	59	70	84
Raindays	13	14	15	15	14	12	10	9	7	8	8	9

CLIMATE				HAMILTON ISLAND									
	J	F	M	A	M	J	J	A	S	O	N	D
Max °C	30	30	29	27	25	22	22	23	25	28	29	30
Min °C	25	25	24	23	21	18	18	18	20	22	23	24
Rain mm	230	305	240	236	150	97	72	55	23	52	97	215
Raindays	15	18	18	20	17	12	10	10	6	8	9	12

CLIMATE				FITZROY ISLAND									
	J	F	M	A	M	J	J	A	S	O	N	D
Max °C	31	30	30	28	26	24	24	25	27	29	30	31
Min °C	24	24	24	23	21	19	19	19	21	22	24	24
Rain mm	480	477	502	303	225	122	74	72	45	27	118	214
Raindays	18	19	22	20	19	13	13	11	9	9	10	14

National parks Permits are required for camping in Qld's national parks (see *Contacts*, opposite).

Snorkelling, Heron Island

Six of the world's seven marine turtle species are found on the reef

Contacts

Visitor information
Southern Reef Islands

Bundaberg
(07) 4153 8888 or
1800 308 888
www.bundabergregion.info

Capricorn Coast
1800 675 785

Gladstone
(07) 4972 4000
www.gladstoneregion.org.au

Rockhampton
(07) 4922 5339 or
1800 805 865
www.rockhamptoninfo.com

Whitsunday Islands

Proserpine
(07) 4945 3711 or
1800 801 252
www.whitsundaytourism.com.au
www.thewhitsundays.com

Tropical North Islands

Cairns
(07) 4051 3588
www.tropicalaustralia.com

Parks and reserves
Queensland Parks and Wildlife Service (QPWS)

For information on parks and marine reserves
(07) 3227 8185 (general)
13 1304 (camping and vehicle permits)

Southern Reef Islands parks
(07) 4971 6500 (Gladstone)
(07) 4936 0511 (Rockhampton)

Whitsunday Islands parks
(07) 4946 7022 (Airlie Beach)
(07) 4944 7800 (Mackay)

Tropical North Islands parks
(07) 4053 6600 (Cairns)
(07) 4066 8601 (Cardwell)
(07) 4796 7777 (Townsville)

Activities/island transport

Contact visitor information centres (see above) for details of activities, island transport (ferries/flights), tours and charter services.

Marine stinger warning Dangerous marine stingers occupy shallow waters along the coast and around the islands from Oct to April.

Lady Elliot Island This is the reef's most southerly island, a tiny coral cay that supports important bird and turtle rookeries and is known for crystal-clear waters for snorkelling and diving.

Southern Reef Islands

The Capricorn and Bunker group of 22 reefs, straddling the Tropic of Capricorn, form the southern end of the Great Barrier Reef, with **Lady Elliot Island** (42 ha) the reef's most southerly coral cay. Clear waters ensure spectacular diving and snorkelling as giant manta rays, turtles and schools of vivid coral fish drift past. Birdlife is prolific (more than 60 species) and turtle nests honeycomb the sand dunes. The cay's low-key resort, with the emphasis on nature, is especially popular with families, birdwatchers and divers. Camping is not allowed.

Lady Musgrave Island's vast coral lagoon is ideal for snorkelling novices and shallow dives, and offers an anchorage for passing yachts. For reef-walkers, the shoreline reveals coral, clams, starfish and sea urchins, at low tide. Shady pisonia trees are characteristic of the southern reef cays. Turtles and seabirds, especially short-tailed shearwaters, nest here. The island (14 ha) is part of the Capricornia Cays National Park and camping is permitted (maximum 50 people; BYO everything).

Heron Island, a 16 ha coral cay, is a sanctuary for 30 bird species, including 100 000 black noddy terns and, of course, reef herons. The island is covered by leafy pisonia trees and rimmed by sandy beaches and an extensive coral platform. Migratory humpback whales pass by from June to September. A quiet resort offers accommodation, but the island is not open to daytrippers.

North West Island (1 sq km), the largest of the reef's cays, was the site of a guano mine from 1894 to 1900 and between 1914 and 1928, a turtle-soup cannery. Sad but true. A mantle of dense pisonia trees again covers the island. Magnificent white-bellied sea eagles nest here, as do vast numbers of short-tailed shearwaters as well as green and loggerhead turtles. Camping is permitted (maximum 150 people).

Those seeking a castaway experience might try **Wilson Island's** exclusive, eco-friendly resort, just 15 km from Heron Island. Only 12 guests at a time can access the pristine reef and deserted beaches on this tiny coral cay (5 ha), with its luxury safari tents and accent on simple pleasures. Daytrippers are not permitted.

Also in the southern reef area are the 19 Keppel Bay islands, most of them part of Keppel Bay Islands National Park, marked by steep hills and natural bushland. A number provide bush camping and the chance to enjoy some great birdwatching. The largest and best known is **Great Keppel Island**

(14 sq km), with 17 beaches, secluded coves, safari tents through to resort accommodation, a multitude of activities and a reputation for its nightlife.

Whitsunday Islands

The tropical archipelago commonly known as the Whitsundays is a magical chain of 74 islands and islets, many of them steep and ruggedly beautiful, in a sea of aquamarine. Only seven of the islands are inhabited and almost all are part of national park groups. Many have their own fringing reefs, providing easy access to coral gardens and intriguing marine life. There is outstanding game- and reef-fishing. Seabirds abound, several species of whales can be sighted (July to August) and dolphins, giant marine turtles and manta rays all frequent these fertile waters.

The Whitsundays also have a rich cultural heritage. Scattered around the islands, shell middens, the remnants of quarries and stone fish traps are reminders of the original inhabitants, the Ngaro people.

Just 32 km north of Mackay, **Brampton Island** (4.6 sq km), the most southerly of the Whitsundays, is almost all national

Great Barrier Reef Marine Park

The park, which is over 345 400 sq km, encompasses almost the entire Great Barrier Reef. About 1.6 million tourists visit each year, with most trips nature-based, focusing on the coral and other marine life.

What are **coral reefs**?

Coral reefs are rock-hard structures that have been formed over millions of years from the skeletons of tiny creatures known as polyps and naturally cemented together over time. On the surface of some reefs are the colourful living polyps; when they die their skeletons add to the reef's framework. There are hard- and soft-skeleton polyps, but it is the hard corals that build the reefs.

park, with a stylish resort at Sandy Point. Fine stands of towering palms are a legacy of the early 1900s when the island was a palm-tree nursery.

On **Lindeman Island** (8 sq km) scenic walking tracks and escape routes lead through forest to quiet beaches, or to Mt Oldfield, the 212 m summit that offers stunning views of islands emerging from the shimmering Coral Sea. Predominantly national park, the island has sandy beaches, rich birdlife and masses of summer butterflies.

Hamilton Island (6 sq km), the most developed of the Whitsundays, provides accommodation (for up to 2000 guests), multiple dining options, a world-class marina and an almost endless variety of reef trips along with sailing, diving, parasailing, helicopter rides and inter-island sorties.

On **Long Island** (12 sq km), lying almost parallel with the coast, there is wonderful bird- and wildlife-watching, and walking trails meander through dense vegetation to peaceful beaches. Three separate resorts (maximum 420 guests) offer a full complement of watersports.

A mere speck in the ocean, **Daydream Island** (17 ha) has pale beaches, coral outcrops, luxuriant tropical growth and a large resort and spa. Only 5 km from Shute Harbour, Daydream is popular with daytrippers. The resort, occupying much of the island, boasts all the usual attractions as well as an outdoor cinema to wile away the balmy evenings.

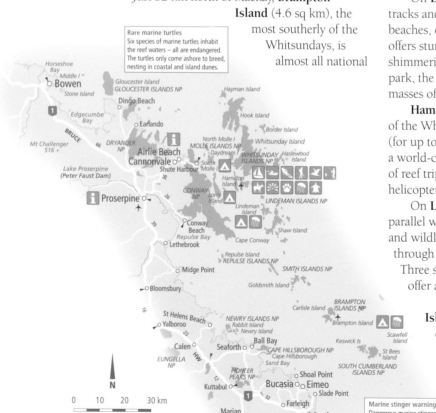

Rare marine turtles
Six species of marine turtles inhabit the reef waters – all are endangered. The turtles only come ashore to breed, nesting in coastal and island dunes.

Marine stinger warning
Dangerous marine stingers occupy shallow waters along the coast and around the islands from Oct to April.

Whitsunday Island (109 sq km), the largest in the group, is an uninhabited island and national park with walking tracks and boardwalks. The iconic Whitehaven Beach, with its dazzling arc of white silica sand, is a favoured anchorage with the yachting fraternity. Surrounding waters invite both reef- and deep-water fishing. Terrific walks, stunning views and bush camping are among the other attractions.

White-sand beaches and a fringing reef with coral fish, dolphins, sea turtles and manta rays surround the picturesque, hilly **South Molle Island**

(4 sq km). Walking trails past rainforest pockets lead to memorable views and plentiful birdwatching opportunities. A family-friendly resort (maximum 520 people) provides multiple watersports and even a 9-hole golf course.

Majestic, densely-vegetated **Hook Island** (53 sq km), with its low-key wilderness resort and camping (maximum 140 people), is popular with backpackers. A small underwater observatory provides a glimpse of coral marine life, and a boardwalk, near fjord-like Nara Inlet on the island's south, gives access to Aboriginal art sites.

Coral cay or continental island?

There are two types of islands on the Great Barrier Reef: the true coral cays, or sand islands, made of reef sediments, and the continental islands. Strictly speaking, the latter are not part of the reef but are drowned mountain peaks that were once part of the mainland. These 'high islands' are often hilly and heavily vegetated and are sometimes surrounded by their own fringe of coral reef.

Sailing the Whitsundays – **adventures in paradise**

Sailing the Whitsunday Passage is a fantastic experience. The weather is warm, the sea glitters blue, the islands offer shelter and there are plenty of safe and beautiful anchorages within a short sail of each other. Fringing reefs around many islands offer superb diving and snorkelling opportunities. Sun-drenched beaches and secluded coves are prime destinations for yachties seeking to get away from it all, while others drop anchor at chic resort islands. Bareboat charters mean you can hire a fully equipped boat but provision and sail it yourself, so you can set your own itinerary dependent only on whim and weather. It is also possible to hire a yacht with a captain, and a crew if needed. Or you can join a fully crewed yacht, a catamaran, a motor cruiser, or even sail on a century-old tall-ship – help hoist the mainsail, or simply soak up the sun.

Left *On charter around the Whitsundays* Following pages *Admiring the view from Fitzroy Island*

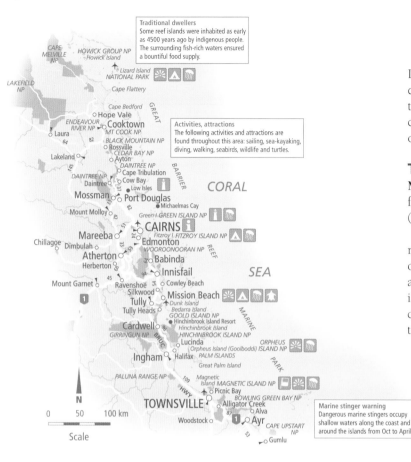

Traditional dwellers
Some reef islands were inhabited as early as 4500 years ago by indigenous people. The surrounding fish-rich waters ensured a bountiful food supply.

Activities, attractions
The following activities and attractions are found throughout this area: sailing, sea-kayaking, diving, walking, seabirds, wildlife and turtles.

Marine stinger warning
Dangerous marine stingers occupy shallow waters along the coast and around the islands from Oct to April.

Hayman Island's northern end, along with Hook Island, offers some of the Whitsundays' best scuba diving and snorkelling. An elegant resort attracts those seeking sophistication and five-star service. Reef cruises, fishing and watersports of all kinds are on offer and a walking trail circles the 4 sq km island.

Tropical North Islands

Magnetic Island, just 8 km from Townsville, caters for both a resident population and holiday-makers (see *Capricorn and the Mid Tropics*, p. 62).

Orpheus Island's spectacular fringing reef ensures excellent diving and snorkelling opportunities. A luxurious resort accommodates a maximum of 42 guests. Orpheus (14 sq km) is a national park and there are also several bush campsites (BYO everything) for those who want to get away from it all.

Hinchinbrook (635 sq km) is the largest island off the Queensland coast (see opposite). A rainforest wilderness, it is almost uninhabited except for an ecologically sensitive resort at Cape Richards. The island is a sanctuary for wildlife, including wallabies, wallaroos, echidnas, sugar gliders and scrub pythons. More than 200 bird species have been sighted. Rare dugongs, marine turtles and myriad fish swim in the surrounding waters, while saltwater crocodiles inhabit

Right A mangrove inlet on Hinchinbrook Island
Inset Frigates are one of the many bird species on the reef

HINCHINBROOK ISLAND – *tropical trails*

Magnificent craggy peaks create a towering backdrop to mangrove-lined creeks and deserted ocean beaches on Hinchinbrook. There are some easy walks, but the challenging Thorsborne Trail, a 32 km trek along the east coast of this rainforest wilderness, is renowned. The 39 900 ha island is uninhabited except for an eco-friendly resort at Cape Richards.

Ramsay Bay to Nina Bay
The 4 km trail traverses tall open forest and mangrove forests; it takes over two hours. The optional climb to Nina Peak is steep and rugged, but offers wonderful views.

Visitor information
See *Contacts*, p. 53

Nina Bay to Little Ramsay Bay
Some rock-hopping on this 2.5 km sector. Watch for green sea turtles swimming in the seagrass off the coast. Set aside two hours.

Mulligan Falls to George Point
Around 2 km through tropical rainforest, five creek crossings and then 5 km of beautiful beach to the end of the trail — allow over two hours.

Thorsborne Trail
Most people take around 4 days to complete this trek, also known as the East Coast Trail. Permits and group sizes are limited. May to October is the best time to visit.

Little Ramsay Bay to Zoe Bay
Creek crossings, open forest and tropical rainforest pockets, mangroves and palm swamps lead to beautiful Zoe Bay beach on this 10.5 km (six-hour) trek. The waters at Zoe Falls tumble into a crystal-clear pool.

Zoe Bay to Diamantina Creek
A steep 6.5 km climb leads beyond Zoe Falls to superb bay views. The diverse plant species along this sector attract a variety of native birds. Allow four hours.

Diamantina Creek to Mulligan Falls
A short — 1 km — but rugged section. Special care is required crossing Diamantina Creek, particularly after rain. Mulligan Falls has a terrific swimming hole.

WARNINGS
This is a wilderness area – you must be self-reliant and self-sufficient:

- Apply for permits well in advance (two to three months at least)
- Read the comprehensive trek notes (available from park staff) when planning
- Trails are ungraded, rough with loose stones, but posted with orange markers and rock cairns at irregular intervals
- Drinking water is available – carry water bottles and drinking vessels
- No open fires – only fuel stoves are allowed
- Camp only at designated campsites and remove all rubbish
- Wear sturdy footwear, hat and sunscreen

Types of reef

The three main types of reef are ribbon, fringing and platform reefs. Ribbon (or barrier) reefs, which form an almost continuous barrier, occur only in the northern part of the Great Barrier Reef, from Cooktown. Fringing reefs form around islands or the edge of the mainland coast. Platform (or patch) reefs, usually round or oval, may develop in shallow water between the mainland and the continental shelf. Coral reefs provide a habitat for an immense variety of gaudy tropical fish, sponges, sea worms, crustaceans, molluscs and other marine creatures.

the mangrove inlets on the island's west. Plant life is equally as abundant and diverse, and there are signs of the island's traditional inhabitants, the Banyin people, including a rockwall fishtrap.

The small (1 sq km), steep island of **Bedarra** is reputedly the reef's most exclusive island, indulging just 32 guests. It is also a natural tropical haven with stunning, boulder-strewn beaches, a cloak of dense vine forest and sparkling turquoise waters.

Steep hills, sheathed in rainforest, tumble down to the palm-fringed, sandy beaches of **Dunk Island** (10 sq km), with its kingfishers, herons and yellow-bellied sunbirds, and wonderful butterflies (watch for the dazzling Ulysses blue). There is a stylish resort, but two-thirds of the island is national park and there is camping (maximum 30 people) near the main jetty.

Enveloped by rainforest, with beaches bordered by spiky pandanus and casuarina, **Fitzroy Island** (4 sq km), close to Cairns, attracts many day visitors. The coral shingle beaches are not ideal for sunbathing, but there is some good snorkelling. The resort is a no-frills affair (cabins and campsites)

Snorkelling is popular with all ages

but there are fine bushwalks, plentiful wildlife and tropical and migratory birds.

Green Island, a 15 ha coral cay, boasts a five-star resort, lush vegetation and white sands surrounded by coral reef. It is also the most popular and most visited reef island, so it can get very crowded. A semi-submersible viewer and underwater observatory make for easy reef-watching and a boardwalk winds through the island's densely wooded interior. There is no camping on the island.

Isolated – 270 km north-east of Cairns, 15 km from the outer reef – and idyllic, **Lizard Island** (21 sq km) has powdery white-sand beaches, clear waters for brilliant snorkelling, great dive sites (the clam gardens at Mrs Watsons Bay and the famed Cod Hole with its 50 kg plus, diver-friendly potato cods are two favourites) and excellent offshore fishing (especially black marlin). Captain James Cook and Sir Joseph Banks visited the island in 1770 and named it after the large lizards (actually sand goannas) they encountered. The resort is luxuriously restrained.

Snorkelling and diving on the reef

Spectacular coral formations, warm, clear waters and an unbelievable wealth of marine life make the Great Barrier Reef one of the world's finest snorkelling and scuba-diving destinations. Every level is catered to, from novice snorkellers to professional divers. Diving gear can be hired readily, while snorkelling gear is often provided on cruises or by resorts. It is possible to undertake an introductory diving lesson, en route to the reef, before your first accompanied dive. Multiple full-time (week or longer) courses enable you to qualify as a certified diver. Airlie Beach, Townsville and Cairns are three of the most popular learning locations, with enough operators to ensure competitive rates.

Fringing reefs and small patch reefs are fascinating, but the outer reef is spectacular. Cruise boats and high-speed catamarans leave regularly for daytrips from resort islands and many coastal towns (Port Douglas is the closest town to the outer reef; the trip takes about an hour). Some companies have pontoons permanently moored on outer reefs for easy access.

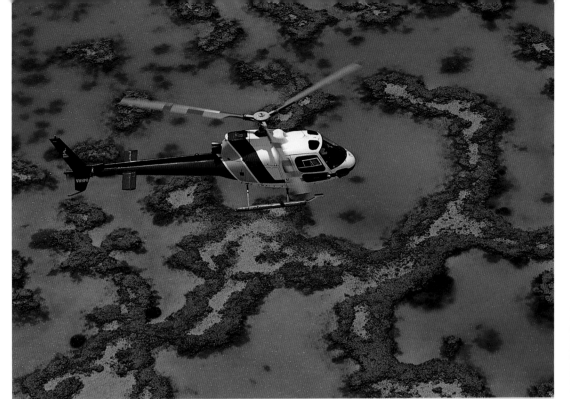

The fastest and most spectacular way to access the islands

Mainland to **island access**

Southern Reef Islands

Lady Elliot Island *80 km NE of Bundaberg*
From Bundaberg or Hervey Bay, by plane.

Lady Musgrave Island *105 km N of Bundaberg*
From Bundaberg, by sea plane, catamaran or trimaran. From Seventeen Seventy and Agnes Water, by catamaran.

Heron Island *72 km NE of Gladstone*
From Gladstone, by catamaran or charter helicopter.

Wilson Island *80 km NE of Gladstone*
From Gladstone or Heron Island, by charter boat.

North West Island *75 km NE of Gladstone*
From Gladstone, by launch or charter boat.

Great Keppel Island *48 km NE of Rockhampton*
From Rockhampton, by light plane. From Yeppoon, by launch.

Whitsunday Islands

Brampton Island *32 km NE of Mackay*
From Mackay, by light plane or launch. From Hamilton Island, by plane.

Lindeman Island *67 km N of Mackay*
From Airlie Beach or Shute Harbour, by light plane or boat. From Mackay, by plane.

Hamilton Island *16 km SE of Shute Harbour*
Direct flight from Sydney, Brisbane and Melbourne; connections to all major cities. From Shute Harbour, by launch.

Long Island *9 km E of Shute Harbour*
From Shute Harbour or Hamilton Island, by launch or helicopter. From Whitsunday Airport, by sea plane.

South Molle Island *8 km E of Shute Harbour*
From Shute Harbour, Whitsunday coast or Hamilton Island, by launch.

Daydream Island *5 km E of Shute Harbour*
From Shute Harbour or Hamilton Island, by launch or helicopter.

Whitsunday Island *25 km E of Shute Harbour*
From Shute Harbour or Airlie Beach, by boat.

Hook Island *20 km NE of Shute Harbour*
From Shute Harbour or Airlie Beach, by launch.

Hayman Island *25 km NE of Shute Harbour*
Direct flight to Hamilton Island from Sydney and Brisbane (connections to all major cities), then by launch to Hayman Island. From Airlie Beach, by water taxi.

Tropical North Islands

Magnetic Island *8 km NE of Townsville*
From Townsville, by vehicular ferry, catamaran or water taxi.

Orpheus Island *80 km N of Townsville*
From Townsville or Cairns, by sea plane.

Hinchinbrook Island *5 km E of Cardwell*
From Cardwell, by launch.

Bedarra Island *35 km NE of Cardwell*
From Dunk Island, by launch.

Dunk Island *5 km SE of Mission Beach*
From Cairns, by plane. From Clump Point near Mission Beach, by launch. From Wongaling Beach and South Mission Beach, by water taxi.

Fitzroy Island *30 km SE of Cairns*
From Cairns, by catamaran.

Green Island *27 km NE of Cairns*
From Cairns, by catamaran, sea plane or helicopter.

Lizard Island *93 km NE of Cooktown*
From Cairns or Cooktown, by plane or sea plane.

Reef walking hints

- Wear protective footwear at all times.
- During stinger or box jellyfish season (October to April) wear protective leg gear.
- Check local tide charts before your walk. The best time for reef walking is during low tide. Keep watch on the incoming tide.
- Use a bucket or container with a clear base for easy underwater viewing.
- Look but do not touch. Some marine life can give painful and dangerous stings.
- Watch where you walk to avoid stepping on, and killing, any coral or sea life.
- Move along sand channels and avoid walking on coral.
- Be aware of marine park collecting restrictions (check with local authorities).
- Do not litter.

Capricorn and the Mid Tropics

The stretch of coast from Bundaberg to Townsville basks beneath a tropical sun, with friendly towns and busy regional centres, national parks with untamed bushland and long sweeps of remote coastline. Offshore lie the islands and reefs of the Great Barrier Reef.

Townsville
Northern Queensland's largest city, and one of Australia's major learning and research centres for coral-reef biology. Magnetic Island is just 8 km offshore.

Airlie Beach
This small resort town is the gateway to the magical islands of the Whitsunday Passage, named by Captain Cook on his historic 1770 voyage.

The Great Barrier Reef defines this stretch of Queensland's coast. The reef's most southerly cays – tiny islands of coral in a sea of blue – begin just north of Bundaberg, and the reef shadows the coast well past Townsville. The reef and its islands shelter the shoreline from pounding surf, and also entice legions of visitors, many of whom use the region's coastal towns as a base or jumping-off point.

Yet the coastline has its own enticements. The climate is balmy, the pace of life is easy going and the range of holiday facilities is often impressive. As well, long stretches of unspoilt beach and the scalloped coastline of indented coves and bays yield both peace and surprising treasures. At least four species of rare marine turtles nest in the sand dunes, the largest rookery being at Mon Repos. Seasonally, dolphins, whales and marine turtles swim in the warm offshore waters. National parks provide a sanctuary for wildlife and diverse flora, from eucalypts and vine thickets to spectacular forests of weeping paperbarks, flowering heath and mangroves. With their idyllic beaches, these parks are perfect for wildlife-watching, bush camping and walking.

Airlie Beach

Dangerous creatures
Saltwater crocodiles inhabit coastal waters and river estuaries. Marine stingers are found along the coast from October to April.

Must see, must do

► See marine turtles nesting at Mon Repos
► Watch the longboard surf classic at Agnes Water
► Snorkel in the crystal-clear waters surrounding Lady Elliot Island
► Try the luscious mangoes at Bowen
► Visit Reef HQ in Townsville

Mackay
The sugar capital of Australia, an easygoing city with a world-class marina, and a string of lovely beaches to the north.

Cape Hillsborough NP
A small coastal park of rugged scenery, spectacular lookouts, short walking trails, more than 150 bird species, tropical butterflies and dune-nesting turtles. Watch out for dangerous saltwater crocodiles.

Mon Repos
Australia's largest loggerhead turtle rookery, where visitors have the rare chance to see nesting marine turtles (Nov-April).

GREAT BARRIER REEF MARINE PARK (CENTRAL SECTION)

CAPE UPSTART NP

Abbot Bay
Horseshoe Bay, Murray Bay and Rose Bay
Guthalungra
Gloucester Island
Merinda
Bowen
THE WHITSUNDAYS
Hayman Island
Hook Island
DRYANDER NP
Airlie Beach
Shute Harbour
Whitsunday Island
WHITSUNDAY ISLANDS NP
Hamilton Island
Lindeman Island
Proserpine
Conway Beach
CONWAY NP
Collinsville
Midge Point
SMITH ISLANDS NP
Bloomsbury
Yalboroo
BRAMPTON ISLAND NP
Brampton Island
SOUTH CUMBERLAND ISLANDS NP
Scawfell Island
BROKEN RIVER
Calen
Seaforth
St Bees Island
EUNGELLA NP
RANGE
Kuttabul
CAPE HILLSBOROUGH NP
Eimeo
Eungella
Walkerston
Mackay
HOMEVALE NP
Eton
GREAT BARRIER REEF
Half Tide
Grasstree
Blue Mtn 625+
Sarina
Armstrong Beach
Koumala
CAPE PALMERSTON NATIONAL PARK
Ilbilbie
Mt Scott +852
WEST HILL NP
Middle Island
SOUTH ISLAND NP
Long Island
South Island
Carmila
Flaggy Rock
MARINE
NORTHUMBERLAND ISLES
Clairview
Quail Island
SOUTH
Stanage
Broad Sound
Townshend Island
PACIFIC
St Lawrence
Shoalwater Bay
Double Mtn +742
MILITARY TRAINING AREA
PARK
OCEAN
Marlborough
GREAT BARRIER REEF MARINE PARK (MACKAY/CAPRICORN SECTION)
Kunwarara
BYFIELD NP
Glen Geddes
Yeppoon
Rosslyn Bay
KEPPEL BAY ISLANDS NP
Great Keppel Island
Yaamba
The Caves
South Yaamba
Emu Park
North West Island
Ridgelands
ROCKHAMPTON
Gracemere
RUNDLE RANGE NP
CAPRICORNIA CAYS NATIONAL PARK
Heron Island
Port Alma
CURTIS ISLAND NP
TROPIC OF CAPRICORN
Bajool
CURTIS ISLAND
Fitzroy Reef
Raglan
Mount Larcom
Southend
Gladstone
Lady Musgrave Island
Yarwun
Boyne Island
Tannum Sands
Calliope
Bustard Head Lighthouse
CASTLE TOWER NP
Turkey Beach
Bustard Bay
Lady Elliot Island
EURIMBULA NP
Seventeen Seventy
Nagoorin
Miriam Vale
Agnes Water
DEEPWATER NP
LITTABELLA NP
Lowmead
Rosedale
BRUCE
Burnett Heads
MON REPOS CP
FRASER ISLAND
Bancroft
Yandaran
Bargara
Lake Monduran
Bucca
Bundaberg
Gin Gin
Elliott Heads
Hervey
Wallaville
Woodgate
Bay
Cordalba
BURRUM COAST NP
Buxton
Burrum Heads

N
0 20 40 60 km
Scale

Fact File

When to go
This region covers tropical and subtropical areas, so warm temperatures prevail year-round. The southern region (as far north as Rockhampton) can get cold at night in mid-winter and very hot in summer. Mar–May and Sept–Nov are the best months. From Rockhampton heading north, May–Nov are usually best. From Mackay to Townsville, summers are hot and humid with tropical downpours (the further north, the heavier the summer rain, with Jan–Mar usually the peak). For weather updates contact the Bureau of Meteorology (BOM): 1900 969 925 (northern); 1900 969 926 (central); www.bom.gov.au

Top coastal events
Mar   *1770 Longboard Classic* (surfing, Agnes Water)
Easter *Harbour Festival* (Gladstone, includes finish of Brisbane–Gladstone Yacht Race)
May   *Seventeen Seventy Commemorative Festival*
Sept *Bowen Family Fishing Classic*
Oct   *Seafood Festival* (Gladstone)
          Octoberfest (Yeppoon)
          Great Tropical Jazz Festival (Magnetic Island)

Safety
Swimming Potentially deadly marine stingers (tropical jellyfish) inhabit shallow coastal waters north of Agnes Water, Oct–April. Look for and observe warning signs; swim at patrolled beaches; swim in stinger enclosures (see *Taking Care*, p. 260). The following beaches are usually patrolled Sat, Sun and public hols Sept–May, and longer hours Dec–late Jan: Elliot Heads, Bundaberg, Moore Park, Agnes Water, Tannum Sands, Emu Park, Yeppoon, Sarina, Mackay, Eimeo (Mackay), Bowen, Alva Beach (Ayr), Townsville, Picnic Bay (Magnetic Island). For details contact Surf Life Saving Queensland: (07) 3846 8000; www.lifesaving.com.au

Boating Beware of estuarine crocodiles and marine stingers (north of Agnes Water) – even shallow water is dangerous (see *Taking Care*, p.260). For tidal information, boating charts and general safety information contact Maritime Safety Queensland: 13 2380 (within Qld); (07) 3253 4500; www.transport.qld.gov.au For weather reports contact BOM: 1900 969 923 (coastal waters); 1300 360 427 (marine warnings); www.bom.gov.au

Restrictions/regulations
Fishing A recreational fishing licence is not required in Qld but minimum and maximum fish sizes, bag limits, tackle restrictions and seasonal closures apply to certain species. For further information contact Dept of Primary Industries: 13 2523; www.dpi.qld.gov.au/fishweb

Protected marine environments The Great Barrier Reef Marine Park (GBRMP) is divided into zones; these specify permitted activities, regulate commercial and recreational use and protect scientific and preservation areas. Be aware of zones; contact the GBRMP Authority for further information: (07) 4750 0700; www.gbrmpa.gov.au Information is also available from regional park offices and visitor information centres.

National parks Permits are required for camping in Qld's national parks (see *Contacts*, opposite).

CLIMATE												ROCKHAMPTON
	J	F	M	A	M	J	J	A	S	O	N	D
Max °C	32	31	30	29	26	23	23	25	27	30	31	32
Min °C	22	22	21	18	14	11	9	11	14	17	19	21
Rain mm	136	141	103	47	52	35	31	29	24	48	68	105
Raindays	11	12	10	7	7	5	5	4	4	7	8	10

CLIMATE												TOWNSVILLE
	J	F	M	A	M	J	J	A	S	O	N	D
Max °C	31	31	30	30	28	25	24	25	27	28	30	30
Min °C	25	24	23	22	10	17	15	16	19	21	23	24
Rain mm	301	265	149	66	24	38	18	18	11	29	59	123
Raindays	13	12	11	5	4	5	2	2	2	3	6	8

Fish-feeding on the reef

Bundaberg
The subtropical sugar capital and home of the famed 'Bundy rum', Bundaberg lies 15 km from the coast, at the southern end of the Capricorn region. Elegant parks and gardens, museums and tours of the rum distillery attract visitors. Its coastal beaches offer white sands, stinger-free, year-round swimming and, at Mon Repos beach, one of Australia's most important turtle rookeries (see *Turtle time at Mon Repos*, p. 66). Humpback whales on their migratory journey can be spotted breaching offshore between August and October, and dolphins swim in these waters. From Bundaberg it is a short cruise to Lady Elliot Island, the Great Barrier Reef's most southerly coral cay, and Lady Musgrave Island; both islands provide turtle- and birdwatching and exceptional reef-diving (see *Great Barrier Reef*, p. 50).

Agnes Water and Seventeen Seventy
A ribbon of fine beaches sweeps up the coast from Bundaberg to the holiday hamlet of Agnes Water, the east coast's most northerly surf beach.

Agnes Water's twin town, Seventeen Seventy, nestles in the lee of a narrow peninsula curving around Round Hill Creek, overlooking historic

Left *Agnes Water*
Inset *The Ulysses blue
butterfly, a tropical species
found in the area*

Bustard Bay. Captain James Cook made his second Australian landfall here in 1770 and the town is named in honour of the event. This is one of the best land-based angling locales on the coast, while Turkey Beach is a favoured spot for succulent mud crabs. Cruises leave regularly to Lady Musgrave Island and Fitzroy Reef Lagoon for outstanding snorkelling, diving and reef-viewing. For the adventurous, an amphibious vessel fords land and tidal creeks to deserted Bustard Head Lighthouse (1868), and panoramic views, at the bay's northern end. Local operators run some excellent eco-wise tours.

A 4WD trail leads south (8 km) to the high sand dunes, pristine freshwater creek and tranquillity of Deepwater National Park. North (11 km) is the untamed wilderness of Eurimbula National Park. At Eurimbula, a patchwork of eucalypt forest, paperbark swamps, cabbage palms and rainforest back the peaceful beaches where loggerhead turtles nest in the dunes. There is fishing and bush camping at both parks; a 4WD vehicle is recommended.

Gladstone

The thriving seaport of Gladstone spreads across the hills overlooking its wonderful natural harbour. The city has the world's largest alumina plant, the country's largest aluminium smelter and Queensland's largest power station. Boating and fishing are major leisure pastimes here. The smart marina accommodates sleek private yachts and charter boats, which cruise to Heron Island, a diminutive coral cay renowned for its prolific birdlife and fine reef diving, Lady Musgrave Island (see *Great Barrier Reef*, p. 50) and uninhabited coral cays. Head 20 km south to Tannum Sands for swimming, snorkelling and fishing at the sandy beaches. Mudcrabbing in the mangrove swamps is also popular.

Rockhampton and Yeppoon

Rockhampton straddles the Tropic of Capricorn and is the major city in the region. It was an important 19th-century river port, sited on Queensland's largest river, the Fitzroy. The town possesses remarkably fine heritage buildings and is regarded as the beef capital of Australia. Rockhampton is 40 km from the ocean, but local operators run daytrips to the reef.

Yeppoon stands on the wide curve of Keppel Bay, an easy going town, best known as the gateway to the scenic Keppel Islands. In fact, Yeppoon itself has plentiful holiday accommodation and facilities, some excellent dining and its own swath of sun-kissed coastline. Boats leave for the islands and reef from Rosslyn Bay Harbour, 7 km south.

Mackay

Balmy, tropical Mackay is a major regional centre at the heart of Queensland's sugar district, 990 km north of Brisbane. The city's rich cultural blend is the legacy of its early sugarcane farming days.

Contacts

Visitor information

Airlie Beach 277 Shute Harbour Rd
(07) 4946 6665
www.thewhitsundays.com

Bundaberg 271 Bourbong St
(07) 4153 8888
www.bundabergregion.info

Gladstone Marina Ferry Terminal
(07) 4972 9000
www.gladstoneregion.org.au

Mackay The Mill
(07) 4952 2677
www.mackayregion.com

Magnetic Island
www.magnetic-island.com.au

Rockhampton Customs House
208 Quay St
(07) 4922 5339
www.rockhamptoninfo.com

Townsville Bruce Hwy
(07) 4778 3555
www.townsvilleonline.com.au

Parks and reserves

Queensland Parks and Wildlife Service (QPWS)
For information on parks and marine reserves
(07) 3227 8185 (general)
13 1304 (camping and vehicle permits)

Cape Hillsborough NP
(07) 4944 7800

Conway NP
(07) 4946 7022

Deepwater NP
(07) 4974 9350

Eurimbula NP
(07) 4974 9350

Capricornia Cays NP
(Lady Musgrave Island)
(07) 4974 9350

Magnetic Island NP
(07) 4778 5378

Activities

Contact visitor information centres (see above) for details of activities, tours and charter services.

Other

Mon Repos Conservation Park
Turtle rookery
(07) 4159 1652

The lush botanic gardens, heritage walk and tours of the sugar refinery (June to November) and open-cut coalmines reveal diverse facets of Mackay. Yachts and charter boats cruise from the extensive modern marina to explore the Great Barrier Reef and islands. Swimming, fishing and boating are favoured pursuits at the town's string of small, quiet beaches.

Eucalypt-cloaked headlands with towering hoop pines, boulder-strewn beaches, mangrove-fringed wetlands and pockets of lush rainforest are protected within Cape Hillsborough National Park, 50 km north of Mackay. Wildlife is prolific – kangaroos, wallabies, sugar gliders, turtles, more than 150 bird species and fantastic tropical butterflies. A fascinating 1.6 km walking trail explains how the Jupiera or Yuwi people traditionally used native plants for survival. Fishing and swimming are not advised here – saltwater crocodiles inhabit these waters. There is bush camping and a small resort on Casuarina Bay, which has caravans and cabins for hire.

Airlie Beach and Conway National Park

On a narrow coastal strip, between the heavily forested hills of the Conway Ranges and the crystalline waters of the Coral Sea, the coastal holiday village of Airlie Beach is the jumping-off point for the beautiful Whitsunday Islands (see *Great Barrier Reef*, p. 50). The town, a favourite with backpackers, is also something of a party capital, with a lively night scene. There

Bareboating from Airlie Beach

Turtle time at Mon Repos

Eastern Australia's largest and most accessible turtle rookery is at Mon Repos, 15 km north-east of Bundaberg. Endangered and rare marine turtles mate at sea, with only the females coming ashore to lay their eggs. The turtles lumber out of the ocean, usually at night, drag themselves to the dunes and, using their hind flippers, dig a vertical egg chamber. They then lay up to 120 leathery-shelled eggs and cover the nest, before crawling, exhausted, back into the ocean. They return several times during the season (November to January) to lay more eggs. The hatchlings emerge from mid-January to March, usually at night, and make a dash to the relative safety of the sea to begin life unaided. Loggerhead (*Caretta caretta*) and green turtles (*Chelonia mydas*) are the main species seen at Mon Repos, where there is an on-site interpretive centre and supervised viewing, run by Queensland Parks and Wildlife Service (see *Contacts*, p. 65).

is accommodation at all levels, some terrific restaurants and a plethora of tour operators. Lures for the visitor include sailing the Whitsunday Passage, diving, island-hopping and reef-watching. As well, sea-kayaking, fishing charters, scuba diving courses and adrenalin-inducing sports such as tandem skydiving, parasailing and jetskiing and more are on offer.

For those seeking peace and quiet, a number of the national park islands have beach camping and bushwalking (see *Contacts*, p. 65). Boats leave from Abel Point Marina and the deepwater port at Shute Harbour.

Conway National Park, overlooking the Whitsunday Passage, is a mosaic of open forest, pandanus woodland, palms and lush lowland rainforest, with 35 km of untouched coastline and stunning views across the Whitsundays. Watch for rare rock wallabies, emerald doves, brush turkeys and scrub-fowl on the walking trails. There is limited bush camping.

Bowen

About midway between Mackay and Townsville, the sun-drenched seaside town of Bowen is a no-fuss, family holiday destination with a fishing-boat filled harbour. At the beaches – long, sandy expanses, intimate coves and bays – swimming, fishing and just soaking up the sun are the order of the day. Diving and snorkelling reveal tropical fish and a coral reef just offshore. Horseshoe Bay (5 km north), a boulder-framed crescent of golden sand, is a family favourite. Murray Bay and Rose Bay are also

lovely. Sample a mango while there – Bowen is famous for them.

Townsville

The red, barren bulk of Castle Hill looms over Townsville, the largest city in North Queensland, a laid-back tropical town with a busy port, a thriving university, a marina full of smart yachts and an impressive collection of heritage buildings. The Strand, a beachfront promenade with swimming pools at both ends, offers tranquil views across Cleveland Bay to the wooded hills of Magnetic Island. Do not miss the impressive Museum of Tropical Queensland, or Reef HQ, a coral aquarium that offers a unique introduction to the Great Barrier Reef's ecological mysteries. Offshore, the wreck of the 90 metre *Yongala*, which sank in 1911, is one of Australia's best dive sites.

Magnetic Island

Just a 20-minute fast-cat ferry ride away, Magnetic Island boasts 320 days a year of sunshine and a low-key lifestyle for residents and holiday-makers. Granite boulders, secluded beaches, lofty hoop pines on the headlands, mangroves and fringing reef define the rugged coastline. The island's marine park waters are a breeding ground for tiger sharks and green sea turtles. More than half the island is national park, with eucalypt woodland and rainforest pockets creating a sanctuary for bird- and wildlife. Bushwalking, sea-kayaking, snorkelling, scuba diving, parasailing and horseriding are activity options.

Magnetic Island, just 20 minutes from Townsville

Cairns, Cape York and the Gulf

The east coast combines the Daintree rainforest, the azure Coral Sea and the Great Barrier Reef. To the west of Cape York Peninsula lies the sparsely populated, mangrove-laced coast of the Gulf of Carpentaria.

Cape Tribulation

Apart from Cairns, the lively visitor capital of northern Queensland, this vast area remains thinly populated, much of it remote and parts of it untouched wilderness. Yet it contains luxury resorts, unique national parks, exquisite beaches and some of the most ecologically fascinating parts of the country.

For those who enjoy indulgence and the pleasure of the tropics, Mission Beach, Port Douglas and Cairns' northern beaches offer a world of sandy shores, shimmering blue waters and resort-style pleasures. The full gamut of watersports plus horseriding, golf, walking trails, fine dining and more are available. Further north, the dense canopy of the ancient Daintree rainforest shelters rare plant and animal species, crocodile-inhabited rivers meander to the sea, and the south-east trade winds fan long, white-sand beaches.

Hugging the east coast is the spectacular Great Barrier Reef. To the west lies the little known Gulf of Carpentaria, a frontier coast of mangroves, incredibly fish-rich waters, crocodiles and dugongs, where indigenous communities retain their cultural heritage and traditional skills are still used daily.

Must see, must do

► Explore the ancient Daintree rainforest

► Visit Michaelmas Cay, one of Australia's largest seabird rookeries

► See the original *Endeavour* anchor at Cooktown Museum

► Swim in the tropical waters of the famed Coral Sea

► Haul in a fish almost anywhere in the region

Dangerous creatures
Saltwater crocodiles inhabit coastal waters and river estuaries. Marine stingers are found along the coast from December to April.

Cooktown
Colonial architecture, a rich heritage and balmy climate make this isolated outpost one of Queensland's treasures.

Daintree NP
A precious pocket of tropical rainforest crammed with rare plants and animals reaching down to the reef-fringed coastline.

Port Douglas
This small tropical resort town began its days in the 1800s as a rowdy port for the goldfields.

Mission Beach
A ribbon of palm-tree lined white-sand beach looking across the Coral Sea to Dunk Island. The rainforest here is one of the last habitats of the endangered cassowary.

CORAL

SEA

GREAT BARRIER REEF

GREAT BARRIER REEF MARINE PARK

TORRES STRAIT

GULF OF CARPENTARIA

CAPE YORK PENINSULA

Scale
0   40   80   120 km

Fact File

When to go
The ideal time is April–Oct (the Dry). During the Wet rainfall and humidity are high and dangerous marine stingers in shallow coastal waters make swimming unsafe (see *Safety* below, and *Taking Care* p. 260). During the Wet the heaviest falls are Jan–Mar when floods cut off almost the entire Cape York Peninsula and most of the Gulf. Cyclones can occur Dec–April. Seasons vary for fishing, but the start and end of the Dry are generally best for angling in this region (April–end June, then Oct–early Dec). For weather updates contact the Bureau of Meteorology (BOM): 1900 969 925; www.bom.gov.au

Top coastal events
May	*Port Douglas Village Carnivale Festival* *World Barramundi Fishing Championships* (Burketown)
June	*Endeavour Festival* (Cooktown) *Torres Strait Cultural Festival* (Thursday Island)
Sept	*Festival Cairns*
Oct	*Marlin Fishing Classic* (Cairns)
Nov	*Full Moon – Coral Spawning* (Contact Quicksilver Reef Biosearch (07) 4087 2150)

Safety
Swimming Potentially deadly marine stingers (tropical jellyfish) inhabit shallow coastal waters Oct –April. Look for and observe warning signs; swim at patrolled beaches; swim in stinger enclosures (see *Taking Care*, p. 260). Surf lifesaving clubs and patrolled beaches are at Port Douglas, Ellis Beach, Palm Cove (Cairns), South Mission Beach and Etty Beach (1 hr south of Cairns). For details contact Surf Life Saving Queensland: (07) 3846 8000; www.lifesaving.com.au

Boating On the east coast all reefs are hazardous; use reliable navigation charts and seek local advice about conditions. Boating self-sufficiency is required in the Gulf of Carpentaria due to its isolation and limited rescue facilities. Beware of crocodiles and stingers throughout the region (see *Taking Care*, p. 260). For tidal information, boating charts and general safety information contact Maritime Safety Queensland: 13 2380 (within Qld); (07) 3253 4500; www.transport.qld.gov.au For weather reports contact BOM: 1900 969 923 (coastal waters); 1300 360 427 (marine warnings); www.bom.gov.au

Restrictions/regulations
Fishing A recreational fishing licence is not required in Qld but minimum and maximum fish sizes, bag limits, tackle restrictions and seasonal closures apply to certain species. For further information contact Dept of Primary Industries: 13 2523; www.dpi.qld.gov.au/fishweb

Protected marine environments Most of the Great Barrier Reef is part of a World Heritage area and is within a marine park (GBRMP). The GBRMP is divided into zones; these specify permitted activities, regulate commercial and recreational use and protect scientific and preservation areas. Be aware of zones; contact the GBRMP Authority for further information: (07) 4750 0700; www.gbrmpa.gov.au Information is also available from regional park offices and visitor information centres (see *Contacts*, opposite).

National parks Permits are required for camping in Qld's national parks (see *Contacts*, opposite).

CLIMATE												CAIRNS
	J	F	M	A	M	J	J	A	S	O	N	D
Max °C	31	31	30	29	28	26	26	27	28	29	31	31
Min °C	24	24	23	22	20	18	17	18	19	21	22	23
Rain mm	413	435	442	191	94	49	28	27	36	38	90	175
Raindays	18	19	20	17	14	10	9	8	8	8	10	13

CLIMATE												NORMANTON
	J	F	M	A	M	J	J	A	S	O	N	D
Max °C	35	34	34	34	32	29	29	31	34	36	37	36
Min °C	25	25	24	22	19	16	15	17	20	23	25	25
Rain mm	260	249	158	31	8	9	3	2	3	10	44	143
Raindays	14	14	9	2	1	1	1	0	0	1	4	9

Cairns Harbour

Snorkelling at Bedarra Island, via Mission Beach

Contacts

Visitor information

Cairns 51 The Esplanade
(07) 4051 3588
www.tropicalaustralia.com.au

Cooktown
(07) 4069 5446
www.cook.qld.gov.au

Daintree 5 Stewart St
(07) 4098 6120
www.pddt.com.au

Mission Beach Kennedy Esp
South Mission Beach
(07) 4068 7099
www.missionbch.com

Port Douglas Reef Anchor House
(07) 4099 4588
www.pddt.com.au

Thursday Island
(07) 4031 7676
www.tropicalaustralia.com.au

Parks and reserves

**Queensland Parks and Wildlife
Service (QPWS)**
For information on parks and
marine reserves
(07) 3227 8185 (general)
13 1304 (camping and
vehicle permits)

Daintree NP
(07) 4098 0052

QPWS Cairns
(07) 4052 3096

Activities

Contact visitor information
centres (see above) for details
of activities, tours and
charter services.

Other

Punsand Bay Fishing Lodge
(07) 4069 1722

**Peddell's Ferry and Tour Bus
Service – Thursday Island**
(07) 4069 1551

Cardwell to Mission Beach

The fishing town of Cardwell, 165 km north of Townsville, overlooks the great mangrove forests of Hinchinbrook Channel. In the background, a seemingly impenetrable forest cloaks the majestically folding hills of Hinchinbrook Island (see *Great Barrier Reef*, p. 50). The fishing fraternity enjoy estuary, island and reef-fishing and great crabbing and prawning around Cardwell.

Tucked into a pocket of tropical rainforest, about 100 km south of Cairns, the several settlements that comprise Mission Beach spread along a sweep of palm-fringed shoreline overlooking the Coral Sea. Exquisite tropical butterflies and rare birds, including the endangered cassowary, can be encountered along the lush rainforest walks. Just offshore are the resort islands of Dunk and exclusive Bedarra. Cruises to the islands and coral cays and reef tours with diving, snorkelling and viewing via glass-bottomed boat all depart from Clump Point. Sea-kayaking, camel- and horserides along the beach and, inland, adrenalin-inducing whitewater rafting on the Tully River are other activity options.

Cairns

Rimmed by lush green hills and overlooking the clear waters of Trinity Bay, Cairns is the heart of northern Queensland. Once a big sleepy country town, it now bears all the hallmarks of a major tropical resort – luxurious accommodation, five-star dining, smart outdoor cafes, boutique shopping and an almost endless array of tour operators. Cairns is also a haven for backpackers, with plentiful accommodation, internet cafes and a lively night scene. The international airport ensures a cosmopolitan crowd, though the atmosphere remains decidedly easy going. First-timers are usually surprised to realise Cairns does not have swimming beaches – the bay tends to be swampy, with sandy beaches beginning well to the north. Swimming pools abound, however, and the man-made swimming lagoon on the Esplanade is popular when the weather is steamy.

The Great Barrier Reef is closer to the shore here than it is further south, making Cairns the perfect base for exploring. Diving (a magic experience, especially on the outer reef), snorkelling, big-game fishing, sea-kayaking or simply sailing or cruising to the reef are potential activities. Green Island, a heart-shaped coral cay 27 km east of Cairns, is lovely but can get very busy (see *Great Barrier Reef*, p. 50). Fragile Michaelmas Cay, a mere speck in the ocean that supports tens of thousands of ground-nesting seabirds, is another favourite site.

The fishing around Cairns is renowned, especially the big-game and marlin fishing, and a flotilla of charter boats leaves daily packed with eager anglers. Cairns is the departure point for trips to the Daintree rainforest, the wilderness of Cape York and the outback Gulf of Carpentaria.

Cairns' Northern Beaches

Starting around 20 km north of Cairns, a succession of small seaside villages, each with its own distinctive ambience, face a stretch of fine sandy white beaches. At Yorkeys Knob, sleek private yachts moor at the impressive Half Moon Bay marina; Trinity Beach offers good windsurfing and sailing and a stinger net in summer; and Palm Cove

Thursday Island

Thursday Island, the hub of Torres Strait, lies 39 km from the mainland, a small hilly island circled by the Prince of Wales Islands. TI, as it is known locally, has been the administrative base for Torres Strait since 1877. The islanders are Melanesian, though the rich cultural blend – Japanese, Chinese, South Sea Islander, Aboriginal and European to name a few – reflects its past as a major pearling port. TI was also a strategic base during World War II. The colonial facade of the waterfront Federal Hotel (1901) and the Sacred Heart Mission church spires are distinctive landmarks. The sheltered harbour is a port for crayfish and prawns and welcomes passing yachties. A growing number of visitors are attracted by the island's colourful history, traditional culture and laid-back lifestyle.

Grassy Hill Lighthouse, Cooktown

is noted for its boutiques and restaurants. Holiday accommodation and activities, including fishing, reef trips, sea-kayaking, snorkelling, swimming and horseriding, cater for most tastes.

Port Douglas

An hour's drive north of Cairns along the Captain Cook Highway, through waving sugarcane and rich, *terra rossa* soil, past stony coves and pandanus-fringed beaches, lies Port Douglas. A clutch of upmarket hotels and resorts and a main street lined with restaurants and boutiques cannot detract from the town's laid-back style and the luxuriant beauty of its tropical vegetation. Bougainvillea thrives, Moreton Bay figs spread overhead, and Four Mile Beach is never crowded. Walking, cycling, swimming, snorkelling, sea-kayaking, windsurfing and, of course, outstanding fishing ensure a steady stream of holiday-makers. Low Isles, a tiny coral cay with a picturebook-perfect lighthouse (1878) is a short cruise away. Port Douglas is also a good base for trips to the Daintree rainforest, diving courses and reef excursions.

Daintree National Park and Cape Tribulation

Cape York's tropical rainforest is one of the most ancient forests on earth. The Cape Tribulation sector of the famed Daintree National Park sees dense lowland rainforest skimming the pristine white sands of the reef-studded coastline. This park contains the world's most diverse collection of primitive flowering plants, the birdlife is prolific and the Daintree River's estuary supports around 200 species of fish and 70 species of crustaceans. It is also home to dangerous estuarine or saltwater crocodiles. The main coastal camping is at Noah Beach. In the Mossman section of the park, join a Kuku Yalanji guide for an indigenous perspective on this unique environment.

Cape Tribulation is remarkably beautiful – tranquil and timeless. A verdant tangle of rainforest runs to the coast, coconut palms and flame trees bend over the sand and the beach arcs into the distance. The coral reef reaches almost to the shoreline. It was less idyllic for Captain James Cook. In 1770, after his ship foundered on the beautiful but treacherous reef, he chose the headland's name because 'here began all our troubles'.

Many operators offer 4WD safaris as well as bushwalks and trekking. Discreetly located around

The unspoilt coastline between Cairns and Port Douglas

Cassowary spotting

Small patches of tropical rainforest along this coast are among the last habitats of the rare and endangered southern cassowary (*Casuarius casuarius*), a huge, flightless bird with a bright blue neck and strange bony 'helmet'. These birds play a critical role in dispersing rainforest seeds and are an important factor in rainforest revegetation. If you are cassowary spotting – a popular pastime around Mission Beach and the Daintree – take care. They stand up to 2 m high, weigh 60 to 70 kg, have powerful legs with sharp spurs and can be fiercely aggressive, especially if protecting their chicks.

Daintree, Cape Tribulation, Thornton Beach and Cow Bay are various types of accommodation, including eco-friendly lodges and resorts, along with interesting eateries. Sailing, sea-kayaking, windsurfing, horseriding, diving, snorkelling and reef trips are on offer, and bird- and wildlife-watching opportunities abound. From here, the rugged Bloomfield Track, impassable in the Wet, is the 4WD-only coastal route to Cooktown. Many visitors venture no further than Cape Tribulation – beyond, a wilderness experience still awaits.

Cooktown and Beyond

Cooktown has a quiet charm all its own. Wide airy streets and a handful of truly grand Victorian buildings hint at its halcyon days when it flourished as a port for the Palmer River goldfields. Earlier still, Cook spent several weeks here in 1770 when he named the river after his reef-damaged barque, the *Endeavour*. History buffs should visit the excellent Cooktown Museum in a former convent (1888) and explore the cemetery. Grassy Hill Lookout, with its quaint lighthouse (1885) and sweeping 360-degree views, is an ideal vantage point for a Coral Sea sunset.

Previous pages Coastline along the Gulf of Carpentaria
Right Fishing the Gulf of Carpentaria

Fishing and the lure of the North

Fishing in northern Queensland is an angler's dream. The 'Marlin Coast', off Cairns, attracts local and international anglers, keen to pit themselves against the mighty black marlin that cruise the deep waters out past the reefs (September to December is the season). Closer inshore smaller game fish such as tuna, Spanish mackerel and sailfish can be caught. An abundance of reef fish includes barracuda, school mackerel, coral trout, sweetlip and red emperor. The target fish for the estuaries is the great barramundi, much prized for its fighting spirit and unique flavour, though you might land mangrove jack, threadfin salmon or trevally. The Bloomfield and Daintree rivers offer excellent estuary fishing.

While the fishing from Cairns to Cooktown is excellent, the fishing in the Gulf of Carpentaria is legendary. These distant waters provide pristine conditions. Fishing guides, charter boats and heli-fishing operators work almost year-round. Deep-sea, estuary and reef-fishing around the islands entice a steady stream of anglers, some of whom fly in just for the fishing. Tropical species such as mangrove jack, queenfish, parrotfish and barramundi, in sizes to brag about, are easily come by. These remote locations demand a 4WD, sturdy boat and BYO everything. They also require caution – crocodiles, sea snakes and, in season, marine stingers inhabit these waters.

Cooktown's fishing is fantastic, whether from the wharf, a tinnie or a luxury cruiser. Spanish mackerel, queenfish, trevally and barramundi can be caught from the public jetty. Fishing charters and cruises to Lizard Island, Princess Charlotte Bay (a veritable fishing paradise) and the reef all leave from Cooktown.

Around halfway up the Cape, Iron Range National Park contains Australia's largest tropical lowland rainforest remnant, valued for its extraordinary biodiversity. Open forest and paperback forest meet the rocky headlands and white sands of the coast. Chili Beach, near Portland Roads, is a remote but lovely campsite. This is BYO everything, including drinking water. Beware of saltwater crocodiles on the beach, rivers and in tidal waterholes.

Cape York

Almost 1000 km north of Cairns, a boardwalk through the dappled light of the rainforest leads to Australia's most northerly mainland beach, known as Frangipani. Visitors then make the trek to the rocky, northernmost tip of the continent, Cape York, where the waters of the Indian and Pacific oceans meet.

Some 14 km away, a favoured camping location is the north-facing Punsand Bay, overlooking the Torres Strait islands. This remote oasis yields exceptional fishing and breathtaking sunsets – it is not for swimming though, with sharks, crocodiles and, in season, marine stingers. A fishing lodge provides campsites, accommodation, fishing safaris and 4WD tours.

The northern tip of the peninsula is a birdwatcher's paradise, especially in summer, when rare rainforest birds migrate from New Guinea. Around 40 km from the tip of the Cape, Bamaga, populated mainly by Torres Strait Islanders, is Australia's most northerly town. Ferries leave daily from Seisia, 5 km north, for Thursday Island and cruises around the islands (see *Contacts*, p. 71). Seisia's jetty is famed for its fishing.

Gulf of Carpentaria

Weipa, 850 km north-west from Cairns, is Cape York's largest town, a base for bauxite mining and a supply stop for those heading north. The fishing is good, as is the birdwatching and the chance to spot marine animals such as dugongs and turtles.

Karumba, at the base of Cape York Peninsula, a general cargo and mining port, services a major prawning and barramundi industry and is an established centre for fishing charters and boat hire. Further west, Burketown – small, remote and hardy – prides itself on its wild outback past and its excellent fishing. Although about 25 km from the waters of the Gulf, it provides boat access on the Albert River and is widely used as a base for fishing. The coastal flats and wetlands are breeding and resting grounds for many of the world's migratory wader birds, ensuring some memorable birdwatching experiences.

Offshore lies the tropical paradise of Sweers Island, part of the Wellesley group. Keen anglers fly in to the island's small specialist fishing lodge, or there are daytrips from Karumba.

Above A marine turtle hauls up on a remote Gulf foreshore
Below Frangipani Beach, Australia's most northerly mainland beach

New South Wales
pacific ocean paradise

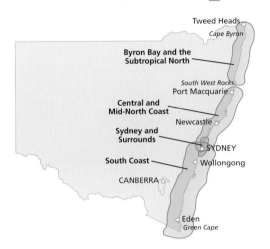

New South Wales' Regions

Sydney and Surrounds
One of the world's most famous urban coastlines, this 87 km shoreline includes scores of suburban beaches renowned for their beauty and quality. The harbour, Sydney's 'front yard', is a vast pleasure ground for the city and the perfect scenic accessory. *See p. 80*

South Coast
Highlights of the South Coast are some of the state's best surfing, clean white-sand beaches and exceptional diving at Jervis Bay, emerald green dairy country dipping down to the Pacific Ocean, and whale-watching near the former whaling port of Eden. *See p. 90*

Central and Mid-North Coast
The capital's getaway coast offers a chain of saltwater lakes (perfect for fishing, boating and kayaking), pockets of national park safeguarding precious natural bush and beautiful beaches, some fascinating history and wonderful wildlife-watching. *See p. 98*

Lord Howe Island
This jewel of an island lies 700 km north-east of Sydney. World Heritage-listed since 1982, the 11 km long island is an exquisite subtropical retreat as well as a nature lover's paradise. *See p. 106*

Byron Bay and the Subtropical North
Unfurling from a backdrop of World Heritage forests and mountains, this subtropical coastline is a place of great beauty, peace and perfect weather. A feature is the clutch of small, idiosyncratic holiday towns that have managed to hold out against major development. *See p. 112*

The tall headlands and rock platforms of this 2000 km stretch bordering the Pacific Ocean fracture into more than 700 sandy beaches, many highly regarded for their natural beauty and quality. Subtropical in the north, temperate in the south, the state's near-perfect weather conditions complement the geography: it is never too hot, rarely too humid; down south the drama of seasonal change plays out; up north, there are strings of warm, sunny winter days.

The New South Wales coast is Australia's most populated region. The urban sprawl of Sydney stretches north to Newcastle and south to Wollongong, intersected, judiciously, by swaths of national park. Elsewhere are major commercial centres, such as Port Macquarie and Tweed Heads, along with scores of fishing and holiday villages of various sizes. There is no part of the New South Wales coast that is difficult to access or without comprehensive facilities.

Despite the bustle, genuine opportunities for peace, escape and adventure abound. National parks, such as Ben Boyd near Eden and Myall Lakes near Newcastle, preserve the landscape in its natural and most beautiful state. Other areas, although settled, feel remote and rural, such as the far south, with its heavy native forests and old-world fishing harbours, and pockets of the north coast, where villages of shacks, caravan parks and populations of lifestyle surfers evoke seaside holidays of the pre-resort era.

Opposite *Byron Bay coastline*
Left *Pelicans are common along the coast*

☎ 13 2077; www.visitnsw.com.au

Sydney and Surrounds

Sydney must rank as one of the world's most sea-focused cities, not just for its unparalleled physical setting but also for its wholesale embrace of the pleasures of sun, surf and sand.

Bondi Beach

Thirty-eight glorious beaches define the city's suburban border in the east, and long-established national parks cap this sun-soaked sprawl in the north and south. Most beaches are clean, patrolled, replete with facilities and packed on weekends with leisure-seekers of every shape and age, united by their shared love of 'the beach'.

Unembarrassed by its surfeit of coastal features, Sydney also claims one of the world's great harbours. The estuary waterway, known as Port Jackson, covers 55 sq km; its 240 km foreshore a giant fracture of headlands, inlets, bays, tributaries and sparkling beaches. Commercial and residential development is heavy, but many prized locations are well preserved, most notably within Sydney Harbour National Park.

There are numerous ways to enjoy this superb coastal environment: surf, sunbake, take a ferry ride, dine alfresco at a beachside cafe, stroll along the cliff-tops, or simply walk the streets to catch that heart-stopping flash of blue and gold that appears at the end of so many suburban streets.

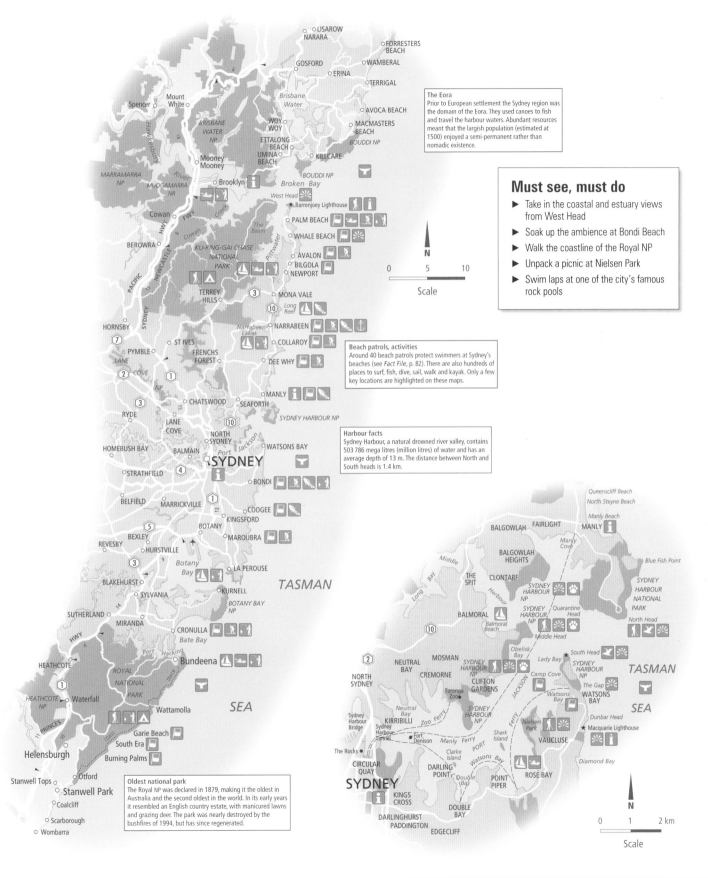

The Eora
Prior to European settlement the Sydney region was the domain of the Eora. They used canoes to fish and travel the harbour waters. Abundant resources meant that the largish population (estimated at 1500) enjoyed a semi-permanent rather than nomadic existence.

Must see, must do

► Take in the coastal and estuary views from West Head
► Soak up the ambience at Bondi Beach
► Walk the coastline of the Royal NP
► Unpack a picnic at Nielsen Park
► Swim laps at one of the city's famous rock pools

Beach patrols, activities
Around 40 beach patrols protect swimmers at Sydney's beaches (see *Fact File*, p. 82). There are also hundreds of places to surf, fish, dive, sail, walk and kayak. Only a few key locations are highlighted on these maps.

Harbour facts
Sydney Harbour, a natural drowned river valley, contains 503 786 mega litres (million litres) of water and has an average depth of 13 m. The distance between North and South heads is 1.4 km.

Oldest national park
The Royal NP was declared in 1879, making it the oldest in Australia and the second oldest in the world. In its early years it resembled an English country estate, with manicured lawns and grazing deer. The park was nearly destroyed by the bushfires of 1994, but has since regenerated.

Fact File

When to go

Sydney has a temperate climate with a subtropical edge. Year-round temperatures are pleasant. Late spring, summer and early autumn are the swimming months: air temperature averages out at 26°C, and water temperatures are in the low twenties. Contact the Bureau of Meteorology (BOM) for weather updates: 1900 926 100; www.bom.gov.au

Top coastal events

Jan *Australia Day Parade on Sydney Harbour* (ferry race, tall ships)
Sydney Festival (arts, summer fun; various locations)
Feb *Cole Classic* (swimming race, Bondi Beach)
Mar *Sydney Harbour Week* (various events)
May *Bridge to Bridge Powerboat Classic* (Hawkesbury River)
July *City to Surf* (fun run)
Sydney International Boat Show (Darling Harbour)
Dec *Sydney to Hobart Yacht Race* (harbour)
New Year's Eve fireworks (harbour)

Safety

Swimming Approximately 34 of Sydney's 38 surf beaches are patrolled. Patrols also operate at three beaches in the southern section of Royal NP and at two harbour beaches: Watsons Bay and Camp Cove. For a list of beaches go to the NSW Safe Waters website: www.safewaters.nsw.gov.au Or contact NSW Surf Life Saving: (02) 9984 7188; www.surflifesaving.com.au

Boating Conditions along the coast can be treacherous in a low pressure system; for up-to-date reports contact BOM's Sydney Waters Service: 1900 969 955. Traffic is heavy on Sydney Harbour; familiarity with rules governing the prevention of collisions is essential. For all boating information – licences, safety, special events, boating and weather forecasts – contact NSW Waterways Authority: 13 1236 (within NSW); (02) 9563 8556; www.waterways.nsw.gov.au

Surfing Sydney has some of the best surfing breaks in the country but these can get very crowded and surfers need to exercise both caution and courtesy. During a low pressure system waves can be huge – up to 5 m. For an up-to-date conditions report go to www.coastalwatch.com

Restrictions/regulations

Fishing Recreational fishers must carry a licence to fish in all NSW waters; bag and size limits apply. Contact NSW Fisheries: 1300 369 365; www.fisheries.nsw.gov.au

CLIMATE												SYDNEY
	J	F	M	A	M	J	J	A	S	O	N	D
Max °C	26	26	25	22	19	17	16	18	20	22	24	25
Min °C	19	19	17	15	11	9	8	9	11	13	16	17
Rain mm	104	113	134	126	121	131	101	80	69	79	83	78
Raindays	12	12	13	12	12	12	10	10	11	12	11	12

Marine reserves Much of the Sydney foreshore – coastal and harbour – is protected by Intertidal Protected Areas (IPAs). Within IPAs, the removal of any invertebrate from rock platforms is an offence, which means anglers should carry their own bait. Aquatic reserves protect certain key sites along the coast; restrictions vary; contact NSW Fisheries for further information (see *Fishing*, above).

National parks Permits are required to camp overnight in parks along the coast. Royal and Ku-ring-gai Chase NPs charge a vehicle entry fee (see *Contacts*, opposite).

Shipwrecks Historic shipwrecks and associated relics are protected. For further information contact NSW Heritage Office: (02) 9873 8574; www.heritage.nsw.gov.au

Sydney Harbour

The harbour is the location of many of the city's important historic sites, its famous structures – the Opera House and Harbour Bridge – and some of its most desirable homes; the preferred arena for big events – firework displays, festival openings, commemorative celebrations; and a much-loved venue for all sorts of recreational activities from family picnics to bushwalking, sailing, swimming, fishing, diving, cruising, kayaking and even surfing.

Sydney faces its 'front yard'

Best Beaches

Swimming in the relatively calm waters of the harbour is a great alternative to the big-surf experience on offer at the coastal beaches. On the south-east side of the harbour at Vaucluse is Nielsen Park, a small, shark-netted gem with

Fort Denison, part of Sydney Harbour National Park

Sydney Harbour National Park

Sydney Harbour National Park preserves large areas of one of the world's most desirable foreshores in something close to a natural state. Prime attractions and activities include the ocean views, seabirds and historic sites of North and South heads; the five accessible harbour islands, including the 1857 fortress/prison, Fort Denison; the Manly Scenic Walkway, an 8 km trek from Spit Bridge to Manly, taking in pockets of rainforest and woodland and a succession of pretty coves and beaches; and the Bradleys Head and Chowder Head Walk, a 5 km stroll from Taronga Zoo through well-preserved bushland, with historic sites and legendary city views.

plenty of shade, protected within Sydney Harbour National Park. Further east, just inside South Head, is the picturesque and patrolled Camp Cove, known for its glamorous patronage. North Shore swimmers head for beautiful Balmoral Beach in Middle Harbour, which has three distinct areas: sea baths, a harbour beach protected by a shark net and an ornate bathers pavilion housing good restaurants.

Ferry Destinations

The cheapest and most rewarding way to experience the harbour is to take a ride on a commuter ferry from Circular Quay. Most visitors choose the 11 km ride to Manly, a northern suburb occupying a spit of land between the harbour and ocean, where attractions include a fun park and aquarium; a famous surf beach and protected family beaches; an art gallery and historic wharf; and miles of pine-shaded esplanade, where visitors can stroll, people-watch and dine on fish and chips.

A similar experience is to be had at Watsons Bay, which lies on the harbour side of South Head. Tiny weatherboard cottages pack the narrow streets of this former fishing community. On the foreshore, the famous Doyle's feeds ferry-loads of hungry tourists, while the pub does a roaring trade in its waterfront beer garden. A short walk leads to the tip of South Head, where the national park protects the bushland and historic sites of a former naval compound. Wander over to The Gap, a famous lookout located on the ocean front of Watsons Bay. South along the cliff-line is Macquarie Lighthouse (built in 1883).

Other ferry destinations include Balmain, Taronga Zoo, Mosman, Cremorne, Kirribilli and Double Bay. At any one of these spots you can disembark and explore the foreshores, with their grassy reserves and small, protected beaches.

Contacts

Visitor information

Sydney city 106 George St
The Rocks
(02) 9255 1788

Brooklyn (Hawkesbury River)
5 Bridge St
(02) 9985 7064

Manly South Steyne
(02) 9977 1088

Palm Beach 122 Pacific Rd
(02) 9974 1373

Sydney Harbour
www.sydneyharbour.nsw.gov.au

Parks and reserves

NSW National Parks and Wildlife Service (NPWS)
General information on parks and marine reserves
1300 361 967
www.nationalparks.nsw.gov.au

Ku-ring-gai Chase NP
(02) 9974 1011

Royal NP
(02) 9542 0648

Sydney Harbour NP
(02) 9427 5033

Activities

Contact visitor information centres (see above) for details of activities, tours and charter services.

Other

Barrenjoey Lighthouse
Tours
(02) 9457 9853

Macquarie Lighthouse
Tours
(02) 8969 2131

Palm Beach Ferry
(02) 9918 2747

Sydney Ferries
13 1300

Keeping fit along Sydney's scenic surf coast

Sydney's South Coast

Sydney's suburban south stretches 46 km from Bondi to Cronulla. Beyond Cronulla, across Port Hacking, lies the Royal National Park. Sandstone headlands and treacherous cliffs dominate much of the foreshore, with beaches making up only one-fifth of the total coastline.

Bondi Beach

Iconic Bondi Beach is just 7 km from the CBD. The beach was privately owned until 1856, when the New South Wales government purchased it for the 'pleasure of the people', a prescient comment if ever there was one. From 1894, the Bondi tram began ferrying families and office workers from the city; the term 'shooting through like a Bondi tram' referred to the end-of-day escape to freedom and leisure.

Bondi was a bohemian and immigrant enclave from the 1950s. Beachgoers continued to visit in droves, but the middle classes did not want to live there. The developers of the 1970s and 1980s skirted the area, leaving intact the suburb's jagged horizon of pastel-coloured Art Deco apartment buildings. Despite the real estate boom of recent years, the population remains diverse, a mix of professionals, artists, students, surfers and immigrants – new and established.

The beach itself stretches 800 m between a set of protective headlands. A promenade borders the beach for its entire length, incorporating the grand 1928 Bondi Pavilion. Beyond, a grassy reserve rises up the hill to meet Campbell Parade. The north end of the beach, with its safe conditions, rock pool and year-round patrols, is the preserve of young families. South Bondi, rougher and less protected, draws a younger, more active crowd, including hordes of board-riders who come for the sizeable, if inconsistent, beach breaks.

South to Cronulla

The Bondi to Coogee walking track is a wonderful way to explore the eastern suburbs coastline, taking in Tamarama, Bronte, Clovelly and Coogee. These beaches are all patrolled and are easily reached by bus or car (see opposite).

The beaches of the far south are busy and suburban. The scene is boogie boards, beach umbrellas and eskys, underscored by the scent of sunscreen. Maroubra, at 1 km, is the longest beach in the eastern suburbs. Good parking, bus access and a lovely green picnic area make this a popular day out with families. Surfers regard the breaks here as among the best in Sydney.

The broad expanse of Bate Bay sits just to the north of Sydney's southern border, Port Hacking. The bay's 4.8 km stretch of sand is the longest in Sydney. South, it has four patrolled beach areas: Wanda, Elouera, North Cronulla and Cronulla.

Australian National Maritime Museum

Located on the waterfront at Darling Harbour, this museum charts the history of Australia's relationship with the sea. The major themes include exploration, immigration, commerce, warfare and culture. The museum is housed in a billowing sail-like structure; outside, along the docks, are several display vessels including HMAS *Vampire* (1952), the last of the navy's big gun ships, and the *Akarana* (1888), a New Zealand racing cutter.

BONDI TO COOGEE *walk*

The hills of this famous cliff-top walk provide the walker with a rigorous workout. And the scenery? Few other major cities can compete with this expanse of heaving waves, treacherous cliffs and endless horizons, offset by beautiful beaches and clusters of apartment buildings and houses jostling for water views.

The Icebergs

This rock pool is home to a recreational club (established in 1929) that asks prospective members to swim most Sundays in winter, regardless of the weather. The old clubhouse has been transformed into one of Sydney's smartest restaurants.

Tamarama

Tiny Tamarama is the beach of choice for Sydney's gay population and many of the city's younger crowd. Short in length and set deep within the shoreline, it has Sydney's most dangerous and – for the initiated – exciting surf.

Visitor information
See *Contacts*, p. 83

To Dover Heights

BONDI BEACH

PDE PARK

BONDI

CAMPBELL

Beach

Rock Pool

Bondi

Bondi Bay

Ben Buckler

Bondi Baths (Icebergs)

BONDI ROAD

To Bondi Junction

INTERTIDAL PROTECTION AREA

TASMAN

TAMARAMA PARK

MARKS PARK

Mackenzies Point

Mackenzies Bay

TAMARAMA

Tamarama Beach
Tamarama Bay

BRONTE

BRONTE PARK

Nelson Bay

Bronte Beach

BRONTE ROAD

BRONTE

MACPHERSON ST

SEA

Bronte Baths

Waverley Cemetery

Beeries Cove

CLOVELLY

INTERTIDAL PROTECTION AREA

To Bondi Junction

Clovelly Beach

Baths

BURROWS PARK

Clovelly Bay

Shark Point

ROAD

Gordons Bay

COOGEE

ARDEN

Coogee Beach

DUNNINGHAM PARK

COOGEE BAY ROAD

Baths

To Maroubra

Coogee Bay

McIver Baths

Wylies Baths

N

0   500 metres

Waverley Cemetery

This historic and scenically positioned cemetery undulates across 40 ha of coastal hills south of Bronte. Established in 1875, it is full of ornate monuments and statues. Famous internees include writer Henry Lawson and Olympic swimmer Fanny Durack.

Bronte

The 250 m long Bronte Beach is home to Australia's oldest surf lifesaving club (established in 1903). Set in a deeply indented valley, the beach is bordered by parkland and flanked by a set of headlands.

Clovelly

The beach fronting this peaceful suburb is extremely short, though quite wide. Two rocky ridges extend some 300 m out to sea, creating something akin to a long lap pool – and one of Sydney's safest beaches.

Coogee

This is a long (400 m), safe family beach, the second most popular beach in the eastern suburbs after Bondi. At the southern end are the heritage-listed Wylies Baths, along with McIver Baths – a pool reserved for women and children.

WALKING NOTES

- Start at the Icebergs on Notts Ave, South Bondi, off Campbell Pde (bus from Bondi Junction or city)
- Finish at Coogee Beach (bus to Bondi Junction or city from Arden St)
- Allow two hours one-way
- Paths are wide and well-sealed, but the 100 or so steps make wheelchair and pram access almost impossible
- There is no shade: wear a hat and sunscreen and carry water
- There are toilet blocks, picnic areas and cafes, around the beach areas

Where to ...

Kayak Tours of the Harbour, Port Hacking, Pittwater and the Hawkesbury are popular; open-sea kayaking is also available.

Fish All the estuaries offer good fishing, including Sydney Harbour. Along the coast, the rock platforms are popular with anglers – safety issues are paramount (see *Taking Care*, p. 260). Gutters form along the surf beaches, offering flathead, mulloway, groper and tailor – go early morning and evening and avoid the beach crowds.

Dive The southern beaches offer superb shore diving, with their underwater landscapes of cave and pinnacles and sea life populations of shark and groper. Top spots include North Bondi, Shark Point (Clovelly), Gordons Bay and South Coogee. In the north, popular sites include Long Reef, where the sea life is prolific. Offshore from nearby Narrabeen Beach is the wreck of the *Dunkfield* (1889), located in 20 m of water.

Surf Just about everywhere: beginners head for Bondi; top spots for experienced surfers are Avalon, Narrabeen and Maroubra. Most spots are crowded and some of the locals are protective of their turf.

Sail/windsurf The harbour is a great place to learn to windsurf or sail, with Balmoral the best starting point. Botany Bay, Narrabeen Lakes and Pittwater are popular windsurfing destinations

Sydney's **rock pools**

Sydney's built rock pools are an extraordinary feature of the coastline, gracing most of the major suburban beaches. Many were built – carved from the shale and sandstone headlands – in the early 1900s when the surf was regarded as too rugged for most swimmers. The pools are still widely used by lap swimmers, families and the elderly. Among the best is the heritage-listed Wylies Baths (1907), which is surrounded by an elevated timber deck perfect for sunbaking. The

eight-lane, 50 m North Narrabeen rock pool is much favoured by lap swimmers, not least for its superb ocean aspect. The Bronte Baths were built in 1887. The pool is on the elevated headland at the south end, squeezed between pounding waves and a tall cliff-face. Not to be forgotten is the Icebergs, South Bondi, home of the famous, eponymous winter swimming club, whose members mark the start of the season by jumping into a pool bobbing with ice.

The northern end, known as Greenhills, is a coastal wilderness and only accessible by foot or 4WD. Cronulla Beach is the only southern beach with a train station, which makes it popular. Stretching 300 m, it is backed by a generous grassy reserve.

Royal National Park
Australia's first national park – it was declared in 1879 – begins at the edge of Sydney's southern reaches. Millions of years of weathering have carved a distinctive set of features out of the park's sandstone bed, including precipitous cliffs, rock platforms, gorges and sea caves. Nestled within these dramatic rockscapes are 11 small, unspoilt beaches, three of which are patrolled. A two-day, 26 km walk starts at Bundeena and snakes along the park's beaches, cliffs and escarpments to Otford in the south; obtain a bush-camping permit before heading out (see *Contacts*, p. 83). Access to the park is by rail, road or passenger ferry across Port Hacking from Cronulla.

Sydney's North Coast
Sydney's northern suburban coastline is a 40 km sweep of surf and sand, incorporating a total of

19 beaches. Most of these beaches are patrolled, clean and easily reached by bus from Manly or the city. North of the suburban border lie the bush-clad estuaries of Ku-ring-gai Chase National Park.

Manly to Narrabeen
Manly is the most accessible of the northern beaches, and certainly the best known. Queenscliff Head marks the north point of the beach and Manly itself lies at the southern end of the 1.4 km stretch of sand. Family friendly Fairy Bower and Shelly beaches are tucked away to the immediate south of Manly. Queenscliff has good surf and is a favourite with seasoned bodysurfers. A headland tunnel connects Queenscliff with Freshwater Beach to the immediate north. Freshwater was the site of Australia's first surfing demonstration: in 1915, Hawaiian surf champion Duke Kahanamoku took to the waves with a surfboard that looked not dissimilar to a wooden plank and showed the crowd of thousands how it was done. The fad, you could say, took hold.

Curl Curl, North Curl Curl, Dee Why, Long Reef, Collaroy and Narrabeen beaches swoop north in a series of crescents of various lengths and widths. Facilities include grassy foreshore areas, changing sheds and rock pools. Shop around for surf instruction, sea-kayaking adventures and windsurfing opportunities. Nature lovers should take a walk around the Long Reef Aquatic Reserve, which protects a series of wide rock platforms and rich eco-communities of marine plants and invertebrates.

The Barrenjoey Peninsula

This long knuckle of land stretches north from Mona Vale to Palm Beach; on one side lies the Pacific Ocean, on the other, the sparkling, calm waters of Pittwater.

Bilgola Beach is one of Sydney's prettiest coastal inlets, nestling deep within a rainforest-clad valley. To the north is Avalon, an exposed beach with excellent conditions for surfing. Whale Beach is a 600 m long stretch of gleaming sand and surf, flanked by imposing 40 m high headlands at either end. Take the Whale Beach Road for spectacular coastal views en route to Palm Beach.

Palm Beach may be Australia's most exclusive beachside suburb, but the large weekend crowds arrive from all parts of Sydney and all walks of life. The beach stretches for 2.3 km along the northern tip of Barrenjoey Peninsula, backed by a narrow ridge of land across which the homes of the rich and famous sprawl. At the tip of the peninsula, and accessible only by foot, is the historic Barrenjoey Lighthouse (built in 1881) – tours are run on the fourth Sunday of every month. To explore Pittwater,

hop aboard a Palm Beach ferry from the wharf in Pittwater Park. Operators in the area facilitate sailing, kayaking, fishing, surfing and diving activities.

Ku-ring-gai Chase National Park

The 15 000 ha Ku-ring-gai Chase curls around the broad sweep of Broken Bay and its three connecting waterways: Pittwater, the Hawkesbury River and Cowan Creek. The park's foreshore geography is a fractured maze of creeks, coves, islands and beaches, clad in thick bush and spiked with rocky outcrops of sandstone. Park highlights include views from West Head, which can been reached by road or walking track from The Basin; the Aboriginal engravings at West Head; and the series of tiny settlements that nestle into valley folds along the Hawkesbury. The best way to see the park is from the water; options include houseboat hire, kayaking tours, ferry rides and a tour with Australia's last riverboat postal service. Camping in the park is at The Basin.

Above A darter dries its feathers, Royal National Park
Below West Head, Ku-ring-gai Chase National Park

South Coast

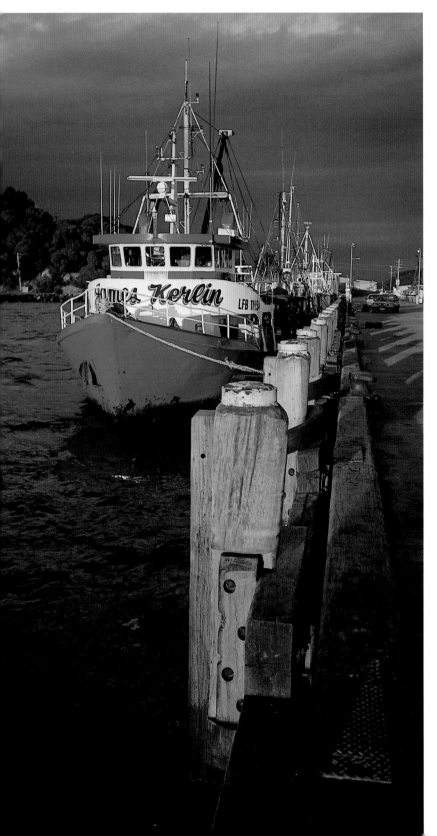

Dramatic rock formations and jutting headlands, punctuated by sweeping beaches, lakes, inlets and countless serene coves, define the South Coast. Stretching from Sydney's outer limits to the Victorian border, the coast is heavily populated in parts but retains a laid-back atmosphere.

The South Coast takes in the Illawarra, Shoalhaven, Eurobodalla and Sapphire Coast districts, around 600 km in all. The narrow coastal plain that extends from Sydney's outer reaches widens south of Wollongong, becoming a fertile tract of farming country where lush green hills curve down to the rollers of the South Pacific Ocean. Further south still, as the population density thins, tracts of dense native vegetation edge to the shoreline.

Wollongong, the state's third largest city and an industrial powerhouse, lies an hour south of Sydney. The towns that dot the coastline all the way to the Victorian border are fuelled by fishing, tourism and an increasingly large retiree population. Magnificent scenery, tranquil lakes and inlets, beautiful beaches and friendly towns entice holiday-makers from Sydney, Canberra, Melbourne and beyond. Accommodation is plentiful and diverse; a highlight is the opportunity to camp in reserves and foreshore caravan parks. The fertile hinterland provides a fresh food bounty for the many cafes and restaurants. Fishing, beyond being a major industry, is a hugely popular recreational pursuit. The surfing is great, there are wonderful dive sites, and a chain of national parks makes the magnificent natural bush and abundant wildlife accessible.

Fishing boats, Eden

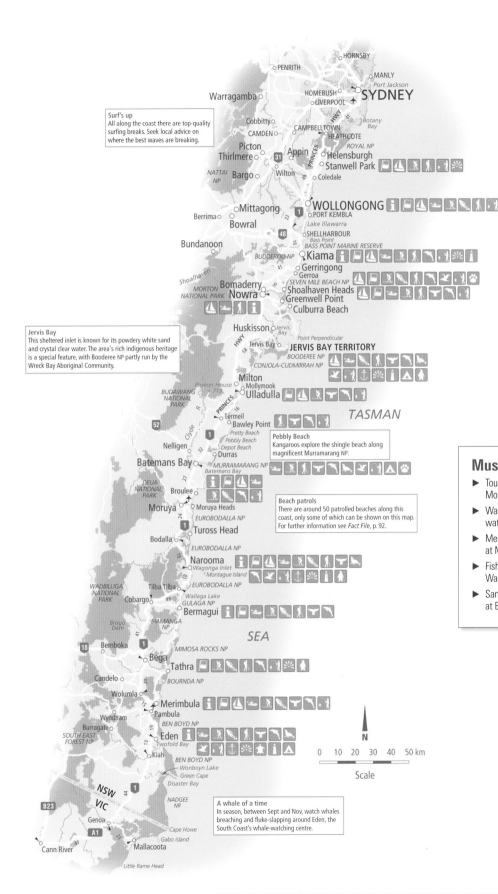

HORNSBY

PENRITH

MANLY
Port Jackson

Warragamba

HOMEBUSH
LIVERPOOL
SYDNEY

Cobbitty
Botany
Bay

CAMDEN
CAMPBELLTOWN
HEATHCOTE

Picton
ROYAL NP
Thirlmere
Appin
Helensburgh
Stanwell Park
Coledale

NATTAI
NP
Bargo
Wilton

Berrima
Mittagong
WOLLONGONG
PORT KEMBLA
Bowral
Lake Illawarra

Bundanoon
SHELLHARBOUR
Bass Point
BASS POINT MARINE RESERVE

BUDDEROO NP
Kiama
Gerringong
Gerroa
SEVEN MILE BEACH NP

Shoalhaven
MORTON
NATIONAL PARK
Bomaderry
Nowra
Shoalhaven Heads
Greenwell Point
Culburra Beach

Huskisson
Jervis
Bay
Point Perpendicular

Jervis Bay
JERVIS BAY TERRITORY
BOODEREE NP
CONJOLA-CUDMIRRAH NP

Pigeon House
▲ 719
Milton
Mollymook
Ulladulla

BUDAWANG
NATIONAL
PARK
PRINCES

Termeil
Bawley Point

Pretty Beach
Pebbly Beach
Depot Beach
Durras

TASMAN

Nelligen

Batemans Bay
MURRAMARANG NP
Batemans Bay

DEUA
NATIONAL
PARK
Broulee

Moruya
Moruya Heads
EUROBODALLA NP

Bodalla
Tuross Head
EUROBODALLA NP

Narooma
Wagonga Inlet
Montague Island

WADBILLIGA
NATIONAL
PARK
Tilba Tilba
EUROBODALLA NP
Wallaga Lake
GULAGA NP

Cobargo
Bermagui

Brogo
Dam
BIAMANGA
NP

SEA

Bemboka
MIMOSA ROCKS NP

Bega
Tathra

Candelo
BOURNDA NP

Wolumla
Merimbula
Pambula

Wyndham
BEN BOYD NP

Burragate
Eden
Twofold Bay

SOUTH EAST
FOREST NP
Kiah
BEN BOYD NP
Wonboyn Lake
Green Cape
Disaster Bay

NSW
VIC
NADGEE
NR

Genoa
Cape Howe
Gabo Island

Cann River
Mallacoota

Little Rame Head

N

0 10 20 30 40 50 km
Scale

Surf's up
All along the coast there are top-quality surfing breaks. Seek local advice on where the best waves are breaking.

Jervis Bay
This sheltered inlet is known for its powdery white sand and crystal clear water. The area's rich indigenous heritage is a special feature, with Booderee NP partly run by the Wreck Bay Aboriginal Community.

Pebbly Beach
Kangaroos explore the shingle beach along magnificent Murramarang NP.

Beach patrols
There are around 50 patrolled beaches along this coast, only some of which can be shown on this map. For further information see *Fact File*, p. 92.

Must see, must do

► Tour the wildlife haven of Montague Island

► Watch whales breaching the waters off Eden

► Meet the beach-loving kangaroos at Murramarang NP

► Fish the turquoise waters of Narooma's Wagonga Inlet

► Sample succulent Clyde River oysters at Batemans Bay

A whale of a time
In season, between Sept and Nov, watch whales breaching and fluke-slapping around Eden, the South Coast's whale-watching centre.

Batemans Bay ☎ (02) 4472 6900; Eden ☎ (02) 6496 1953; www.southcoast.com.au

Fact File

When to go
The northern part of the coast has a mild, sunny coastal climate. Summers can be warm to hot, tempered by sea breezes. Further south is warm to hot in summer, again with ocean breezes, and cool in winter. The best time for whale-watching is Oct–Nov. Contact the Bureau of Meteorology (BOM) for weather updates: 1900 955 361; www.bom.gov.au

Top coastal events
Jan	*Gerringong Surf Spectacular*
	Bluewater Fishing Classic (Bermagui)
Feb	*Jazz Festival* (Kiama)
Mar	*Eden Fishing Competition*
	Blowhole Big Fish Classic (Kiama)
Easter	*Blessing of the Fleet* (Ulladulla)
April	*Seaside & Arts Festival* (Thirroul)
May	*Fishing Festival* (Ulladulla)
July	*Festival of the Sea* (Batemans Bay)
Oct	*Eden Whale Festival*
	Country Music Festival (Merimbula)
Nov	*Seaside Festival & Colonial Ball* (Kiama)
	Harbourfest (Port Kembla)

Safety
Swimming There are fine surf beaches all along the coast, from Wollongong to Cape Howe, but these are ocean beaches and strong rips and currents can occur. There are also numerous sheltered bays and inlets suitable for swimming. Around 50 beaches along the South Coast are patrolled by surf lifesavers on weekends, public holidays and during peak summer periods. Swimmers should take special care at isolated and unpatrolled beaches. A list of beaches is at NSW Safe Waters website: www.safewaters.nsw.gov.au Or contact NSW Surf Life Saving: (02) 9984 7188; www.surflifesaving.com.au

Other water activities Prevailing winds in summer are north-north-easterlies, with a tendency to swing sharply to the south unexpectedly. For all boating information – licences, safety, special events, boating and weather forecasts – contact NSW Waterways Authority: 13 1236 (within NSW); (02) 9563 8556; www.waterways.nsw.gov.au For up-to-date weather reports contact BOM's NSW Coastal Waters Service on 1900 926 101.

Restrictions/regulations
Fishing Recreational fishers must carry a licence to fish in all NSW waters; bag and size limits apply. Contact NSW Fisheries: 1300 369 365; www.fisheries.nsw.gov.au

Marine reserves Fishing is allowed in NSW marine parks, with some restrictions. Fishing and/or removal or harm of plants or animals is prohibited in aquatic reserves. Jervis Bay Marine Park extends from Kinghorn Point to Sussex Inlet, and includes most of Jervis Bay; fishing is restricted in some areas. Fishing is prohibited in Bushrangers Bay (Bass Point), an aquatic sanctuary. For further information contact

CLIMATE												WOLLONGONG
	J	F	M	A	M	J	J	A	S	O	N	D
Max °C	26	26	25	22	20	17	17	18	20	22	24	25
Min °C	17	17	16	14	11	9	8	8	10	12	14	16
Rain mm	107	109	118	131	116	109	91	61	67	68	72	86
Raindays	9	8	9	9	8	8	7	6	6	7	8	8

CLIMATE												MERIMBULA
	J	F	M	A	M	J	J	A	S	O	N	D
Max °C	24	25	23	21	19	16	16	17	18	20	21	23
Min °C	15	15	14	11	8	6	4	5	7	9	12	14
Rain mm	77	79	91	83	65	69	41	42	56	69	88	78
Raindays	10	10	10	9	9	9	7	9	11	11	13	11

Marine Parks Authority NSW: (02) 9228 4918; www.mpa.nsw.gov.au

National parks Permits are required to camp overnight in national parks along the coast. Some of the more popular parks charge a vehicle entry fee. (see *Contacts*, opposite).

Shipwrecks Historic shipwrecks and associated relics are protected. Recreational diving is permitted on many sites. For further information contact NSW Heritage Office: (02) 9873 8574; www.heritage.nsw.gov.au

Kiama – the blowhole

In 1797, English explorer George Bass commented on the 'tremendous' noise emanating from the blowhole, a natural phenomenon that has since become the town's most famous tourist attraction. When the south-easterlies are running, seawater is pushed though a hole in the cliff-face, sometimes shooting plumes 60 m into the air.

The coastline at Stanwell Park

The clear waters of Booderee National Park

Stanwell Park and Wollongong

At the southern tip of Royal National Park, just 54 km south of Sydney, the Southern Tablelands stretch to the Pacific Ocean, creating breathtaking coastal vistas. Headlands plummet into the water, broken by rocky and sandy coves. The historic beachside town of Stanwell Park is popular with hang-gliders.

Wollongong is home to steelworks, copper smelting and other heavy industry and an international shipping port is located at the Port Kembla Harbour. About 85 km south of Sydney, the state's third largest city spreads along a narrow coastal plain, with the hills and forests of the Illawarra escarpment to the west. To the east lie 17 sparkling surf beaches, patrolled by lifeguards during the peak summer season. Port Kembla Harbour offers great breakwater fishing for the land-based angler – mulloway, snapper, bream, luderick and tailor are typical hauls. It may be heavily fished, but the shallow waters of Lake Illawarra also yield consistently reliable catches.

Some of the region's best fishing is just past Lake Illawarra, at Bass Point. The Bass Point Marine Reserve is recognised as a premier dive and snorkelling location. Port Jackson sharks, eagle rays, groper, giant cuttlefish and a vivid mosaic of sponges, waving sea tulips and colourful nudibranchs are typical of this diverse ecosystem.

Kiama to Nowra

The township of Kiama nestles around several small charming bays, with Norfolk Island pines standing sentinel on the headlands. The intriguing blowhole (see opposite), the 1887 lighthouse and the visitor information centre, housed in one of the old keepers' cottages, can all be seen at Blowhole Point, near Kiama Harbour.

A 10-minute drive south, winding past natural bushland and undulating dairy country, leads past the small seaside townships of Gerringong and Gerroa to the glorious sweep of Seven Mile Beach. The beach is protected within Seven Mile Beach National Park, a small but important habitat for birdlife. Walking, surfing, windsurfing and fishing are the order of the day here.

A little further south, Nowra is a major business, service and tourism capital, a bustling city 179 km south of Sydney, 17 km inland on the beautiful Shoalhaven River. Small towns cling to the coastline near the broad mouth of the river: Shoalhaven Heads, a popular resort and kite-flying venue; the fishing village of Greenwell Point, known for its luscious oysters; and Culburra Beach, home to Nowra's surf club.

Jervis Bay

Jervis Bay, a picturesque inlet blessed with pure white-sand beaches and crystal clear water, is one of the South Coast's special gems. The more sheltered northern beaches are a favourite with families. On the north-eastern side of the peninsula the intriguing rock strata of the Beecroft Peninsula creates a dramatic cliffscape pounded by the Pacific. Aboriginal archaeological sites scattered through the heathland are a reminder of the area's rich indigenous heritage. Point Perpendicular provides spectacular views, an elegant and much photographed lighthouse (built in 1899) and a fine vantage point for spotting whales, dolphins and seals (access to the point is not always available; check with visitor information).

Contacts

Visitor information

Batemans Bay Princes Hwy
(02) 4472 6900
www.naturecoast-tourism.com.au

Bermagui Lamont St
1800 654 808

Eden Princes Hwy
(02) 6496 1953
www.sapphirecoast.com.au

Kiama Blowhole Pt
(02) 4232 3322 or
1300 654 262
www.kiama.com.au

Merimbula Beach St
(02) 6497 4900
www.sapphirecoast.com.au

Narooma Princes Hwy
(02) 4476 2881

Wollongong cnr Kembla and
Crown sts
www.tourismwollongong.com
(02) 4227 5545 or
1800 240 737

Parks and reserves

NSW National Parks and Wildlife Service (NPWS)
General information on parks and reserves
1300 361 967
www.nationalparks.nsw.gov.au

Ben Boyd NP
(02) 6495 5001

Booderee NP
General
(02) 4443 7059
Camping
(02) 4443 0977

Murramarang NP
Campsite bookings
(02) 4478 6582 (Depot Beach)
(02) 4457 2019 (Pebbly Beach)

Murramarang Aboriginal Reserve
(02) 4887 7270 (Fitzroy Falls Visitor Centre)

Activities

Contact visitor information centres (see above) for details of activities, tours and charter services.

Other

Green Cape Lightstation
Accommodation and tours
(02) 6495 5000

Montague Island Tours
(02) 4476 2881

Umburra Cultural Centre
(02) 4473 7232

Montague Island

Six nautical miles offshore from Narooma, 82 ha
Montague Island is a natural wildlife refuge. Steely-
blue little penguins nightly shuffle ashore to one of
Australia's largest colonies. The rocky shores are a
major haul-out site for Australian and New Zealand
fur seals, with numbers peaking between August
and October. Thousands of migratory short-tailed
shearwaters breed here; crested terns scrape their
shallow nests in the sand each October; and silver
gulls breed in vast and noisy numbers. Warm water
currents from the South Pacific blend with nutrient-
rich water from the Southern Ocean, enticing
whales, dolphins and turtles to the area. The
lighthouse, first lit in 1881, is built from the grey
granite that imbues the island with its stark beauty.
The area's Aboriginal inhabitants visited the island
for thousands of years to harvest seabirds and their
eggs. Regular tours run by park rangers explore the
island's indigenous, European and natural heritage
(see *Contacts*, p. 93).

The main town is
Huskisson. Its settlement
history, dating from
the early 1800s, and
its historic boatbuilding
industry are recorded
in the town's maritime
museum.

Scuba divers
enjoy the underwater
wonderland, including
the SS *Merimbula*
(wrecked 1928) in shallow waters off Whale Point.
Professional operators hire equipment and organise
dives. Sailing, cruising, swimming, windsurfing
and sea-kayaking are all enjoyed on the bay.

Dolphin-watching cruises (look out for little
penguins too) leave Huskisson daily, while June
to November are the months for whale sightings.

Pale sandy beaches and crumbling cliffs rim
the coast of the delightful Booderee National Park,
on the southern side of Jervis Bay. Sandstone cliffs,
towering 90 m or more, flank isolated Steamers
Beach, one of several fine beaches in Booderee.
The gentle terrain, easy walking trails, a wealth of
flowering plants and rich birdlife (200 species have
been recorded) make this a great area for walking.
At Wreck Bay, on the southern headland, shell
middens recall the feasts of Aboriginal inhabitants
over thousands of years. The name Booderee is
from the Dhurga language, meaning 'bay of plenty'
or 'plenty of fish'.

Ulladulla to Murramarang National Park

At Ulladulla, the annual Blessing of the Fleet ceremony at Easter proudly celebrates the heritage of the Italian fishing community who settled near the lovely bay in the 1930s. World-class surfing conditions attract the surfing fraternity and surf titles are held here regularly.

Around 26 km south of Ulladulla, Bawley Point is one of the prettiest spots on the coast, with distinctive Pigeon House Mountain (named by Sir Joseph Banks in 1770) in the distance, peaceful beaches, a wealth of birdlife and pods of dolphins enjoying the surf. Just out of town, the coastal Murramarang Aboriginal Reserve (open to visitors) protects a tribal burial site that has a vast midden containing ancient stone artefacts, shellfish and animal remains (see *Contacts*, p. 93).

A string of lovely beaches, such as Pretty Beach and Pebbly Beach (known for its beach-loving eastern grey kangaroos), are framed by the coastal rainforest of Murramarang National Park. Swimming, fishing, canoeing on Durras Lake, beach and forest walks, and wildlife-watching occupy visitors to the park.

Batemans Bay

On the mouth of the majestic Clyde River, Batemans Bay is a busy and growing town, well geared to tourists with its ample accommodation, good restaurants and holiday facilities. Anglers can indulge themselves with river, estuary, jetty and surf-fishing, and offshore gamefishing. Diving, sailing, sea-kayaking and canoeing are popular and houseboats cruise inland on the navigable Clyde. A local specialty are the oysters grown in farms on the river – get them fresh.

Narooma

The seaside resort of Narooma overlooks the inviting Wagonga Inlet, with its tranquil waters and magnificent views that face inland to a buffer of dense state forest and east to the Pacific Ocean. A stunning cliff-top golf course, cruises on the inlet, fishing charters and a swag of good restaurants keep holiday-makers busy. National park ranger-guided tours explore the fascinating wildlife haven of Montague Island (see opposite). The waters around

Above *Kangaroos graze in Murramarang National Park* Below *The holiday town of Merimbula*

Old lighthouse keeper's residence, Green Cape

Montague are fish-rich territory, with tuna and marlin, kingfish and snapper to mention a few.

Bermagui to Merimbula
The harbour hums with activity in the fishing port of Bermagui, curved around sandy Horseshoe Bay. Bermagui's fishing is legendary. The continental shelf is at its closest point to eastern Australia here. The steep ocean drop-off is only 20 km from Bermagui, which means exceptional deep-sea fishing just offshore, with yellowfin tuna and the famed black marlin the prized catches.

Head to Wallaga Lake for sailing, canoeing, bushwalking and wildlife-watching. Nearby, Umbarra Aboriginal Cultural Centre documents the heritage of the local Yuin people.

At tiny Tathra, which is located between Mimosa Rocks and Bournda national parks, the cafe and rustic museum in an old cargo shed on the weathered timber wharf have a mesmerising view across the sparkling deep green waters. Dolphins and little penguins often swim close to shore. Tathra's beaches are ideal for surfing, windsurfing, swimming, fishing, diving or just lazing about.

Merimbula's almost urban sprawl and ever-increasing array of holiday apartments and houses cannot detract from the quality of its beaches, or its easy going holiday feel. There are tidal lakes, fine beaches and good fishing – in fact, it is hard not to catch a fish from Merimbula Wharf. The Merimbula and Pambula river mouths provide exceptional surfing breaks, though things can get rather crowded in summer.

Eden and Beyond
Eden, the state's most southerly town, a busy commercial fishing port and centre for the local timber industry, situated on Twofold Bay, is low-key and unpretentious. Sturdy fishing boats line up around the jetty, and charter boats head out daily, luring anglers with the promise of big hauls. Eden began as a whaling port. In the 1840s, 27 whaleboats were based here, but the wholesale slaughter killed the industry itself. The Killer Whale Museum tells the story. Whales again swim past on the migratory journey to their Antarctic feeding grounds (September to December are the best months for whale-watching). Dolphins, seals, penguins and turtles can also be seen. Eden's golden beaches draw surfers, families and fishers, while divers explore the coast's shipwrecks and stunning underwater scenery. Lake Wonboyn, 30 km south of Eden, is another mecca for dedicated anglers.

Ben Boyd National Park (see opposite) commemorates pioneer entrepreneur Benjamin Boyd, who established a whaling fleet at Twofold Bay in the 1840s.

BEN BOYD *National Park*

Ben Boyd National Park (22 000 ha) lies north and south of Twofold Bay. The dense coastal heath of the headlands is bent low by the constant wind and salt-laden air. Further inland, open forest and woodland cloak the terrain, providing a refuge for around 50 mammal species. Visitors bushwalk, swim, surf, beachcomb and explore the rock pools.

Visitor information
See *Contacts*, p. 93

The Pinnacles
The distinctive Pinnacles – worn white-sand cliffs with red gravel tops – can be viewed from a nearby cliff. The track and windswept headland offer panoramic views.

Green Cape Lighthouse
The state's most southerly lighthouse has been in service since 1883. Restored cottages provide heritage accommodation, and there are regular guided tours, including a climb to the top of the lighthouse (see *Contacts*, p. 93).

Boyd's Tower
Whaling entrepreneur Benjamin Boyd built the tower in 1847 as a lighthouse, but it was never lit and was used instead for spotting whales in the bay.

Davidson Whaling Station Historic Site
This was Australia's longest-operating shore-based whaling station, open from 1826 to the late 1920s. Interpretive signs and the remnants of the old blubber-boiling works can be viewed.

Light to Light walk
A 30 km, three-day walk joins Green Cape to Boyd's Tower, passing through eucalypt forest and heathland.

Birdwatching
Waterbirds, seabirds and raptors, such as the powerful white-breasted sea eagle, feed from the fish-rich waters. Terrestrial birds include brilliant crimson rosellas and eastern yellow robins.

Marine wildlife
Dolphins, fur seals, little penguins, turtles, and humpback and other whales in season (late Sept–early Dec) make for exhilarating wildlife-watching.

ADVICE/WARNINGS
- There is no camping in the park north of Eden; in the south there are some campsites and some bush camping is permitted
- Camping fees apply and bookings are essential for Christmas, Easter and public holidays (see *Contacts*, p. 93)
- There are wood barbecues at Bittangabee and Saltwater Creek, but you must take your own firewood
- Collecting crustaceans and marine animals from the rocks is prohibited

Map labels:
Merimbula
Merimbula Lake
Merimbula Point
Merimbula Beach
To Bega
Pambula
Merimbula Bay
Pambula Beach
Haycock Point
North Long Beach
Quondolo
Pambula Lake
The Pinnacles
BEN BOYD NATIONAL PARK
Lennards Island
BROADWATER STATE FOREST
TASMAN
Eden
North Head
Lookout Point
Nullica Bay
Twofold Bay
SEA
Davidson Whaling Station
Boydtown
Red Point
Boyd's Tower
N
0   5 km
Mowarry Point
LIGHT TO LIGHT
HIGHWAY
Saltwater Ck
BEN BOYD Ck
NATIONAL PARK
Bittangabee Ck
EDROM
GREEN CAPE ROAD
EAST BOYD STATE FOREST
PRINCES
To Cann River
WONBOYN
Wonboyn
Wonboyn Lake
Wonboyn Beach
Disaster Bay Lookout
Bittangabee Bay
LIGHT TO LIGHT WALK
ROAD
Green Cape Lighthouse
Green Cape
Disaster Bay

Central and Mid-North Coast

This region extends from the magnificent lower reaches of the Hawkesbury River, on Sydney's outer limits, past historic Newcastle and a chain of serene coastal lakes, to popular Port Macquarie.

Relaxing at the beach, Port Stephens

A deeply indented span of coastline – a succession of inlets and estuarine lakes, ragged headlands and wave-worn rocky shores, with sandy beaches lapped by the Pacific Ocean – runs north from Sydney to Port Macquarie.

The lower reaches of the region are on the perimeter of Sydney's urban sprawl. In fact, commuters make the 160 km return trip from Gosford to the capital. A freeway puts Sydney within easy reach (a two-hour drive) of Newcastle, the state's second largest city, an industrial powerhouse that has managed to retain its stunning surf coastline. A string of towns, fishing hamlets with weekenders and beach shacks, smart resorts such as Terrigal, and larger centres such as vibrant Port Macquarie spread a sizeable population along the coast. This is classic family holiday territory, inviting swimming, fishing, walking and picnics.

Pockets of national park protect remnants of littoral rainforest, majestic headlands, extensive coastal lakes and idyllic beaches, providing visitors with a chance to experience the coast's precious natural beauty. Another wonderful experience is wildlife-watching, including the thrill of seeing giant humpback and other whales migrating in season.

Must see, must do

▶ Dive among dolphins at Port Stephens

▶ Explore the spectacular dunescape of Stockton Bight

▶ Go birdwatching in fascinating Myall Lakes NP

▶ Take a dip in Newcastle's vast Merewether sea baths

▶ Watch for whales, seals and dolphins from Sugarloaf Point

Port Macquarie
Governor Macquarie established a penal outpost here in 1821. Today, Port Macquarie is one of the state's favourite holiday destinations, blessed by fine weather, beautiful beaches and bountiful fishing.

Myall Lakes NP
A brackish–freshwater lake system, the largest in NSW, is at the heart of one of the state's most visited national parks. Paperbarks, palms and other wetland vegetation line the four major lakes, an important habitat for many bird species.

Newcastle
A major industrial city and port, with handsomely restored colonial buildings and fine surf beaches, Newcastle is the second largest city in NSW. Australia's most destructive earthquake struck here in 1989, destroying 9000 homes and killing 13 people.

Bouddi NP
Bouddi's lovely beaches, backed by eroded cliffs and forest-sheathed hills, are popular for swimming and snorkelling. The park is rich in archaeological sites relating to the traditional custodians, the Guringai (Kurring-gai) people.

Scale
0   10   20   30 km

Fact File

When to go
This region experiences a subtropical climate with warm to hot summers and cool to mild winters, with the heaviest rainfall usually Jan–April. Visit in spring and early summer for idyllic beach days, boating and bushwalking and in winter for whale-watching (and to avoid high-season crowds). Contact the Bureau of Meteorology (BOM) for weather updates: 1900 955 361; www.bom.gov.au

Top coastal events
Jan   *Golden Lure Tournament* (Port Macquarie)
Mar   *Surfest* (Newcastle)
April   *Port Stephens Outrigger Regatta*
          Heritage Afloat (Lake Macquarie)
May–June *Festival of the Whales* (Port Stephens)
July   *Terrigal Beach Food and Wine Festival*
Oct   *Gosford City Arts Festival*
          Oyster Festival (Forster)
          Mattara Festival (Newcastle)
Nov   *Tastes of the Bay* (food and wine, Nelson Bay)
Dec   *Tuggerah Lakes Mardi Gras Festival* (The Entrance)

Safety
Swimming Around 48 beaches from Gosford to Port Macquarie are patrolled by surf lifesavers on weekends, public holidays and during peak summer periods. Swimmers should take special care at isolated and unpatrolled beaches. For a list of patrolled beaches go to the NSW Safe Waters website: www.safewaters.nsw.gov.au Or contact NSW Surf Life Saving: (02) 9984 7188; www.surflifesaving.com.au

Other water activities There is good rock-fishing along this coast, but it can be dangerous and should be approached with care (see *Taking Care*, p. 260). The Central and Mid-North Coast includes estuaries and extensive coastal lakes that can be affected by tides. Exercise extreme caution near fast-flowing channels into the sea. Always seek local advice about conditions. For all boating information – licences, safety, special events, boating and weather forecasts – contact NSW Waterways Authority: 13 1236 (within NSW); (02) 9563 8556; www.waterways.nsw.gov.au. For up-to-date weather reports contact BOM's NSW Coastal Waters Service on 1900 926 101.

Restrictions/regulations
Fishing Recreational fishers must carry a licence to fish in all NSW waters; bag and size limits apply. Some species are totally protected. Contact NSW Fisheries: 1300 369 365; www.fisheries.nsw.gov.au

Marine reserves Fishing is allowed in NSW marine parks, with some restrictions. Fishing and/or removal or harm of plants or animals is prohibited in aquatic reserves. For further information contact Marine Parks Authority NSW: (02) 9228 4918; www.mpa.nsw.gov.au

National parks Permits are required to camp overnight in national parks along the coast. Some of the more popular parks charge a vehicle entry fee (see *Contacts*, opposite).

Shipwrecks Historic shipwrecks and associated relics are protected. Recreational diving is permitted on many sites. For further information contact NSW Heritage Office (02) 9873 8574; www.heritage.nsw.gov.au

CLIMATE	J	F	M	A	M	J	J	A	S	O	N	D
GOSFORD												
Max °C	27	27	26	24	20	18	17	19	21	24	25	27
Min °C	17	17	15	12	8	6	5	5	8	11	13	15
Rain mm	139	148	150	136	119	128	79	76	69	83	92	102
Raindays	11	11	11	11	9	10	8	8	8	9	10	10

CLIMATE	J	F	M	A	M	J	J	A	S	O	N	D
PORT MACQUARIE												
Max °C	26	26	25	23	21	19	18	19	20	22	23	25
Min °C	18	18	17	14	11	9	7	8	10	13	15	17
Rain mm	153	177	176	170	147	132	98	83	83	94	102	127
Raindays	12	13	14	13	11	10	9	9	9	11	11	11

Gosford

On the northern shore of Brisbane Water (an estuary system feeding into Broken Bay), in a setting of steep hills and valleys, is the busy commercial city of Gosford. Its beachside suburbs stretch for miles and some of its residents make the daily commute to Sydney. Visitors and residents alike enjoy its fishing, fine beaches and easy access to watersports and national parks. Gosford offers the full gamut of accommodation, though Terrigal or The Entrance, right on the coast, may be more relaxed holiday options.

Brisbane Water National Park

Brisbane Water National Park, 11 500 ha of rugged sandstone country, is noted for its spectacular wildflowers – spring-flowering waratahs along Patonga Road, followed by massed Christmas Bells.

Lake Macquarie

The Dharug and Darkinjung people occupied parts of the park for at least 11 000 years and the sandstone rock engravings at Bulgandry, in the distinctive Hawkesbury style, are among the finest in the Sydney region. Bushwalking (a network of walking trails crosses the park), canoeing and birdwatching are favourite activities. Waratah Trig and Staples Lookout provide stunning water views. There is limited bush camping (BYO everything). The best fishing tends to be in the southern section of the estuary, during summer and autumn.

Terrigal to The Entrance

Just 12 km from Gosford, the seaside town of Terrigal has a fashionable air with its smart sidewalk cafes, boutiques and shady Norfolk Island pine-lined esplanade. Families frequent the wide beach and its rock pools, while board-riders prefer the surfing breaks at the beach's northern end. Walk across grassy parkland to The Skillion, a distinctive, often windswept headland with impressive ocean views. Anglers can find some potentially great rock fishing from the ledges below, though it can get crowded early in the morning and at tide turn. Luderick, rock blackfish and bream are typical catches, with bonito, tailor, kingfish and tuna further out. Terrigal's plentiful accommodation includes resort-style hotels and holiday apartments.

A few kilometres south, Avoca has terrific surf, a wide family-friendly beach, beachfront cafes and quiet accommodation including a swag of B&Bs. To the north, a series of small towns such as Bateau Bay fringe the coastline and waterways through to

Pelicans gather at The Entrance

Newcastle. Most have good beaches and holiday accommodation. At The Entrance, where Tuggerah Lake eases its way into the Pacific Ocean, sailing, boating, kayaking, fishing, surfing and scuba diving are all on offer.

On either side of The Entrance, relatively tiny Wyrrabalong National Park (620 ha) contrasts forest-clad headlands with pale sandy beaches. Walkers will discover pockets of virgin coastal rainforest, a majestic red-gum forest, flowering banksias and wetlands rich in birdlife. Watch for diamond pythons, Goulds sand goannas and sand-swimming lizards in the dunes in the park's north, and look out to sea for migrating whales (June to October) and large pods of dolphins. There is no camping in the park.

Lake Macquarie

Lake Macquarie, the state's largest saltwater lake, 24 km long and over 3 km across at its widest point, is rimmed by small fishing and holiday towns. Windsurfers, waterskiers, kayakers and boating enthusiasts skim the lake's extensive waters. Fishing is popular, though not always reliable. Locals often head for the western end of the fast-flowing Swansea Channel, where the lake runs into the Pacific, for some of the state's biggest flathead. The channel is also the place to net prawns over summer. There is plenty of

Contacts

Visitor information

Forster Little St
(02) 6554 8799
www.greatlakes.org.au

Newcastle 363 Hunter St
1800 654 558
www.newcastletourism.com

Port Macquarie cnr Clarence and Hay sts
(02) 6581 8000 or
1300 303 155
www.portmacquarieinfo.com.au

Port Stephens Victoria Pde
Nelson Bay
(02) 4981 1579
1800 808 900
www.portstephens.org.au

Parks and reserves

NSW National Parks and Wildlife Service (NPWS)
General information on parks and reserves
1300 361 967
www.nationalparks.nsw.gov.au

Booti Booti NP
(02) 6591 0300 (Pacific Palms)
(02) 4984 8200 (Nelson Bay)

Bouddi NP
General
(02) 4320 4200
Camping
(02) 4320 4203

Brisbane Water NP
General
(02) 4320 4200
Camping
(02) 4320 4203

Crowdy Bay NP
(02) 6586 8300

Myall Lakes NP
(02) 6591 0300 (Pacific Palms)

Tomaree NP
(02) 4984 8200

Activities

Contact visitor information centres (see above) for details of activities, tours and charter services.

Other

Stockton Sand Dunes
For permits and 4WD access advice contact Port Stephens or Newcastle visitor information centres (see above).

accommodation, from beach shacks and B&Bs to resorts and a full range of holiday activities. As Newcastle's suburbs creep further south, however, some of Lake Macquarie's towns are becoming almost outer suburbs of their northern neighbour.

Newcastle

Newcastle, New South Wales' second-largest city, has moved beyond its grim origins. From convict outpost and heavy-industry heartland (coalmining, shipbuilding, steelworks) Newcastle has emerged as a progressive city with many handsomely restored heritage buildings and a well-established cultural life that spans high culture and contemporary arts. Huge ships still glide past – this is one of the country's busiest ports – but Queens Wharf and the harbourside areas have been restored and landscaped for all to enjoy.

There are some fine beaches and consistent surfing breaks (the annual Surfest is a major event on the surf calendar) and Newcastle is home to four-time World Surfing Champion, Mark

Richards. Nobbys Beach, a city favourite, is patrolled by surf lifesavers all year. The 5 km Bathers Way Coastal Walk wends its way from Nobbys Head, with its historic 1858 lighthouse (the third built in NSW), past the 1920s Art Deco

Bouddi National Park

Steep, heavily wooded slopes and time-ravaged cliffs back a cluster of small, charming beaches at Bouddi National Park (1500 ha), just south of Terrigal. An aquatic reserve protects all marine life at crescent-shaped Maitland Bay, making it ideal for rock pooling, snorkelling and diving. The remnants of the paddlesteamer *Maitland*, which foundered off Bouddi Point in 1898, lie on a rock platform at the northern end of the bay. Shell middens, rock engravings (some up to 20 m long), rock shelters and other archaeological finds – in fact 100 sites so far – are evidence of the Kuring-gai people's long association with the Bouddi Peninsula.

Nobbys Head, Newcastle

pavilion at Newcastle Beach to the huge saltwater ocean baths at Merewether. En route you can see the forbidding Fort Scratchley, built in the 1880s when here, as elsewhere in Australia, there was fear of a Russian invasion. The fort now houses both military and maritime museums.

Multiple fishing options include harbour, surf-and rock-fishing, as well as the Hunter River estuary and Lake Macquarie. There are opportunities for recreational activities of all types and, around 50 km north-east, within easy touring distance, lies the famed Hunter Valley and its many fine wineries.

Port Stephens

Around 200 km north of Sydney, sheltered Port Stephens is a brilliant expanse of sparkling waters more than twice the size of Sydney Harbour. The waters teem with fish and are home to over 100 bottlenose dolphins (dolphin-watching cruises are big business). Small fishing and holiday settlements border bushy Tomaree Peninsula, much of it protected within Tomaree National Park – a lovely spot for picnics or walking. The waters off Fly Point and Halifax, safeguarded as aquatic reserves, are outstanding diving and snorkelling sites. Nelson Bay, the bay's largest town, overlooks the port and a busy marina, where an armada of

Scuba diving, Port Stephens

sleek dolphin-watching and whale-watching cruisers, charter boats and yachts moor. Water-based activities include surfing, sailing, waterskiing, sea-kayaking, game- and deep-sea fishing. From June to October, the exhilarating sight of humpback whales breaching, spy-hopping and fluke-slapping on their migratory voyage between the warm tropics and Antarctica, can be experienced from lookouts and cruise boats. The incredible Stockton Sand Dunes (see left) are well worth exploring. Plentiful accommodation options include houseboats, which will enable you to explore the waterways.

A ferry links Nelson Bay and Tea Gardens, which is itself linked to Hawks Nest by a bridge across the Myall River mouth. A 3 km sand spit leads to the volcanic outcrop of Yacaaba Headland, where there are sensational views.

Just north of Port Stephens is Myall Lakes National Park, one of the state's most visited national parks (see p.104).

Seal Rocks and Sugarloaf Point

Sugarloaf Point Lighthouse (built in 1875) crowns a prominent headland, a fine vantage point for spotting migrating whales in season, dolphins

Stockton's rolling dunes

Between Newcastle and Port Stephens, along Stockton Bight, the Stockton Sand Dunes sweep dramatically along the coast for over 30 km, towering up to 30 m high, a constantly moving sand mass. The birdlife is prolific – oystercatchers, gulls and terns patrol the water's edge, while other birds scavenge above the tide mark. Scattered middens of sun-bleached shells and the bones of small mammals and birds are evidence of the many feasts Aboriginal inhabitants shared along the coast. Surf-fishing here can yield rich rewards, and walking, horseriding and 'sand safaris' enable visitors to experience this intriguing area. Access onto the dunes by 4WD is allowed (permits are required, see *Contacts*, p.101). Offshore, in the shallows, 20 km south of Anna Bay, the massive hulk of the *Sygna*, wrecked in 1974, lies rusting in the surf, silhoutted against the changing sky.

Sugarloaf Point Lighthouse

braiding patterns in the surf and ospreys and peregrine falcons wheeling overhead.

North of the point is Seal Rocks, a peaceful little fishing village on picturesque Sugarloaf Bay, favoured by fishers, surfers and bushwalkers. Divers explore the underwater caverns, which provide a nursery for endangered grey nurse sharks.

Myall Lakes National Park

North of Port Stephens, a 50 km chain of shallow coastal lakes, flanked by high coastal dunes and forested hills, form the blissfully serene heart of Myall Lakes National Park (44 000 ha). On the east side, the Pacific surf breaks onto white sand along 40 km of pristine beaches. Extensive stretches of navigable waterways are ideal for all sorts of boating. Marked walking trails and the park's diverse environments – including coastal rainforest remnants, mangroves, paperbarks and flowering heathland – provide opportunities for outstanding bird- and wildlife-watching. The brackish-to-fresh water nourishes 36 species of fish as well as abundant prawns. Fishing and camping are permitted; it can be busy (especially at Christmas and Easter) but it is usually possible to find a quiet spot. There is a vehicle ferry at Bombah Point. Boats, houseboats and canoes can be hired, and there is boat access on the Myall River from Port Stephens and Bulahdelah (the nearest major town, located on the Pacific Highway).

Broughton Island

Lying just 12 nautical miles offshore, 138 ha Broughton Island is a rare gem. With its volcanic peaks, windswept vegetation and deserted beaches, this is an oasis for thriving shearwater, silver gull and tern rookeries and close to the northern limit of the little penguin. The surrounding waters are remarkably fish-rich and divers can explore a wonderland of caves, coral and marine life. A track leads to the 94 m summit and panoramic views. Broughton is part of the Myall Lakes National Park (see left).

Forster–Tuncurry

Forster–Tuncurry, twin towns on either side of the Wallamba River, at the entrance to Wallis Lake, attract regular visitors with their winning combination of brilliant beaches, lovely lakes, good fishing (Tuncurry is derived from an Aboriginal word for 'plenty fish') and easy going lifestyle. Deep-sea sponge gardens and archways make for great diving, and nearby Booti Booti National Park (see below) is another major drawcard.

Booti Booti National Park

Booti Booti (1567 ha) offers a stunning surf beach, the tranquil waters of Wallis Lake, camping facilities and a steep, 30-minute trek to dramatic Cape Hawke, with breathtaking views from a lookout tower of the Myall Lakes system, densely clad hills, Seal Rocks and beyond. The Booti Hill walk (7 km return, medium to hard) is also worthwhile, especially in winter for sunsets over the lake. This is birdwatcher's heaven – honeyeaters feed in the heath, lorikeets flash by and myriad waterbirds forage and feed. Snakes, including dangerous brown snakes, are common in the heath areas, so take care.

Crowdy Bay National Park

Peaceful rock pooling, beachcombing, wildlife-watching, fishing and walking are perfect pursuits in Crowdy Bay National Park (9948 ha). The sculpted rock formations of Diamond Head tower 100 m above the bay, and a walk to the squat lighthouse (1878) reveals limitless ocean views. There is camping, but campers must bring their own drinking water. From the northern end of the park, at Laurieton, it is less than 50 km along a wonderfully scenic coast road to Port Macquarie.

Port Macquarie and Beyond

On the mouth of the Hastings River, 400 km from Sydney, Port Macquarie's rugged coastline, splendid beaches, surrounding network of rivers and lakes and pleasant, constant climate make it one of the state's classic holiday destinations. Port Macquarie is also one of Australia's oldest towns, established as a penal settlement in 1821, though its convict era was short-lived. Today it has a population of around 34 000 with thriving fishing and farming industries and a multitude of leisure activities – sailing, river cruises, sea-kayaking, and camel safaris along the beach to name a few. The beaches are

*Left White-breasted sea eagles are frequently spotted along this coastline
Below Crowdy Bay National Park*

inviting and fishing enthusiasts will enjoy some of the state's premier sites, with beach and rock-fishing, especially over autumn and winter, and good boat fishing in the Hastings River estuary. For those who seek the thrill of gamefishing, marlin, yellowfin tuna and shark can be caught only a few kilometres offshore. Port Macquarie has a full range of accommodation options and first-class holiday facilities.

Crescent Head, about 40 km north, is a classic surf town with a 1970s feel, spreading across the north-facing slope of Crescent Head, with great views of the surrounding coastline. Off the head is a well-regarded surfing break – a favourite with long-boarders. The main surf beach is patrolled and there is an estuary beach for families.

Lord Howe Island

World Heritage-listed Lord Howe Island, 700 kilometres north-east of Sydney, packs a stunning array of landscapes into its diminutive 1455 hectares.

Lord Howe's volcanic headlands

A surge of volcanic activity pushed the island out of the sea 7 million years ago; a splinter of land remains, measuring 11 km north to south and 2 km across. The island was settled in the 1830s but, due to its isolation, the pace of development was, at best, slow. The island remains low-key and free of major tourist development. A reserve protects around 75 percent of the total land area and resident and tourist numbers are kept at sustainable levels.

Travellers, lured to the island by the promise of tranquillity, white sands and tropically clear waters, might come away budding naturalists. Bushwalking, birdwatching, snorkelling and eco-touring are great ways to experience the island's natural wonders – with time-out for surfing, fishing, tennis and golf.

Visitors travel to the island by regular flights from Sydney and Brisbane and around the island on foot or bicycle.

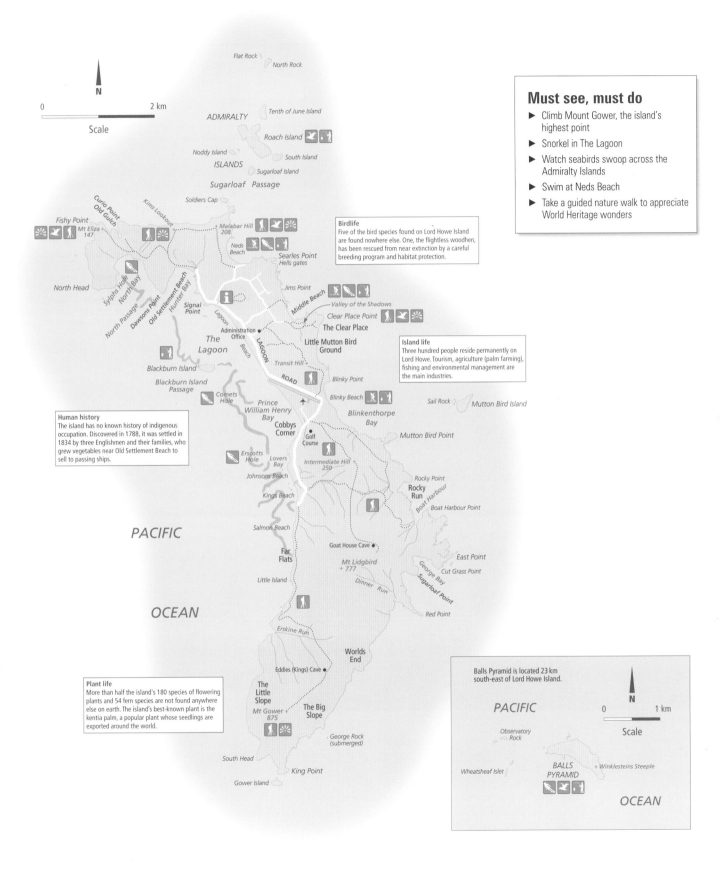

N

0   2 km

Scale

Must see, must do

► Climb Mount Gower, the island's highest point
► Snorkel in The Lagoon
► Watch seabirds swoop across the Admiralty Islands
► Swim at Neds Beach
► Take a guided nature walk to appreciate World Heritage wonders

Birdlife
Five of the bird species found on Lord Howe Island are found nowhere else. One, the flightless woodhen, has been rescued from near extinction by a careful breeding program and habitat protection.

Island life
Three hundred people reside permanently on Lord Howe. Tourism, agriculture (palm farming), fishing and environmental management are the main industries.

Human history
The island has no known history of indigenous occupation. Discovered in 1788, it was settled in 1834 by three Englishmen and their families, who grew vegetables near Old Settlement Beach to sell to passing ships.

Plant life
More than half the island's 180 species of flowering plants and 54 fern species are not found anywhere else on earth. The island's best-known plant is the kentia palm, a popular plant whose seedlings are exported around the world.

Balls Pyramid is located 23 km south-east of Lord Howe Island.

PACIFIC

N

0   1 km

Scale

Observatory Rock

Wheatsheaf Islet

BALLS PYRAMID

+ Winklesteins Steeple

OCEAN

Flat Rock
North Rock

ADMIRALTY

Tenth of June Island

Roach Island

Noddy Island   South Island

ISLANDS

Sugarloaf Island

Sugarloaf Passage

Soldiers Cap

Curio Point Old Gulch   Kims Lookout

Fishy Point   Mt Eliza 147   + Malabar Hill 208   Neds Beach   Searles Point Hells gates

North Head   Sylphs Hole   North Bay

North Passage   Dawsons Point   Old Settlement Beach   Hunter Bay   Signal Point

Jims Point

Middle Beach   Valley of the Shadows

Clear Place Point   The Clear Place

Administration Office   Little Mutton Bird Ground

The Lagoon

LAGOON   Beach   Transit Hill +   Blinky Point

ROAD

Blackburn Island   Blinky Beach   Sail Rock   Mutton Bird Island

Blackburn Island Passage   Blinkenthorpe Bay

Comets Hole   Prince William Henry Bay   Mutton Bird Point

Cobbys Corner   Golf Course

Erscotts Hole   Lovers Bay   Intermediate Hill 250   Rocky Point   Rocky Run   Boat Harbour

Johnsons Beach   Boat Harbour Point

Kings Beach

PACIFIC

Salmon Beach   East Point   Cut Grass Point

Far Flats   Goat House Cave   George Bay   Sugarloaf Point

OCEAN   Mt Lidgbird + 777

Little Island   Dinner Run   Red Point

Erskine Run

Worlds End

Eddies (Kings) Cave

The Little Slope   Mt Gower + 875   The Big Slope   George Rock (submerged)

South Head   King Point

Gower Island

Fact File

When to go
Year-round. Summer maximums average 25°C, winter 18°C. High humidity, tempered by sea breezes, keeps the air temperature comfortable year-round. The driest months are Nov–Feb. For further information contact the Bureau of Meteorology: (02) 6563 2083 (Lord Howe Island station); www.bom.gov.au

Top coastal events
Jan	*Ocean View Pairs* (bowls)
Feb	*Seaweek*
Mar	*Birdweek*
Mar–April	*Coral Court Easter Open* (golf)
April	*Photoweek*
June–Aug	*Pinetrees Jazz, Tennis, Bushwalking Program*
Oct	*Lord Howe Music Festival*
Dec	*Plant Week*

Safety
In the water Lord Howe Island's waters are typical of a small, steep-sided island: currents can be strong, waves large and the wind can rise quickly. Beach patrols do not operate on Lord Howe Island; most beaches are safe for swimming, particularly along The Lagoon, but visitors should swim in the presence of others and heed local advice. Watch out for sea urchins, known locally as sea eggs: their long brittle spines can easily penetrate flesh, resulting in a nasty sting.

Land The southern end of the island is remote and virtually trackless. Visitors are required to travel with an authorised guide (see *Restrictions/ regulations*, below).

Restrictions/regulations
Fishing All NSW Fisheries' laws apply at Lord Howe Island: recreational fishers must carry a licence (these can be purchased at Thomson's Store on Neds Beach Rd); bag and size limits also apply; for general information contact NSW Fisheries: 1300 369 365; www.fisheries.nsw.gov.au

Marine reserve A 300 510 ha marine reserve protects the waters of Lord Howe. Most recreational activities are permitted within the reserve, but anglers must observe the following bans: fishing at Neds Beach; spearfishing of doubleheader and butterfly cod; spearfishing in The Lagoon; the use of fishtraps.

Land reserve The Lord Howe Island Permanent Park Reserve protects 75 percent of the island. Camping is not permitted. Walkers to Mount Gower must be in the company of an authorised guide, as must visitors to the Admiralty Islands, to the immediate north of Lord Howe. Inquiries can be made to the local ranger on (02) 6563 2066 or to the information centre on (02) 6563 2114.

CLIMATE									LORD HOWE ISLAND			
	J	F	M	A	M	J	J	A	S	O	N	D
Max °C	25	26	25	23	21	19	19	19	20	21	22	24
Min °C	20	20	20	18	16	14	13	13	14	15	17	19
Rain mm	108	114	122	149	160	177	178	141	135	127	116	117
Raindays	11	13	15	18	21	22	23	21	17	14	12	12

Walking on Mount Gower

Orientation
Settlement is confined to the northern third of the island where, along a narrow bank of land, an airstrip, a few shops and a miniscule network of roads service the needs of the 300 or so people lucky enough to call this beautiful spot home. Some 17 properties (B&Bs, scaled-down resorts, apartments and motels) accommodate the 400 visitors allowed on the island at any one time.

The island has 10 beaches, many guarded at each end by high, craggy cliffs. On the east coast are Blinky Beach and the kentia-fringed Neds Beach, with good swells in the right conditions. A band of heavily vegetated hills and cliffs come to an abrupt halt along the northern coast, offering good views but preventing easy access to the water's edge. The world's southernmost coral reef rims the upper half of the west coast, creating The Lagoon, a 6 km long stretch of translucent, emerald-green water perfect for diving, snorkelling and swimming.

A permanent reserve protects the southern half of the island. Here, amid the mists, subtropical forests of giant ferns, gnarled trees, orchids and ragged rocks drape the slopes of volcanic mountains, which reach their peak at the summit of Mount Gower (875 m).

Land Activities
Walking is not just a recreational activity on Lord Howe Island, but the main means of transport. Birdwatching, the other main land-based pursuit, is highly recommended and, in fact, hard to avoid, so large is the number of seabirds that congregate on the island's many cliffs and outcrops.

Malabar Hill, the highest point at Lord Howe's northern end, looms above Neds Beach. Red-tailed tropic birds performing aerobatic antics and island views are the rewards for the 45-minute uphill hike. A stroll beneath the 20 m high banyan palms of the Valley of the Shadows leads visitors to The Clear Place, where the view is of the southern mountains

Left *Fishing from a kayak*
Inset *Woodhen*
Following pages *Lord Howe from the air*

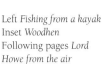

and beyond to the tip of Balls Pyramid. Superb views of the impenetrable north coast unfold from atop Mount Eliza, a 30-minute climb from North Beach. Here hundreds of sooty terns breed in summer and spring, and masked boobies and black-winged petrels soar and wheel around the cliffs.

The island's ultimate trek is to the mist-covered summit of Mount Gower. The walk is eight-hours return and should only be attempted in the company of an authorised guide. The unsigned, often precipitous track threads through a diverse range of vegetation, including, near the summit, patches of what is often referred to as 'Hobbit' forest, a dense subtropical profusion of stunted trees, giant ferns and wispy orchids.

Water Activities

Equipped with snorkel and facemask, visitors can get up close to the 500 or so fish species and other marine creatures recorded in the Lord Howe waters, including a number of endemic species. Accessible spots include Neds Beach, Middle Beach, Sylphs Hole and North Bay. Glass-bottomed boats regularly take snorkellers further out to Comets and Erscotts holes, excellent spots in The Lagoon.

Those keen to go deeper can don scuba gear and explore the region's intricately structured underwater landscape, with its gutters, canyons and overhanging ledges. The Admiralty Islands are probably the best spot: they have a steep drop to a submerged plateau teeming with fish.

Fishing is a big drawcard in these fertile waters. Charter boats make regular runs to offshore waters where kingfish, trevally and red emperor are target catches; for a less adrenalin-charged experience, there are jetties from which to dangle a line, and good surf-fishing along the east coast.

Surfers head for the east coast, specifically Neds, Middle and Blinky beaches, for a range of uncrowded beach breaks framed by a backdrop of volcanic mountains and lush forest.

Off the island

Lord Howe is not a lone jewel. It shares its perch on the 2000 km long Lord Howe Rise with a cluster of islets, outcrops and reefs, all protected within the 146 300 ha World Heritage area. Most distinctive is Balls Pyramid, a 551 m cathedral of rock, 25 km south-east of the main island. Tour operators run fishing, diving, sightseeing and birdwatching charters to the outcrop in good weather. The Admiralty Islands consist of eight rocky outcrops that are home to tens of thousands of seabirds — sooty terns, noddies, masked boobies and wedge-tailed shearwaters, among many. Cruise boats visit the largest island, Roach Island, in good weather.

Byron Bay and the Subtropical North

A subtropical environment, World Heritage forests, glorious Pacific Ocean surf beaches and towns where the ambience is a curious combination of warmth, sophistication and quirkiness have made this one of Australia's most popular holiday regions.

Parks protect much of the coastline around Coffs Harbour, and a string of small surfing and fishing communities provide facilities for the groups of walkers and campers who come to explore the area. Coffs Harbour itself is an important commercial centre, servicing the region's large-scale agricultural and fishing industries. It is also a very well-equipped tourist destination, with major resort facilities and opportunities for divers, anglers, kayakers and surfers.

The far north coast extends from Wooli, east of the major centre of Grafton, to the border with Queensland, its centrepiece the backpacker/surfer/ New Age haven of Byron Bay. The region has spectacular beaches, legendary surf and a backdrop of World Heritage-listed rainforests and mountains. The Clarence, Richmond and Tweed rivers, and their myriad tributaries, intersect the broad coastal plains, creating harbours for the local fishing fleets and protected estuaries for swimming and boating. Busy, prosperous and accessible, the area remains a place of great peace and beauty, with development confined to major centres.

The Sydney to Brisbane railway offers economic travel to many parts to the region, and airports service Coffs Harbour, Ballina and Coolangatta (Queensland) and their surrounding areas.

Cape Byron Lighthouse

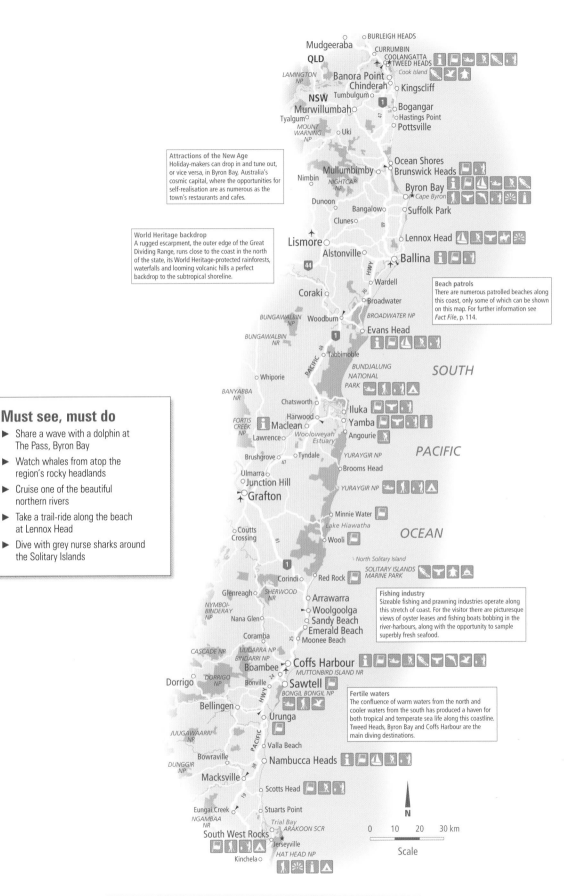

Attractions of the New Age
Holiday-makers can drop in and tune out, or vice versa, in Byron Bay, Australia's cosmic capital, where the opportunities for self-realisation are as numerous as the town's restaurants and cafes.

World Heritage backdrop
A rugged escarpment, the outer edge of the Great Dividing Range, runs close to the coast in the north of the state, its World Heritage-protected rainforests, waterfalls and looming volcanic hills a perfect backdrop to the subtropical shoreline.

Beach patrols
There are numerous patrolled beaches along this coast, only some of which can be shown on this map. For further information see *Fact File*, p. 114.

Must see, must do

▶ Share a wave with a dolphin at The Pass, Byron Bay

▶ Watch whales from atop the region's rocky headlands

▶ Cruise one of the beautiful northern rivers

▶ Take a trail-ride along the beach at Lennox Head

▶ Dive with grey nurse sharks around the Solitary Islands

Fishing industry
Sizeable fishing and prawning industries operate along this stretch of coast. For the visitor there are picturesque views of oyster leases and fishing boats bobbing in the river-harbours, along with the opportunity to sample superbly fresh seafood.

Fertile waters
The confluence of warm waters from the north and cooler waters from the south has produced a haven for both tropical and temperate sea life along this coastline. Tweed Heads, Byron Bay and Coffs Harbour are the main diving destinations.

Scale

0   10   20   30 km

N

Fact File

When to go
Year-round. The region enjoys a subtropical climate, with winter temperatures achieving a pleasant daily maximum of 20°C. Byron Bay and Coffs Harbour are extremely busy over the Christmas period; Byron Bay remains busy until Easter, when the popular blues festival is held. Migrating whales are in the area June–Oct. For weather updates contact the Bureau of Meteorology: 1900 955 361; www.bom.gov.au

Top coastal events
Jan   *Brunswick Valley Fish & Chips Festival* (Brunswick Heads)
Festival of the Sail (Coffs Harbour)
April   *Minnie Water Family Fishing Festival*
Easter   *East Coast Blues & Roots Festival* (Byron Bay)
May   *Ocean Swim Classic* (Byron Bay)
June   *Soulfeast, Rhythm & Blues* (Yamba)
Aztec Rose All Girls Surf Showdown (Lennox Head)
Wintersun Festival (rock 'n' roll, Tweed Heads)
July   *Gromfest* (junior surfing, various locations)
Iluka Fishing Classic
Splendour in the Grass (music festival, Byron Bay)
Aug   *Byron Bay Writers' Festival*
Sept   *Coffs Harbour International Buskers' Festival*
Oct   *Ballina Aquatic Festival*
Yamba Lions Family Fishing Festival
Port Yamba Annual Yachting Regatta

Safety
Swimming Lifesavers patrol numerous beaches along the north coast. For a list of beaches go to the NSW Safe Waters website: www.safewaters.nsw.gov.au NSW Surf Life Saving provides information about the beaches under its jurisdiction: (02) 9984 7188; www.surflifesaving.com.au Do not swim at unpatrolled surf beaches along this coast – many areas are subject to big swells and strong rips.

Other water activities North-easterlies are the prevailing winds in this region in early summer, and can reach 15–20 knots. West winds are rough July–Sept and southerlies are prevalent in winter. Exercise extreme caution crossing river bars. For information regarding licences, safety, special events and boating weather forecasts contact NSW Waterways Authority: 13 1236 (within NSW); (02) 9563 8556; www.waterways.nsw.gov.au For up-to-date weather reports contact BOM's NSW Coastal Waters Service on 1900 926 101.

Restrictions/Regulations
Fishing Recreational fishers must carry a licence to fish in all NSW waters; bag and size limits apply. Contact NSW Fisheries: 1300 369 365; www.fisheries.nsw.gov.au

Marine reserves There are two marine parks in this region: Cape Byron MP and Solitary Rocks MP; fishing is permitted in both. Solitary Rocks MP has several fishing exclusion zones, which apply to around 12 percent of the park; similar zones are yet to be determined for Cape Byron MP.

Contact the parks direct (see *Contacts,* opposite) or Marine Parks Authority NSW: (02) 9228 4918; www.mpa.nsw.gov.au

National parks Permits are required to camp overnight in national parks along the coast (see *Contacts,* opposite).

Shipwrecks Historic shipwrecks and associated relics are protected. Recreational diving is permitted on many sites. For further information contact NSW Heritage Office: (02) 9873 8574; www.heritage.nsw.gov.au

CLIMATE												BYRON BAY	
	J	F	M	A	M	J	J	A	S	O	N	D
Max °C	28	28	27	25	22	20	19	20	22	23	25	26
Min °C	21	21	20	17	15	12	12	13	14	16	18	20
Rain mm	161	192	215	185	188	158	100	92	66	102	118	143
Raindays	15	16	17	15	15	12	10	9	9	11	12	13

CLIMATE												COFFS HARBOUR	
	J	F	M	A	M	J	J	A	S	O	N	D
Max °C	27	27	26	24	21	19	19	20	22	24	25	27
Min °C	18	19	18	15	11	8	7	8	10	13	16	18
Rain mm	169	207	232	190	138	130	94	81	68	96	104	137
Raindays	12	13	14	12	10	8	7	7	9	9	11

Hat Head National Park

Left *Boats at Coffs Harbour*
Inset *A silver gull*

Around South West Rocks

Hat Head National Park unfurls south of South West Rocks, a rich coastal environment comprising one of the largest dune systems in New South Wales. Smoky Cape and Hat Head have campsites (bring your own water), along with wonderful coastal views. The Smoky Cape Lighthouse (built in 1891), with its distinctive octagonal tower, sits alongside a complex of keepers' quarters and service buildings; tours and accommodation are available (see *Contacts*, right).

The pleasant resort town of South West Rocks, located on the Macleay River estuary, is a popular location for campers, bushwalkers and anglers. The estuary offers some brilliant fishing, particularly for mulloway at the mouth of the river, while the town itself is the base for some of the best light-tackle gamefishing in New South Wales. Worth a visit is historic Trial Bay Gaol, within the Arakoon State Conservation Area, 4 km east of the town. This imposing prison, which operated from 1886 until 1903, is open to the public and has lovely beaches and a scenic camping area nearby.

Around Nambucca

Nambucca Heads is one of a string of holiday villages south of Coffs Harbour. Located at the wide mouth of the picturesque Nambucca River, it is a popular destination offering fishing, surfing and windsurfing. Oyster leases are abundant in this area and oysters can be purchased year-round from stalls here and in nearby towns. South of Nambucca is Scotts Head, popular with surfers; north is Bongil Bongil National Park, a lovely 6 km long coastal strip featuring wetlands, plentiful birdlife, rainforest and the pristine estuaries of the Pine and Bonville creeks, where conditions are perfect for canoeing. The park has a network of walking trails but no campsites.

Coffs Harbour

Coffs Harbour is New South Wales' most popular coastal holiday destination. In peak periods its population of 22 000 swells five-fold. It is the only region south of Queensland's Cape Tribulation where the Great Dividing Range meets the coastline. As such the region offers a remarkable diversity of natural environments including rugged patches of World Heritage-protected temperate rainforest within Dorrigo National Park (about an hour from

Contacts

Visitor information

Ballina 154 River St
(02) 6686 3484

Byron Bay 80 Johnson St
(02) 6680 8558

Coffs Harbour cnr Marcia St and Rose Ave
(02) 6652 1522

Maclean (Iluka/Yamba) Ferry Park
(02) 6645 4121

Nambucca Heads
4 Pacific Hwy
(02) 6568 6954

Tweed Heads 4 Wharf St
1800 674 414

Parks and reserves

NSW National Parks and Wildlife Service (NPWS)
General information on parks and reserves
1300 361 967
www.nationalparks.nsw.gov.au

Arakoon State Conservation Area
(02) 6566 6168

Bongil Bongil NP
(02) 6652 0900

Bundjalung NP
(02) 6641 1500

Cape Byron Marine Park
(02) 6685 8505

Hat Head NP
(02) 6566 6168

Solitary Islands Marine Park
(02) 6652 3977

Activities

Contact visitor information centres (see above) for details of activities, tours and charter services.

Other

Cape Byron Lighthouse
Tours and accommodation
(02) 6685 8565

Smoky Cape Lighthouse
Tours and accommodation
(02) 6566 6301

Above Yuraygir
National Park
Below Horseriding
at Lennox Head

(September to April), or simply watch from the many elevated headlands in the area. Birdwatchers can visit Muttonbird Island (connected to the mainland by a causeway), home to 10 000 wedge-tailed shearwaters who nest here from August to April each year.

For lovers of big things, no trip to Coffs would be complete without a visit to the Big Banana, on the town's northern outskirts, a tribute to one of the region's major industries.

Grafton Coast

The coastline to the east of the commercial centre of Grafton (population 16 500) is dominated by national parks. Yuraygir National Park protects 60 km of shore, the longest stretch of undisturbed coastline in the state. Seven well-serviced campgrounds provide a base for canoeing, fishing and walking; and swimming patrols operate at the beaches of the peaceful park-encircled towns of Wooli, Red Rock and Minnie Water.

the coast). Accommodation options cover all ranges, while the list of activities and attractions is extensive.

There are numerous patrolled beaches close to town, including the popular Park Beach. Jetty Beach, located near the marina and well protected from the ocean swells by a breakwater, is perfect for family swimming. Dive operators run snorkelling and scuba tours to the Solitary Islands (see opposite), while fishing charters make runs to fertile offshore grounds. Sea-kayaking tours are popular, and surfers head for breaks at Diggers Beach and Macauleys Headland.

Sea mammals are a local presence. The Pet Porpoise Pool has displays and daily shows. Those who prefer the wilderness experience can board a whale tour (June to October) or dolphin tour

North of Yuraygir National Park, on the Clarence River estuary, are the prawning and fishing towns of Yamba and Iluka. A daily ferry service operates across the harbour, which is home to a deep-sea fishing fleet. A picturesque lighthouse, mature Norfolk Island pines, superb estuary and coastal fishing, houseboat hire, river cruises, whale-watching opportunities, fresh seafood and good cafes and restaurants make these villages a popular holiday destination. Yamba provides access to Angourie, where the surfing break, known as 'Anga', is regarded as one of the best on the north coast.

Victoria
southern ocean scenery

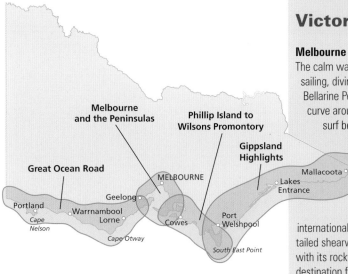

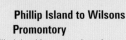

Victoria's Regions

Melbourne and the Peninsulas
The calm waters of Port Phillip are perfect for swimming, sailing, diving and fishing. Mornington Peninsula and the Bellarine Peninsula, dotted with small seaside towns, curve around the bay, both offering calm bayside and surf beaches, wineries, marinas, historic sites and wonderful walking trails. *See p.122*

Phillip Island to Wilsons Promontory
Phillip Island has great beaches and terrific fishing but is also known for its wildlife: the internationally renowned little penguins, fur seals, short-tailed shearwaters and koalas. Further east, 'the Prom', with its rocky headlands and sandy beaches, is a favourite destination for campers and walkers. *See p.130*

Gippsland Highlights
A sweep of white sandy beaches and an intricate network of lakes, lagoons and rivers create the perfect environment for boating, sailing, swimming and fishing. Beyond is the pristine wilderness coast of Croajingolong National Park. *See p.138*

Great Ocean Road
This coast offers remarkable diversity: the surfing mecca of Bells Beach and the cafe life of Lorne, the magnificent rock formations around Port Campbell, whale-watching at Warrnambool and historic villages such as Port Fairy. *See p.144*

The Victorian coastline stretches for more than 1800 kilometres, washed by the powerful waters of the Southern Ocean and Bass Strait. It takes in the wilderness coast and remote beaches of the state's far east, the sheltered lakes and inlets of Gippsland, the untouched bushland of Wilsons Promontory and the wildlife haven of Phillip Island. One of the world's great touring routes, the Great Ocean Road, traces the coast west to the border with South Australia.

Melbourne's magnificent Port Phillip is a haven for sailing and windsurfing, and the state has some of Australia's best surfing breaks, particularly around the famed Bells Beach area. A range of outstanding dive sites offers the chance to explore the coast's rich and varied marine life. Fishing is plentiful right along the Gippsland coast, but particularly around the vast Gippsland Lakes district. A network of national parks provides excellent walking and camping opportunities along much of Victoria's coast. Wildlife enthusiasts should head to Warrnambool for the seasonal migration of southern right whales, consider swimming with dolphins in Port Phillip or visit Phillip Island for the world-famous little penguin parade.

Opposite Victoria's south-west coast offers magnificent views and amazing rock formations Left Little penguins abound on Phillip Island

 ☎ 13 2842; www.visitvictoria.com

Melbourne and the Peninsulas

Melbourne is perfectly positioned to enjoy the magnificent sweep of Port Phillip, a sheltered harbour covering almost 2000 square kilometres. Almost enclosing the bay are the picturesque Mornington and Bellarine peninsulas.

Port Phillip
Site of Australia's busiest cargo port, the bay is also ideal for swimming, windsurfing and sailing and attracts bottlenose dolphins and seals.

French Island
Over 580 indigenous plant species and more than 230 bird species have been recorded here and Victoria's largest koala population inhabits the island.

Patrols, activities
Around 30 beaches are patrolled around Port Phillip (see *Fact File, p. 124*), and there are numerous places to sail and fish. Only some of this information can be shown on this map.

Danger!
There are some great surfing breaks along this wild Bass Strait coast, but the ocean beaches can be hazardous.

Scale
0 5 10 15 km

Brighton Beach bathing boxes

Port Phillip is a staggering 35 times as large as Sydney Harbour and shelters the country's busiest cargo port. More than 3.2 million people live clustered around its shoreline. This makes its marine environment all the more remarkable – the bay is a dynamic and self-sustaining ecosystem, a natural habitat for more than 1000 species of marine plants and 500 species of fish. Bottlenose dolphins live in these waters and fur seals frolic, feed and breed at the southern end of the bay.

Many of Melbourne's beaches offer big-city sophistication, with stylish cafes, well-dressed promenaders and luxury marinas. At the same time, the bayside beaches are still the focus for those classic Australian pastimes – picnicking, swimming, sunbaking and fishing.

The Mornington and Bellarine peninsulas are truly holiday playgrounds. Golf courses, wineries, fine coastal and beach walks, fishing of all kinds, surfing, world-class dive sites and heritage towns such as Queenscliff and Sorrento are all within easy touring distance of Melbourne. More exceptional still are the opportunities to watch rare and endangered bird species in their natural habitats and to see, and even swim with, seals and dolphins in the wild.

Must see, must do

► Swim with dolphins and seals in Port Phillip
► Soak up the atmosphere as you stroll along St Kilda's palm-lined Esplanade
► Enjoy spectacular views from historic Cape Schanck Lighthouse
► Join a rockpool ramble along Queenscliff's shoreline
► Visit Geelong's restored Eastern Beach promenade

☎ 13 2842; www.melbournebays.org.au

Fact File

When to go
Year-round. Summers are usually warm to hot with bayside areas and the peninsulas offering sea breezes as a respite from the hottest days. Still plenty to explore during winter, including coastal walks and wild, wintry beaches. For weather updates contact the Bureau of Meteorology (BOM): 1900 955 363; www.bom.gov.au

Top coastal events
Jan   *Sail Melbourne Regatta* (Melbourne and coastal towns through the region)
      Waterfront Festival (Geelong)
      Swim Classic (Portsea)
      Sayonara Cup (different venues, sometimes interstate)
Feb   *St Kilda Festival*
Feb–   *Rye Beach Sand Sculpting Championships*
Mar
Mar   *Street Festival* (Sorrento)
Oct   *Mornington Food and Wine Festival*
Nov   *Music Festival* (Queenscliff)
      Film Festival (Rosebud)
Dec   *Melbourne to Hobart Yacht Race*

Safety
Swimming Ocean beaches facing Bass Strait can be especially dangerous and are subject to rips and strong currents – special care is required. Swim at patrolled beaches. Lifesavers patrol weekends and public holidays Nov–April at almost all city bayside beaches (from Williamstown to Seaford) as well as Geelong, Frankston, Mornington, Mt Martha, Dromana Bay and Rosebud. Gunnamatta, Sorrento Back Beach, Portsea Surf Beach and Pt Lonsdale are patrolled daily 26 Dec–26 Jan and weekends and public holidays late Nov–late April. Queenscliff beach is patrolled daily 26 Dec–26 Jan. For further details contact Surf Life Saving Victoria (SLSV): (03) 9534 8201; www.surflifesaver.com.au

Other water activities Users of watercraft need to watch for the southerlies and easterlies that blow in winter; summer westerly changes on hot north-wind days are also dangerous. Contact Marine Safety Victoria for tidal and safety information: (03) 9655 3399; www.marinesafety.vic.gov.au BOM offers a recorded forecast for coastal waters on 1900 969 966.

Restrictions/regulations
Fishing A Recreational Fishing Licence is required for fishing in all Victorian waters; for details contact the Department of Primary Industries, Department of Sustainability and Environment: 13 6186; www.nre.gov.au/fishing

Marine parks Fishing and the removal and/or destruction of marine life are prohibited in protected marine environments in Vic; contact Parks Victoria for location of parks and reserves: 13 1963; www.parkweb.vic.gov.au

Shipwrecks It is an offence in Vic to cause damage to or remove objects from shipwreck sites; for further information contact Heritage Victoria: (03) 9655 6519; www.heritage.vic.gov.au/shipwreck

CLIMATE	J	F	M	A	M	J	J	A	S	O	N	D
MELBOURNE												
Max °C	26	26	24	20	17	14	13	15	17	20	22	24
Min °C	14	14	13	11	8	7	6	7	8	9	11	13
Rain mm	48	47	52	57	58	49	49	50	59	67	60	59
Raindays	8	7	9	12	14	14	15	16	15	14	12	11

CLIMATE	J	F	M	A	M	J	J	A	S	O	N	D
MORNINGTON												
Max °C	25	25	23	19	16	14	13	14	16	18	20	23
Min °C	13	14	13	11	9	7	7	7	8	10	11	12
Rain mm	46	43	50	62	71	71	69	71	72	70	60	55
Raindays	7	7	8	11	14	15	15	15	14	13	11	8

Melbourne

Although sections of the Melbourne coastline service shipping and industry, numerous sandy beaches, palm-tree lined promenades, foreshore markets, lively side streets and long historic piers accommodate lifestyle and leisure activities.

Williamstown to Point Cooke

West of the city, Williamstown, Melbourne's first port, retains the feeling of a small coastal village, with its wide streets and heritage buildings a legacy of its colonial beginnings. In Nelson Place see the convict-built timeball tower (c. 1849), enjoy the water views or soak up the atmosphere at one of the stylish cafes or restaurants. Bay cruises and fishing boat charters leave from Gem Pier and ferries depart for Southbank and St Kilda. Take to the high seas aboard *The Enterprize*, a replica square-rigged sailing ship, or experience a bird's-eye view from a sea plane – both depart from Gem Pier. HMAS *Castlemaine*, a WW II minesweeper, is permanently moored here as a museum. If you are just after some fishing, a favourite spot for land-based anglers is the Warmies, north of Gem Pier, or try for bream or mullet off the pier itself.

Further west, towards Werribee, Point Cooke Coastal Park attracts abundant birdlife, and adjacent Cheetham Wetlands is a habitat for migratory birds from as far afield as Japan and Alaska (September to March is the peak season). A distinctive viewing tower (3 km return walk from the Tower carpark) provides sensational 360-degree views. Along the shoreline a marine reserve protects the diverse flora and fauna. The RAAF Museum, with its outstanding collection of aircraft, is located at the RAAF Base, via Point Cook Road.

Port Melbourne to St Kilda

Port Melbourne, one of the city's oldest precincts, is defined by its sandy beaches, sleek contemporary apartments and vibrant cafe life. The rather stately *Spirit of Tasmania* ferries leave regularly from the port's Station Pier for Tasmania.

Kite-flying, Port Phillip

Yachts, St Kilda

Sail away

Sydney may have its harbour, but Melbourne has its bay, an impressive expanse of water that inspires some of the country's keenest sailors. On a sunny day, dozens of yachts skim across the horizon and the 20 or so clubs dotted around the coast hum with activity. The waters of Port Phillip are comparatively shallow and, with the small tidal variations and the winds channelled in from the Southern Ocean and Bass Strait, provide consistent fair sailing conditions. Regular regattas such as the coveted Sayonara Cup (said to be Australia's oldest yachting trophy), the Schnapper Point Classic at Mornington and the Sail Melbourne Regatta, hosted by a number of bayside yacht clubs, are all keenly contested. Ocean-going races include the annual Melbourne to Hobart Yacht Race.

On the Bellarine Peninsula, Geelong and Queenscliff are highly regarded sailing venues (Geelong hosts an annual regatta in January that attracts more than 400 racing yachts), while Somers is one of the busiest clubs on the Mornington Peninsula.

If you would like to know more about rigging and gibing, knots and navigation, contact one of Melbourne's sailing schools or clubs. Yachting Victoria has a full list of clubs, and also runs hands-on classes (see *Contacts*, right).

St Kilda Pier is a Melbourne icon and a popular destination for promenading and fishing. The views back towards the city skyline are spectacular (sunsets are especially beautiful). St Kilda breakwater, a rocky outcrop beyond the pier, is home to a hundred or so little penguins, one of the few known mainland breeding sites of these tiny birds. They can be spotted from the observation platform or from a charter boat. Ferries leave from the pier for Williamstown and the Yarra River; bay cruises (watch for dolphins in season) and fishing charters also operate. Other St Kilda must-sees are Luna Park, and the Upper Esplanade's Sunday craft market.

Along the palm-lined Esplanade, paths cater to bayside walkers, cyclists and skaters (bikes and in-line skates can be hired at the end of the pier).

The Bay Trail walk edges the bay, from St Kilda to Brighton (6 km, one way), with cafes along the route.

Melbourne's bayside beaches are wide and sandy, yet each has its own character. St Kilda and South Melbourne are inner-city favourites; Kerferd Rd (Albert Park) is a no-go zone for boats, power skis and sailboards, so it is ideal for swimming; Elwood is favoured by young families – kites often flutter above the grassy reserves; Brighton is noted for its colourful bathing boxes; the wreck of the 1870 HMVS *Cerberus* is visible offshore at pretty Half Moon Bay; and Ricketts Point has lovely shaded picnic areas and a cafe known for its water views. Almost all the beaches have lifesaving clubs, with regular patrols during the summer season.

On a fine, windy day, windsurfers cluster

Contacts

Visitor information

Melbourne Federation Square cnr Flinders St and St Kilda Rd (03) 9658 9658

Dromana (for Mornington Peninsula and French Island) Point Nepean Rd (03) 5987 3078 or 1800 804 009

Geelong cnr Moorabool and Brougham sts 1800 620 888 www.geelongotway.org

Point Nepean Point Nepean Rd Portsea (03) 5984 4276

Sorrento 2 St Aubins Way (03) 5984 5678

Queenscliff 55 Hesse St (03) 5258 4843

Parks and reserves

Parks Victoria General information on parks and marine reserves 13 1963 www.parkweb.vic.gov.au

French Island NP See *Parks Victoria* above

Mornington Peninsula NP See *Parks Victoria* above

Activities

Contact visitor information centres (see above) for details of activities, tours and charter services.

Other

Cape Schanck Lighthouse Tours and accommodation (03) 9568 6411 or 1800 804 145

French Island ferry 0408 553 136

Quarantine Station Point Nepean (03) 5984 3606

Queenscliff–Sorrento Car and Passenger Ferry (03) 5258 3244

Sorrento Ferry Co (passenger only) (03) 5984 1602

Yachting Victoria (03) 9597 0066 www.yachtingvictoria.com.au

around St Kilda Beach, Elwood Sailing Club area, Point Ormond and Sandringham. You can hire a board, or take lessons. For boating enthusiasts, Patterson River is one of the safest harbours on this side of the bay and the most popular boating gateway to Port Phillip.

There is plenty of fishing – if not always fish – from the piers at Port Melbourne, Middle Park, St Kilda, Brighton and Sandringham, with flathead, snapper and whiting the main target fish. Fishing charter boats also regularly ply these waters.

Bellarine Peninsula

Within easy driving distance south-west of Melbourne, the Bellarine Peninsula is small scale and charming, a gently undulating landscape bounded by quiet beaches, brimming with history, delightful small towns and plenty of chances to swim, surf, sail or simply relax.

Geelong and Corio Bay

Geelong, Victoria's second largest city and a major seaport, turns towards the blue waters of Corio Bay for its leisure and pleasure. Along the waterfront, a 4 km walk dotted with quirky painted bollards recounting Geelong's history, and a palm-lined promenade, cycling and skateboard paths, restaurants and cafes all bring the precinct to life. A restored 1930s' Art Deco swimming pool and park complex stand at the heart of Eastern Beach. Nearby, the Victorian Sailing and Water Safety School teaches sailing, canoeing, kayaking and other water-based activities. For anglers, Corio Bay is a year-round snapper area.

Swimming with
dolphins and seals

Port Phillip Bay is home to hundreds of wild bottlenose dolphins and Australian fur seals, and Queenscliff, Sorrento and Portsea are bases for dolphin- and seal-watching cruises. During the warmer months, from October to April, the adventurous can swim in the water, experiencing these marvellous creatures close at hand. Most of the vessels visit Popes Eye, a rock structure between Sorrento and Queenscliff, started as an island fort in 1880, now home to fish, kelp and coral and a protected rookery for gannets (as well as a favourite diving location). Chinamans Hat, an old channel marker, is another well-known diving site. The seals that congregate here are used to divers and can be surprisingly curious and playful. Underwater photographers are usually well rewarded by the animals' antics – but remember they are wild, so keep your distance and take care.

Above Bollards, Geelong
Below Cunningham
Pier, Geelong

Above *Point Lonsdale Lighthouse*
Inset *Pelicans, Queenscliff*

Corio Bay has long been important for sailing and boating – the Royal Geelong Yacht Club was officially established in 1859. In January the bay is a sea of colourful spinnakers as more than 400 racing yachts participate in Australia's largest regatta. In a bluestone woolstore (built in 1872) near the waterfront, the award-winning National Wool Museum documents Geelong's heritage as a port.

Queenscliff

Several grand Victorian-era hotels and rows of neat timber cottages line the wide streets of elegant Queenscliff. The small town is rich in maritime and military history, exemplified by its impressive 19th-century fort (open for inspection) and the unusual black (actually bluestone) lighthouse overlooking Port Phillip. The pine-tree lined foreshore attracts daytrippers, who picnic or wander out on the historic jetty. A steam railway, shops for browsing and a clutch of smart cafes are other distractions.

The safe harbour is a base for dolphin and seal tours and scuba diving schools (see opposite). Ferries leave regularly for Sorrento and Portsea. Fishing is popular from the pier (best in the summer) and Port Phillip's biggest flathead can be caught in Swan Bay. Boat trips, snorkelling excursions and informative and fun rock pool rambles organised by the Marine Discovery Centre provide a unique insight into the local marine life. Swan Bay's shallow waters,

protected within a marine reserve, are a significant habitat for wading birds and rare species such as orange-bellied parrots.

Portarlington to Point Lonsdale

Lovely cliff walks, safe swimming beaches and a marina where fishing and sailing boats shelter give Portarlington its gentle character. Cast a line off the 1890s' pier in summer for garfish, whiting or flathead. On weekends, buy local fresh mussels or fish and chips near the pier and take in the sunset.

At Indented Head, an early steam ship scuttled in the waters off the coast is a favourite site for snorkellers and divers.

Point Lonsdale's classic 1902 lighthouse (open for weekend tours) watches over the many cargo ships, tankers and yachts that pass continually through the notoriously dangerous Rip. The seaside resort is a peaceful getaway with its sheltered and ocean surf beaches, rock pools, sweeping views and unusually long jetty for fishing (mullet, Australian salmon and barracouta are regular catches), as well as good rock fishing. In the cliffs below the lighthouse is Buckleys Cave, where escaped convict William

Queenscliff to Sorrento ferries

Ferries ply hourly between historic Queenscliff and Sorrento, on either side of the heads. There is an older-style passenger ferry, which also stops at Portsea, or the more streamlined *Sea Road* car ferry. The ferry trip, around 40 minutes long, provides wonderful views of the towns as you depart and arrive. The biggest thrill is spotting dolphins (usually October to May) scudding in the ship's bow wave, or seals frolicking around marker buoys and beacons. The passenger ferry has an old-fashioned charm, while the car ferry is more spacious, with comfortable lounges and a snack bar.

Cape Schanck

Mornington Peninsula National Park

Wild, windswept beaches, dense coastal shrubbery and the craggy basalt cliffs of Cape Schanck typify Mornington Peninsula National Park, just 80 km from Melbourne. A network of paths and boardwalks make the coast accessible to walkers of all standards. A fine walk is around Bushrangers Bay, from Cape Schanck Lighthouse to Boneo Road (6 km one way), taking in the cliff-top, gullies, flowering banksias and rugged beach. For the fit, a challenging 32 km walk leads from the lighthouse to Portsea Surf Beach. The old fortifications at Point Nepean, a labyrinth of tunnels, turrets and lookouts, were originally built in the 1880s when a Russian invasion was feared. Access is by foot, bike (these can be hired) or special transport vehicle (details from Point Nepean Visitor Centre; booking recommended). There are fabulous views of the heads from Point Nepean, and access to Cheviot Beach, where Prime Minister Harold Holt mysteriously disappeared in 1967.

Buckley, who lived with the Wathaurong people for over 30 years, may have sheltered at one time. The Glaneuse Reef rock pools, about 300 m west of the lighthouse, are ideal for snorkelling and scuba diving.

Mornington Peninsula

Mornington Peninsula curves down and around, reaching out towards Queenscliff on the opposite shore of the heads. Bordered by the waters of Port Phillip, Western Port and Bass Strait, the peninsula offers countless opportunities for coastal walks, fishing and watersports. National parks and historic sites, gourmet food farms and wineries, golf links and good restaurants encourage visitors to explore and enjoy the peninsula at a leisurely pace.

Frankston to Mt Martha

Dozens of sandy beaches rim the Port Phillip side of the peninsula, from busy Frankston to exclusive Portsea. At Mornington, Schnapper Point boat harbour attracts numerous vessels, and anglers line up along the pier. Mt Martha's petite curved beach boasts brightly coloured bathing boxes and a busy yacht club. Both Dromana and Rosebud are traditional family holiday resorts, favoured for their foreshore camping facilities, calm beaches and easy offshore fishing (snapper is the most likely haul). Arthurs Seat, the peninsula's highest point, is the best vantage point for panoramic bay views (the scenic chairlift was not open at the time of writing).

Sorrento to Portsea

Past the small bay beach towns of Rye and Blairgowrie (both excellent fishing haunts) lies Sorrento, its European history dating back to 1803 when an early attempt at settlement at Sullivan Bay failed. Although it can be hectic in summer, Sorrento retains a holiday feeling with its fine limestone buildings, historic jetty, kerbside cafes and sheltered front beaches. The town has a long tradition as a resort – in the early 1900s holiday-makers arrived by steamship from Melbourne.

The bay in a day

You can still enjoy the varied charms of both sides of the bay, even if time is short. Drive from Melbourne to Queenscliff on the Bellarine Peninsula (105 km); enjoy a stroll through the historic village; picnic on the foreshore or have an early lunch at one of the town's many cafes; then take the car ferry to Sorrento. Discover some of Sorrento's charm before heading back to Melbourne (111 km), perhaps with a stop at one of Mornington Peninsula's boutique wineries.

You can fish from the jetty or take a boat, join a swim-with-the-dolphins tour (heavily booked in season), or take scuba diving lessons at the pier. Sorrento Back Beach has suitable breaks for learners, though crowds and carpark traffic jams are summer hazards. Car and passenger ferries operate from Sorrento to Queenscliff (see *Contacts*, p.125).

Portsea, near the tip of the peninsula, is renowned as an upmarket holiday enclave, with many of its old-money mansions hidden discreetly from view. The Portsea Hotel, built in 1927, is legendary – the grassy beer garden is a great place to enjoy a summer evening. Also famous is the annual Portsea Swim Classic, a 1.2 km race that attracts over 2500 swimmers. Swim at the beautiful and calm front beach; or head for the back beach with its ocean swells if you prefer surfing or rock fishing.

Fascinating dive sites within the bay and off the ocean beach reveal a colourful shallow reef system, kelp gardens, shipwrecks and scuttled submarines; contact Heritage Victoria (see *Fact File*, p.124) to find out about the state's shipwreck discovery trail. Dive Victoria (next to the pub) offers tours, lessons and snorkelling dives with seals and dolphins.

Don't miss the old fortifications at Point Nepean (see *Mornington Peninsula National Park*, opposite) and the former Quarantine Station, an interesting collection of heritage buildings, established in 1852 to protect the colony from contagious, ship-borne disease.

Hastings to Flinders

Hastings, Western Port's commercial hub, is served by an extensive marina. The Royal Australian Navy's largest base is located at Crib Point; further on a ferry links Stony Point to French Island (see above right) and Phillip Island (see *Phillip Island to Wilsons Promontory*, p.130). The tiny townships further south have generally quiet swimming beaches, but Point Leo is surfing territory. The closest surf beach to Melbourne, it has a reputation for consistent swells. Flinders boasts several good tearooms, a safe swimming beach, scuba diving from the pier, surfing at the ocean beach and spectacular views from the golf course.

Cape Schanck and Gunnamatta

Looming over the peninsula's most southerly point stands the imposing 1859 Cape Schanck Lighthouse, fronting the often-turbulent waters of Bass Strait and backed by rugged landscape. Daily tours (recommended) and accommodation in the keepers' cottages are available (see *Contacts*, p.125).

French Island

French Island's remote beaches and unspoilt landscape offer remarkable tranquillity just a short ferry ride from Stony Point. The sparsely populated island is home to Victoria's largest koala population, several hundred bird species, the rare long-nosed potoroo and more than 100 orchid species. There are no made roads – visitors can explore on foot or bike (mountain bikes recommended) or join a tour. The crew aboard the French expedition ship, *Le Naturaliste*, discovered the island in 1802 and named it Ile de Francoise, but the island was not settled by colonists until 1842. Chicory was grown and roasted here, and a prison farm operated from 1916 to 1975. Today, two-thirds of the island is a national park and the surrounding waters are part of a marine sanctuary. Accommodation options include camping, B&Bs and farmstays.

Divers at Portsea

Phillip Island to Wilsons Promontory

Phillip Island, one of Victoria's favourite holiday retreats, is well known to local and international visitors for its endearing little penguins, which waddle ashore nightly in their hundreds. Further east, the much-loved 'Prom', protected within a national park for more than a century, is renowned for its untamed beauty and magnificent beaches.

Summerland Beach spectacle
Hundreds, and in season thousands, of little penguins return nightly to their dune burrows after swimming up to 100 km in search of food in Bass Strait.

Cape Woolamai
Every evening, from September to May, thousands of short-tailed shearwaters fly in to their cliff-top rookeries. Cliff-top walks and stunning views.

Bunurong Marine Park
Fascinating rock-pooling along intertidal platforms (best time within an hour of low tide) and also some great snorkelling sites.

W ildlife is abundant in and around Phillip Island – there are little penguins of course, but Australian fur seals, short-tailed shearwaters (which migrate from the Arctic annually to breed) and koalas are just some of the other treasures. World-class breaks lure surfers to the island's ocean coastline (Woolamai is legendary), families flock to the sheltered beaches in summer, the fishing is outstanding and coastal walks offer superb views. For history buffs, tiny Churchill Island has many echoes of its historic past.

Heading east, the coastline encompasses rugged cliffs and long beaches pounded by surf, sheltered inlets and small, secluded holiday towns such as Cape Paterson and Venus Bay. Anderson Inlet, Shallow Inlet and the various marine and coastal parks are significant habitats for seabirds, waders and migratory birds. And there is some great fishing in these waters.

At Wilsons Promontory National Park, or the Prom as it is affectionately known, the southernmost tip of Australia's mainland juts out dramatically into Bass Strait. Around 130 km of pristine coastline is backed by craggy headlands, tall open forest, rainforest gullies lush with ferns, a wealth of native wildlife and teeming birdlife. Excellent camping, walking, swimming, snorkelling, diving and wildlife-watching ensure the Prom's continuing popularity.

Cape Woolamai

SOUTH GIPPSLAND

Inverloch

enus Bay

Tarwin Lower

Walkerville

Cape Liptrap ★ Cape Liptrap Lighthouse

CAPE LIPTRAP COASTAL PARK

Mt Liptrap 171 +

Waratah Bay

Sandy Point

Waratah Bay

Shallow Inlet

SHALLOW INLET MARINE AND COASTAL PARK

Yanakie

CORNER INLET MARINE AND COASTAL PARK

Corner Inlet

Foster

Toora

Welshpool

Port Franklin

Port Welshpool

Entrance Point

Long Island

Mt Hunter 347

Mt Roundback 316 +

WILSONS PROMONTORY MARINE PARK

WILSONS PROMONTORY NATIONAL PARK

Mt Vereker 637 +

Mt Latrobe + 754

Sparkes Lookout
Tongue Point

Tidal River
Lookout ●

Mt Oberon 558

Mt Wilson 705

Refuge Cove

Cape Wellington

WILSONS PROMONTORY

Great Glennie Island

★ South East Point

Anser Group

WILSONS PROMONTORY MARINE RESERVE

BASS STRAIT

Rodondo Island

N

0   5   10   15 km

Scale

Shallow Inlet
Brilliant bird-watching – migratory wading birds and shorebirds include plovers, cormorants, great egrets, terns and pied oystercatchers.

Wilsons Promontory NP
Camping at Tidal River and bush campsites. More than 100 km of walking tracks. Shell middens and stone tool fragments scattered along the coast. Sea-kayaking and spectacular dive sites in the marine park.

Gippsland

Leongatha   B460

Koonwarra

umburra

HWY

BASS

Anderson Inlet

Tarwin River

SOUTH GIPPSLAND HIGHWAY

A440

Must see, must do

► Watch the famous penguin parade on Phillip Island

► Cruise to Seal Rocks to see thousands of fur seals

► Surf at Woolamai Beach, Phillip Island

► Bushwalk in magnificent Wilsons Promontory NP, and stay overnight in the historic lighthouse keeper's cottage

► Fish any of the inlets along Bass Strait coast

Phillip Island ☎ (03) 5956 7447; Prom Country ☎ (03) 5655 2233;
www.promcountrytourism.com.au

Fact File

When to go
Warm dry summers and cool wet winters. Phillip Island's climate tends to be milder than Melbourne's, although strong winds can whip along the southern coast. East of the island, temperatures can be even milder, although in winter the winds coming off Bass Strait can be wild – and bitterly cold – especially around the Prom. For weather updates contact the Bureau of Meteorology (BOM): 1900 955 363; www.bom.gov.au

Top coastal events
Dec– Jan	*Sun, Surf & Sand Festival* (Cowes, Wonthaggi, San Remo)
	Churchill Island Bush Dance
Feb	*Shannons Phillip Island Classic* (historic motor racing, Phillip Island)
	Phillip Island Titles (surfing)
	Cowes Classic (swim/run competition)
Mar	*Inverloch Jazz Festival*
	Fishing contest (Port Albert)
April	*Phillip Island Longboard Classic* (surfing)
Oct	*Australian Motorcycle Grand Prix* (Phillip Island)

Safety
Swimming There are sheltered and family beaches on Phillip Island and along the coast, but the ocean beaches experience strong and unpredictable winds, treacherous rips and strong currents. The waves from Kilcunda to Mallacoota can be fickle and many of the beaches are isolated. Beaches patrolled over summer are Cowes, Smiths, Cape Woolamai, Venus Bay, Inverloch, Waratah Beach (Sandy Point), Tidal River (Norman Beach) and Cape Paterson. Contact Surf Life Saving Victoria (SLSV) for details of patrol periods: (03) 9534 8201; www.surflifesaver.com.au

Other water activities Offshore anglers need to watch out for strong southerly winds in winter and strong northerlies in summer. Contact Marine Safety Victoria for information on tides and general boating safety: (03) 9655 3399; www.marinesafety.vic.gov.au BOM offers a recorded forecast for coastal waters on 1900 969 966.

Restrictions/regulations
Fishing A Recreational Fishing Licence is required for fishing in all Vic waters; for details contact the Department of Primary Industries, Department of Sustainability and Environment: 13 6186; www.nre.gov.au/fishing

Marine parks Fishing and the removal and/or destruction of marine life are prohibited in protected marine environments in Vic; contact Parks Victoria for location of reserves: 13 1963; www.parkweb.vic.gov.au

Shipwrecks It is an offence in Vic to cause damage to or remove objects from shipwreck sites; for further information contact Heritage Victoria (03) 9655 6519; www.heritage.vic.gov.au/shipwreck

CLIMATE												COWES
	J	F	M	A	M	J	J	A	S	O	N	D
Max °C	24	24	23	19	16	14	13	14	16	18	20	22
Min °C	13	14	13	11	9	8	7	7	8	9	11	12
Rain mm	44	43	56	68	76	79	75	74	70	69	58	51
Raindays	8	7	9	13	15	16	17	17	15	14	12	9

CLIMATE											TIDAL	RIVER
	J	F	M	A	M	J	J	A	S	O	N	D
Max °C	20	20	19	17	15	13	12	13	14	16	17	18
Min °C	14	15	14	13	11	9	8	8	9	10	11	12
Rain mm	62	57	70	81	85	90	96	92	80	84	76	76
Raindays	14	12	15	17	19	19	21	20	19	20	17	16

Cape Liptrap

Phillip Island

The bustling main street of Cowes dips down the hill to the sparkling waters of Western Port. Ferries leave from the pier for Stony Point on Mornington Peninsula, and historic French Island (see *Melbourne and the Peninsulas*, p. 122). Or you can cruise to Seal Rocks to see fur seals sunning themselves – 10 000 or more in the summer breeding season.

The pockmarked cliffs of Cape Woolamai headland are home to thousands of migratory short-tailed shearwaters, from late September to around May. These birds (now protected) were traditionally killed and boiled down for fat – even when they're not around, you can detect their strong, fatty odour. The island's dramatic southerly point is best appreciated from the Cape Woolamai Trail, a sandy cliff-top walk. Waterfowl, waders and seabirds flock to tiny Churchill Island, which can be reached by a bridge near Newhaven. Around Rhyll Inlet's saltwater lagoons watch for spoonbills, ibis, cormorants and other waterbirds.

Phillip Island has a beach for everyone, from the still, silvery waters of Silverleaves, near Cowes, to the white sands of Summerland Beach and prized surfing breaks at Woolamai. There is good jetty, beach and boat fishing, though the fisherman's wharf at San Remo (just before you cross the bridge onto Phillip Island) is the place to stock up if the big one got away.

Inverloch to Sandy Point

The sweeping sandy beaches and often dramatic scenery of this stretch of coast have been discovered by increasing numbers of visitors in recent years. Surfing, windsurfing, rock-pooling, exceptional birdwatching and some of the state's best fishing can all be enjoyed in this region.

Inverloch, on sheltered Anderson Inlet, is ideal for windsurfing, dinghy sailing, waterskiing and fishing. The beaches are fine for swimming, though beware of the deep tide channels. At low tide you can winkle for pipis, or watch waterbirds probe the exposed sand flats. Bunurong Environment Centre's displays help explain the area's fossilised shells and intriguing dinosaur diggings. The first dinosaur bones found in Australia were found in this area in 1906 and there is usually an annual 'dig' for fossils around February to March (tours available).

The Bunurong Coastal Drive reveals secluded coves and stunning vistas as it follows the cliff-line for around 16 km from Inverloch to Cape Paterson, along the narrow Bunurong Marine and Coastal Park. Watch out for wildlife on the road, especially at dusk. Walkways and stairs lead down to various beaches and Cape Paterson is known for its good surfing breaks and great sunsets.

Venus Bay, tucked into the sand dunes, has a sweep of coastline boasting five surf beaches. For anglers, there is great river, surf and estuary fishing (yellow eye mullet and Australian salmon are local catches). The coast from here to Cape Liptrap, classified as a coastal park, is a stretch of untouched landscape with rocky headlands, wavecut platforms and impressive views to the Prom.

At isolated Sandy Point, windsurfing conditions are internationally renowned. If you feel like dropping a line you might haul in whiting, trevally, flathead or salmon. Shallow Inlet Marine and Coastal Park provides a feeding ground for an amazing variety of wading birds, notably Northern Hemisphere migratory species. Beachcombers may be rewarded by seeing shell middens, some dating back 6000 years, the remains of the campsites of the Brataualung people.

Penguin parade

Every night at sunset, dozens of steely-blue little penguins ride in the waves, then waddle up Summerland Beach to their sand dune burrows. At the height of the breeding season around 4500 penguins come ashore. The little penguin (*Eudyptula minor*), at around 33 cm tall the smallest of the 17 species of penguins, is the only species to breed on the Australian mainland, and attracts an international crowd of onlookers. Viewing platforms ensure visitors do not disturb the penguins. The visitor centre has informative displays, a shop and cafe. Take warm clothes, and book in advance during the summer.

Contacts

Visitor information

Inverloch (for Bass Coast)
A'Beckett St
(03) 5674 2706

Phillip Island
Phillip Island Tourist Rd,
Newhaven
(03) 5956 7447
www.phillipisland.net.au

Parks and reserves

Parks Victoria
General information on parks and marine reserves
13 1963
www.parkweb.vic.gov.au

Wilsons Promontory NP
Bookings for accommodation at Tidal River
1800 350 552

Activities

Contact visitor information centres (see above) for details of activities, tours and charter services.

Other

Bunurong Environment Centre
(03) 5674 3738

Phillip Island Nature Park
Penguin parade, koalas, and Churchill Island
(03) 5956 8300

Seal cruise,
Phillip Island

Previous pages Tidal River, Wilsons Promontory
Right The clear waters of the Prom are great for diving

Wilderness waters – diving around the Prom

Snorkelling and diving reveal a spectacular world in the cold but clear waters surrounding Wilsons Promontory. The Prom's dramatic scenery continues below sea level, with rugged granite outcrops, plummeting drop-offs, and caves and ledges harbouring a thriving ecosystem. Many species in these southern waters can be found nowhere else in the world. Waving seagrass meadows and rocky reefs with their multitude of crevices and hollows are home to a rich diversity of plants and animals. Sponge gardens, coral colonies, stingrays, sharks and vivid fish are just some of the prolific marine life.

At Picnic Bay (Leonard Point), about 150 m from the shore, in 6 m or so of water, schools of fish, which include the blue-throat wrasse and herring cale, swim in the plentiful kelp. From the north end of Norman Bay beach you might swim past long-finned pike, or even see Port Jackson sharks cruising near the rocks. Snorkel, or scuba to a depth of 15 m, in the sheltered waters of Sealers Cove to experience its richly varied marine life. At Refuge Cove, about 50 m offshore, the skeletal remains of whales slaughtered by whalers in the 1800s still lie on the ocean floor. For experienced divers, there is excellent diving at Shellback Island, Norman Island and the Glennie islands. Beware: currents can be strong and unpredictable.

Australian fur seals breed on the small offshore islands and feed in the strait. On land the seals can be dangerous; in water they are usually harmless and may frolic with divers, providing a truly exhilarating experience, but they should still be approached with caution. Beware: the seals attract white sharks.

There are also more than 30 shipwrecks in these waters. Contact Heritage Victoria for details of their outstanding shipwreck trail (see *Fact File*, p.132).

Wilsons Promontory National Park

This is one of the state's best known national parks, and also one of the oldest (declared in 1898). It is hard to fault 'the Prom', if you want to experience some of Victoria's most magnificent coastal scenery. White sandy beaches, granite headlands, timbered mountains, open forest and fern gullies contribute to the wild beauty of the park's 50 000 ha. The wildlife is special too – more than 30 species of mammals and hundreds of bird species inhabit the park. Although a hugely popular national park, (with half a million visitors each year), the Prom's superb natural environment is fiercely guarded.

Facilities are mainly at Tidal River, 30 km from the park entrance. There are about 450 camping and caravan sites, but no powered sites and generators are not permitted. Fires cannot be lit at campsites (take a gas or fuel stove). Cabins, lodges and motor huts provide accommodation. Such is the park's popularity that summer bookings are made by ballot (bookings June, ballot drawn July). In the high season an open-air cinema runs, and rangers organise spotlight tours, talks and guided walks.

Tidal River has plenty for visitors – the beach is great, surf can be good, rock pools offer endless intrigue, crimson rosellas are as tame as pets and you are almost sure to encounter wombats, kangaroos and emus.

WILSONS PROMONTORY *walking trails*

The Prom is a bushwalker's paradise, with more than 30 walks for all levels of enthusiasm, energy and available time. Short forays from Tidal River, overnight hikes to campgrounds, or – for the more experienced and intrepid – treks into the remote north-east area, reveal the park's diverse character.

Visitor information
See *Contacts*, p.133

Sealers Cove Hike
An invigorating day walk (9.5 km, allow two to three hours each way). Starts at Oberon carpark, heads up to Windy Saddle, then down to secluded Sealers Cove. The walk is medium to hard; the return trip is uphill, so allow plenty of time to get back.

Sealers Cove to Refuge Cove
Start at Sealers Cove campground. The walk (6.4 km, allow two hours each way) is medium to hard and passes tall tree ferns in shaded gullies, then drier coastal vegetation. Captivating views to the north and also of Seal Islands. Watch for seals, and whales in winter.

Squeaky Beach Nature Walk
A discovery walk: coastal vegetation, wonderful views, good wombat-watching. Start at the Tidal River footbridge. Squeaky Beach is so called because the almost pure quartz sand squeaks when grains rub together. The trek to the beach's north end (3.2 km, 50 minutes each way) is medium grade.

Tidal River to Norman Bay
For beginners, a stroll along sandy tracks from the camping area or carpark to lovely Norman Bay beach (perfect for swimming). Shellfish, many of them traditional bush tucker, are revealed as the tides change. Routes are up to a kilometre and take around half an hour.

Prom Lighthouse Trek
A fascinating, ranger-led walk (38 km return) to the southern-most tip of the mainland. It usually takes two to three days, varies from easy to moderate (there are steep sections), with occasional stunning views. Walkers can stay in the lighthouse keeper's quarters at the historic lighthouse (c. 1850) high above Bass Strait. Bookings essential.

WARNINGS/ RESTRICTIONS
- Permits needed for all overnight hikes
- Book campsites in advance, especially in peak periods
- Always make sure you are adequately prepared; even for a short walk, carry drinking water
- All animals, plants, rocks, soils and historical sites are protected
- Stay on the tracks

Gippsland Highlights

Corner Inlet to Mallacoota takes in wild and beautiful beaches, a unique network of waterways, lakes and river deltas and some of the country's best fishing. It is the perfect destination for those who prefer their landscape unspoilt, who enjoy watersports, bushwalking, wildlife-watching and relaxing in peace.

Gippsland Lakes
With numerous sheltered moorings, and no reefs or rips, this is a wonderful place for boating – yachts, canoes, kayaks, luxury motor cruisers and more.

Wildlife-watching
Dolphins can be spotted cavorting off this stretch of coast and even in the saltwater Gippsland Lakes.

Port Albert
Off the coast from Port Albert, divers can explore the wreck of the paddlesteamer *Clonmel* (c. 1840), part of Heritage Victoria's Shipwreck Discovery Trail.

Must see, must do
▶ Wander around the old port at historic Port Albert
▶ Cruise the placid waters of the Gippsland Lakes
▶ Surf-fish from Ninety Mile Beach
▶ Watch for dolphins and seals off the wilderness coast of Croajingolong NP
▶ Explore remote Gabo Island

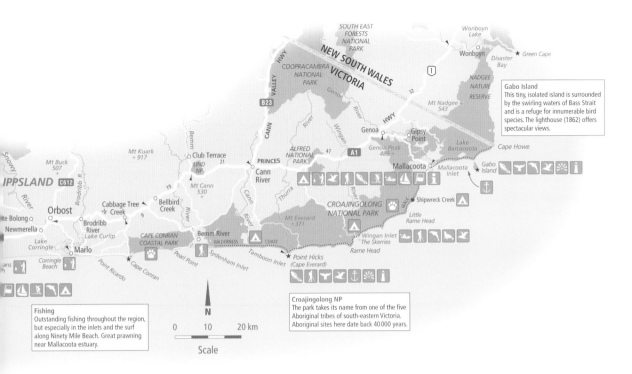

Gabo Island
This tiny, isolated island is surrounded by the swirling waters of Bass Strait and is a refuge for innumerable bird species. The lighthouse (1862) offers spectacular views.

Fishing
Outstanding fishing throughout the region, but especially in the inlets and the surf along Ninety Mile Beach. Great prawning near Mallacoota estuary.

N

0   10   20 km

Scale

Croajingolong NP
The park takes its name from one of the five Aboriginal tribes of south-eastern Victoria. Aboriginal sites here date back 40 000 years.

Historic fishing villages such as Port Welshpool and Port Albert and sleepy holiday towns are dotted along the coastline. The golden sands of the superb Ninety Mile Beach are buffeted by surf rolling in from Bass Strait and backed by the Gippsland Lakes. This intricate system of lakes and rivers, surrounded by bushland and mountains, forms a natural resort, much favoured by boating enthusiasts.

To the east lies the wilderness coast of Croajingolong National Park, offering a rare opportunity to experience coast and country in its near-natural state. Rocky coves, remote beaches, towering dunes and coastal heath fringe the park for 100 km. Native plants, animals and birdlife thrive in this remarkable sanctuary. Camping, bushwalking and wildlife-watching are the preferred pursuits here, though the fishing is also undeniably good. One of the anglers' favourite retreats, the fishing village of Mallacoota, is cradled by the untamed beauty of Croajingolong.

The Gippsland region offers a full range of accommodation options, from bush camping in remote locations in the beautiful national parks, to waterside villas and fully equipped luxury motor cruisers or yachts. Whichever you choose, the stunning landscape and views are free for all to enjoy.

Gippsland Lakes

Fact File

When to go
Year-round. Beautiful in summer, but the milder temperatures (a few degrees warmer than Melbourne, particularly around Lakes Entrance) and the lack of crowds make other seasons – especially spring and autumn – good options. For weather updates contact the Bureau of Meteorology (BOM): 1900 955 363; www.bom.gov.au

Top coastal events
Jan *Lakes Summer Festival* (Lakes Entrance)
Mar *Port Albert Regatta*
Easter *Festival of the Southern Ocean* (Mallacoota)

Safety
Swimming Seaspray, Lakes Entrance beach and Bastion Beach (Mallacoota) are patrolled daily 26 Dec–26 Jan and weekends and public holidays late Nov–late April. Eastern Beach is patrolled daily 26 Dec–26 Jan. Woodside Beach is patrolled weekends and public holidays late Nov– late April. Contact Surf Life Saving Victoria (SLSV): (03) 9534 8201; www.surflifesaver.com.au

Other water activities Users of watercraft should take extreme care in crossing the bars at Lakes Entrance, Mallacoota, McLoughlins Beach and Port Albert. The entire coastline is subject to strong southerlies in winter and strong northerlies in summer. Contact Marine Safety Victoria for tidal and safety information: (03) 9655 3399; www.marinesafety.vic.gov.au BOM offers a recorded forecast for coastal waters on 1900 969 966.

Restrictions/regulations
Fishing A Recreational Fishing Licence is required for fishing in all Vic waters; for details contact the Department of Primary Industries, Department of Sustainability and Environment: 13 6186; www.nre.gov.au/fishing

CLIMATE								LAKES	ENTRANCE			
	J	F	M	A	M	J	J	A	S	O	N	D
Max °C	24	24	22	20	17	15	15	16	17	19	20	22
Min °C	14	15	13	11	8	6	5	6	7	9	11	13
Rain mm	57	35	55	61	79	65	55	57	57	61	73	74
Raindays	8	7	10	10	12	13	12	14	13	13	13	11

Marine parks Fishing and the removal and/or destruction of marine life are prohibited in protected marine environments in Vic; contact Parks Victoria for location of parks and reserves: 13 1963; www.parkweb.vic.gov.au

Shipwrecks It is an offence in Vic to cause damage to or remove objects from shipwreck sites; for further information contact Heritage Victoria (03) 9655 6519; www.heritage.vic.gov.au/shipwreck

Corner Inlet to Port Welshpool

Lying north and east of Wilsons Promontory, the vast tidal lagoon of Corner Inlet and fringing coastline are of international significance as feeding grounds for over 30 species of migratory wading birds, including godwits, plovers and curlews. The seagrass-rich waters of the inlet, the most easterly and therefore the warmest of Victoria's large bays, are also important breeding grounds for many species of fish.

There is endless activity: swimming, boating, sea-kayaking, windsurfing, canoeing and bushwalking (Snake Island is a favourite). Fish from the surf beaches or try your luck in the calmer inlet. Beachcombers watch for crabs, small fish and sea stars in the waving seagrass, mangroves and mudflats. Extensive Aboriginal shell middens remain along the southern shore, signs of the area's traditional Kurnai inhabitants.

At Port Welshpool, you can drop a line from the long jetty or set off from the local boat ramp. Nearby Barry Beach is the shipping terminal and base for major Bass Strait oil and gas rigs.

Port Albert

In the mid-1800s sailing ships swayed in Port Albert's harbour as thousands of Chinese disembarked for the Gippsland goldfields. Today, the town is something of a backwater. Its historic

Pelicans, Gippsland Lakes

Trawlers at Lakes Entrance

Fishing heaven

For the fishing fraternity, the coastline from Corner Inlet east to Mallacoota is fishing heaven. Lake, river, ocean, boat, jetty – every type of fishing, for any type of angler, at all times of the year. If you have never dropped a line in the water, this is the place to start.

On calm days, the huge tidal lagoon of Corner Inlet yields flathead, whiting, mullet, trevally, snapper and more. From Corner Inlet to the old fishing town of Port Albert, the prized catch is whiting, which is prolific in the warmer months. Offshore, big schools of yellowtail kingfish, snook and striped tuna are possible catches. Port Welshpool has two jetties for land-based fishing. In summer, whiting, flathead, mullet, flounder and garfish are running; in winter, pike and trevally.

With the waters from Bass Strait thundering in, surf-fishing along Ninety Mile Beach is a great experience. Corringle and Pettmans are two of the most popular and easily accessible beaches. Australian salmon, tailor, shark, flathead and trevally can all be landed from the shoreline.

Once you reach the Gippsland Lakes, your fishing options multiply. From the Loch Sport jetty at Lake Victoria you can fish for mullet and bream by day, and spear for flounder in the evening. Large schools of tailor, bream, flathead, whiting, mulloway and bass swim in the waters around Lakes Entrance and Paynesville. The famed fishing territory of Mallacoota Inlet – more sheltered and a little warmer than the Gippsland Lakes – offers ideal boating and jetty fishing. Bream, flathead, whiting and mulloway are typical catches and the prawning is first class. Offshore there is big game – marlin and tuna.

Take your own fishing gear, although in most areas you can hire just about everything you need. There are plenty of hire outlets, and a number of good local fishing charter services. And always ask the locals what fish are biting, and where. Contact Gippsland Ports (see *Contacts*, right) for information on boat launching, tidal and lake mooring.

Contacts

Visitor information

Lakes Entrance cnr Marine Pde and Esplanade
(03) 5155 1966

Mallacoota cnr Allan and Buckland drives
(03) 5158 0219

Parks and reserves

Parks Victoria
General information on parks and marine reserves
13 1963
www.parkweb.vic.gov.au

Croajingolong NP
Campsite bookings for Tamboon Inlet, Wingan Inlet and Shipwreck Creek
(03) 5158 6351

Rotamah Island Bird Observatory
(03) 5156 6398

Activities

Contact visitor information centres (see above) for details of activities, tours and charter services.

Other

Gabo Island Lightstation
Accommodation bookings
13 1963
www.parks.vic.gov.au

Gippsland Ports
Information on boat launching, tidal and lake mooring
(03) 5152 1974
www.gippslandports.vic.gov.au

Point Hicks Lightstation
Accommodation bookings
(03) 5158 4268

buildings and maritime heritage provide plenty of character, but it is the exceptional fishing that keeps the town in business. Wander around the old port or visit Gippsland's Regional Maritime Museum for a glimpse of the past.

Gippsland Lakes

This intricate network of saltwater lakes, estuaries, wetlands and lagoons is separated from the breathtaking beauty of Ninety Mile Beach by a sliver of sandy land. It is surprisingly uncrowded, but a holiday haven for those in the know.

Four major rivers reach the lakes here, en route to the sea, creating a spectacular 400 sq km web of

waterways. The area is justifiably claimed to be one of Australia's top boating spots: you can sail, cruise, paddle, take a 'tinnie' out for some fishing, board a skippered yacht or try a sea kayak. There is rarely more than a gentle breeze and numerous sheltered moorings can be found.

The fishing is outstanding. Surf, ocean, river and estuary sites and at least 20 varieties of fish keep anglers well occupied all year round. Lakeside towns include Paynesville and fashionable Metung, where elegant cruisers moor along the jetties.

Birdlife flourishes throughout the region, but Rotamah Island, a bird sanctuary with a resident ornithologist, is especially fascinating.

Fishing, Croajingolong National Park

Ninety Mile Beach

Stretching seemingly forever, Ninety Mile Beach is an unspoilt span of golden sand, washed by the waters of Bass Strait. You can surf-fish on secluded beaches and watch for dolphins, seals and even whales in season. Much of the area is protected within parks and reserves, ensuring a valuable refuge for wildlife and birdlife.

Lakes Entrance

Lakes Entrance is where the lakes meet Bass Strait. The country's biggest fishing fleet moors here and the surrounding waters are a natural drawcard for recreational anglers of all types. Around 40 jetties provide for boating and fishing.

Holiday-makers crowd the beach in season. Surf is reasonable but there can be strong rips, so swim between the flags, and surf with a friend. Paddleboats, catamarans, bodyboards and canoes can be hired near the beach, just over the footbridge. Try the Fishermen's Co-op on Bullock Island for superlative fresh seafood.

Croajingolong National Park

Croajingolong National Park reaches along more than 100 km of wilderness coast. This is one of the country's great treasures, a remote and spectacular strip of coastal land, distinguished by UNESCO as a World Biosphere Reserve for its ecological importance. Fine sandy beaches are fringed by dunes, broken by granite cliffs and lush bush-covered promontories.

Gabo Island – remote retreat

Less than 1 km from the wilderness coastline of Croajingolong National Park lies rocky, windswept Gabo Island. It is tiny – around 2.5 km long and 1 km wide – remote, and often lashed by icy seas. Yet it is rich in flora and fauna, circled by lovely boulder-strewn and sand beaches and dominated by a tall, elegant lighthouse built in 1862 from the island's rare pink granite.

Gabo Island supports the world's largest-known breeding colony of little penguins, as well as extensive short-tailed shearwater rookeries. Raptors, such as marsh harriers, brown falcons and sometimes even the majestic white-bellied sea eagle, wheel overhead in search of prey. Fur seals frequent the rocks around the island, whales pass on their annual migration south (September–October) and pods of dolphins swim by.

The rocky shoreline provides a habitat for myriad sea creatures and endless fascination for beachcombers. When the sun shines, Santa Barbara Bay is perfect for swimming, snorkelling and fishing. For experienced scuba divers, shipwrecks are a reminder of how treacherous these waters can be.

Access, by sea or air (light plane from Mallacoota), is dependent on the weather. Book well in advance if you would like to stay in the lighthouse keeper's cottage – it's a memorable experience. A tour of the lighthouse itself offers panoramic views.

Wildlife thrives in this environment – more than 300 bird species, 52 mammal species and 1000 types of native plant (including 49 species of orchid) have been identified. The smoky mouse, long-footed potoroo and ground parrot are a few of the rare or endangered species that make the park their home.

Conservation of the park's natural resources and management of recreation activities are carefully balanced. Licensed fishing is permitted. You can walk in solitude, swim in clear blue–green waters, dive, snorkel, canoe or sail. Kayaking – both offshore and on the many inlets, creeks and rivers – is a wonderful way to experience the park. Off the coast, around the rocky outcrop known as the Skerries, inquisitive fur seals may swim up and around you. Beware though – the seals attract white sharks.

Favourite camping venues include peaceful Tamboon Inlet (best reached by boat, and perfect for flat-water canoeing); Wingan Inlet with its rich birdlife; and Shipwreck Creek, a good departure point for various walking tracks. Remember, camping facilities are basic; access is by gravel roads, or by foot; and bookings are needed for peak periods. Or you can stay at one of the nearby towns, such as Cann River, Genoa or Mallacoota.

For serious bushwalkers, the challenging 100 km Wilderness Coast Walk (permit required), extends from Sydenham Inlet in Croajingolong National Park to Wonboyn in the Nadgee Nature Reserve, New South Wales.

On the edge of the park, high on a granite headland, Point Hicks Lightstation, built in 1890 and mainland Australia's tallest classical lighthouse, has breathtaking views. The weatherboard keepers' cottages offer accommodation.

Mallacoota

Mallacoota, tucked away on the state's far eastern coast, is surrounded by Croajingolong National Park. Year-round it is a mecca for anglers, but during summer it turns from a sleepy hollow into a busy holiday resort. Thousands of campers enjoy the idyllic lakeside setting. The beautiful beaches and clear waters of the inlet make it ideal for watersports – surfing, swimming, windsurfing, sailing, diving, kayaking – and, of course, fishing.

Mallacoota Inlet consists of two lakes joined by a narrow opening (the Narrows) and a lovely shoreline punctuated by bays and coves. Jetties around its rim provide ample spots to dangle a line. There are also plenty of good picnic venues and scenic walking tracks. Canoeing and kayaking are well suited to these waters, and the Betka, Wallagaraugh and Genoa rivers are navigable some way upstream. On the inlet's upper reaches, picturesque Gipsy Point has a tranquil charm all its own.

For wildlife observers, the coastal heathland is a natural sanctuary for considerable birdlife (watch for flashes of colour as rosellas and parrots swoop overhead) and home to wallabies, eastern grey kangaroos and goannas. Migratory waders and waterbirds nest and forage for food around the inlet and its peaceful sandy islands.

Betka Beach (3 km from town), Tip Beach and nearby Bastion Point have good surfing breaks, while Quarry Beach is known for snorkelling (look for abalone around the rocks) and surf-fishing. Offshore, big-game fishing is excellent with tuna and marlin in summer, but the entrance is shallow, narrow and notoriously dangerous.

Mallacoota is an ideal base for exploring Croajingolong National Park. For culture buffs, its Festival of the Southern Ocean, held at Easter, is exceptionally good.

Great Ocean Road

The Great Ocean Road, one of Australia's most scenic coastal trips, runs between Anglesea and Warrnambool, although the name is commonly used as a catch-all for the entire south-west coastal region, which stretches 400 kilometres to the border with South Australia.

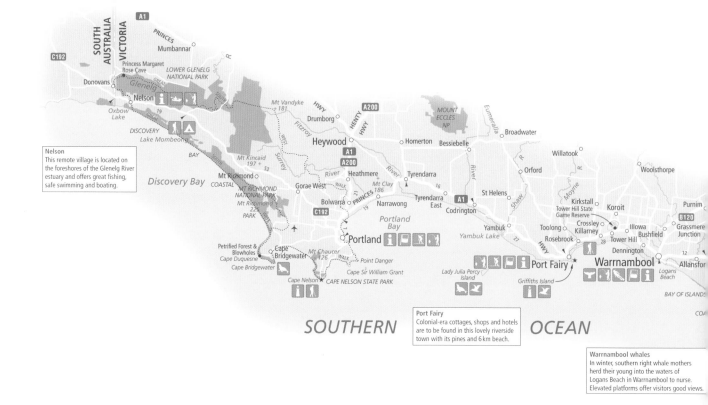

Nelson
This remote village is located on the foreshores of the Glenelg River estuary and offers great fishing, safe swimming and boating.

Port Fairy
Colonial-era cottages, shops and hotels are to be found in this lovely riverside town with its pines and 6 km beach.

Warrnambool whales
In winter, southern right whale mothers herd their young into the waters of Logans Beach in Warrnambool to nurse. Elevated platforms offer visitors good views.

The region begins just 100 km from Melbourne with a series of top-class surf beaches. Further west, the rolling coastal plains give way to an undulating line of sea cliffs, around which the road weaves a precarious but famously scenic course. Holiday towns, bordered by sandy beaches, appear every so often, set within the folds of craggy valleys. The road leaves the coast to take in the peaks and forests of the Otway Ranges, and returns at the site of the Twelve Apostles, a collection of massive limestone stacks, which stand like sentinels amid the crashing swells of the Southern Ocean. Historic evidence of the treachery of these waters lies submerged with the hundreds of boats wrecked off the coast. The heritage buildings of the western towns reveal the story of Victoria's earliest settlements, as do the rising numbers of whales and seals, whose populations were hunted to near extinction before protection bans were introduced in the 20th century.

This area is a major holiday centre with good facilities, including a wide range of accommodation and dining choices. There are many activities on offer, including some of the best surfing opportunities in the state, diving and snorkelling tours of shipwrecks, fishing, walking, riding and cycling.

The Twelve Apostles – a signature Victorian landscape

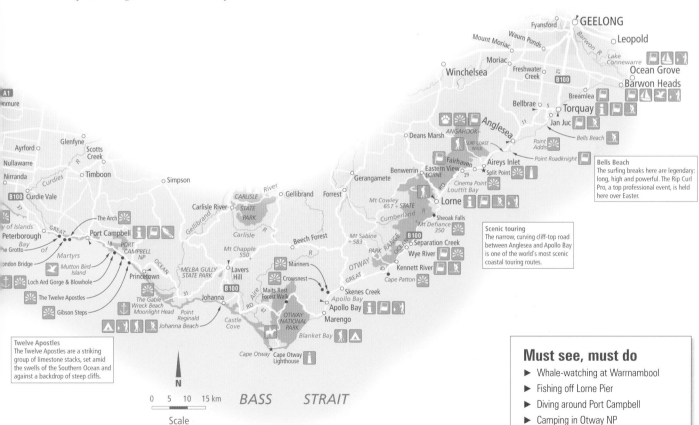

Twelve Apostles
The Twelve Apostles are a striking group of limestone stacks, set amid the swells of the Southern Ocean and against a backdrop of steep cliffs.

Bells Beach
The surfing breaks here are legendary: long, high and powerful. The Rip Curl Pro, a top professional event, is held here over Easter.

Scenic touring
The narrow, curving cliff-top road between Anglesea and Apollo Bay is one of the world's most scenic coastal touring routes.

Must see, must do

► Whale-watching at Warrnambool
► Fishing off Lorne Pier
► Diving around Port Campbell
► Camping in Otway NP
► Surfing at Bells Beach

☎ 1800 620 888; www.greatoceanroad.org

Fact File

When to go
Winters are cold and blustery here, but dramatic. Summers are crowded, but the only real swimming season. For surfers and divers, the best time is April–Sept. For weather updates contact the Bureau of Meteorology (BOM): 1900 955 363; www.bom.gov.au

Top coastal events
Jan	*Pier to Pub Swim* (Lorne)
	Mountain to Surf Footrace (Lorne)
Mar	*Folk Festival* (Port Fairy)
Easter	*Rip Curl Pro Bells Beach* (Torquay)
July	*Fun 4 Kids* (Warrnambool)
Sept	*Angair Wildflower Festival* (Anglesea)
Dec	*Falls Festival* (Lorne)

Safety
Swimming Some sheltered bays and estuaries provide safe swimming, but conditions at most beaches are rough and unpredictable. Patrols operate weekends and public holidays Nov–April at 15 beaches along this coastline; there are daily patrols at some beaches from Boxing Day to Australia Day. For details contact Surf Life Saving Victoria (SLSV): (03) 9534 8201; www.surflifesaver.com.au

Other water activities This region is subject to strong southerly blows and unpredictable swells and currents, resulting in dangerous conditions for boating and diving. Newcomers should team-up with experienced locals. North to north-east breezes create the best conditions for most water activities; these are most prevalent from Mar–Aug. Surfers need to watch out for rips and bigger than expected swells. BOM offers a recorded forecast for coastal waters on 1900 969 966.

Restrictions/regulations
Fishing A Recreational Fishing Licence is required for fishing in all Vic waters; for details contact the Department of Primary Industries, Department of Sustainability and Environment: 13 6186; www.nre.gov.au/fishing

Marine reserves Fishing and the removal and/or destruction of marine life are prohibited in protected marine environments in Vic; contact Parks Victoria for location of parks and reserves: 13 1963; www.parkweb.vic.gov.au

CLIMATE												LORNE
	J	F	M	A	M	J	J	A	S	O	N	D
Max ºC	23	23	22	19	16	14	13	14	16	18	20	21
Min ºC	12	13	12	10	9	7	6	6	7	8	9	10
Rain mm	39	49	54	71	87	100	105	109	99	91	65	53
Raindays	7	7	8	11	14	16	17	17	16	14	11	8

CLIMATE												PORTLAND
	J	F	M	A	M	J	J	A	S	O	N	D
Max ºC	24	23	22	20	17	15	14	15	16	18	20	22
Min ºC	13	14	13	11	9	7	6	7	8	9	10	12
Rain mm	33	34	48	60	78	77	88	86	74	67	55	44
Raindays	8	8	10	13	17	17	20	19	17	15	13	11

Shipwrecks It is an offence in Vic to cause damage to or remove objects from shipwreck sites; for further information contact Heritage Victoria: (03) 9655 6519; www.heritage.vic.gov.au/shipwreck

Right Scenic touring along the Great Ocean Road
Below Sign at Bells Beach

Rip Curl Pro, Bells Beach

Bells and other great breaks of the south-west

The south-west coast is Victoria's surfing mecca with a combination of factors making for some of the best and most consistent wave opportunities in the world. North, north-easterly and north-westerly winds push up the swell along the coast, aided by low-pressure systems from the Southern Ocean. Coastline reefs, headlands and beaches also help 'shape' the waves with beach breaks, point breaks and reef breaks. The best surfing conditions are between April and September.

In the Torquay area, beginners get a good run at Jan Juc beach and Torquay Point. More experienced surfers head for breaks that include Steps and Boobs (the latter named for local character 'Boobs'

Johnson), while the experts tackle the region's class acts, Winkipop and Bells Beach.

Bells Beach is the region's signature break. It has a rock shelf coming right into shore, on a steady incline, which means waves break consistently, whatever the size of the swell. On a good day, distinct swell lines can be seen forming hollow 3 to 4 m waves. Bells is the venue for the Rip Curl Pro held at Easter, an event that attracts the world's top surfers.

When the surfing professionals descend at Easter, and holidaying hordes arrive in summer, the locals head south, where good breaks include Cathedral Rock near Lorne, Lorne Point, Kennett River and the remote Johanna Beach.

Around Torquay

This area, which extends along the ocean frontage of the Bellarine Peninsula, claims some of Australia's best surf beaches. Starting just 100 km from Melbourne, it has a classic Australian seaside feel, with its holiday shacks, caravan parks and long stretches of sandy surf beach.

Barwon Heads and Ocean Grove sit on either side of the broad flow of the Barwon River. Both offer the choice between surf and estuary beaches. The area attracted national attention when it featured in the popular ABC television series

SeaChange, which was credited with sparking a seaside property boom. Ocean Grove is the larger of the two towns, on the eastern side of the Barwon. It fronts a sensational 6 km long surf beach, which, as one of the closest surf beaches to Melbourne, is hugely popular in summer. Barwon Heads has several good restaurants and a caravan park with estuary frontage. The Bluff, located nearby, has wonderful ocean views, and is a renowned birdwatching spot.

Surfers first started coming to the town of Torquay in the 1960s, attracted by rumours

Contacts

Visitor information

Apollo Bay 100 Great Ocean Rd
(03) 5237 6529

Lorne 144 Mountjoy Pde
(03) 5289 1152

Nelson Leake St
(08) 8738 4051

Port Campbell 26 Morris St
(03) 5598 6089

Port Fairy Bank St
(03) 5568 2682

Portland Lee Breakwater Rd
(03) 5523 2671

Torquay Surf City Plaza Beach Rd
(03) 5261 4219

Warrnambool 600 Raglan Pde
(03) 5564 7837
www.warrnamboolinfo.com.au

Parks and reserves

Parks Victoria
General information on parks and marine reserves
13 1963
www.parkweb.vic.gov.au

Bay of Islands CP
See *Parks Victoria* above

Discovery Bay CP
See *Parks Victoria* above

Otway NP
See *Parks Victoria* above

Port Campbell NP
See *Parks Victoria* above

Activities

Contact visitor information centres (see above) for details of activities, tours and charter services.

Other

Bimbi Park
Horseriding tours and accommodation
(03) 5237 9246

Cape Nelson Lightstation
Tours and accommodation
(03) 5523 5100

Cape Otway Lighthouse
Tours and accommodation
(03) 5237 9240

Summer at Torquay

of legendary breaks at and around Bells Beach (see p.147). In the late 1960s, a handful of dedicated surfers began designing and making surfboards for locals. Today, these booming businesses, including Rip Curl and Quiksilver, generate an annual turnover of $400 million; their products, which include surfboards, wetsuits, surf wear and street wear, can be purchased at factory outlets around town. Surfworld Australia in Torquay, the biggest museum of its kind in the world, charts local, national and overseas surfing history, and has displays on surfing techniques and surf culture. Surfing competitions take place in the immediate area from November to April, culminating in the Rip Curl Pro, held at Easter. The 30 km Surf Coast Walk begins at Jan Juc, just south of Torquay, and ends at Fairhaven.

Anglesea to Lorne

The touring scenery of the Great Ocean Road is at its most spectacular between the towns of Anglesea and Apollo Bay. Here, a ragged line of hills tumbles headlong into the ocean, forming high cliffs at the point of contact. The hills divide into valleys, which accommodate creek beds, sandy coves and, in recent times, holiday towns. The road curves and twists, veering into dark folds of rock and forest, before emerging to views of vast skies and the heave and froth of Bass Strait.

Anglesea is a small town with good holiday facilities. The nearby beach at Point Roadknight is popular with families, while the main beach is great for surfers (beginners) and bodysurfers. One of the town's signature attractions is the troop of kangaroos that comes to graze on the greens of the local golf course. Another, is the superb Anglesea Heathland, which, with over 600 native plant species, including 100 species of orchid, rates as one of the most diverse flora areas in Australia. The nearby town of Aireys Inlet has an 1891 lighthouse and superb views from surrounding cliff-tops.

The resort village of Lorne lies between the wide curve of Louttit Bay and a band of forested hills. The main street, packed to the rafters in summer, offers a lively mix of cafes, restaurants and shops. The accommodation on offer, which includes a large historic guesthouse, self-contained eco-cottages and contemporary apartments, is of a very high standard. The main beach is long and wide, and easily able to accommodate the big summertime

gatherings of sunbakers, anglers, bodysurfers and family groups. Lorne Pier is regarded as one of the region's premier fishing spots, yielding catches of garfish, mullet, Australian salmon and barracouta. The surrounding hills enclose a tranquil landscape of waterfalls and rainforest, which can be explored via a series of walking trails.

Apollo Bay and the Otway Coast

The Otway Ranges dominate the immediate hinterland of much of the south-west coast, extending as far as Anglesea in the north-east. But it is the rugged national park-protected landscape of hills and forests in the vicinity of Cape Otway that is popularly claimed as the 'Otways'.

The town of Apollo Bay is the eastern gateway to the region. Although busy in summer, development is decidedly low-key and, in any case, completely dwarfed by the great beauty of the town's natural setting, an elegant arch of concertinaed hills, distant forests and long sandy beaches.

The town's main beach is reasonably protected, and popular with families in summer. At its southern end is a picturesque boat harbour, the walls and jetty of which attract crowds of anglers. The harbour is the base for the local fishing fleets and attendant crews whose day's-end activities make for good theatre. The town has sophisticated choices in terms of food and accommodation, but prices remain reasonable.

Above *Fishing boats at Apollo Bay*
Left *Point Addis lookout*

Beyond nearby Marengo the Great Ocean Road departs from the coast for a 60 km tour of the hills, valleys, creeks and forests of the Otway National Park (see opposite). The road re-emerges at the tiny settlement of Princetown.

Port Campbell Coast

Vast skies, striking rock formations, dramatic changes of light and the ongoing drama of the Southern Ocean make this one of the most scenic coastal areas of Australia.

The region's famous limestone formations are the marooned, eroded remnants of the original cliff line. Instantly recognisable are the Twelve Apostles – a series of natural sculptures, which, with their pale, porous surfaces, reflect every nuance of the changing light. Along with Uluṟu, they are one of the most photographed sites in Australia.

Other sites of geological and scenic interest include the Blowhole, Loch Ard Gorge, Mutton Bird Island, which is home to thousands of nesting pairs of short-tailed shearwaters (muttonbirds) from September to April, London Bridge, and the limestone stacks in the Bay of Islands and Bay of Martyrs. The attractions are protected within the adjoining Port Campbell National Park and Bay of Islands Coastal Park; there are viewing platforms, boardwalks and information boards at the main sites. The area offers plenty of opportunities for diving (see p.154) and there is safe swimming at Port Campbell.

The tragedy of the *Loch Ard*

Around 180 historic wrecks pepper the south-west coast, and there are as many stories describing the treachery of this notorious route and the limitations of early navigation equipment and maritime technology, and the human tragedies that resulted. Of these, none is as poignant or enduring as that of the *Loch Ard*. The *Loch Ard*, launched in 1873, was a splendid boat for her time: a big iron-hulled clipper weighing 1693 tonnes, with a main mast of 50 m. On a voyage from England to Australia, in 1878, she entered difficult waters in dark and foggy conditions. The boat drifted too close to the break line and was picked up by the swell and dashed against the reef off Mutton Bird Island. Of the 54 passengers and crew on board, only two survived: an 18-year-old passenger, Eva Carmichael, and her rescuer, crewman Tom Pearce. The four bodies that were recovered lie buried on the cliff-top in what is now known as Loch Ard Cemetery. The Historic Shipwreck Trail runs between Moonlight Head and the South Australian border. Through brochures (available from visitor information centres) and land-based plaques, the trail records the history and charts the position of 53 of the region's best known wrecks.

The OTWAY coast

The 13 000 ha park preserves spectacular rainforest, forests of mountain ash and a littoral landscape that is remote and dramatic. Access to the coast is by a couple of minor roads leading off the Great Ocean Road and a small network of walking tracks. Attractions include a historic lighthouse, shipwreck relics, fossils, beachside camping and a top-class surfing beach.

Visitor information
See *Contacts*, p.147

Wreck Beach
From the Wreck Beach carpark (Moonlight Head Road) steep stairs lead to Wreck Beach. Here, 800 m to the west, are the anchors of the *Marie Gabrielle* (1869) and, a further 400 m on, of the barque, the *Fiji* (1891).

Blanket Bay
There is no vehicle access to this sheltered, east-facing bay, which is one of the reasons for its popularity as a walking and camping destination. Walking tracks lead north to Shelly Beach and south to the lighthouse.

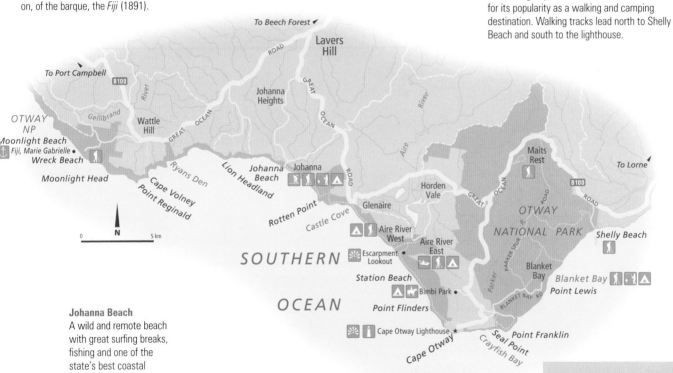

Johanna Beach
A wild and remote beach with great surfing breaks, fishing and one of the state's best coastal camping spots. An 8 km beach walk leads to Rotten Cove, passing the mouth of the Johanna River. The beach is not suitable for swimming.

Bimbi Park
This long-established cattle and horse stud has caravan sites, camping and offers trail rides along the area's beaches and cliffs.

Cape Otway Lighthouse
The beacon was built in 1848 to light the treacherous strait between King Island and Cape Otway. Now decommissioned, the lighthouse and surrounding buildings are open to the public, with tours, accommodation and a museum.

WARNINGS/ RESTRICTIONS

- Beaches in the area are exposed and not suitable for swimming
- Fireplaces are located only at Blanket Bay and Aire River East (bring your own wood); open fires are not permitted at other campgrounds
- Drinking water may not be available – bring your own
- Mobile phones may not work in the area; if you are planning to walk in a remote area, give a copy of your itinerary to a friend or relative

Loch Ard Gorge

Diving around Port Campbell

Shipwrecks and interesting underwater formations attract divers to the cold and turbulent seas of the Port Campbell area. The activity is dependent on highly variable local conditions, which force the cancellation of more than half all scheduled dives (be prepared to be flexible). The *Loch Ard* wreck is the most popular site. It is located off Mutton Bird Island, in an exposed and treacherous area, and it is suitable for advanced divers only. The wreck offers a good variety of dive depths – from 10 to 24 m, with most of the wreckage between 16 and 18 m. Another popular site is the *Falls of Halladale*, which is suitable for all levels of experience, offering a depth range of 3 to 12 m. The wreck is close to shore, but it should only be accessed by boat. The Arches Marine Sanctuary protects a series of spectacular underwater canyons, arches and tunnels, along with a diverse array of marine plants and animals; these are at a depth range of 16 to 24 m; the site is suitable for advanced divers only. There are a number of sites accessible from the shore in the bay at Port Campbell: at Loch Ard Gorge (where conditions can be treacherous) and the Blowhole, where divers drop straight off the rock face into 18 m of water. Training, equipment and boat charters are available at the township of Port Campbell.

Warrnambool

Warrnambool, a major commercial centre, is one of the best whale-watching spots along Australia's southern coast. Most years, from winter through to spring, female southern right whales come to the town's Logans Beach to calve and then nurse their young. Visitors watch from specially constructed viewing platforms above the beach.

Why whales choose one place to calve over another is a mystery. One theory is that their choice is based on the lie of the underwater landscape and the turbulence and temperature of the sea. Park rangers who monitor the animals believe that a mother returns to the place where she was born. If true, this may explain why the family line has been preserved at Logans Beach, an area that geographically did not lend itself to whaling.

As many as eight mothers with their calves have been spotted at Logans in a single year, although some years not a single creature shows up. Potential visitors should contact the local visitor information centre for an update on new arrivals.

Among Warrnambool's other attractions is Flagstaff Hill Maritime Museum, offering displays of maritime history, a detailed re-creation of an Australian colonial port, and a sound and light show, which re-enacts the *Loch Ard* tragedy. The town has a protected beach, river estuaries and Lake Pertobe, a sheltered network of lakes and islands linked by bridges. There are great opportunities for diving and offshore fishing; charter services operate from town. A six- to seven-hour foreshore walk, the Mahogany Trail, leads to Port Fairy (return by bus).

Port Fairy

Sealers and whalers plied their trade in and around Port Fairy from the early 1800s – with tragic environmental consequences. Regardless of the destruction that these early settlers wrought or, more accurately, because of it, the town grew large and prosperous. Today, its many heritage buildings make it one of Australia's most complete architectural records of early 19th-century life in a maritime community; tours and brochures detailing self-guide historic walks are available from the town's information centre.

The town is located on the peaceful Moyne River and boasts one of the state's prettiest beaches, a 6 km long sandy stretch with good surf. Fishing, patrolled swimming and surfing are popular activities. Griffiths Island, just offshore and connected to the town by a footbridge, is home to the elegant Griffiths Island Lighthouse (1859), and a large short-tailed shearwater colony. Much further offshore lies Lady Julia Percy Island, which the local Aboriginal people regard as a significant place, a totem-centre to which the spirits of their dead return. The island protects a colony of around 4000 Australian fur seals, which can be seen on one of the boat tours that regularly depart the town.

Discovery Coast

The Discovery Coast runs to the border of South Australia. At its eastern end lies the town of Portland. Although a major deep-water port and site of a large aluminium smelter, the town has attractive foreshores and good conditions for fishing, swimming and surfing. Other attractions include a foreshore cable tram ride and the Maritime Discovery Centre – a state-of-the-art museum with historic and environmental marine displays. Portland was the first permanent settlement in Victoria (1834) and has a number of significant historic buildings, many of them dating back to the 1840s and 1850s. South-west of Portland is the red-capped Cape Nelson Lighthouse, completed in 1884. There is holiday accommodation available in the keeper's quarters and lighthouse tours (see *Contacts*, p. 147), as well as access to some good cliff-top walks in the area.

The Discovery Bay Coastal Park runs from Cape Bridgewater to Nelson. It offers a beautiful and sparse wilderness of rolling dunes, wide white beaches, long barrelling dunes, volcanic cliffs, lakes and estuaries. At its eastern end are the 130 m high volcanic cliffs of Cape Bridgewater, where there are impressive blowholes, and a large colony of Australian fur seals, which can be seen from specially constructed viewing platforms. At its western end, the park borders the estuary of the Glenelg River at Nelson. The river, which is protected upstream by Lower Glenelg National Park, is regarded as the state's premier kayaking/canoeing destination; vessels can be hired in Nelson. The Glenelg also offers some of the best estuary fishing in Victoria and safe swimming. The acclaimed Great South-West Walk, which incorporates a number of shorter walks, is a 250 km return trek, which explores the dunes, beaches and lakes of this remote coastline; contact Parks Victoria for more information.

Moyne River, Port Fairy

Tasmania
island off an island

Tasmania's Regions

Hobart and the South
Most of the south-east is within easy reach of Hobart, a city rich in maritime history. The natural landscape is a scenic spread of long, jagged peninsulas, massive sea cliffs, deep channels and yawning estuaries. The far south is a rugged, once glacial coastal wilderness, which can only be explored on foot. *See p.158*

The East and North-East
The mild east coast offers sensational diving and fishing, as well as access to the famed coastlines of Freycinet Peninsula and historic Maria Island. Flinders Island, with its wrecks, red rocks and windswept grandeur, lies off the north-east tip of the state, while the north-east coast, facing Bass Strait, is a mix of busy holiday towns and long stretches of deserted white-sand beaches, giving way to the broad opening of the Tamar estuary. *See p.164*

The West and North-West
The Bass Highway traces the scenic north-west coast from Ulverstone to Smithton, offering access to holiday villages and clear-water beaches with great fishing and swimming. The west coast is an untamed wonder of huge ocean swells, craggy headlands and forests. It is difficult to access, but well worth the effort. Towards its southern end is the popular village of Strahan, which perches on the edge of Macquarie Harbour and vast tracts of World Heritage wilderness. *See p.174*

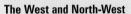

The map shows Tasmania's regions: **West and North-West**, **East and North-East**, and **Hobart and the South**, with *KING ISLAND* and *FLINDERS ISLAND* shown as insets. Labelled locations include Cape Grim, Burnie, Devonport, Launceston, St Helens, Cape Sorell, Strahan, Orford, MARIA ISLAND, HOBART, Port Arthur, Southport, BRUNY ISLAND, South West Cape, South East Cape.

A ustralia's smallest state claims just 1 percent of the total area of the country, but its coastline, which includes 1000 islands, is longer than the coastlines of Victoria and New South Wales combined. The sea dominates lifestyle and leisure activities across the state, and features prominently in local literature and art. Historic ports recall early maritime history. Sailing events re-create the excitement of new arrivals. Locals retreat to holiday shacks or remote coastal campsites. And, despite water surface temperatures that drop to 12 degrees, fishing, kayaking, sailing, diving, surfing and swimming are year-round pursuits.

Despite its enormous beauty, the Tasmanian coastline has not been subject to over-development. Holiday facilities are decidedly low-key, even along the balmy east coast, Tasmania's preferred coastal retreat, where you are more likely to find 1950s-style shacks and corner shops than high-rise apartments and designer outlets. Perhaps more than any other, Tasmania's coastline offers genuine and relatively simple opportunities for escape. There are numerous offshore islands, spectacular national parks offering great coastal walking and camping, and large tracts of World Heritage-protected wilderness where development is not even a rumour.

Opposite Flinders Island
Left Big-bellied seahorse

Hobart and the South

Tasmania's south, radiating from the salt-saturated city of Hobart, is a landscape of long, ragged peninsulas, river openings and misty channels.

James Kelly Basin
Payne Bay
Spring River
River
Old River
Warts River
Solly River
(PART OF WORLD HERITAGE AREA)
Point St Vincent
Port Davey
Mt Rugby 772
Bathurst Harbour
Roy River
SOUTHWE
Stephens Bay
Melaleuca
Mt Counsel 801
SOUTH COAST
Island Bay
SOUTHWEST CONSERVATION AREA
Window Pane Bay
Mt Melaleuca 595
Cox Bight
South West Cape
Karamu Bay
New Harbour
Louisa Bay
De Witt Island
Flat Witch Island
MAATSUYKER GROUP
Maatsuyker Island

Southwest NP
This huge park preserves a large section of Tasmania's south coast in its original wilderness state.

SOUTHERN

Tasman Peninsula

Hobart
Established in 1804, the charming capital of the country's only island state has a rich maritime heritage.

Tasman Peninsula
Convict ruins, strange rock formations and dramatic sea cliffs make this spectacularly ragged peninsula a popular spot for daytrippers from Hobart.

Bruny Island
This holiday island preserves areas of coastal wilderness. It is close to the Tasmanian mainland but maintains the atmosphere of a place at world's end.

Must see, must do

► Diving to wrecks near Eaglehawk Neck

► Kayaking on the still waters of D'Entrecasteaux Channel

► Spotting some of the 138 bird species on Bruny Island, including little penguins

► Cruising the historic sites and natural attractions of the River Derwent

► Walking the South Coast Track – one of Australia's great wilderness treks

A band of ancient mountains, elegantly fluted and heavily forested, rise from the narrow coastal plain, creating scenes more typical of Europe than Australia. Echoes of this topography resound in the towering sea cliffs that guard parts of the coast against the onslaught of the Southern Ocean. Much of the coastline faces the open sea, but the region is best known for its deep pockets of calm water, which lie in the lee of rocky peninsulas and the long, knuckled shape of Bruny Island.

On Hobart's magnificent River Derwent, sailing and fishing form part of daily life. Beyond the hum of the capital, development is minimal; the landscape's remote and distant character belies its proximity to a major city. Many places, including historic Port Arthur, are easily explored on daytrips from Hobart. Several national parks in the region offer excellent camping and walking opportunities. Birdwatching is best at Bruny Island and sea-kayaking is a popular pursuit across the region.

☎ (03) 6230 8233; www.discovertasmania.com.au

Fact File

When to go
Summer is the state's peak touring season; mid-Jan – end Feb is particularly warm and pleasant. The Roaring Forties scour the south and south-west coast relentlessly; visitors should carry wet-weather gear regardless of the season. For weather updates contact the Bureau of Meteorology (BOM): 1900 955 364; www.bom.gov.au

Top coastal events
Jan   *Sailing South* (Hobart)
       Sandy Bay Regatta (Hobart)
Feb   *Australian Wooden Boat Festival* (Hobart)
       Clarence by the Water Jazz Festival (Hobart)
       Royal Hobart Regatta
Mar – *10 Days on the Island* (arts, Hobart
April and elsewhere)
Nov *Surf Safari* (surf-ski and surfboat event, Hobart)
Dec – *Summer Festival* (music and entertainment,
Jan   Hobart)
       Sydney to Hobart Yacht Race (Hobart)
       Taste of Tasmania (Hobart)

Safety
Swimming Lifesavers patrol Clifton and Carlton beaches Dec–Mar; for details contact Surf Life Saving

Tasmania: (03) 6272 7788; www.slst.asn.au There are many protected estuary and channel beaches in the region; nevertheless, newcomers to the area should heed local advice before entering the water.

Other water activities Users of watercraft should contact Marine and Safety Tasmania for boating forecasts: (03) 6233 9966; www.mast.tas.gov.au BOM has recorded boating weather information on 1900 969 940.

Bushwalking The south-west is one of the world's most remote walking destinations. Bushwalkers need to prepare thoroughly for their trip, advise a friend or relative of their itinerary and consider carrying an electronic tracking device (see *Taking Care*, p. 260).

Restrictions/regulations
Fishing/marine reserves Fishing in and the removal of sea life from marine reserves in Tas are restricted. There are two reserves in this area: Tinderbox near Blackmans Bay and Ninepin Point near Verona Sands. Recreational anglers do not need a licence to fish for scale fish in coastal waters, but bag and possession limits apply. Tas has a number of protected species that must be returned if caught. Licence and seasonal regulations apply to abalone and rock lobster. For

CLIMATE												HOBART
	J	F	M	A	M	J	J	A	S	O	N	D
Max. ºC	24	23	22	20	17	15	14	15	16	18	20	22
Min. ºC	13	14	13	11	9	7	6	7	8	9	10	12
Rain mm	33	34	48	60	78	77	88	86	74	67	55	44
Raindays	8	8	10	13	17	17	20	19	17	15	13	11

CLIMATE												BRUNY ISLAND
	J	F	M	A	M	J	J	A	S	O	N	D
Max º C	18	18	17	15	13	12	11	12	13	14	15	16
Min º C	11	12	11	10	8	7	6	6	7	8	9	10
Rain mm	62	57	69	81	85	90	96	92	80	84	76	76
Raindays	14	12	15	17	19	19	21	20	19	20	17	16

further information contact the fisheries sectio n of the Department of Primary Industry, Water and Environment: (03) 6233 7042; www.dpiwe.tas.gov.au

National parks A small entry fee applies to national parks across Tas; contact the Parks and Wildlife Service for further information: 1300 135 513; www.parks.tas.gov.au

Hobart's historic docks

Capital Estuary

The capital of an island state, Hobart is a city of the sea. Views of the Derwent estuary appear around every corner; the smell of salt and brisk ocean breezes pervade the senses; yachts skim from bank to bank; maritime heritage abounds; and the anticipation of ships arriving is as keen as it was in the 19th century. The historic docks precinct, which includes a working port, provides a focus for city life. Here amid the historic maritime buildings, locals and visitors feast on freshly caught seafood, watch the crews work and board boats for scenic cruises. Local maritime history is on display at the Maritime Museum of Tasmania, while Battery Point, a tiny suburb of beautifully preserved cottages, shops and pubs, offers a glimpse of life in a 19th-century sea-faring community.

Hobart is the finishing line for one of the world's great sailing events, the Sydney to Hobart Yacht Race, which begins on Boxing Day and concludes several days later at Constitution Dock. The deep, broad waters of the river are a sailor's dream, while the jetties, beaches and rocks on both sides of the waterway bring quality land-based angling to the doorstep of the city. Good swimming spots include Nutgrove at Sandy Bay and Hinsby Beach at Taroona. The best ocean beaches within close proximity are Seven Mile,

The Penitentiary,
Port Arthur

Contacts

Visitor information

Hobart cnr Elizabeth and
Davey sts
(03) 6230 8233

Huonville The Esplanade
(03) 6264 1838

Port Arthur Historic Site
(03) 6251 2310
www.portarthur.org.au

Kettering (D'Entrecasteaux
Channel and Bruny Island)
Kettering Wharf
(03) 6237 4494

Parks and reserves

Parks and Wildlife Service
General information on parks
and marine reserves
1300 135 513
www.parks.tas.gov.au

Macquarie Island
Inquiries to parks office at Seven
Mile Beach
(03) 6214 8100

**Recherche Bay Nature
Recreation Area**
(03) 6264 8473

South Bruny NP
(03) 6293 1419

Southwest NP
(03) 6264 8473

Tasman NP
(03) 6250 3497

**Tinderbox Underwater Marine
Nature Reserve**
1300 135 513

Activities

Contact visitor information
centres (see above) for details
of activities, tours and
charter services.

Other

Bruny Island Ferry
(03) 6273 6725

Coastal incarceration

The ragged geography of Tasmania's south-east served as a ready-made prison for the island's large convict community. Authorities sent 65 000 convicts to Tasmania in the first half of the 19th century, approximately half the entire Australian consignment, and incarcerated many of them — around 12 000 — within the bone-chillingly beautiful confines of Port Arthur. Today, the ruins of the Port Arthur Historic Site include the Model Prison, where hooded convicts were held in solitary confinement and wardens wore slippers so no sound was heard. Authorities were able to isolate Port Arthur and its prisoners from the rest of Tasmania: fierce dogs were kept chained to the narrow isthmus at Eaglehawk Neck and scraps of meat were tossed into the waves to encourage sharks to congregate and thereby deter any convict who dared contemplate swimming to freedom.

Clifton and Carlton beaches; the last two are patrolled in summer. Tinderbox Underwater Marine Nature Reserve is located at the mouth of the estuary, just past Blackmans Bay, and offers the state's only snorkel trail.

Tasman Peninsula

The Tasman Peninsula, home of the famous convict site of Port Arthur (see *Coastal incarceration*, above), is a dramatic and rugged coastline. In the north, a 100 m wide isthmus connects the peninsula to the rest of Tasmania. A series of unusual rock features, including the Tessellated Pavement and Tasman Blowhole, are on the coast near the town of Eaglehawk Neck. The underwater landscape, with its shipwreck sites, kelp forests and caves, is equally spectacular. A favourite site is the SS *Nord*, wrecked in 1915; the boat sits in 40 m of clear water and is Tasmania's most intact wreck. Another site is

Hippolyte Rocks, which has breathtaking underwater formations and a resident seal population. Dive operators are based in Eaglehawk Neck and Hobart. The main recreation beach is at Pirates Bay, which has good conditions for swimmers, surfers, kayakers and anglers.

Tasman National Park preserves the southern sections of the peninsula. The steep-faced sea cliffs around Cape Pillar and Cape Raoul, accessible only by walking track, are among the highest in Australia, rising 300 m from the sea; these are good places to spot Australian fur seals. Remarkable Cave is another startling rock formation, and just offshore is one of the best surfing breaks along the east coast. Camping in the park is at the scenic Fortescue Bay. On the western side of the peninsula is the shack settlement of White Beach; the surfing settlement of Roaring Beach; and Coal Mines Historic Site, the preserved ruins of Tasmania's first mine.

King penguins on Maquarie Island

Macquarie Island

Macquarie Island sits halfway between Australia and Antarctica, 1500 km south-south-east of Hobart, and is part of the state of Tasmania. In 1997 the island was listed as a World Heritage site, primarily for its geological significance: it is the only place where rocks originating at the earth's mantle (6 km below the ocean floor) are exposed above sea level; the rocks were squeezed upwards, as if through a tube, by the movement and compression of the oceanic crust, some 600 000 years ago. The island supports extensive congregations of wildlife, including around 3.5 million seabirds, most of them penguins, and large colonies of elephant seals. Its human population is limited to scientists and, in summer, small groups of tourists who come for the wildlife and the island's sparse subantarctic beauty. Private operators run boat tours to the island in conjunction with Tasmania's Parks and Wildlife Service (see *Contacts*, p. 161). Permits are required and visitors must stay aboard the touring vessel at night – daytrips with a guide are permitted.

D'Entrecasteaux Channel and Bruny Island

'The Channel', enclosed by Bruny Island, is a coastal landscape of calm waters and gauzy mists. Sweeping views of the island appear from the shores of secluded beaches and discrete coves. The fishing is great, as are the opportunities for sailing and kayaking (see opposite). Local towns include Kettering (ferries leave here for Bruny Island), Snug, Woodbridge and Dover. Branching off from the channel, and within easy touring distance, is the mouth of the Huon River, one of the prettiest estuaries in Australia. Here you will find the apple orchards of Huonville and the alternative cafes and craft shops of Cygnet.

The 64 km long Bruny Island is two islands strung together by a narrow 5 km long isthmus, known as the Neck. The top end of the island is an easy half-hour ferry trip from the mainland. It is popular as a daytrip, but also has good facilities for more extended holidays. The main holiday area is Adventure Bay, which sits just below the Neck.

Bruny has 138 species of bird, including all 11 species endemic to Tasmania. The Neck supports large colonies of little penguins and short-tailed shearwaters, which can be seen in the early evening between November and April. Nearby, a long set of stairs leads to a lookout with views across much of the south-east coastal area.

In the south, South Bruny National Park protects a magnificent coastline of towering cliffs and headlands, separated by the secluded beaches of Cloudy Bay. There are a series of coastal walks, campgrounds with pit toilets and fireplaces (bring your own water and firewood), and the Cape Bruny Lighthouse, which was built by convicts in 1836 (tours are by appointment only – contact park staff).

The South and South-West

Cockle Creek is Australia's most southerly settlement. The remote community lies cradled between forested mountains and the calm waters of Recherche Bay – a notable walking and camping area, partially protected by the Recherche Bay Nature Recreation Area.

The town is associated with one of the country's most challenging coastal walks, the South Coast Track – an 85 km odyssey, which takes six to eight days to complete along the remote, World Heritage-protected coastline of Southwest National Park. Around 1000 walkers tackle the track each year, most during the summer months; they fly from Hobart to Melaleuca, then backtrack east to Cockle Creek. Walkers need to be fit, experienced and very well prepared; guided tours are available with private operators. Port Davey, located on the otherwise inaccessible south-west coast, is a 6 km walk from the airfield at Melaleuca. Visitors fly in from Hobart, either privately or as part of an organised tour. Walkers, campers and kayakers get to explore the wonders of this ancient wilderness, which include dolerite peaks, Gondwana-era plants, and sea caves and dunes containing Aboriginal middens; adventure companies run guided tours. Visitors to these remote places must contact Parks and Wildlife ahead of travelling for updates on essential safety information (see *Contacts*, p. 161).

Sea-kayaking around the state's south

Tasmania is a famed sea-kayaking destination and the state's south is a great place to begin the adventure. Beginners can start with a short tour of the docks and other attractions of the Derwent estuary. Those who want to get a taste of the open sea can book a half- or full-day tour around the Tasman Peninsula, where 300 m cliffs, strange rock formations and colonies of seals are all part of the scenery. The calm waters of D'Entrecasteaux Channel are perfect for beginners. Hire a kayak from Kettering to reach Bruny Island within half an hour, or join a tour to explore further afield. More experienced kayakers can sign up for extended tours (up to seven days) of Port Davey, on the south-west coast, one of Australia's most isolated and spectacular harbours. Tours are weather-dependent and most have strict limits on numbers, so book ahead. Operators will hire out kayaks, but they will want to discuss your level of experience and help you choose an appropriate location.

Sea-kayaking, Tasman Peninsula

The East and North-East

This sunny corner of Tasmania takes in the east coast holiday villages, the transcendentally beautiful Freycinet Peninsula, the remote and rugged Flinders Island, and the white-sand, red-rock beaches of the far north.

Freycinet Peninsula

The east coast sweeps north from Hobart, edged by the Tasman Highway. Dubbed the Suncoast, it has a mild, dry climate, which produces more sunshine than any other area of the state. Despite its smattering of holiday villages and tidy grid of farms and vineyards, development here is pleasantly low-key. The historically rich Maria Island is a popular destination with walkers, cyclists and campers, as is the famed Freycinet Peninsula, with its finely curved coves. Anglers travel to the east coast in droves, and divers come for some of the best temperate diving in Australia.

Further north, remnants of the mountainous land bridge that connected Tasmania to the mainland over 12 000 years ago appear in the rocky headlands framing the coastline and the forested mountains rising in the distance. The area is remote, largely undeveloped and visited mostly by intrepid anglers and self-sufficient campers. Distinctive red lichen-covered rocks, which glow orange–pink with the rising and the setting of the sun, fringe long expanses of white-sand beaches. The same landscape themes are played out on Flinders Island – a sizeable remnant of the original Tasmania-to-mainland land link, some 20 km offshore. Development picks up along the Bass Strait coast, particularly along broad curves of the River Tamar, where a collection of estuary villages offer opportunities for swimming, fishing and boating.

BASS STRAIT

BANKS STRAIT

Cape Barren Island
See Flinders Island inset below.
Preservation I. FURNEAUX GROUP
Clarke Island
Lookout Heads
Moriarty Point

Cape Portland ★ Swan Island
Waterhouse ★ Lyme Regis
Island
Ninth Island Croppies Point Waterhouse Point Great Musselroe Bay
WATERHOUSE Ringarooma Bay Cape Naturaliste
West Sandy Point CONSERVATION Tomahawk
AREA Musselroe Bay

Mount William NP
Pristine white-sand, red-rock beaches are a feature of this northern park, which offers some of the state's best coastal camping and walking.

Noland Anderson Bay Waterhouse Mt William
Bay Boobyalla 214
Tenth Island Bellingham B82 34 MOUNT WILLIAM
Stony Head Bridport Gladstone NATIONAL PARK
Lulworth Weymouth B82 Eddystone Eddystone Point
Five Mile Bluff Pipers Brook Pioneer Eddystone Point Lighthouse
Low Head Pilot Station Pipers River B84 Herrick Ansons Bay
Low Head George Town Lebrina Golconda B81 Scottsdale Derby Ansons Bay
Spirit of Tasmania ferries Beauty Point Springfield Weldborough BAY OF FIRES
Devonport to Melbourne and Sydney Beaconsfield Branxholm CONSERVATION AREA
NARAWNTAPU Mount Ringarooma Bay of Fires
NATIONAL PARK Direction Lilydale The Gardens
Pt Sorell Exeter Karoola Talawa Sloop Lagoon
Port Sorell Beauty Point Dilston Targa Pyengana Binalong Bay
Devonport Legana Patersonia TASMAN St Helens Point Lookout
Latrobe Harford Frankford ROCHERLEA HWY St Helens ST HELENS
Sassafras MOWBRAY CONSERVATION AREA
Railton Frankford TREVALLYN Nunamara St Helens Island
LAUNCESTON Dianas Basin

TASMAN

Mathinna Beaumaris
Scamander
Henderson Lagoon
Falmouth

Suncoast
Stretching from Triabunna to St Helens, this balmy corner of the state receives 300 days of sunshine a year and is a popular holiday spot for locals.

Mt Nicholas Four Mile Creek
B43 +858
Cornwall A3
St Marys Lagoon Beach
Fingal Lookout
Chain of Lagoons

SEA

DOUGLAS-
APSLEY Seymour
Mt St John NATIONAL Long Point
779 + PARK MacLean
Bay
Bicheno
Governor Island
GOVERNOR ISLAND MARINE RESERVE
Cape Lodi

Wineglass Bay
Set within Freycinet NP, this crescent of azure sea and white sand is claimed as one of the world's most beautiful beaches.

Cygnet Apslawn
Cranbrook Lookout FREYCINET
B34 Moulting NATIONAL
Lagoon PARK
Nine Mile Swanwick
Beach Coles Bay Lookout
Swansea Cape Tourville
Sleepy Bay
Wineglass Bay
Promise Bay Cape Forestier
Great Oyster FREYCINET
Bay FREYCINET NATIONAL PARK
Mayfield PENINSULA
Bay Schouten Cape Degerando
Passage
Little Schouten Island
Swanport Cape Sonnerat
Little Little Swanport
Swanport Hill
Point Bailly 537 +
Ile des Phoques

Maria Island
Early colonial history is preserved in the sparse but striking heritage structures on this easy-to-access, national park-protected island.

Grindstone Point
Woodsdale + Mt Murray
317
Triabunna A3
Cape Bougainville
Orford Louisville Ile du Nord
Darlington
Spring MARIA ISLAND MARINE RESERVE
Buckland Beach Historic Penal Settlement
TASMAN MARIA MARIA ISLAND NATIONAL PARK
Runnymede ISLAND
Nugent Shoal Riedle Bay
Orielton Bay
Kellevie Cape Peron
Sorell Marion
Bream Creek Bay
Lewisham Marion Bay
Dunalley Cape Frederick Hendrick

N
0 10 20 km
Scale

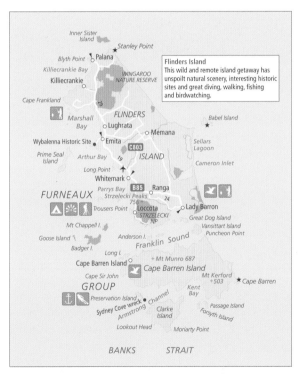

Inner Sister
Island
Stanley Point
Blyth Point Palana
Killiecrankie Bay
Killiecrankie WINGAROO
NATURE RESERVE
Cape Frankland

Flinders Island
This wild and remote island getaway has unspoilt natural scenery, interesting historic sites and great diving, walking, fishing and birdwatching.

Marshall FLINDERS Babel Island
Bay Lughrata
Wybalenna Historic Site Memana
Emita
Prime Seal ISLAND Sellars
Island Arthur Bay Lagoon
Long Point Cameron Inlet
FURNEAUX Whitemark Ranga
Parrys Bay B85
Strzelecki Peaks Loccota
756 STRZELECKI
Trousers Point NP
Mt Chappel I. Great Dog Island
Vansittart Island
Goose Island Puncheon Point
Badger I. Anderson I.
Long I. Franklin Sound
Cape Barren Island
Cape Sir John Cape Barren Island
Mt Kerford
+503 ★ Cape Barren
GROUP Kent
Bay
Preservation Island Passage Island
Sydney Cove wreck Channel
Armstrong Clarke Island Forsyth Island
Lookout Head Moriarty Point

BANKS STRAIT

Must see, must do

► Walking the coastal tracks that crisscross scenic Freycinet Peninsula

► Diving to rare underwater landscapes near Bicheno

► Fishing the East Australian Current offshore from St Helens

► Camping in deserted coves in Mount William NP

► Exploring underwater shipwrecks around Flinders Island

Fact File

When to go
Summer is the state's peak touring season; mid-Jan–end Feb is particularly warm and pleasant. The east coast enjoys the state's most temperate weather. For weather updates contact the Bureau of Meteorology (BOM): 1900 955 364; www.bom.gov.au

Top coastal events
Mar *Tasmanian Game Fishing Classic* (St Helens)
June *Suncoast Jazz Festival* (St Helens)
Oct *Blessing of the Fleet* (Triabunna)
Nov *Fun Fish* (bream-fishing competition, Swansea)
Tamar River Festival (arts, Launceston)

Safety
Swimming Bluff Beach, Devonport is patrolled Dec–Mar. Contact Surf Life Saving Tasmania for details: (03) 6272 7788; www.slst.asn.au Protected estuary and channel beaches in the region offer safe swimming; nevertheless, newcomers should always seek local advice before entering the water.

Other water activities Users of watercraft should contact Marine and Safety Tasmania for boating forecasts: (03) 6376 05555 (east coast) or (03) 6323 2555 (north coast); www.mast.tas.gov.au BOM has recorded boating weather information on 1900 969 940. Flinders Island can experience very high winds; divers and boating anglers should travel with a local charter service.

Bushwalking The north-east is remote. Bushwalkers need to prepare thoroughly and advise a friend or relative of their itinerary.

Restrictions/regulations
Fishing/marine reserves Marine reserves lie off Governor and Maria islands. Fishing in and the removal of sea life from marine reserves in Tas are restricted. Recreation anglers do not need a licence to fish for scale fish in coastal waters, but bag and possession limits apply. Tas has a number of protected species, which should be returned if caught. Licence and seasonal regulations apply to abalone and rock lobster. For further information contact the fisheries section of the Department of Primary Industry, Water and Environment: (03) 6233 7042; www.dpiwe.tas.gov.au

CLIMATE											BICHENO	
	J	F	M	A	M	J	J	A	S	O	N	D
Max ºC	21	21	20	19	16	14	14	14	16	17	18	20
Min ºC	13	13	12	10	8	7	6	6	7	8	10	11
Rain mm	55	59	56	61	58	61	55	49	45	55	58	73
Raindays	8	8	8	9	9	9	9	9	8	10	10	10

CLIMATE										FLINDERS ISLAND		
	J	F	M	A	M	J	J	A	S	O	N	D
Max ºC	22	23	21	19	16	14	13	14	15	17	18	20
Min ºC	13	14	12	11	9	7	6	6	7	8	10	12
Rain mm	47	39	52	61	82	73	85	76	64	62	55	58
Raindays	9	8	10	13	16	17	18	18	15	14	12	10

National parks A small entry fee applies to national parks across Tas; contact the Parks and Wildlife Service for further information: 1300 135 513; www.parks.tas.gov.au

To Bicheno and Beyond

The southern half of the east coast begins at Sorrell, 30 km from Hobart. It stretches for 200 km along the Tasman Highway, and makes for a great daytrip or pleasant two- or three-day tour from the capital. The popular Maria Island and Freycinet Peninsula are en route. A succession of small holiday villages along the coast offer interesting heritage sites (settlement of this area precedes that of Hobart), quiet beaches and good basic holiday facilities. Bicheno, a whaling and sealing base as early as 1803, is the jumping-off point for the region's top-quality temperate diving (see opposite). Other activities include glass-bottom boat tours of the magnificent underwater landscape off Governor Island, foreshore walks, great fishing and safe swimming. Just north of Bicheno is Douglas–Apsley National Park, which features dry sclerophyll forest, patches of rainforest, river gorges and spectacular coastal views, along with opportunities for walking and camping.

Maria Island
Among the extraordinary natural features of this national park-protected island are high limestone cliffs rich in fossil deposits, beautifully banded sandstone cliffs, known as the Painted Cliffs, and a wealth of plant and animal species, including endangered species from other parts of the state, introduced to the island in the hope that its isolation will ensure their continued survival. Maria Island provides some of the best birdwatching in Tasmania, with species ranging from huge colonies

Cyclists on Maria Island

Plying the clear waters of the east coast

Contacts

Visitor information

Bridport Main St
(03) 6356 0280

Devonport 92 Formby Rd
(03) 6424 8176

George Town cnr Victoria
St and Main Rd
(03) 6382 1700

Launceston cnr St John
and Paterson sts
1800 651 827

St Helens 61 Cecilia St
(03) 6376 1744

Parks and reserves

Parks and Wildlife Service
General information on parks
and marine reserves
1300 135 513
www.parks.tas.gov.au

Douglas–Apsley NP
(03) 6256 7000

Freycinet NP
(03) 6256 7000

Maria Island NP
(03) 6257 1420

Mount William NP
(03) 6356 1173

Narawntapu NP
(03) 6428 6277

Strzelecki NP
(03) 6359 2217

Activities

Contact visitor information
centres (see above) for details
of activities, tours and
charter services.

Other

Maria Island Ferry
(03) 6257 1589

of short-tailed shearwaters to the endangered forty-spotted pardalote, of which less than 4000 are thought to survive.

The island's human history begins with the Paredarerme people, who made regular canoe crossings to the place they called Toarra-Marra-Monah. It was later a site for whalers, a penal settlement (from 1825 to 1832 and again in the 1840s), an agricultural settlement and a base for a cement business. Heritage buildings found around the island recall these various periods of settlement.

Maria Island is a car-free zone; visitors walk or use bikes. It is serviced by a passenger ferry, which leaves three times each day from Louisville, 6 km north of Orford. Campsites and basic accommodation in the scenic old penitentiary at Darlington are available. Walking tracks lead to the island's many natural features and historic sites.

Freycinet National Park

The beautiful Freycinet Peninsula has wonderful coastal scenery and is national park-protected. A sandy isthmus separates two wooded mountain ranges, The Hazards to the north and the Freycinet group in the south. Devonian-period granite headlands, which turn a honey–gold at sunset,

Diving on the east coast

There are spectacular diving opportunities along this coastline. Dive operators are based in Bicheno and St Helens; operators from elsewhere run tours into the area. The main dive areas are:

Around St Helens This holiday town has very good shore diving, including within Georges Bay where night diving offers the best results.

Around Bicheno Most of the activity here takes place within the Governor Island Marine Reserve, a 60 ha expanse featuring 18 m high kelp forests, caves, deep gutters and rock walls encrusted with sponges and anemones. The Golden Bommies, regarded as one of the state's top sites, features giant pinnacles wallpapered with a variety of clinging species.

Schouten Island This island supports a large seal colony, members of which enjoy accompanying divers, who come to explore underwater ledges, caves and small kelp forests.

Maria Island Marine Reserve This reserve protects the seascapes of Fossil Bay and the Ile du Nord, where attractions include forests of string kelp, seagrass beds and unusual sandstone reefs.

*Coles Bay, Freycinet
National Park*

cradle perfectly formed beaches. The park is
a treasure trove of plants and animals: more than
145 of the state's 230 bird species are found here,
as are one-third of its plant species.

Freycinet is a major bushwalking destination
(see opposite). Diving and snorkelling are popular,
particularly around Sleepy Bay and Honeymoon
Bay, while sea-kayaking around Coles Bay, to
the peninsula's north-west, is regarded as one of
Tassie's signature outdoor experiences. The park
has powered and unpowered campsites – none of
which has showers. Camping is extremely popular
over the summer holiday period, and campsites
are allocated by a ballot drawn on 1 October
(see *Contacts*, p.167).

St Helens and the Bay of Fires

St Helens, set at the head of Georges Bay, is a small
but thriving commercial centre and the state's main
fishing port, with oyster leases and sizeable scale-
and crayfish industries. Recreational anglers come
here in droves, eager to try their hand on the East
Australian Current, which yields catches of tuna,
marlin and shark. A number of fishing charter
services operate in the area. Needless to say, the

seafood available in local restaurants is supremely
fresh. North of the town is the Bay of Fires, a
wilderness coastline with kilometres of white
beaches and sand dunes unfolding into turquoise
seas. Access to much of this coastline is by foot;
operators run extended walking tours of the
region, which extends north to Mount William
National Park.

Mount William National Park

The remote Mount William National Park occupies
13 812 ha of land on the east coast, and preserves
pristine white-sand beaches, offset by rocks and
headlands, sheathed in red lichen. Declared in
1971, the park was established as a sanctuary for
the Forester kangaroo, but has won equal renown
as a haven for birds, especially waterbirds. Some
of the state's finest camping spots are tucked away
in the park's secluded coves and inlets. All official
sites are marked with signs; there is no power and
visitors must bring their own drinking water and
firewood. The Eddystone Point Lighthouse sits at
the southern end of the park. A distinctive pink
granite structure, built in the late 1880s, it remains
operational. The first settlement of significance

FREYCINET PENINSULA *walks*

Freycinet offers some of the best coastal walking in Australia.
Take a short stroll for cliff-top views of beautiful Wineglass Bay;
a three-hour hike up one of the peninsula's craggy mountains; or
an overnight tour of the remote beaches of the south.

Visitor information
See *Contacts*, p. 167

Mount Amos

The three-hour trek to Mount Amos — part of The Hazards range — is demanding but the views from the summit are sensational. The track begins at the Walking Tracks Carpark and is suitable for fit walkers only.

Hazards Beach

From Wineglass Bay, walk across the isthmus (30 minutes) to reach the dunes and Aboriginal middens of Hazards Beach. To walk the entire length of the beach, and return, takes about five hours. Hazards Beach can also be reached direct from the Walking Tracks Carpark.

Freycinet Peninsula Circuit

This 30-km route is one of the country's more famous long-haul coastal tracks. It takes about two days (there are basic campsites) and passes around The Hazards, along Hazards Beach and heads south to the remote Bryans Beach. The walk is suitable for experienced bushwalkers only.

Cape Tourville

Take an easy 15-minute stroll to the elevated Cape Tourville, where 270-degree views of Wineglass Bay, the Friendly Beaches and The Nuggets await. The lighthouse at the cape was constructed in 1971 — a rare example of a modern beacon.

Wineglass Bay Lookout/ Wineglass Bay

The one and a half hour hike from the Walking Tracks Carpark delivers walkers to legendary views of the elegant arch of Wineglass Bay; walkers can continue on for another hour to reach the bay itself.

WARNINGS

- Those tackling longer walks should register at the booth in the Walking Tracks Carpark (see map), or with park staff at Coles Bay
- Many walks are on steep, loose granite surfaces — wear sturdy boots
- Carry sufficient water – water is scarce in the park
- Carry a jumper and wet-weather gear — the weather can turn quickly
- Care for the environment by removing all rubbish and sticking to marked tracks
- The Aboriginal middens in the park are protected by law — do not disturb

along the Bass Strait coast is Bridport, a scenic holiday village with quiet beaches framed by lush forest.

Flinders Island

Flinders Island is 64 km long and lies 20 km off the north-east tip of the Tasmanian mainland. It is part of the 52-strong Furneaux Group, a necklace of islands strung between the Victorian and Tasmanian coastlines. It has a population of 1000, which swells to about 6000 with the annual influx of summer tourists. Access is by plane from Melbourne or Launceston, or cruise boat from Launceston.

Flinders is famed for its sparse, wild beauty. Its coves are framed by lichen-embedded rocks and granite headlands, and bordered by beaches of pure white sand. A granite mountain range, crowned by the Strzelecki Peaks (756 m), tracks a ragged course down the island, giving way to windswept plains and tannin-stained lagoons along the coastline. In the absence of foxes and other predators, native wildlife abounds. The most prominent species is the Cape Barren goose, whose numbers in the area top 14 000, approximately three-quarters of the entire Australian population.

Flinders and the other Furneaux islands presented an enormous challenge to early mariners. Patches of reef and rock run to within 16 km of Wilsons Promontory; the widest gap between the various islands is only 20 nautical miles. This sieve-like geography has claimed 120 ships, including the *Sydney Cove*, which ran into trouble off Preservation Island in 1797. In good weather, dive operators run tours of the wrecks.

The main town, Whitemark, lies midway along the west coast. A variety of accommodation is available, along with basic retail facilities. The island's southern extremity takes in Strzelecki National Park, which offers camping at Trousers Point and some challenging walks, including the five-hour-return walk to Strzelecki Peaks. North of Whitemark, on a windy saddle of land, are the chapel, cemetery and commandant's house that form Wybalenna Historic Site. In the 1830s, upwards of 130 Aboriginal people, the last full-blood indigenous Tasmanians, were exiled here from mainland Tasmania, supposedly for their own protection. Disease, mismanagement and homesickness killed all but 46 of the group; the survivors were relocated to Oyster Cove, south of Hobart, in 1847.

Previous pages Honeymoon Bay, Freycinet Peninsula Below Eddystone Point Lighthouse, Mount William National Park

The Estuary Coast

The Bass Strait coast to Devonport offers peaceful beaches, historic sites and some great national park-protected coastal scenery. The region's many estuaries and calm waterways provide superb angling and boating conditions. Fishing is good offshore as well, and there are a number of charter services available. The River Tamar is a magnificent broad waterway, which served as a natural passageway for the settlement of the state's second largest city, Launceston, and the rural regions of northern Tasmania. Near the mouth of the river is historic George Town, first settled in 1807. Cruises are available from George Town to the 600-strong seal colony on Tenth Island in Bass Strait and to the scenic sites of the Tamar. Just to the north is the Low Head Pilot Station, established in 1805 and still operating. Some of the early buildings now house a maritime museum and tourist accommodation. During their breeding season, little penguins can be viewed here (tour only) at dusk. The area has great beaches, including East Beach on the Bass Strait coast and Lagoon Beach on the river.

Narawntapu National Park borders the Tamar estuary on its western shore. The park safeguards a glorious coastal landscape of inlets, small islands, headlands, wetlands, dunes and lagoons, along with a large wildlife population. There are three campsites with basic facilities, good walking and safe swimming at Bakers and Badger beaches. In the west the park abuts the peaceful waterway of Port Sorrell. The township of the same name is a popular holiday area offering protected swimming beaches and more of Tasmania's iconic red lichen-covered rocks. Nearby is the large commercial centre of Devonport – the arrival and departure point for *Spirit of Tasmania* ferries. Devonport's Mersey Bluff has magnificent coastal views, along with the Tiagarra Aboriginal Cultural Centre and Museum, and the red-striped Mersey Bluff Lighthouse, built in 1889.

Dolphins off the coast of Flinders Island

The West and North-West

This diverse corner of the island state includes the clear-water beaches of Bass Strait, the wild coast of the remote west, the heritage-rich Macquarie Harbour and the verdant hills and rocky coves of King Island.

The north coast, from Ulverstone to Smithton, is a productive strip of farms, fishing and tourism. The foreshore, with its peaceful north-facing beaches, unfurls from a landscape of gentle hills and rivers. The swimming is safe, the fishing is good and the weather is fine and warm in the summer months. By contrast, the west coast is wild, remote and virtually unpopulated. Its ragged headlands and deserted beaches are framed by trackless forests and mountains, and pummelled by the huge swells and high winds of the Southern Ocean. To the south is the fishing village of Strahan,

set on the shimmering, tannin-stained waters of Macquarie Harbour. This little pocket of civilisation – a cluster of historic cottages, a picturesque wharf and outlying heritage sites – quickly recedes into the vast sweep of ancient forests and wild rivers that make up the World Heritage-protected wilderness of the south-west. Aboriginal middens, rock art, culturally significant landscapes and burial sites, the rich legacy of the Peerapper people, are to be found across the region. About 100 km off the north-west corner of the state, and in a world of its own, lies King Island, an offshore haven of peace and simplicity.

Table Cape near Wynyard

See inset below for map of King Island.

BASS STRAIT

The Nut
Looming above the historic town of Stanley, The Nut is one of Australia's more unusual coastal formations – a 152 m high sheer-walled mass of volcanic rock perched in the waters of Bass Strait.

Monster swells
Consistently huge Southern Ocean swells make this coastline a mecca for adventure surfers from around the world.

Strahan
This historic fishing village, and the only town of significance on the west coast, is located on Macquarie Harbour, on the edge of the ancient south-west wilderness.

SOUTHERN OCEAN

Must see, must do

► Cruise the forest-fringed waters of Macquarie Harbour
► Surf huge swells at Marrawah
► Explore Aboriginal sites at Rocky Cape NP
► Fish offshore from King Island
► Visit the remote property at Woolnorth and smell the fresh air at Cape Grim

King Island
The verdant grasslands of this Bass Strait island, 100 km off the north-west coast, support a dairy industry that produces some of Australia's best cheeses.

Scale
0   10   20 km

Fact File

When to go
Summer is the state's peak touring season; mid-Jan–end Feb is particularly warm and pleasant. The Bass Strait coast is often subject to rough weather, although conditions can also be surprisingly mild. The west coast is regularly exposed to wet, cold and windy conditions, particularly in the winter months. For weather updates contact the Bureau of Meteorology (BOM): 1900 955 364; www.bom.gov.au

Top coastal events
Jan   *West Coast Wavesailing Classic* (Marrawah)
Oct   *Wynyard Tulip Festival*
Nov   *Melbourne to Stanley Yacht Race*
       Piners' Festival (heritage and arts, Strahan)

Safety
Swimming Beaches are patrolled in the following towns during summer: Boat Harbour, Burnie, Penguin, Somerset and Ulverstone. Contact Surf Life Saving Tasmania for details: (03) 6272 7788; www.slst.asn.au Protected estuary and channel beaches lie along the Bass Strait coast, however, newcomers should always seek local advice before entering the water. The west coast is dangerous for swimmers.

Other water activities Surfers and other watercraft users need to exercise extreme care along the west coast. Always surf with a friend. Contact Marine and Safety Tasmania for up-to-date boating forecasts: (03) 6498 7755; www.mast.tas.gov.au BOM has recorded boating weather information on 1900 969 940.

Bushwalking Tasmania's west coast is extremely remote. Bushwalkers need to prepare thoroughly for their trip, advise a friend or relative of their itinerary and consider carrying an electronic tracking device (see *Taking Care*, p. 260).

Restrictions/regulations
Fishing Recreational anglers do not need a licence to fish for scale fish in coastal waters, but bag and possession limits apply. Tas has a number of protected species that should be returned if caught. Licence and seasonal regulations apply to abalone and rock lobster. For further information contact the fisheries section of the Department of Primary Industry, Water and Environment: (03) 6233 7042; www.dpiwe.tas.gov.au

National parks A small entry fee applies to national parks across Tas; contact the Parks and Wildlife

CLIMATE												STRAHAN
	J	F	M	A	M	J	J	A	S	O	N	D
Max °C	21	21	19	17	15	12	12	13	14	16	18	19
Min °C	11	11	10	9	7	5	5	5	6	7	8	9
Rain mm	104	66	106	150	154	167	180	188	164	138	115	124
Raindays	18	13	17	20	20	21	23	25	23	21	18	19

CLIMATE												KING ISLAND
	J	F	M	A	M	J	J	A	S	O	N	D
Max °C	20	21	20	17	15	14	13	13	14	16	17	19
Min °C	13	13	13	11	10	9	8	8	8	9	10	11
Rain mm	36	39	48	68	99	102	124	115	84	75	60	52
Raindays	11	10	14	17	21	22	24	24	21	19	15	13

Service for further information: 1300 135 513; www.parks.tas.gov.au

Aboriginal sites/land Those planning to visit Aboriginal sites in the area should contact the Tasmanian Aboriginal Land Council, (03) 6231 0288, for details regarding access. Laws in Tasmania protect Aboriginal sites, including middens.

King Island coastline

King Island

King Island lies in Bass Strait, 100 km off the north-west coast. Sixty-four km long, it supports a permanent population of around 2000, and caters to an annual tourist influx of 13 000. It is a lush and remarkably fertile environment; the rolling grassland of the north supports a dairy industry famous for its gourmet produce (much of which can be sampled locally). The coastline, often exposed to wild onshore winds, offers an attractive sweep of rocky headlands and beaches, some of which are well protected from prevailing conditions.

Around 60 shipwrecks lie off the island, including that of the *Cataraqui*, which sailed from Liverpool and sank in 1845 with the loss of 399 immigrants and crew, making it Australia's worst peacetime disaster; dive charter services run tours to some of these sites. The King Island Maritime Trail provides an introduction to points of historic interest on the island, including the 48 m high Cape Wickham Lighthouse, built in 1861. There is superb shore-fishing for Australian salmon, whiting and flathead from the beaches along the east coast and excellent reef-fishing on the British Admiral Reef, off the south-west coast – fishing charters operate in good weather.

The island is serviced by regular flights from Melbourne, Devonport and Wynyard. Accommodation is available in Currie – the main centre – and Naracoopa.

Along the Bass Highway

This route, from Ulverstone to Smithton, along the Bass Highway, is an unsung wonder in Australia's catalogue of great coastal touring routes, taking in a lovely north-facing coastline with white-sand, clear-water beaches and rocky headlands, dissected by rivers and backed by a long band of rolling hills.

Most of the small towns en route have holiday facilities. Penguin, named and known for its penguin rookeries, is a particularly scenic spot, with its main street facing the peaceful town beach. The busy commercial centre of Burnie has a deep-water port, which handles a good deal of Tasmania's exports. Further west, amid tulip fields, are the towns of Wynyard and Boat Harbour, both with access to very good north-coast dive sites. Near Wynyard is the slab-like Table Cape, offering superb coastal views. Boat Harbour is the jumping-off point for Rocky Cape National Park, which protects important Aboriginal sites and contains evidence of 8000 years of continuous human habitation (see *The Peerapper*, following). Swimming, fishing and bushwalking are popular park activities. The walks range from 20-minute strolls to eight-hour treks and offer visitors the chance to explore Aboriginal shelters, rocky headlands, beaches, wildflowers and birdlife. The park is primarily for daytrippers and does not have camping.

The fishing village of Stanley straddles a 7 km long isthmus and lies nestled against the base of a 152 m high rock formation of wide girth and sheer sides, called The Nut. A steep stairway and chairlift lead to the cliff-top, where there are wonderful walks and views. The surrounding reserve is home to short-tailed shearwaters and little penguins. The town was settled in 1826 and, with its picture-postcard cottages, is a living museum of the district's European heritage. The nearby town of Smithton is located on Duck Bay and offers good fishing. Tours depart Smithton for the remote 22 100 ha sheep, cattle and plantation-timber property of Woolnorth, owned by the Van Diemen's Land Company since 1825. The tour includes a visit to Cape Grim where a science station measures the earth's rising pollution levels.

The Peerapper:
people of the north-west

The Peerapper occupied this corner of Tasmania for around 20 000 years prior to white settlement; evidence of their tenure is to be found in the region's numerous rock engravings, burial sites and middens. The various family groups followed ancient tracks laid down by their ancestors. They traversed beaches, swamps, mountains and dense tangled forests. Their land stretched along the north coast from Wynyard, to Cape Grim and then south along the west coast as far as Macquarie Harbour, and provided abundant food, including swan and duck eggs, short-tailed shearwaters and elephant seals. The area was slow to be settled, and traditional lifestyles are thought to have endured here longer than anywhere else in Tasmania.

Contacts

Visitor information

King Island
1800 645 014
www.kingisland.net.au

Penguin Main St
(03) 6437 1421

Stanley The Nut Chairlift
Browns Rd
(03) 6458 1286

Strahan The Esplanade
(03) 6471 7622

Ulverstone Car Park La
(03) 6425 2839

Wynyard cnr Hogg and
Goldie sts
(03) 6442 4143

Parks and reserves

Parks and Wildlife Service
General information on parks
and reserves
1300 135 513
www.parks.tas.gov.au

**Arthur–Pieman
Conservation Area**
(03) 6457 1225

**Franklin–Gordon Wild
Rivers NP**
(03) 6471 2511

Rocky Cape NP
(03) 6452 4998

Activities

Contact visitor information centres
(see above) for details of activities,
tours and charter services.

The Nut, Stanley

The Wild West

Largely unchanged since white settlement, the ragged northern corner of the west coast confronts the winds and the waves of the Southern Ocean, then recedes into a hinterland of untamed rivers, deep forests and remote settlements peopled by lifestyle surfers, abalone divers and small-claim farmers.

The settlement of Marrawah is one of the state's best surfing destinations. The huge swells here are legendary, attracting 'extreme' surfers from around the world. Beginners should be prepared to watch and learn. From Marrawah there is access to the West Point Reserve, which protects Aboriginal sites, including middens dating back 2000 years. Further north is Preminghana, which has an extensive rock-art site; intending visitors should contact the Tasmanian Aboriginal Land Council (see *Fact File*, p. 176) for information on access.

The Arthur–Pieman Conservation Area is the region's scenic centrepiece, and a spectacular place to explore. It is accessed via Marrawah, along a 54 km mostly unsealed track. The track is suitable for conventional vehicles, but many secondary tracks in the area require 4WD capacity. The reserve has three camping areas, with facilities, all fairly close to the settlement of Arthur River. Boat tours ply the tea-coloured waters of Arthur River in the north and Pieman River in the south. Tours of the Pieman lead from the settlement of

Corinna to the river's mouth, where passengers can disembark and explore the wild and otherwise difficult-to-access coastline. Beyond the reserve, there is access to the coast at Granville and Trial harbours, both good fishing and surfing spots, along unsealed roads from Zeehan. The west coast generally is subject to large swells and is not suitable for swimming.

Strahan

Strahan is the only coastal town of any size on the west coast. Once a bustling port from which gold, silver and other metals were exported, along with large quantities of 2000-year-old Huon pine, it is now a peaceful fishing and holiday village populated by craftspeople, artists and anglers. It is set on the banks of Macquarie Harbour (see opposite) and is the stepping-off point for boat tours of the harbour and the Gordon River, along with other leisure activities, including sailing and kayaking. The Strahan Wharf Centre houses a museum, where displays chart the history of Tasmania's south-west, including the battle in the early 1980s to stop authorities damming the Franklin–Gordon river system. The surrounding coastline, which includes the 33 km Ocean Beach to the north, provides a scenic setting for walkers and anglers, with wonderful sunsets from its west-facing vantage point.

Strahan waterfront

MACQUARIE HARBOUR *highlights*

Australia's second largest coastal waterway served as a penal colony from 1822 to 1833, and then as a port for the shipment of minerals and timber. These days sightseeing cruises, along with yachts, kayaks and other pleasure craft, ply its gleaming tannin-stained waters.

Visitor information
See *Contacts*, p. 177

Hells Gates lighthouses
The slender 1899 Cape Sorell Lighthouse guards the outer head of the harbour entrance (access is by walking track). Bonnet Island and Entrance Island lighthouses date from 1891 and are identical, six-sided wooden structures, which mark the 120 m wide inner-harbour entrance.

Wilderness railway
The restored 1896 rack-and-pinion railway, known as the Abt Railway, travels 35 km from Queenstown to Strahan through forests and along the banks of King River and Macquarie Harbour.

Sarah Island
Ruins are all that remain on this prison island, which once housed Tasmania's most recalcitrant offenders. Convicts worked 12 hours a day felling Huon pines. Food, shelter and clothing were in short supply, but corporal punishment was administered in abundance.

Heritage Landing
The Gordon River, which runs into Macquarie Harbour, is part of the Tasmanian Wilderness World Heritage Area. Cruises go as far as Heritage Landing, where visitors can disembark to explore this forested paradise – attractions include a 2000-year-old Huon pine.

THE BATTLE FOR THE WILDERNESS
In the late 1970s, the Tasmanian government moved to dam the wild rivers of the south-west, to generate hydro-electricity. Campaigners against the damming ran a non-violent blockade, which attracted participants from around the world. This, along with the release of photographs into the media depicting the beauty and wonder of the area, helped garner public opinion in support of the campaign. The battle to save the river was finally won with a High Court decision, in 1983.

Map labels: To Zeehan, Henty Glacial Moraine, Professor Plateau, L. Margaret, Lake Margaret Power Station, Henty River, Yolande River, ZEEHAN HWY, Mt Lyell 920, Burbury, Henty Dunes, Ocean Beach, B24, B27, Misery Flat, AMH, Queenstown, LYELL HWY, A10, To Hobart, Strahan, Lynchford, Regatta Point, Lettes Bay, Teepookana, Mt Jukes 1168, Southern Ocean, Cape Sorell, Hells Gates, Edwards Bay, King Pt, Yellow Bluff, King River, West Coast Wilderness Railway, Pyramid Peak, West Coast Range, Franklin R., Sophia Pt, Backagain Point, Mt Strahan 855, Liberty Pt, Macquarie Harbour, Coal Head, Mt Sorell 1144, Sloop Point, WORLD HERITAGE AREA BOUNDARY, Phillips I., Gorge Point, Gould Pt, FRANKLIN-GORDON WILD RIVERS NATIONAL PARK, Convict Ruins, Sarah I., Rum Pt, Heritage Landing, SOUTHWEST CONSERVATION AREA, Birthday Bay, Birchs Inlet, Flat Top Hill, Gordon River, 0 — 10 km, N

South Australia
wide skies and wildlife

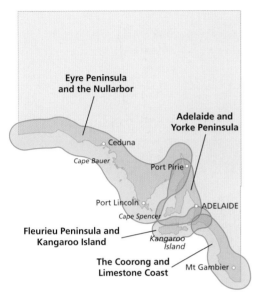

Eyre Peninsula and the Nullarbor

Adelaide and Yorke Peninsula

Ceduna

Cape Bauer

Port Pirie

Port Lincoln

ADELAIDE

Cape Spencer

Fleurieu Peninsula and Kangaroo Island

Kangaroo Island

The Coorong and Limestone Coast

Mt Gambier

S outh Australia's 3816 km coastline – 5067 km if the state's islands are counted – offers a diverse series of landscapes, from the rampart-like cliffs of the Nullarbor to the wild Southern Ocean beaches of Kangaroo Island and the shimmering dunes and lakes of the Coorong. Common to all regions is an intoxicating sense of spaciousness: the bays, typically, are broad and still; the beaches long and lonely; the patchy native bush filters the light but rarely blocks the view; the hills are whitened, low-slung forms that flatten into wide, rippling plains; the skies are vast; and the light translucent.

Facilities are ideal for independent touring. Visitors come here for distant horizons, long roads, the fierce, untouched beauty of the landscapes and the challenges offered by outdoor activities such as deep-sea fishing, remote trekking and cage diving with white sharks.

South Australia has what is often referred to as a Mediterranean climate, attested to by the growing of Mediterranean-style produce – grapes, olives, fruit and nuts – in the fertile south-east. The far west, the Nullarbor, is arid and best avoided in the summer months. The winters can be cold, particularly in the south, and especially on Kangaroo Island, while autumn and spring are the best seasons for an extended tour.

South Australia's Regions

Adelaide and Yorke Peninsula
South Australia's sunny capital, Adelaide, is blessed with wide sandy beaches that are ideal for outdoor activities. Yorke Peninsula's coastline offers wonderful opportunities for walking, jetty fishing, browsing in museums and diving, as well as stunning natural scenery within Innes National Park. *See p. 182*

Fleurieu Peninsula and Kangaroo Island
Close to Adelaide, the vine-covered Fleurieu Peninsula faces the calm waters of Gulf St Vincent on one side and the drama of the Southern Ocean on the other. Kangaroo Island is 15 km off the mainland but an age away in terms of pace and lifestyle. A true island escape, it offers deserted beaches and abundant wildlife. *See p. 188*

The Coorong and Limestone Coast
The wild beauty of the Coorong, with its chain of saltwater lakes and Southern Ocean coast, draws keen anglers, walkers, birdwatchers and those who enjoy peace and tranquillity. The old port of Robe has the quaint feeling of a fishing village and a legacy of interesting historic buildings. Rock lobsters from these waters are a renowned delicacy. *See p. 196*

Eyre Peninsula and the Nullarbor
The Eyre is the rugged wedge of land lying between Spencer Gulf and the Great Australian Bight. It is a complete adventure destination, offering fishing, walking, surfing, camping and wildlife-watching. On the Nullarbor towering cliffs rise from the sea, while scores of southern right whales tend their young. *See p. 200*

Opposite *Sellicks Beach, Fleurieu Peninsula*
Left *Sea lions, Eyre Peninsula*

Adelaide and Yorke Peninsula

This region extends from the wide sandy beaches of Adelaide to the heritage mining towns and fishing ports of Yorke Peninsula and the busy industrial centre of Port Pirie. At the tip of the peninsula lies the ruggedly beautiful coastline of Innes National Park.

Innes National Park

Adelaide is renowned for its parks and churches, elegant stone architecture and prestigious arts festival, but its coastline remains something of a secret. The 60 km of shoreline, reaching from Outer Harbour in the north to the quaint township of Port Noarlunga at the beginning of the Fleurieu Peninsula, is an enticing stretch of easily accessible sandy beaches, offering the full gamut of coastal holiday experiences.

One and a half hour's drive away is Yorke Peninsula – reaching out into Gulf St Vincent and Spencer Gulf – a patchwork of waving barley and grain, vineyards and silvery olive groves, framed by a scenic coastline. The north has a distinctive mining history and strong Cornish heritage. The ocean floor in both gulfs is littered with shipwrecks, providing first-rate diving sites. Anglers will find excellent jetty and offshore fishing. At the southern tip is Innes National Park, where the terrain is pockmarked with salt lakes and craggy cliffs and high sand dunes are shaped by the pummelling waves of the Southern Ocean. The park is a wonderful environment for walking, swimming, surfing, fishing and wildlife-watching.

Must see, must do

► Net top-notch blue swimmer crabs from the jetties

► Take in the spectacular views from Cape Spencer

► Experience the abundant birdlife on Troubridge Island

► Watch world-class surfing around the southern breaks

► Visit the Wallaroo Heritage and Maritime Museum

Diving and snorkelling
There are wonderful jetty dive sites, many also suitable for snorkelling. Dozens of shipwrecks provide magnificent sites for diving and underwater photography.

Port Victoria
This small, historic township attracts keen anglers and divers. A maritime heritage trail around Wardang Island features land-based and underwater plaques.

Walking trails
Explore the region on foot – promenade along Glenelg pier, ramble along isolated beaches, walk along Ardrossan's red-tinged cliff-tops, or hike in scenic Innes NP.

Patrolled beaches
Surf lifesavers patrol around 10 beaches along the Adelaide coast, not all of which can be shown here; see *Fact File*, p.184 for further information.

Innes NP
9000 ha of mallee scrub, rimmed by a majestic, surf-washed coastline. Great fishing, surfing, diving, bushwalking and wildlife-watching. There are several camping sites.

Edithburgh
Edithburgh offers handsome stone buildings, an historic pier and excellent fishing. Offshore, Troubridge Island is a refuge for prolific birdlife.

Fact File

When to go
Year-round. Adelaide experiences a Mediterranean-type climate with warm to hot summers and cool to mild winters. Yorke Peninsula's coastal climate is moderated in all seasons by its proximity to the sea. Summer is perfect for family holidays. In winter the fish are still biting. For weather updates contact the Bureau of Meteorology (BOM): 1900 955 365; www.bom.gov.au

Top coastal events
May   *Kernewek Lowender* (Cornish Festival; odd-numbered years; Kadina, Moonta and Wallaroo)
Sept   *Blessing of the Fleet* (Port Pirie)
Oct   *Gala Day* (Edithburgh)
        Glenelg Jazz Festival
        Yorke Surfing Classic (Innes NP)
        Festival of Country Music (Port Pirie)
Nov   *Copper Coast Fishing Festival* (Wallaroo)
Dec   *Proclamation Day* (re-enactment, Glenelg)

Safety
Swimming Ten surf lifesaving clubs, from Semaphore to Port Noarlunga, patrol the Adelaide beaches on weekends and public holidays over summer. Contact Surf Life Saving South Australia for details: (08) 8354 6900; www.surfrescue.com.au The beaches on Yorke Peninsula are not patrolled. Always seek local advice on swimming conditions.

Other water activities Always seek local advice and check forecasts before taking to the water. For surfing conditions, check www.coastwatch.com.au BOM offers a recorded forecast for coastal waters on 1900 969 975. Contact Transport SA for boating safety tips and information on the location of ramps and moorings: 1300 360 067; www.transportsa.gov.au Divers need an appropriate level of experience; dive with an established operator.

Restrictions/regulations
Fishing A recreational angling licence is not required in SA, but size, bag and boat limits apply and there are closed seasons for certain species. Registration is required to use rock lobster (crayfish) pots. It is an offence to take, or attempt to take, rock lobster with a spear or pointed instrument. Contact Primary Industries and Resources (PIRSA): (08) 8226 2311; www.pir.sa.gov.au Or call Fishwatch on 1800 065 522.

Aquatic reserves Aquatic reserves protect Troubridge Hill and Port Noarlunga Reef. Fishing and/or the removal or disturbance of sea life are not permitted in these zones. For further details contact PIRSA (see *Fishing*, above).

Diving Some diving locations, including the *Zanoni*, require permits. Divers should not interfere with the wreck sites in any way. For details contact the Department for Environment and Heritage: (08) 8204 9311; www.heritage.sa.gov.au If anyone is injured while diving, contact the Diver Emergency Service at Royal Adelaide Hospital on 1800 088 200.

National parks Camping permits are required for Innes NP and can be obtained from Parks and Wildlife offices, at the park's visitor centre during office hours, or any time at Stenhouse Bay. For further details contact Parks and Wildlife: (08) 8124 4700; www.environment.sa.gov.au For information on individual parks see *Contacts*, opposite.

Camping As well as national park campsites (see *National parks*, above), there are quite a few bush campsites on Yorke Peninsula; many of these require camping permits. Contact visitor information offices, or go to www.yorke.sa.gov.au

CLIMATE												ADELAIDE
	J	F	M	A	M	J	J	A	S	O	N	D
Max °C	29	29	26	22	19	16	15	16	18	21	24	27
Min °C	17	17	15	13	10	9	8	8	9	11	13	15
Rain mm	20	21	24	44	68	72	67	62	51	44	31	26
Raindays	4	5	4	9	13	15	16	16	13	11	8	6

CLIMATE												KADINA
	J	F	M	A	M	J	J	A	S	O	N	D
Max °C	31	30	28	24	19	16	15	17	20	23	26	28
Min °C	16	16	14	11	9	7	6	6	8	10	12	14
Rain mm	15	19	19	33	46	52	49	45	39	34	23	18
Raindays	3	3	4	6	10	12	13	13	10	8	6	4

Glenelg Jetty

Adelaide
Golden, sandy beaches sweep north and south of Adelaide, facing the waters of Gulf St Vincent. This coast is relatively undeveloped, in many cases evoking old-fashioned Australian beach holidays. Swimming, surfing, picnicking, beach cricket and, of course, fishing are enjoyed along these shores.

Glenelg
The best known of the capital's beaches is historic Glenelg, on Holdfast Bay. South Australia was officially proclaimed a province here in 1836 and the seaside suburb has been at the heart of Adelaide's beach life ever since. Iconic trams bring beachgoers from the city centre, as they have for more than a century. There is plenty of action – a busy shopping precinct, exhibitions in the imposing 1875 town hall, a grand five-star hotel, foreshore parks, a long jetty for promenading, a sleek new marina with elegant cafes and smart restaurants, and beach volleyball courts.

Port Adelaide
Heritage-rich Port Adelaide, established in 1840, is a tangible reminder of colonial life. Its nautical

Port Noarlunga

Contacts

Visitor information

Ardrossan 39 First St
(08) 8837 3015

Edithburgh cnr Weaver and
Towler sts
Stansbury
(08) 8852 4577

Kadina and Wallaroo
50 Moonta Rd
(08) 8821 2333 or 1800 654 991
www.yorkepeninsula.com.au

Port Pirie 3 Mary Elie St
(08) 8633 8700

Parks and reserves

**National Parks and Wildlife
SA (NPWSA)**
General information
(park passes, camping)
(08) 8124 4700
www.environment.sa.gov.au

Innes NP
(08) 8854 3200

Activities

Contact visitor information
centres (see above) for
details of activities, tours
and charter services.

Other

Diving
Shipwrecks and diving trails
(08) 8204 9311
www.heritage.sa.gov.au

**Garden Island Ships'
Graveyard, Port Adelaide**
www.shipsgraveyards.sa.gov.au

Troubridge Island Hideaway
(08) 8852 6290

Investigator Strait
Maritime Heritage Trail

Investigator Strait lies between southern Yorke Peninsula and Kangaroo Island. As the entrance to Gulf St Vincent, the strait has played an important role as a trade and communication route. In the early 1800s whaling and sealing vessels plied the waters. They were followed by passenger sailing ships and transport vessels carrying grain, wool and mineral cargoes to Europe and returning with manufactured goods to Adelaide and the peninsula. Smaller boats carted produce between peninsula ports and Adelaide and transported passengers from the capital to the outlying districts. Steamships gradually replaced sailing ships, but the strait remained a vital – though often treacherous – link. Between 1849 and 1982, at least 26 vessels were wrecked in these waters. The wrecks include the schooner SS *Clan Ranald*, which went down in 1909 with the loss of 40 lives. Another well-known wreck is the SS *Marion*, a passenger ship that crashed onto rocks near Stenhouse Bay in 1862 and still lies in shallow water. The wrecks are time capsules, as well as major habitats for marine flora and fauna. Land-based and underwater plaques document the many tragic tales of these shipwrecks, which attract local and international divers as well as history buffs.

past is brought to life with old waterside pubs, landmark colonial buildings, restored sailing ships and a clutch of informative museums. Join a walking tour, visit the Maritime Museum, climb the 1869 lighthouse tower, or book a cruise on the handsome 1919 sailing ketch *Falie*. The historic steam tug *Yelta*, river cruise boats and fishing charter boats are based here. In fact, it is still a busy port. Nearby is an intriguing archaeological site – Garden Island Ships' Graveyard, with abandoned vessels dating from 1856. The wrecks create a haven for bird- and marine life. You can view the sights on a cruise from the historic centre, or hire a sea-kayak and explore the partly exposed hulks, tidal creeks and mangroves. Watch for the bottlenose dolphins that inhabit these waterways.

Other Beaches

Some of Adelaide's other beaches have special attractions. Largs Bay, settled in 1870, is proud of its colonial hotel and heritage-listed jetty. Historic Semaphore has a classic carousel and cafes and galleries, as well as historic Fort Glanville, dating from c.1880. Ancient rock formations reveal geological activity dating back millions of years at Hallett Cove. A conservation park here includes interpretive signs explaining the glacial activity that helped shape the coast's rocky terrain. O'Sullivan Beach is one of the coast's fishing hotspots.

Semaphore and North Haven are the best beaches for windsurfing in the summer, though the surfing fraternity tends to head for Christies Beach or further south. Clear waters, an underwater trail and a pristine reef attract families as well as divers and snorkellers to the delightful village of Port Noarlunga. Lifesavers patrol the main city beaches over summer (see *Fact File*, p.184).

Yorke Peninsula

Yorke Peninsula has almost 600 km of coastline and visitors can take their pick – quiet sandy coves, historic towns with jetties stretching deep into the gulf waters, or jagged-cliff beaches and pounding surf. There are wonderful opportunities for swimming, sailing, surfing, fishing, wildlife-watching and – with 85 known shipwrecks along the coastline – some exceptional scuba diving.

Ardrossan to Edithburgh

Towering wheat silos near Ardrossan's wharf are a reminder that the town is the largest grain-handling port on the peninsula. At the long jetty, however, it is a more leisurely pace, with fishing for tommy ruff, whiting and garfish. March and April are the best months to net blue swimmer crabs from the shallows or the jetty. A National Trust museum is located in the old Stump Jump Plough factory and an interesting walking trail meanders along the cliff-tops.

Further down the east coast, the sleepy beach town of Port Vincent boasts some fine stone buildings, a crescent-shaped bay and a flurry of yacht sails in summer. A wide range

of accommodation caters for holiday-makers, who can swim, fish or stroll along the foreshore walking trail to the lookout across the bay.

Stansbury, on picturesque Oyster Point, is another low-key town that draws families and those who enjoy fishing, swimming, windsurfing and quiet beaches. If you feel like doing something different, visit one of the local oyster farms.

On the heel of the peninsula the charming cliff-top town of Edithburgh overlooks Gulf St Vincent and a chain of tiny islands. Troubridge Island, distinguished by a towering red and white lighthouse built in 1856, is now a conservation park. Little penguins and other seabirds frequent the island, and more than 30 000 Northern Hemisphere birds migrate here annually. Visitors can stay in the original lighthouse keeper's house (see *Contacts*, p.185). Offshore and jetty diving from Edithburgh are richly rewarded (see *Diving around Yorke Peninsula*, opposite) and the jetty fishing is said to be among the peninsula's best. Boating and swimming are popular at Sultana Bay and a tidal rock pool set in a rocky cove at the cliff-base is perfect for a refreshing swim. Continue south-west from Edithburgh to reach Butlers Beach, a renowned beach- and rock-fishing spot.

Innes National Park

On the toe of the peninsula lies the natural treasure of Innes National Park. A magnificent coastline of towering red-tinged granite cliffs, buffeted by the Southern Ocean, guards around 9000 ha of undulating mallee scrubland and salt lakes. Gypsum was mined commercially in the southern part of the park from 1889 until the 1930s and there are still signs of this industrial era, but the landscape is slowly regenerating. The park is a haven for birds – mound-building mallee fowl, the rare western whipbird, ospreys, rock parrots, white-breasted sea eagles, and many more. There is also plenty of other wildlife – western grey kangaroos, dragon lizards and pygmy possums, to name a few. Top-quality breaks lure surfing enthusiasts (the lovely Pondalowie Bay is a summer favourite), while good reef diving and angling are other drawcards. Some of the beaches are truly magical, but not all are safe for swimming. Well-planned coastal and inland walking trails, ranging from a 10-minute stroll to a three-hour hike, reveal the park's diversity – pristine beaches, wave-cut rock platforms, towering sand dunes, mining relics and coastal vegetation. Plenty of campsites

Fishing at Butlers Beach

Diving, Yorke Peninsula

and accommodation in restored lodges make the park accessible. There are spectacular views across to Althorpe and Kangaroo islands from the lookout at Cape Spencer. Watch from here for dolphins all year and southern right whales in winter.

Port Victoria to Port Germein

Port Victoria, on the west coast, has been called the last of the windjammer ports. Windjammers, square-rigged sailing ships that were used to transport grain to Europe, once crowded the bay, the last leaving in 1949. Just offshore, the eight shipwrecks around Wardang Island are part of a maritime heritage trail. Land-based and underwater plaques recount the stories of the wrecks.

Port Hughes, another relaxed holiday location, offers lovely beaches, wonderful jetty diving and the promise of more good fishing.

The 'copper triangle' towns of Wallaroo, Moonta and Kadina preserve the rich historical legacy of the Cornish migrants who came to mine the peninsula's abundant copper ore deposits, in the mid to late 1800s. Still a major grain-handling port, Wallaroo is also a much-loved holiday venue, with sandy beaches, golden sunsets and superb fishing. In the summer try netting for blue swimmer crabs and prawns. The Nautical Museum, in Wallaroo's handsome 1856 post office, next to the 1877 Tiparra Lighthouse, traces the district's colourful maritime and mining history.

At the head of Spencer Gulf, and at the edge of the bluffs of the southern Flinders Ranges, lies Port Pirie, an important industrial city and port. Anglers will enjoy good fishing, and in September the Blessing of the Fleet celebrates the role of Italians in establishing the local fishing industry. For an old-fashioned beach holiday, head to the hamlet of Port Germein, 27 km north, with its holiday shacks and laid-back atmosphere. Swim, fish from the 1881 timber jetty, search for sand crabs along the shore or just relax.

Diving around
Yorke Peninsula

Yorke Peninsula has some of the state's best dive sites, including several maritime heritage trails (excellent guides are available). The diversity of coastline, numerous jetties, islands and reefs, and around 85 shipwrecks in the surrounding waters make for a fascinating and diverse underwater world. In the 19th century many ships in this area fell foul of unpredictable storms and navigation hazards such as reefs and shoals. The well-preserved merchant vessel, *Zanoni* (1865), off the coast from Ardrossan, is a popular dive location (permits are required). There is some great jetty diving. Edithburgh jetty is one of the best, offering prolific marine life – watch for box fish and cowfish, leafy sea dragons, dumpling squid, crabs of all sizes and eagle rays. Further offshore, there are at least 35 wrecks in Gulf St Vincent. The shoals and reefs around Troubridge Shoals are recommended for advanced divers, with the SS *Marion* (1851) and the SS *Iron King* (1873) two of the safest and most accessible sites. This is also the place to watch for giant spider crabs. On the west coast, Innes National Park offers some significant dive sites, in particular from Pondalowie Bay and around Althorpe Island. (See also *Investigator Strait Maritime Heritage Trail*, p. 185.)

Fleurieu Peninsula and Kangaroo Island

Within two hours' drive of Adelaide, the Fleurieu Peninsula and Kangaroo Island offer the sparse beauty, vast skies and remote atmosphere so characteristic of the South Australian coastline.

The western edge of the Fleurieu Peninsula abuts the long sprawl of Adelaide's southern suburbs, although the landscape is more rural Mediterranean than Australian urban fringe: thousands of hectares of grapevines, belonging to the 50 vineyards of the McLaren Vale district, ripple across the hills towards the coastal plain, stopping just short of the serene beaches of Gulf St Vincent. The east coast – the surf coast – opens to the Southern Ocean. It has major holiday towns, including South Australia's busiest resort town, Victor Harbor, but also stretches of natural coastline popular with campers, walkers, surfers and anglers.

Kangaroo Island, Australia's third largest island, sits 15 km off the Fleurieu coast. The island is a popular tourist destination, but remains free of major development. There are no high-rise resorts catering to the 120 000 annual visitors – just small towns, shacks and the odd heritage lighthouse, sandwiched between scenic stretches of coastline where various forms of wildlife, including famously large colonies of sea mammals, thrive. The opportunities for the outdoor enthusiast are endless, with walking, fishing, diving, camping, surfing and sailing all on offer. For families, there are protected calm-water coves for picnics and bathing.

Kingscote
Kangaroo Island's largest town was the site of the state's first settlement, in 1836; it has good holiday facilities, safe beaches, historic sites and an excellent jetty for fishing.

Flinders Chase NP
One of South Australia's first national parks, Flinders Chase encloses a wild and rugged coastline teeming with wildlife.

The fortress-like cliffs of Kangaroo Island

ADELAIDE

GLENELG
STIRLING
Balhannah
Bridgewater
BRIGHTON
Hahndorf
Nairne
HALLETT COVE
BELAIR NP
Mount
Barker
M1
Callington
Clarendon
Kangarilla
Monarto
South
PORT NOARLUNGA
Meadows
Macclesfield
Old Noarlunga
MOANA
McLaren Vale
Woodchester
FERRIES
McDONALD
CP
A15
PORT WILLUNGA
Willunga
Strathalbyn

t Willunga
s historic village has few facilities,
a wonderful beach facing the
n waters of Gulf St Vincent.

Aldinga Beach
Aldinga Bay
ALDINGA REEF AQUATIC RESERVE
(no fishing)
Sellicks Beach
Mount
Compass
Ashbourne
Belvidere
B45
Langhorne Creek

GULF

ST VINCENT

Myponga
Finniss
TOLDEROL
GAME RESERVE

B23
FLEURIEU
A13
Milang
Lake
Alexandrina

Normanville
Yankalilla Bay
Yankalilla

Goolwa
Raukkan
Ferry
Ashville

Rapid Bay
Second
Valley
PENINSULA
Port Elliot
Cockle Train
Encounter
Bay
Hindmarsh
Island
Narrung

35
B37
Victor
Harbor
Barrages
Lake
Albert

Cape Jervis
Kangaroo Island
Vehicular &
Passenger
Ferry
DEEP CREEK
CP
WEST ISLAND
AQUATIC RESERVE
(no fishing)
YOUNGHUSBAND
COORONG

NEWLAND HEAD CP
Newland Head
NATIONAL

Penneshaw
Wildlife at Victor Harbor
Victor Harbor protects a large colony of little
penguins, while the waters of Encounter Bay
provide a temporary refuge for passing
southern right whales.
PARK
PENINSULA

American
Beach
DUDLEY
LASHMAR CP
Antechamber Bay
Cape St Albans

UDLEY
PENINSULA

Cape Willoughby
CAPE HART CP

RICAN RIVER
TIC RESERVE
o fishing)
Cape Hart

nington

N

0   10   20   30 km

Scale

Must see, must do

► Dive on Aldinga Reef
► Stroll among the Australian sea lions
at Seal Bay
► Walk Kangaroo Island's west coast
► Fish offshore via Victor Harbor
► Dine on the cliff-tops at Port Willunga

☎ (08) 8323 9944; www.fleurieupeninsula.com.au   ☎ (08) 8553 1185; www.tourkangarooisland.com.au

Fact File

When to go
Year-round. The mainland heats up in Feb, but coastal breezes keep temperatures manageable. Kangaroo Island is subject to cool and blustery conditions during winter. For weather updates contact the Bureau of Meteorology (BOM): 1900 955 365; www.bom.gov.au

Top coastal events
Jan	*Milang to Goolwa Freshwater Sailing Classic*
Feb	*Coast to Coast Bike Ride* (Goolwa, Victor Harbor)
Mar	*Fleurieu Fishin' Fest* (Yankalilla Bay) *Victor Harbor Triathlons* *South Australian Wooden Boat Festival* (Goolwa)
June	*Launch of the Whale Season* (Victor Harbor) *Sea & Vines Festival* (McLaren Vale)

Safety
Swimming Moana, Aldinga Bay and Normanville beaches on Gulf St Vincent and Chiton Rocks and Horseshoe Bay beaches in Port Elliot are patrolled weekends and public holidays from the first weekend in Nov to the last weekend in Mar; contact Surf Life Saving South Australia for details: (08) 8354 6900; www.surfrescue.com.au Visitors should keep to the calm-water bays and coves on Kangaroo Island, and swim only when there are others present. Do not swim at unpatrolled surf beaches. Although rare, shark attacks do occur in South Australian waters.

Other water activities SA's south-east coast is exposed to strong winds off the Southern Ocean. Strong to gale force winds from the south are not uncommon and can make for very rough seas. Gulf St Vincent is relatively protected from large swells, but it does get a short chop, which can be uncomfortable for small boats. For recorded information on coastal conditions, contact BOM on 1900 969 975. Contact Transport SA for safety tips, tidal charts and the location of ramps and moorings: 1300 360 067; www.transportsa.gov.au

Restrictions/regulations
Fishing A recreational angling licence is not required in SA, but size, bag and boat limits apply and there are closed seasons for certain species. Registration is required to use rock lobster (crayfish) pots. It is an offence to take, or attempt to take, rock lobster with a spear or pointed instrument. Contact Primary Industries and Resources (PIRSA): (08) 8226 2311; www.pir.sa.gov.au Or call Fishwatch on 1800 065 522.

Aquatic reserves Aquatic reserves protect Seal Bay, Bales Beach and American River on Kangaroo Island, and Aldinga Reef and West Island (off Victor Harbor) on the Fleurieu Peninsula. Fishing and/or the removal or disturbance of sea life are not permitted in these zones. Access to the waterfront at Seal Bay is restricted. For further details contact PIRSA (see *Fishing*, above).

National parks National park entry and camping fees apply across SA. A range of passes covers access to groups of parks for periods of up to a year. For further details contact Parks and Wildlife: (08) 8124 4700; www.environment.sa.gov.au For information on individual parks see *Contacts*, opposite.

CLIMATE											VICTOR HARBOR	
	J	**F**	**M**	**A**	**M**	**J**	**J**	**A**	**S**	**O**	**N**	**D**
Max °C	25	25	23	21	19	16	15	16	18	20	22	24
Min °C	15	15	14	12	10	8	8	8	9	10	12	14
Rain mm	21	20	23	43	62	71	75	67	56	46	28	24
Raindays	5	4	6	10	14	15	17	16	14	11	8	7

CLIMATE											KANGAROO ISLAND	
	J	**F**	**M**	**A**	**M**	**J**	**J**	**A**	**S**	**O**	**N**	**D**
Max °C	24	24	22	20	18	15	15	15	17	19	21	22
Min °C	15	15	14	13	11	9	8	8	9	10	12	14
Rain mm	15	17	18	35	58	73	77	65	47	37	23	19
Raindays	4	4	5	9	13	16	18	17	13	10	7	5

Netting the catch, Port Willunga

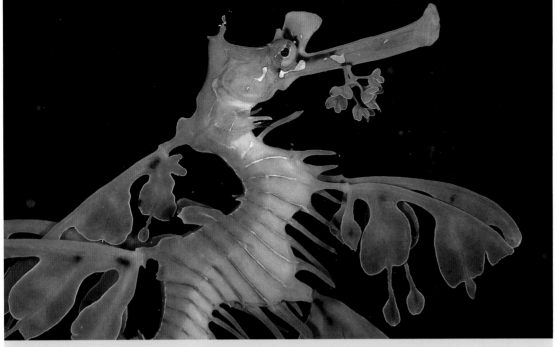

Leafy sea dragon

Contacts

Visitor information

Goolwa The Wharf
(08) 8555 3488
www.visitalexandrina.com

McLaren Vale (Gulf St Vincent coast) Main Rd
(08) 8323 9944
www.visitorcentre.com.au

Penneshaw (Kangaroo Island) Howard Dr
(08) 8553 1185
www.tourkangarooisland.com.au

Victor Harbor The Causeway
(08) 8552 5738
www.tourismvictorharbor.com.au

Yankalilla (Gulf St Vincent coast)
106 Main Rd
(08) 8558 2999
www.yankalillabay.com.au

Parks and reserves

National Parks and Wildlife SA (NPWSA)
General information
(park passes, camping)
(08) 8124 4700
www.environment.sa.gov.au

Deep Creek CP
(08) 8336 0901

Flinders Chase NP
(08) 8559 7235

Granite Island
Penguin tours
(08) 8552 7555

Newland Head CP
(08) 8336 0901

Seal Bay CP
Seal tours
(08) 8559 4207

Activities

Contact visitor information centres (see above) for details of activities, tours and charter services.

Other

Cape Borda and Cape du Couedic lighthouses
Tours and accommodation
(08) 8559 7235

Kangaroo Island ferry
13 1301

Diving and snorkelling Gulf St Vincent

The diving opportunities in this area are excellent. Because the waters of Gulf St Vincent are protected, divers rarely have to negotiate ocean swells and currents. South Australia has a large number of rare and unusual marine species, including the bizarrely appendaged leafy sea dragon. Shipwrecks are protected sites and divers should not interfere with or remove items from these sites.

Star of Greece shipwreck This wreck lies just off the beach at Port Willunga and, because boat access is not required, is popular with both divers and snorkellers. The scattered wreckage sits at a maximum depth of 6 m, and attracts many reef fish.

Aldinga Reef Protected within an aquatic reserve, this reef is located 500 m offshore. It is regarded as the best dive site within easy reach of Adelaide. Depths range from 4 to 20 m. Reef fish congregate in its many large caverns and crevasses. The best times for diving here are summer and early autumn.

This 700 m long jetty attracts huge schools of fish along with weedy and leafy sea dragons. This popular shore dive has a maximum depth of 10 m and is best attempted when the prevailing winds are south-south-east.

Second Valley Jetty and cave shore dives are on offer here. The jetty, although short, is a good spot for training divers. The cave network is extensive and includes a blowhole, but conditions have to be very still, otherwise visibility is poor.

Gulf St Vincent Coastline

Creamy-coloured limestone cliffs unfurl against a backdrop of vines, alongside the mesmerising, clear waters of Gulf St Vincent. Despite the proximity to Adelaide, this sunny district with its rare stripped-back beauty feels remote and undiscovered.

The calm-water beaches are great for families, who come with their beach shades, picnics and ball games and stay for the day. Top beaches include Port Willunga, Aldinga, Sellicks and Normanville. Facilities for visitors vary, but are generally low-key: caravan parks, holiday rentals and take-aways.

Port Willunga does not have shops or motels, but it does have one of South Australia's most famous shipwrecks, the *Star of Greece*, a three-masted iron cargo ship, which ran aground in 1888 with the loss of 23 lives. The wreck is partially exposed at low tide. On the cliffs above the beach, offering extraordinary views, is the highly regarded Star of Greece Cafe. The beaches of Aldinga and Sellicks offer a 6 km stretch of wide sands and clear water. Windsurfing is popular throughout the area, but particularly so at Sellicks, where a wind gully known as 'The Funnel' creates ideal conditions.

Cape Jervis, which sits at the end of the peninsula, is the departure point for the car ferry to Kangaroo Island. The nearby Deep Creek Conservation Park has 18 km of unspoilt coastline set against bush-covered hills; it offers good walking and camping opportunities.

Victor Harbor

Victor Harbor, set on the shores of Encounter Bay, was established in 1837 as a whaling station. Its

beaches are protected from the full force of the Southern Ocean by the 26 ha Granite Island. The town and island are linked by a narrow wooden causeway; a historic horse-drawn tram transports visitors the short distance to the island. The island has a little penguin population of around 2000; take a ranger-guided tour at twilight to see these endearing creatures return to their burrows after a day's fishing. During winter and early spring, a handful of southern right whales visit Encounter Bay, and are often spotted from the town's headlands. The South Australian Whale Centre in Victor Harbor has interpretive displays on the life cycles of these and other sea mammals. Victor Harbor is one of South Australia's best fishing destinations. The Granite Island jetty is a top-class land-based spot, reaching well out into the bay, while activity around the offshore reefs yields catches of snapper, mackerel, snook and trevally.

Newland Head Conservation Park, which encompasses a stretch of unspoilt coastline, lies south of Victor Harbor. It offers opportunities for walkers and campers, as well as good conditions for surfers and anglers, particularly along Waitpinga Beach.

Port Elliot to Goolwa

The Cockle Train, a beachside steam train running along a track constructed in 1854, connects Victor Harbor with its easterly neighbours, Port Elliot and Goolwa. Port Elliot was established in 1854 as a seaport for Murray River trade, but soon became a holiday escape for city dwellers. It has several beautiful beaches, including the protected swimming beach on Horseshoe Bay, and Boomer and Knights beaches, both offering surfing breaks with waves of up to 3 m. The town has intact 19th-century streetscapes and a range of boutique shops and quality restaurants.

Goolwa was a key port in the second half of the 19th century when river boats carried passengers and goods between three states. The town sits on the western shore of the Murray River's Lake Alexandrina, 12 km west of where the river spills into the Southern Ocean. It offers good opportunities for recreational boating: tours aboard skippered yachts, bareboating, windsurfing and canoeing are all available. The less energetic can take cruises of the lake, the Murray mouth and the adjoining Coorong (see *The Coorong and Limestone Coast*, p.196). Walkers can pick up the coastal track that starts 6 km from town and leads to the

point where the river opens to the sea. Hindmarsh Island lies right at the mouth of the Murray and is reached by bridge from Goolwa. The building of the bridge caused a well-publicised controversy in the 1990s, when members of the Ngarrindjeri, the original landholders, objected to the proposal on the grounds that it violated women's sacred sites.

Kangaroo Island

Kangaroo Island is a romantically unruly place, its character – environmental and historic – comprehensively shaped by the unforgiving force of the Southern Ocean. But alongside its rough and rugged features, such as towering cliffs, windswept plains and gnarled coastal scrub, the island offers pockets of peace and tranquillity – sandy coves where, in good weather, the sapphire waters are as calm and clear as those in the tropics.

Two things strike first-time visitors to Kangaroo Island. First, the island's large size: it covers 4409 sq km, and stretches 156 km from east to west, certainly more than can be managed in a daytrip. Second, the pervading air of isolation: the island, just 16 km from Cape Jervis in South Australia's south-east, is of another era entirely. Low-key villages service the needs of the 4000 residents and 120 000 annual visitors, but there are no traffic lights and few sealed roads. Half the island remains

Above Western Cove, *Kangaroo Island*
Inset Sea lions, Seal Bay
Opposite Goolwa Wharf

uncleared and parks and reserves claim a good third of the total area. By community consent there are no resorts. The accommodation on offer – campsites, caravan parks, small motels, intimate B&Bs – suits most who come here.

The first human occupation of the island ended, mysteriously, 10 000 years ago. Members of the mainland tribe Ngarrindjeri called the island Karta, meaning old woman's place, and Narungawai, hunting place of the dead. In the early 19th century, the island served as an unofficial protectorate for various colonial miscreants: pirates, kidnappers, sealers and

Kangaroo Island's best beaches

Vivonne Bay — voted by marine scientists one of Australia's best beaches; long and curved, with safe swimming, surfing, fishing and snorkelling

Stokes Bay — this large, enclosed rock pool provides protection from the surf

Emu Bay – a 4 km stretch with vehicle access, fishing and safe, clear water for swimming

Kingscote — picnicking, wading and shallow swimming at the town beach

Chapman River – flows into Antechamber Bay and offers safe estuary swimming

Penneshaw Beach — good views across Backstairs Passage and safe swimming for all ages

D'Estrees Bay — camping, swimming and fishing along this unspoilt coastline frequented by shore-wading birds

Above Remarkable Rocks
Below Cape du
Couedic Lighthouse

Ranger-led tours to the beach give visitors an up-close-and-personal encounter with these impressive creatures as they sunbake, feed their young, and embark on fishing trips. A New Zealand fur seal colony is stationed in Flinders Chase National Park (see opposite).

Australian marsupials are well represented. The inventory includes 15 000 koalas, several hundred thousand tammar wallabies, numerous platypuses and possums, and the Kangaroo Island kangaroo, a species endemic to the island. Visit Flinders Chase to see this creature in the wild, or wildlife centres in Parndana and Stokes Bay. Waterbird-watching opportunities abound: little penguin tours operate from Kingscote and Penneshaw; pelicans are handfed in Kingscote; and waders and native ducks can be spotted in the wild at Murray Lagoon in Cape Gantheaume Conservation Park.

Water Activities

Kangaroo Island's 450 km long coastline affords endless opportunities for outdoor activities. Anglers are extremely well catered for, with very good onshore – jetty, rock platform and beach – locations. The jetty at Kingscote is one of South Australia's best, yielding King George whiting in consistent numbers, particularly after dark. Small-boat anglers enjoy the sheltered waters of American River where, again, the whiting is very reliable. Kingscote, American River, Western River, Penneshaw and Emu Bay are all bases for charter operators, who take visitors out among the sharks, blue fin tuna and yellowtail kingfish.

Divers on Kangaroo Island can explore the natural beauty and maritime heritage of the surrounding waters. The clear waters of the north coast have underwater landscapes of coral walls, coves, swim-throughs and ledges. Some 240 species of fish, leafy and weedy sea dragons, seals and dolphins keep divers company. At least 50 ships have been wrecked off the island's coastline. Not all are accessible to divers, but those that are include *Portland Maru* (1935) off Cape Torrens, and *Fanny M* (1885), the remains of which lie in an accessible 5 to 7 m of clear water offshore from Kingscote. Shore diving is popular at Penneshaw Jetty and Western River Cove.

Other activities include sailing (Nepean Bay offers reliable year-round conditions) and surfing (good breaks at Stokes, Vivonne and Pennington bays).

absconders from the Royal Navy. Matthew Flinders named the island in 1802 as a gesture of gratitude for the kangaroo dinner that he and his crew enjoyed, after having been at sea for four months with no fresh food. South Australian settlers imposed the rule of law on the island when South Australia was colonised in 1836. Farming was the economic mainstay for much of the 20th century, but tourism has taken over in recent times.

Wildlife-watching

Some 8000 years of isolation and the absence of predators have given Kangaroo Island one of Australia's most impressive concentrations of wildlife. On the south coast, Seal Bay Conservation Park is home to around 500 Australian sea lions.

KANGAROO ISLAND'S *west coast*

The largely unsettled west coast is preserved within Flinders Chase National Park and other conservation zones. Highlights include wildlife-watching, unusual rock formations, historic lighthouses, walking trails and opportunities for camping.

Visitor information
See *Contacts*, p. 191

Map labels

Investigator Strait

Cape Forbin

Cape Torrens

Portland Maru

Harveys Return

Cape Borda

Cape Borda Lighthouse ★

Scott Cove Lookout

CAPE TORRENS WILDERNESS PROTECTION AREA

JUMP OFF RD

PLAYFORD HIGHWAY

To Parndana ►

HIGHWAY

Larrikin Lagoon

Loch Vennachar

Vennachar Point

West Bay

FLINDERS CHASE

RAVINE des CASOARS

WILDERNESS PROTECTION AREA

NATIONAL PARK

WEST BAY TRACK

SHACKLE

Cape Bedout

Snake Lagoon

Mars

Sandy Beach

The Gorge

Rocky River Ranger Station

Tandanya

WEST END

To Kingscote ►

SOUTH COAST ROAD

Maupertuis

Loch Sloy

Bay

Emily Smith

CAPE du COUEDIC RD

Bunker Hill

KELLY HILL CONSERVATION PARK

Hanson Bay

Cape Younghusband

Cape du Couedic

Cape du Couedic Lighthouse ★

Weirs Cove

Admirals Arch

Casuarina Islets

Sanderson Bay

Remarkable Rocks

SOUTHERN OCEAN

0 N 5 km

Cape Torrens

Kangaroo Island's 19th-century reputation as a pirate fortress was derived from its resident population of lawbreakers and its mighty sea cliffs, including the 200 m high natural battlements of Cape Torrens.

West coast trek

A walking route (60 km) stretches from Cape du Couedic in the south-west to Harveys Return, near Cape Borda, in the north-west. Developed tracks cover some of the distance, but mostly walkers must find their own way along beaches and cliff-tops.

Lighthouses

Two lighthouses stand on the west coast. Cape Borda is a distinctive square-shaped structure, built in 1858; guided tours are available. Cape du Couedic, an imposing tower of sandstone, dates from 1909. Accommodation is available in the keeper's quarters at both lighthouses.

Fur seal colony

A seasonal population of 6000 New Zealand fur seals occupies the rock platforms of Cape du Couedic. The seals are equally at home in the huge seas that pound Admirals Arch as they are in the series of pools that pockmark the surrounding rock shelves.

Remarkable Rocks

These magnificently sculptured rocks were once part of the massive granite dome on which they sit. Underground weathering action has hollowed out subterranean 'caves' in the granite and subsequent erosion has left the shapes exposed.

CAMPING AND WALKING

- Permits are required to camp; these are available from Flinders Chase Visitors Centre at Rocky River
- Bookings are essential for all campsites
- The Rocky River Campground has water, showers, gas barbecues and a store for supplies
- Bush campsites are at Snake Lagoon, West Bay and Harveys Return; they have basic toilet facilities and water is seasonally available (treat prior to use)
- Walking tracks lead off from the major visitor areas: Rocky River, Cape du Couedic and Cape Borda
- Areas of the west coast are remote: stick to the tracks or trails; carry sufficient water; advise a responsible person of your itinerary

The Coorong and Limestone Coast

The Coorong wetlands curve south from the mouth of the Murray River near Goolwa, a brooding coast of sand, sky and water views. The Limestone Coast faces the wild beauty of the Southern Ocean; its isolation and smattering of small historic towns entice holiday-makers seeking peace and tranquillity.

Dunes and birdlife, the Coorong

The Coorong's low-lying waterways are shielded from the pounding surf of the Southern Ocean by a spit of sand known as the Younghusband Peninsula, which stretches for 145 km. On the remote ocean side, ever-shifting sands create towering dunescapes. The network of shallow, salty lagoons provides a habitat for prolific birdlife, including migratory birds from as far afield as the Arctic Circle.

The Limestone Coast, as the region from Meningie to the Victorian border is known, has become a favourite holiday retreat, with its back-

to-nature pleasures. Camping, fishing, walking, canoeing, swimming, surfing and outstanding birdwatching are all possible. For 4WD enthusiasts there is ample opportunity to head off-road, to experience isolated beaches, secluded campsites and pockets of untamed coastal bushland. Small fishing towns are scattered along the coast. Some are scarcely more than refuelling stops, while others, such as the historic village of Robe, contain much to explore. The hinterland offers rolling pastures, timber country, some intriguing history and the celebrated wineries of the Coonawarra district.

Must see, must do

► Explore the sand-rippled dunes of the Coorong's ocean coast

► Sample just-caught southern rock lobster

► See one of Australia's largest pelican breeding sites, near Jack Point

► Visit the Maritime Museum at Port MacDonnell

► Enjoy a golden sunset over Robe's Guichen Bay

Traditional Custodians
The Coorong is rich in Indigenous history. The Ngarrindjeri people, who have lived here for over 6000 years, are now involved in the park management.

42 Mile Crossing
This is the main year-round 4WD access to the ocean beach. The last section can be walked in 20 minutes. Fish, beachcomb or enjoy the coast's wild beauty.

Robe
Robe, a thriving 19th-century port, has become one of the state's favourite holiday retreats with its historic stone buildings, gourmet foods and sheltered anchorage for fishing boats.

Chinamans Well
Built in the 1850s by Chinese immigrants. More than 16 000 Chinese landed along this coast in the mid-1800s and walked to the Victorian goldfields to avoid the landing tax.

Bird Haven
The Coorong is a birdwatcher's delight — about 240 species frequent the area, which has been classified as a wetland of international importance.

Fact File

When to go

The Mediterranean-style climate has warm to hot summers and cool to mild wet winters. Summer is ideal for swimming and watersports. Fierce winds can blow in from the Southern Ocean over winter, bringing dramatic stormy skies and turbulent seas. June–Aug are the main months for rainfall. For weather updates contact the Bureau of Meteorology (BOM): 1900 955 360: www.bom.gov.au

Top coastal events

Jan	*Cape Jaffa Seafood & Wine Festival* (Kingston)
	Kingston Lions Surf Fishing Competition
	Port MacDonnell Bayside Festival
	Robe Rodeo
Feb	*Longboard on Long Beach* (surfing, Robe)
Mar	*Kingston/Cape Jaffa Offshore Boat Fishing Competition*
Easter	*Robe Easter Classic* (surfing)
May	*Port MacDonnell Tuna & Sportfish Competition*
Sept	*Blessing of the Fleet* (lobster fleet, Robe)
Nov	*Goolwa to Meningie Sailing Classic*
	Robe Village Fair

Safety

Swimming The south-east coast along the Coorong is often wild and treacherous. There is safe swimming in Lacepede Bay at Kingston SE, Robe, Beachport and Port MacDonnell. The coast off Canunda NP is not suitable for swimming. These beaches are not usually patrolled. Always seek local advice on swimming conditions.

Other water activities This stretch of Southern Ocean coast can experience very rough seas. Boating here requires a large, seaworthy boat and special care. Always seek local advice and check forecasts before going out. For surfing conditions, check www.coastwatch.com.au The BOM offers a recorded forecast for coastal waters on 1900 969 975. Contact Transport SA for boating safety tips, and information on the location of ramps and moorings: 1300 360 067; www.transportsa.gov.au

Restrictions/regulations

Fishing A recreational angling licence is not required in SA, but size, bag and boat limits apply and there are closed seasons for certain species. Registration is required to use rock lobster (crayfish) pots. It is an offence to take, or attempt to take, rock lobster with a spear or pointed instrument. Contact Primary Industries and Resources (PIRSA): (08) 8226 2311; www.pir.sa.gov.au Or call Fishwatch on 1800 065 522.

Aquatic reserves and sanctuaries Aquatic sanctuaries protect Cape Jaffa and Margaret Brock Reef; the removal of rock lobster is not permitted in these zones. For further details contact PIRSA (see *Fishing*, above).

National parks Camping permits are required and can be obtained from Parks and Wildlife offices or from towns along the Coorong coast. There are also self-registration stations at a number of campsites. Many areas within the parks are 4WD only. Access across the dunes, apart from 42 Mile Crossing, is 4WD only; access tracks are marked and vehicles must stay on the tracks. To protect the hooded plover that nest here each spring, the ocean beach along the Coorong from Tea Tree Crossing to the Murray Mouth is closed 24 Oct–24 Dec. For further details contact Parks and Wildlife: (08) 8124 4700; www.environment.sa.gov.au For information on individual parks see *Contacts*, opposite.

CLIMATE													ROBE
	J	F	M	A	M	J	J	A	S	O	N	D
Max °C	22	23	21	19	16	14	14	14	16	17	19	21
Min °C	14	14	13	11	10	9	8	8	9	10	11	12
Rain mm	20	18	26	47	74	96	104	85	60	45	30	27
Raindays	5	5	7	12	16	19	21	20	16	13	10	7

Robe coastline

The Coorong

The Murray River fans sluggishly into the waters of lakes Alexandrina and Albert, feeding into the Coorong's chain of saltwater lagoons, around 150 km south-east of Adelaide. The small, lakeside township of Meningie is a short drive from the entrance to the 50 000 ha national park that protects the Coorong's fragile environment.

Coorong National Park, more than half of it water, extends in a narrow ribbon for more than 130 km. A complex of mud flats, sandy, marshy bushland and still water create an internationally recognised habitat for birdlife, including northern hemisphere migratory birds, seabirds, waders, Cape Barren geese and endangered Australian species such as orange-bellied parrots. One of the country's largest colonies of breeding pelicans, immortalised in Colin Thiele's classic children's story *Storm Boy*, can be seen on the small islands opposite Jack Point. A hide provides a viewing vantage point.

The Princes Highway runs parallel to the Coorong for most of its length, but there are only five locations where it is possible to cross the peninsula. Conventional vehicles can access the ocean beach via 42 Mile Crossing (year-round), though the last 1.3 km can only be reached by 4WD or on foot (it is a 20-minute walk, well worth it for the ocean views).

Left *Moonlight over the Coorong*
Inset *Cape Dombey Obelisk, Robe*

Other peninsula crossings are for 4WD vehicles only.

Sailing and charter boats, ecological nature cruises and kayaking safaris explore the Coorong, most leaving from Goolwa or Milang. Canoes and kayaks are ideal in the shallow tidal waters, though careful navigation is essential, especially in the sandbar-riddled southern stretches. Well-signed walking trails also provide the opportunity to experience at close hand the coastal vegetation and native wildlife. The area is rich in Ngarrindjeri culture – visit the Coorong Wilderness Lodge, or join an Aboriginal guide for an indigenous viewpoint on the area's natural and cultural history.

First rate off- and onshore fishing attracts dedicated and amateur anglers. The peninsula's ocean side yields mulloway, salmon, sand flathead, yellow-eye mullet, shark and bluefin tuna. Bream and mulloway are typical hauls from inland waterways.

Limestone Coast

Kingston SE, on the relatively calm waters of Lacepede Bay, is a popular summer spot for swimming, windsurfing, scuba diving and sailing. Watch for dolphins cavorting in the bay, sea lions and seals. A 10 m lobster ('Larry') and the 1872 Cape Jaffa Lighthouse (moved here from Margaret Brock Reef a century later and open for inspection during school holidays) are local landmarks.

The coastline curves south to Robe, on tranquil Guichen Bay, 336 km east of Adelaide. One of South Australia's oldest towns, and a major wool port in the 19th century, Robe has a long maritime history. Heritage-listed stone buildings line its streets, while some fine restaurants and a swag of quality B&Bs and other accommodation ensure contemporary comforts. There are a number of interesting walks,

including a stroll to Cape Dombey, site of an obelisk, built in 1855, or you can fish, swim, surf or windsurf at Long Beach, or sail on the bay.

Beachport, site of a whaling station in the 1830s, is now a lobster-fishing port and holiday hamlet. Fish off the 772 m long jetty, surf, windsurf, or beachcomb the shores of Rivoli Bay, where wild seas wash up natural treasures.

South of the Coorong lie a string of coastal conservation parks, with dense, wind-ravaged scrub, ancient shell middens, deserted beaches and rugged limestone cliffs. Canunda National Park is a remote haven for bushwalking, fishing, surfing and some magnificent bird- and wildlife watching. (Access by conventional vehicles is limited.) Penguins, seals and dolphins swim offshore, while southern right whales pass on their annual migratory journey during May to September.

At Port MacDonnell the country's largest lobster fleet has replaced the sailing ships of the 19th century. Hazardous reefs and Southern Ocean swells have taken their toll – at the Maritime Museum tragic tales of shipwreck include that of the *Admella*, sunk in 1859 with the loss of 90 lives. There is excellent fishing, including the state's best rock lobster fishing. Scuba diving is popular, experienced surfers can find some good breaks and it is possible to glimpse penguins at Cape Northumberland. For a change of pace, visit Dingley Dell, the restored cottage of famed poet and horseman Adam Lindsay Gordon.

Contacts

Visitor information

Beachport Millicent Rd
(08) 8735 8029

Kingston SE 1 Princes Hwy
(08) 8767 2404

Meningie 76 Princes Hwy
(08) 8575 1259
www.coorong.sa.gov.au

Millicent 1 Mt Gambier Rd
(08) 8733 3205

Port MacDonnell 7 Charles St
(08) 8738 2576

Robe Mundy Tce
(08) 8768 2465
www.robe.sa.gov.au

Parks and reserves

National Parks and Wildlife SA (NPWSA)
General information
(park passes, camping)
(08) 8124 4700
www.environment.sa.gov.au

Beachport CP
(08) 8735 6053

Butcher Gap CP
(08) 8768 2543

Canunda NP
(08) 8735 6053

Coorong NP
(08) 8575 1200

Little Dip CP
(08) 8768 2543

Activities

Contact visitor information centres (see above) for details of activities, tours and charter services.

Other

Camp Coorong
Aboriginal tours
(08) 8575 1557

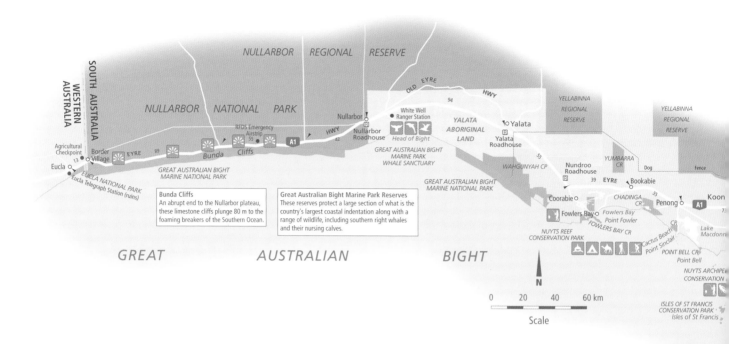

Bunda Cliffs
An abrupt end to the Nullarbor plateau, these limestone cliffs plunge 80 m to the foaming breakers of the Southern Ocean.

Great Australian Bight Marine Park Reserves
These reserves protect a large section of what is the country's largest coastal indentation along with a range of wildlife, including southern right whales and their nursing calves.

The austere Nullarbor coastline near Cactus

Eyre Peninsula and the Nullarbor

South Australia's western coastline stretches 1000 kilometres from the large town of Whyalla to the border of Western Australia. It is a spectacular expanse of vast distances, brilliant light, ancient landforms, frontier fishing towns and vivid emerald waters teeming with wildlife.

Point Labatt
See the only accessible mainland Australian sea lion colony from 50m high cliffs; take a cruise from Baird Bay, nearby, to swim with baby sea lions at a secret location.

Whalers Way
This remote, unsealed road takes in what is said to be some of the state's most spectacular scenery. Traversing private land, it remains something of a hidden treasure in the catalogue of great coastal journeys.

Spencer Gulf fishing
The islands within the Sir Joseph Banks Group, a string of safe harbours, long jetties and fertile offshore waters make Spencer Gulf a first-class recreational fishing destination.

Must see, must do

- Cage dive with white sharks off the Port Lincoln coast
- Taste oysters along Eyre Peninsula's west coast
- Surf at Cactus Beach
- Watch whales at the Head of Bight
- Troll for tuna in Spencer Gulf

☎ 1800 067 739; www.tep.com.au

Point Lowly Lighthouse

Fact File

When to go
The southern section of this region is temperate, while the west is arid; avoid the latter during the hot months of Jan–Mar. June–Aug is the period of highest rainfall; spring brings a carpeting of wildflowers. For weather updates contact the Bureau of Meteorology (BOM): 1900 955 365; www.bom.gov.au

Top coastal events
Jan	*Tunarama Festival* (culture and community, Port Lincoln)
Feb	*Yachting events* (Port Lincoln)
April	*Australian Amateur Snapper Fishing Championship* (Whyalla)
June–Aug	*Australian Salmon Fishing Championship* (Elliston)
Oct	*Oyster Fest* (Ceduna)

Safety
Swimming A surf lifesaving club is located in Whyalla; contact Surf Life Saving South Australia for details of patrolled beaches: (08) 8354 6900; www.surfrescue.com.au There are protected beaches along the west coast, but many surf beaches are not suitable for swimming. Sharks frequent the waters of the peninsula; seek local advice on low-risk swimming spots.

Boating Weather conditions in Spencer Gulf are generally good for boating, but can deteriorate rapidly. Avoid trouble by monitoring weather forecasts. The Great Australian Bight is completely unprotected and subject to the vicissitudes of the open sea. For recorded information on coastal conditions contact BOM: 1900 969 975. Contact Transport SA for safety tips, tidal charts and the location of ramps and moorings: 1300 360 067; www.transportsa.gov.au

Surfing Conditions can be dangerous at the popular surf spot, Cactus Beach: shark attacks, although rare, occur, and the swells are often large and unpredictable; seek local advice. For surfing conditions, check www.coastwatch.com.au

Road travel
Substantial distances separate fuel, supply and accommodation stops on the Eyre Highway. Also watch for road trains and heavy transports on this route. Many of the roads around the undeveloped south-east of Eyre Peninsula are suitable for 4WDs only.

CLIMATE											PORT LINCOLN	
	J	F	M	A	M	J	J	A	S	O	N	D
Max °C	25	26	24	22	19	17	16	17	18	20	22	24
Min °C	15	16	15	13	11	9	8	8	9	11	12	14
Rain mm	13	15	20	37	57	75	79	69	50	36	22	19
Raindays	4	4	5	10	14	16	18	17	13	11	7	6

CLIMATE											NULLARBOR	
	J	F	M	A	M	J	J	A	S	O	N	D
Max °C	28	28	27	25	22	19	18	19	22	24	25	26
Min °C	15	16	14	11	9	6	5	6	8	10	12	14
Rain mm	10	12	21	21	31	31	26	24	17	19	16	13
Raindays	2	2	4	6	9	8	9	8	6	5	4	3

Restrictions/regulations
Fishing A recreational angling licence is not required in SA, but size, bag and boat limits apply and there are closed seasons for certain species. Registration is required to use rock lobster (crayfish) pots. It is an offence to take, or attempt to take, rock lobster with a spear or pointed instrument. Contact Primary Industries and Resources (PIRSA): (08) 8226 2311; www.pir.sa.gov.au Or call Fishwatch on 1800 065 522.

Aquatic reserves Fishing is off-limits in Great Australian Bight Marine Park, Point Labatt Aquatic Reserve and Whyalla–Cowleds Landing Aquatic Reserve. For further information contact PIRSA (see *Fishing*, above).

National parks Park entry and camping fees apply across SA. A range of passes cover access to groups of parks for periods of up to a year. For further details contact Parks and Wildlife: (08) 8124 4700; www.environment.sa.gov.au A permit is required to visit Memory Cove in Lincoln NP; contact Port Lincoln Visitor Information Centre: (08) 8683 3544.

Whalers Way This scenic touring route traverses private property; obtain permission and a key from the visitor centre at Port Lincoln: (08) 8683 3544.

Whale-watching permits A permit is required to traverse Yalata Land at the Head of the Bight; apply at local roadhouses or at the White Well Ranger Station, near the viewing platform (June–Oct): (08) 8652 2601.

Eyre Peninsula
The Eyre Peninsula is a rough-hewn triangular expanse dotted with a couple of major centres and a string of picturesque fishing villages. To the east, the relatively calm waters of Spencer Gulf lap at white sandy beaches, while the west coast is pounded by the big swells of the Great Australian Bight.

Spencer Gulf
The east coast of the Eyre Peninsula faces the clear, blue–green waters of Spencer Gulf. The large commercial centres of Whyalla and Port Lincoln lie to the north and south respectively, while small fishing towns, intersected by farms and patches of bush, cover the distance in between. Recreational anglers are lured here by abundant on- and offshore opportunities (see *Fishing Spencer Gulf*, opposite); non-anglers watch wildlife, dive, taste local produce and recline on any one of a number of protected beaches.

The Sir Joseph Banks Group lies about 25 km off the coast between the small town of Tumby Bay and Port Lincoln. All but one of the 18 islands are preserved within a 2033 ha conservation zone, a haven for wildlife. Species include Australian sea lions, large rookeries of Cape Barren geese and

Swimming with dolphins near Baird Bay

Contacts

Visitor information

Ceduna 58 Poynton St
(08) 8625 2780 or
1800 639 413

Elliston 6 Memorial Dr
(08) 8687 9200

Port Lincoln 3 Adelaide Pl
(08) 8683 3544 or
1800 629 911

Whyalla Lincoln Hwy
(08) 8645 7900 or
1800 088 589

Parks and reserves

National Parks and Wildlife SA (NPWSA)
General information
(park passes, camping)
(08) 8124 4700
www.environment.sa.gov.au

Ceduna NPWSA
(08) 8632 3144

Port Lincoln NPWSA
(08) 8688 3111

Coffin Bay NP
See Port Lincoln office above

Great Australia Bight MP
See Ceduna office above

Lincoln NP
See Port Lincoln office above

Nullarbor NP
See Ceduna office above

Point Labatt CP
See Ceduna office above

Sir Joseph Banks Group CP
See Port Lincoln office above

Activities

Contact visitor information centres (see above) for details of activities, tours and charter services.

the fascinating white shark. Diving (including cage diving to observe white sharks) and fishing charters to the islands depart Tumby Bay and Port Lincoln, while sailors can tour the islands aboard a bareboat charter. Lincoln National Park protects a rugged promontory at the southern extreme of the peninsula, 25 km south of Port Lincoln (see *Eyre's south-east tip*, p. 207).

The West Coast

The Great Australian Bight, the largest indentation on the Australian coast, fronts the peninsula's west coast. The Bight is notorious for its violent storms, rough seas and big swells, but along the Eyre coastline, if not the Nullarbor coastline in the north-west, there are many well-protected bays where conditions are often perfect for swimming, fishing and other water activities.

In the far south is Coffin Bay National Park, a coastal wilderness with exposed cliffs, beaches and abundant wildlife. Camping, walking, surfing and wildflower viewing are some of the activities to be enjoyed here. Most vehicle tracks are 4WD only, although regular vehicles can take the Yangie Trail, a scenic drive beginning in the Coffin Bay township.

While in Coffin Bay, enjoy great conditions for recreational angling and make a point of trying the locally grown oysters, said to be among the best in Australia. At the very least, meander along the 8 km Oyster Walk, a picturesque tour of the town's foreshore.

To the north is the holiday town of Elliston, the many attractions of which include

Fishing Spencer Gulf

Most of the towns along the Eyre Peninsula's east coast feature well-maintained jetties for shore-based angling, while the larger towns are bases for charter tours of fertile offshore areas, particularly around the islands of the Sir Joseph Banks Group. Whyalla in the north is a haven for snapper. Cowell, 111 km south, is set on the protected waters of Franklin Harbour, where boat launching conditions are ideal; blue swimmer crabs are plentiful along the foreshore, with snapper, whiting and garfish on offer further out. Port Lincoln, situated on a most beautiful natural harbour, is home to Australia's biggest tuna fleet and a mecca for holiday anglers; opportunities include tackling salmon from the rocks or beach, pulling bag-limit hauls of whiting around the islands and trolling for tuna.

Eyre Peninsula is one of Australia's most important aquaculture centres; tours of processing plants and farms operate throughout the region.

a spectacular coastal drive to Anxious Bay, and good surf fishing. Tucked away at the northern end of Anxious Bay is the village of Baird Bay, where visitors can board a cruise to view and, if conditions are right, swim alongside Australian sea lion pups and dolphins. Sea lions populate the rock platform at nearby Point Labatt Conservation Park; boardwalks and interpretive signs introduce visitors to the only permanent breeding colony of this species on mainland Australia.

Previous pages *Sleaford Bay,
Lincoln National Park*
Right *Whale-watching
platform, the Nullarbor*
Inset *Southern right whale*

The Nullarbor

'Any man who would travel this country for pleasure would go to hell for a pastime', wrote explorer Richard Thelwall Maurice of the Nullarbor in the 1890s. Today thousands travel the Eyre Highway, across this vast plain, precisely for the pleasure it offers; what was regarded as a hellish landscape is now admired as a place of sparse, open beauty and rare wilderness. The region, although well frequented by visitors, is remote in terms of facilities; travellers need to be well prepared and reasonably self-sufficient. From January to March, temperatures across the western region can be extreme.

Ceduna is the bustling business centre of South Australia's far west. Offshore are the 22 pristine islands of Nuyts Archipelago, used mostly as a destination for fishing and diving charters.

West along the coast from Ceduna lies a string of surf beaches, culminating in three famous breaks at Cactus Beach. Surfers from around the world come to experience the legendary 3 m high swells along what is one of the most austerely beautiful parts of Australia's southern coastline. Non-surfers can take a walk or camel tour along the wild, white-sand beaches. Bush camping is available around Cactus; for other facilities head for nearby Penong.

Fowlers Bay, at the end of an unsealed road, is the last coastal township before the Western Australian border. It was once a wool port and a base for early explorers; today it is a small village and popular fishing area. A series of roadhouses and tiny settlements dot the Eyre Highway to the border. Most offer a limited range of accommodation, including sites for campers and caravanners.

Whale-watching

About 150 km past Fowlers Bay lies the Head of Bight, the site of one of Australia's most spectacular wildlife displays. Each year, between June and October, the area is transformed into a maritime nursery for visiting southern right whales and their calves – sometimes up to 100 in a single season. Three marine reserves, extending nearly 5.5 km offshore, protect the habitat of these huge mammals and several other whale species, along with dolphins and Australian sea lions. The whales come within 50 m of the cliff-line, providing observers with an unforgettable experience. Whale-watching permits are available from the Yalata Roadhouse and the White Well Ranger Station (open June to October), near the viewing platform.

Bunda Cliffs

The Bunda Cliffs are an enduring symbol of the wild and untouchable nature of the Nullarbor. They stretch for 200 km, unbroken by inlet, estuary or gap, forming an 80 m rampart against the ferocity of the churning Southern Ocean waters. The cliff-line begins just west of the Head of Bight and within a few kilometres steepens and straightens until it forms a precise right angle with the vast limestone slab of the desert plain of the Nullarbor. The sight is as majestic and terrifying now as it was in 1870 when explorer John Forrest wrote: 'We reached the cliffs, which fell perpendicularly into the sea and, although grand in the extreme, were terrible to gaze from'. The cliffs are protected within the bounds of the Nullarbor National Park. Signposts on the highway lead to a series of cliff-top viewing points; the limestone is unstable and travellers need to take care near the edges.

EYRE'S *south-east tip*

Lincoln National Park covers Eyre Peninsula's anchor-shaped promontory, to the south of Port Lincoln. The far south of the peninsula, reached along an unsealed road known as Whalers Way, has some of the state's most beautiful and unspoilt coastal scenery. The entire area is known for its walking, camping and 4WD adventure opportunities.

Visitor information
See *Contacts*, p. 203

Investigator Trail
This long-distance trail threads a 93 km course along the spectacular Lincoln National Park coastline. The walk starts and finishes at the park entrance at Tulka (the nearest entrance to Port Lincoln).

Whalers Bay
This route traverses a rugged coastal landscape – a spectacle of cliffs, blowholes, crevasses, caves and golden beaches. There are views from Cape Wiles and Cape Carnot and bush camping at Redbanks.

Sleaford Bay
Sleaford Bay borders a landscape of limestone cliffs, wave-battered beaches and the magnificent wind-sculptured Wanna Dunes. Access is 4WD only. Southern right whales can be spotted off the coast from June to October.

Memory Cove Wilderness Area
This is a high-status conservation zone containing exquisite bay and beach scenery flanked by densely vegetated headlands. There is camping in the far south at Memory Cove.

Map labels:
Cape Donington Lighthouse
Boston Bay
Donington Cottage
Bickers Island
September Beach
Fishermans Point
Surfleet Cove
Grantham Island
Stamford Lookout
Spalding Cove
Woodcutters Beach
Stamford Hill 145
MacLaren Point
To Port Lincoln
Proper Bay
Tulka
Pillie Lake
Westmere
Sleaford Mere
LINCOLN NATIONAL PARK
Taylors Landing
SLEAFORD - WANNA DUNE ACCESS
N
0   5 km
Wisemans Beach
Sleaford Bay
Wanna
Taylor Island
Grindal Island
Shag Cove
MEMORY COVE WILDERNESS AREA
Fishery Bay
Cape Tournefort
Memory Cove
Curta Rocks
Thorny Passage
Cape Carnot   Cape Wiles
Jussieu Bay
Smith Island
Cape Catastrophe
West Point
Williams Island

ACCESS AND FACILITIES

- Port Lincoln NP, a 10-minute drive from Port Lincoln, has a number of camp sites, most with toilets; bring your own water; accommodation is also available at Donington Cottage – book ahead
- Whalers Way is on private property; obtain a permit and key to the property gate from the visitor centre at Port Lincoln
- Visitor numbers to the high-status conservation zone of Memory Cove are capped at 15; obtain a key and permit from the visitor centre at Port Lincoln; a 4WD vehicle is recommended
- The Wanna Dunes area at Sleaford Bay is reached by a narrow, 4WD-only track; reduce tyre pressure to avoid becoming bogged

Western Australia
outback coast

Broome and
Kimberley Coast

Cape Londonderry

Broome

Barrow
Island

Port Hedland

**Shark Bay and
Outback Coast**

Dirk
Hartog
Island

Carnarvon

Geraldton

Perth to Geraldton

Eucla

Fremantle

PERTH
Rockingham

Cape Naturaliste

Esperance

Albany

**Esperance and
the Nullarbor**

The South-West

Western Australia's Regions

Perth to Geraldton
Residents of Western Australia's capital enjoy the magnificent Swan River, historic Fremantle and a swag of beautiful beaches. Idyllic Rottnest Island lies just offshore. To the north is the city of Geraldton and the fascinating Houtman Abrolhos Islands. *See p. 210*

The South-West
Large towns dot the coast to the immediate south of Perth. Further on, around Margaret River, vineyards and farmland meld with karri forests and a rugged, wave-pounded shoreline. Along the whale-rich Southern Ocean are vast inlets bordered by remote beaches and holiday towns. *See p. 218*

Esperance and the Nullarbor
Esperance is known for its stunning beaches: ribbons of clean white sand edging sapphire-blue waters. Beyond are the desert landscapes of the Nullarbor Plain. *See p. 226*

Shark Bay and Outback Coast
World Heritage-listed Shark Bay offers unparalleled marine experiences – the chance to swim with the world's largest fish and to see rare and endangered marine wildlife. The outback coast takes in heritage and mining towns. *See p. 232*

Broome and Kimberley Coast
Broome, a surprisingly busy but remote town, with a colourful history of pearling, is at the heart of the Kimberley coast. This region offers a true wilderness experience – spectacular landscape, pristine beaches, exceptional fishing and ancient Aboriginal rock art. *See p. 240*

The Western Australian coast has as its far northern point the tropical Timor Sea; it stretches south along the Indian Ocean, then sweeps east along the Southern Ocean to meet the border with South Australia.

It is an enormous, remote area, much of which is still waiting to be 'discovered' by travellers. The top third of the state is a tropical wilderness, where roads are few or non-existent and access to the coast is by boat. Wildlife thrives, unfazed by what little development there is. The World Heritage-listed Shark Bay supports prolific populations of dolphins, dugongs and turtles, along with rock-like structures called stromatolites, said to represent life in its most ancient form. Age has given the landscape a grandeur and sparse beauty. Where the desert meets the sea, clear turquoise waters offset vivid red cliffs and sands of pale gold. Although the south-west is well settled, nature dominates. There are limestone plateaus pitted with caves, mighty cliffs and vast inlets. Perth boasts one of the best urban coastlines in the world: a long sweep of white-sand surf beaches opening to a series of safe estuaries and harbours.

Opposite *Leeuwin–Naturaliste National Park*
Left *A red hermit crab emerges from its shell*

Perth to Geraldton

Western Australia's sunshine-blessed capital sits on the broad reaches of the Swan River. Beyond Perth's northern beaches lie coral islands and reefs, tales of shipwreck and the thriving city of Geraldton, on the edge of the outback.

Cottesloe Beach

Perth is very much a coastal city. Although the capital is 19 km from the Indian Ocean, the wide, pale waters of the Swan River create an almost beach-like atmosphere. This is said to be the country's sunniest capital, and it enjoys a Mediterranean climate, with dry, hot summers. Gleaming high-rise buildings overlook the river, with its skimming yachts and windsurfers. There are a host of opportunities for outdoor activities, and cafes and restaurants take advantage of the many fine water views.

At the mouth of the river, the remarkably well-preserved 19th-century port of Fremantle has plenty of 21st-century activity. This is a busy cargo and leisure port, with some wonderful heritage buildings and a decidedly laid-back atmosphere. Just a ferry ride away, Rottnest Island suits the West's easy going holiday mode – low-key, with quiet beaches, great snorkelling, fishing and wildlife-watching. Other not-to-be-missed highlights in this region are Nambung National Park, with its bizarre limestone outcrops, and the unique marine environment of the historic Houtman Abrolhos Islands. Geraldton is an ideal base for exploring the coast and offshore islands and the state's wonderful wildflowers.

Must see, must do

► Explore the lunar landscape of The Pinnacles in Nambung NP

► See 17th-century shipwreck treasures at the WA Maritime Museum, in Fremantle and Geraldton

► Cycle around peaceful Rottnest Island

► Hit the waves at Lancelin, Australia's windsurfing capital

► Fly over the magnificent Houtman Abrolhos Islands

Houtman Abrolhos Islands
Containing some of the world's southernmost reef-building coral, this archipelago stretches for 100 km. It is beautiful but treacherous – 19 known shipwrecks surround the reefs.

Nambung NP
Thousands of limestone outcrops, known as The Pinnacles, create a bizarre lunar landscape in this coastal national park.

Perth's beaches
Around 13 of Perth's beaches are patrolled, making them safe for swimming. Other activities along the city's 35 km coastal stretch include fishing, surfing and sailing.

Aquarium of WA
WA's aquarium offers an excellent overview of the state's rich and complex marine world. Dolphins, seals, crocodiles, turtles, sea dragons and more can be seen.

Idyllic escape
Rottnest Island, 19 km from Perth, is known for its early colonial buildings, unspoilt beaches, wonderful snorkelling and diving sites and excellent wildlife-watching opportunities (see map, p. 215).

Heritage port
The historic port of Fremantle has a wealth of heritage buildings, a world-class maritime museum and a lively waterfront area where locals and visitors enjoy the easygoing lifestyle.

Fact File

When to go

Perth enjoys a Mediterranean climate with warm to hot summers and mild winters. Temperatures range from around 30°C in summer to 17°C in winter. May–end Nov are the wettest months. Further north, along the 'sun coast', the climate is similar – warm, dry and sunny for most of the year. For weather updates, contact the Bureau of Meteorology (BOM): 1900 955 366; www.bom.gov.au

Top coastal events

Jan	Sardine Festival (Fremantle)
	Cougar XS Lancelin Ocean Classic (windsurfing, Lancelin)
Jan–Feb	Perth International Arts Festival
Feb	Rottnest Island Channel Swim
Mar	Sea Jazz Spectacular (Geraldton)
	Rottnest Kite Surf Classic
April	Fremantle Street Arts Festival
June	Batavia Celebrations (maritime history, Geraldton)
Oct	Sunshine Festival (Geraldton)
Nov	Surf Assault (Rottnest Island)
	Marine Expo & Blessing of the Fleet (Jurien Bay)
Dec	Rottnest Swim Thru

Safety

Swimming Some of Perth's beaches are prone to strong currents and rips. At least 13 metropolitan beaches, as well as Yanchep Beach, Mahomets and Batavia Marina beaches (at Geraldton) are patrolled

weekends and public holidays, Nov–Mar. Take special care at isolated beaches. For details of patrols, along with updates on weather and conditions at key beaches, contact Surf Life Saving WA: (08) 9244 1222; www.mybeach.com.au

Other water activities The waters around Perth are fairly protected by offshore reefs and islands. The best launching areas around Perth are at Hillarys Boat Harbour at Sorrento and at Jervois Bay. Lancelin and Geraldton are known for their excellent windsurfing conditions. For weather reports contact BOM: 1900 955 363; www.bom.gov.au There is a recorded forecast for coastal marine warnings on 1300 659 223.

Road safety Towns and cities within this region are accessible by well-maintained roads, but there are 4WD tracks within national parks that require special care. For up-to-date road reports contact Main Roads WA: 1800 013 314; www.mrwa.gov.au

Restrictions/regulations

Fishing A recreational licence is required in WA and bag, size and possession limits apply. For further information contact WA Dept of Fisheries: (08) 9482 7333 (Perth); (08) 9193 8600 (Broome); www.fish.wa.gov.au

Boating For information about state rules and regulations and safety practices, contact WA Dept for Planning and Infrastructure: (08) 9216 8999; www.dpi.wa.gov.au/imarine

National parks Visitor fees as well as camping fees apply to some WA national parks. Contact Dept of

CLIMATE												PERTH
	J	F	M	A	M	J	J	A	S	O	N	D
Max °C	30	31	29	25	21	19	18	18	20	22	25	27
Min °C	18	19	17	14	12	10	9	9	10	12	14	17
Rain mm	8	12	19	45	123	184	173	136	80	54	21	14
Raindays	3	3	4	8	14	17	18	17	14	11	6	4

CLIMATE												GERALDTON
	J	F	M	A	M	J	J	A	S	O	N	D
Max °C	32	33	31	28	24	21	20	20	22	24	27	30
Min °C	18	19	18	15	13	11	9	9	11	14	16	
Rain mm	6	11	17	25	72	104	95	65	32	20	10	6
Raindays	2	2	3	6	10	14	15	13	10	7	4	2

Conservation and Land Management (CALM): (08) 9334 0333; www.naturebase.net

Marine reserves Rottnest Marine Reserve, Marmion MP and Jurien Bay MP are within this region. Check with CALM for information regarding restrictions on fishing activity: (08) 9334 0333; www.naturebase.net Further information is also available from regional park offices and visitor information centres (see Contacts, opposite).

Shipwrecks Historic shipwrecks and associated relics are protected. Recreational diving is permitted on many sites. For further information contact WA Maritime Museum: (08) 9431 8444; www.mm.wa.gov.au

Hillarys Boat Harbour

Perth

Perth lies just inland from the coast but the generous swath of the Swan River has its own beaches, with grassy foreshores and shady trees. Two of the most popular of these for swimming, sailing and windsurfing are Peppermint Grove and Como. Cruises leave from the city's Barrack Street jetties for the port of Fremantle and upriver to the undulating countryside and wineries of the Swan Valley.

The capital's peaceful river views are matched by the 35 km stretch of peerless city beaches that extend north from Cottesloe. Long, wide stretches of white sand are lapped by the Indian Ocean. Swimming, surfing, yachting, kayaking and diving are popular pursuits, but just soaking up the sun rates highly as well. Some of the best known beaches are Cottesloe, a family swimming beach with the added attraction of cafes and shady Norfolk pines; City Beach, rarely crowded; and Scarborough and Trigg beaches, favoured by windsurfers and experienced surfers.

The wind, 'the Fremantle doctor', which blows in during the afternoon, can bring cool respite on a sweltering day, but can also make the beach windy

Diving on the reef, Marmion Marine Park

Marmion Marine Park

Offshore, between Trigg Island and Burns Beach, and protected within Marmion Marine Park, small islands, shallow lagoons and reefs are home to seabirds and a wide range of marine life. There is some great diving – a plethora of colourful fish including cardinalfish, wrasse, bullseyes and more flash by, while sponges, sea urchins and other marine creatures inhabit ledges and caves. Bottlenose dolphins are common, Australian sea lions use Little Island as a resting place and humpback whales pass on their migratory journey between the Antarctic and warm northern waters. Boyinaboat Reef, 75 m from Hillarys Boat Harbour, is one of the capital's top dive sites.

and the water dangerously rough. Many beaches have regular surf patrols from early October to the end of March (see *Fact File*, opposite). There is little shade at many Perth beaches, so be sure to take your own sun protection.

Hillarys Boat Harbour

Just past Sorrento Beach, Hillarys Boat Harbour and Sorrento Quay are busy with yachts, boardwalk cafes, restaurants and shops. Cruises, deep-sea fishing charters and scuba diving trips are available from the quay, and ferries leave regularly for Rottnest Island (see *Fishing*, below and *Rottnest Island*, p. 215). At one end of the quay, the Aquarium of Western Australia provides an insight into the state's complex marine world. Weedy sea dragons, starfish and coral can be observed at close hand, a walk-through transparent tunnel brings you face-to-fin with sharks and giant eagle rays, while dolphins and seals swim outdoors. Eco-adventures such as seal-spotting and whale-watching in season can be booked here.

Fishing

The Mediterranean climate, the Swan with its estuary fishing, and the many opportunities for beach and boat fishing mean there is plenty to keep the angler occupied. Expect tommy ruff, Australian salmon, tailor in spring and yellow eye mullet in winter from the ocean. Tailor is also common in the Swan estuary.

Fishing is allowed in Marmion Marine Park but there are restrictions (see *Fact File*, opposite).

Fremantle

Fremantle's character is defined by its colonial and Victorian architecture, old maritime pubs, interesting cafes and some wonderful water views. The port, virtually a suburb of Perth these days, has a number of impressive museums, some of them in historic buildings – handsome, sometimes convict-built and distinctive in the pale local sandstone.

The WA Maritime Museum's two excellent venues in Fremantle reveal much about the coast and Australia's maritime history, especially early Dutch exploration. The Shipwrecks Museum, in the convict-built 1852 commissariat store, is the country's premier institution for marine archaeology and houses prized relics from the Dutch merchant ship *Batavia*, shipwrecked in 1629 in the Abrolhos (see *Shipwreck Coast*, p. 217). The Museum's new gallery, at Victoria Quay, in a soaring, nautically inspired design that hovers over the water, showcases the state's rich maritime heritage. Moored outside is the *Leeuwin II*, an elegant, square-rigged tall ship that offers weekend cruises in summer and autumn.

There is quite a buzz around the waterfront. Fremantle Sailing Club's sleek yachts moor at Success Boat Harbour, while Challenger Harbour was built for the 1987 America's Cup Challenge.

Contacts

Visitor information

Perth
Forrest Pl
1800 812 808
www.westernaustralia.net

Fremantle
Town Hall
Kings Square
(08) 9431 7878

Geraldton
cnr Bayley St and Chapman Rd
(08) 9921 3999
www.geraldton.wa.gov.au

Rottnest Island
Thomson Bay
(08) 9372 9752
www.rottnest.wa.gov.au

Parks and reserves

Dept of Conservation and Land Management (CALM)
General information on parks and marine reserves
(08) 9334 0333
www.naturebase.net

Houtman Abrolhos Islands
Tour bookings
(08) 9964 7887
www.fish.gov.au

Jurien Bay Marine Park
(08) 9652 1911

Lesueur NP
(02) 9652 1911

Marmion Marine Park
(08) 9336 0111

Nambung NP
(08) 9652 7043

Activities

Contact visitor information centres (see above) for details of activities, tours and charter services.

Other

Aquarium of Western Australia (AQWA)
91 Southside Dve
Hillarys Boat Harbour
(08) 9447 7500
www.aqwa.com.au

Rottnest Island

A regular ferry to Rottnest Island leaves from Northport Ferry Terminal in Rous Head Harbour, and the 500-strong fishing fleet berths at Fishing Boat Harbour. History buffs should inspect the museum-standard replica of the *Duyfken* (or 'little dove'), the Dutch scout ship whose sailors supplied the first recorded chart of the Australian coastline in 1606. Cruises, sailing trips, whale-watching tours (September to late November), deep-sea fishing charters and more all leave from Fremantle.

Rottnest Island

Eighteen kilometres west of Fremantle, emerging from a watery patchwork of azure blues and sublime greens, is the small, environmentally protected Rottnest Island. Just 11 km long and 4.5 km at its widest point, this is a much-loved destination for Perth citizens, a short ferry ride or flight away (see *Rottnest Island*, opposite).

Historic buildings on the National Estate register and several heritage trails are worth investigating on Rottnest, but swimming, surfing, sailing, sunbathing and soaking up the atmosphere are the priorities. Clear waters, diverse marine life (the warm Leeuwin Current brings tropical species), shipwrecks such as the *City of York*, wrecked in 1899, and some of the world's most southerly coral mean exceptional snorkelling and scuba diving (October to June are the prime months). An alternative for underwater viewing is a glass-bottomed boat tour.

Fishing is plentiful: reef fish as well as squid, salmon and tailor are usually in abundance. The surrounding waters are a marine reserve, so check for any restrictions (see *Fact File*, p. 212).

Rottnest's famous quokkas – around 10 000 inhabit the island – are small marsupials that can often be spotted moving around at dusk. Rottnest also has over 100 bird species, with the island's inland salt lakes home to Caspian terns, plovers, herons and other waterbirds; sea eagles and osprey nest along the coast and there are shearwater rookeries.

Accommodation includes the historic Rottnest Hotel, a range of cottages, rustic cabins and campsites. Competition is fierce over summer, so book well ahead.

Yanchep to Lancelin

There are small holiday towns along the coast. Yanchep, 51 km north of Perth, is a quiet beachside spot known for the bushland of Yanchep National Park and the marina at nearby Two Rocks. Another 66 km takes you to the small rock lobster fishing town of Lancelin, a hotspot for windsurfing, with an annual windsurfing event in January that draws national and international competitors.

Cervantes and The Pinnacles

Cervantes, 245 km north of Perth via the Brand Highway, has quiet beaches for swimming, boating and windsurfing. Its main attraction, however, is its proximity to Nambung National Park, 17 km south-east, where The Pinnacles, a moonscape of around 150 000 limestone outcrops, up to 4 m high, stud the yellow sand. When Dutch navigators sighted the area in 1658, they believed the pillars were the ruins of an ancient city. The park, covering 17 000 ha, predominantly sand dunes and sand plains, has drifts of dazzling wildflowers and a haze of golden wattle in

Rottnest history

The Nyungar people were the traditional custodians of Rottnest, or Wadjemup. Europeans first settled the island in the 1830s, later establishing a prison for Aboriginal people, which ran from 1838 to 1903. The island was used as an internment camp during WW I, but was declared an A-class reserve in 1917 and has been a family holiday resort for many decades.

ROTTNEST ISLAND *holiday haven*

Rottnest Island, just a short ferry ride from Perth, is a favourite holiday retreat. Tiny sheltered beaches, rocky coves and coral reefs rim the island and, best of all, everything moves at a leisurely pace – all year round. There is a lovely sense of peace – there are no private cars, so exploring the island is by foot, bicycle (available for hire) or small bus.

Underwater wonderland
Around 360 species of fish, including 97 species of tropical fish and 20 species of coral, can be found in the marine reserve around the island.

Visitor information
See *Contacts*, p. 213

'Rat's nest'
In 1696 Dutch mariner Willem de Vlamingh mistook the island's small furry marsupials, now known as quokkas, for rats, naming the island *Rotte-nest* or 'rat's nest' in Dutch.

Shipwreck trail
A shipwreck trail with underwater plaques documents 14 shipwrecks.

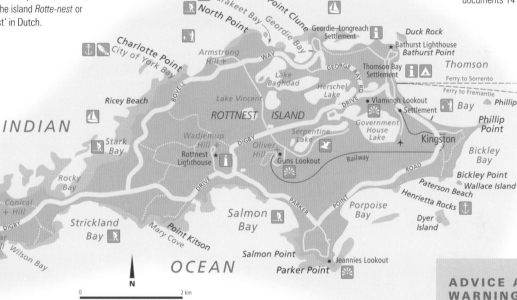

Cape Vlamingh
Cape Vlamingh, at the west end of Rottnest, 11 km from Settlement, has fantastic ocean views, with a rookery of wedge-tailed shearwaters. Dolphins enjoy the azure waters, and humpback whales can be seen off the cape in winter months.

Heritage listed
Rottnest has some of the state's oldest buildings, from its colonial and prison days (it was a penal colony for Aboriginal prisoners from 1838 to 1903). Regular walking tours explore the island's rich history.

Quokka Arms
Rottnest Hotel was built in 1846 as the state governor's summer residence. It is known locally as the Quokka Arms.

ADVICE AND WARNINGS

- Ferries and an air taxi operate from the mainland (Fremantle and Hillarys Boat Harbour); no private cars are permitted on the island
- A fee is charged for all visitors to the island
- Rottnest Island is an A-class reserve; visitors are reminded that there is an emphasis on ecologically responsible tourism
- The island and surrounding waters are a reserve to protect the natural environment
- Spearguns and netfishing are prohibited in the marine reserve; sanctuary (no fishing) zones apply at Kingston Reef and Parker Point; fishing is restricted to non-daylight hours at the Basin and Parakeet Bay

spring. Peaceful beaches and good fishing – Kangaroo Point and Hangover Bay (4WD only) are both well known – are added attractions. There is no camping in the park; tours can be arranged (see *Contacts*, p. 213). For 4WD enthusiasts, there is access from the park's southern entrance via Lancelin on the coast.

Jurien Bay Marine Park

Twenty-eight kilometres north of Cervantes, the recently declared Jurien Bay Marine Park, encompassing a number of islands, acknowledges the area's importance. Major sea lion and seabird breeding areas can be found here and the warm Leeuwin Current enables an unusual mix of temperate and tropical plants and animals to co-exist. Seagrass meadows provide a nursery habitat for marine life, while vivid sponges and marine invertebrates crowd the limestone reefs and caves. Commercial fishing thrives with western rock lobster a major catch; recreational fishing is also allowed, but anglers should check for restrictions. The sheltered bay offers opportunities for swimming, surfing, windsurfing and boating, while the rich underwater environment is ideal for diving and snorkelling.

For those seeking wildflowers, Lesueur National Park, 23 km north-east of Jurien Bay, supports more than 800 floral species, many of them endemic. Wildlife, including honey possums, and at least 124 bird species also inhabit the park.

Dongara to Greenough

The small townships of Dongara and Port Denison date back to the 1850s, when they were set up to service pioneer settlers and handle cargo being

shipped into the area. These days the rock lobster industry is big business. Visitors come for the sparkling blue waters, sandy beaches and proximity to the area's magnificent wildflowers. At Greenough, 40 km north of Dongara, a small hamlet of restored 19th-century buildings is testament to the spirit of the district's pioneers. The settlement is bordered by trees bent almost to the ground, whipped by the fierce, salt-laden Indian Ocean winds.

Geraldton

Geraldton, 427 km north of Perth, is a good base for exploring the region's coast, the fragile Houtman Abrolhos Islands and the wildflower-rich countryside. The city, with a population of 23 000, is also an important deepwater port, handling grain, livestock and minerals, while huge hauls of rock lobster are unloaded at the busy fishing harbour.

European history here dates back to 1629 when the Dutch ship *Batavia* was wrecked offshore (see *Shipwreck Coast,* right). Some of this history can be glimpsed in the WA Museum's Geraldton site, where 17th-century artefacts are highlights. The museum also explores the lives of the region's Yamaji people through the ages.

Local landmarks include St Francis Xavier Cathedral, designed in the Byzantine style by Monsignor John Hawes, an architect turned priest, and completed in 1938. The city's recent memorial to HMAS *Sydney*, which sank during WW II with the loss of 645 crew, is dramatically sited on Mt Scott. Boldly striped Point Moore Lighthouse, in continuous operation since 1878, is also notable (though not open for inspection).

The Leeuwin Current

The Leeuwin Current is a southward-flowing ocean current that originates in the tropics, near North West Cape, and runs strongly down the Western Australian coast, then east into the Great Australian Bight, each year from April to October. The warm water carries true reef-building corals and tropical marine larvae beyond its normal tropical confines. Tropical species can thrive in this warm water in latitudes where they might not otherwise survive.

The Pinnacles

Safe harbour, Houtman Abrolhos Islands

Houtman Abrolhos Islands

Lying 60 km offshore, scattered 100 km across the ocean, the 120 coral islands and reefs of the Houtman Abrolhos form an intriguing if treacherous archipelago. Washed by the warm Leeuwin Current (see *The Leeuwin Current*, opposite), the area's more than 80 species of coral include some of the world's southernmost reef-building corals. The reefs teem with tropical and temperate fish and invertebrates. There are sea lions and dolphins as well as vast numbers of terns, shearwaters, noddies and dozens of other bird species.

The magnificent underwater environment is not without its perils, however. The earliest European sailors to follow the coast were aware of the islands' dangers – 'Abrolhos' is derived from a Portuguese expression meaning 'open your eyes' – and 19 known shipwrecks litter the ocean floor.

Intensive commercial rock lobster fishing from March to June sees 1.5 million kg of lobster hauled in, but the islands' fragile and unique quality is safeguarded within a marine reserve. Access is restricted, camping is prohibited and wildlife is protected on all the islands. Regular diving, snorkelling and eco-tours and scenic flights (from Geraldton) explore this amazing marine world. Fishing charters are also available.

Geraldton's clear waters are fine for swimming, there are some good surfing breaks, and the area's strong winds (especially November to April) have ensured its reputation as an international windsurfing venue (Mahomets Beach is legendary). Watch for seals swimming around the harbour mouth, dolphins and, in season, humpback whales. Anglers should find an abundant supply of tailor, Spanish mackerel, bream and western rock lobster.

Shipwreck Coast

Ships en route to the Dutch East Indies in the 17th century voyaged half way around the world before heading north along the western coastline of Australia. Many never reached their destination, foiled by the treacherous reefs, unpredictable currents and massive tides.

Since the 1600s, more than 1400 vessels have been shipwrecked along this coast. The most famous is perhaps the *Batavia*, which hit Morning Reef in the Houtman Abrolhos Islands in 1629. Dozens of the 316 men, women and children aboard drowned. Jeronimus Cornelisz, the merchant left in charge of the survivors, keen to claim the ship's silver treasure, mutinied and massacred another 125 people. When the captain returned with help from Batavia (now Jakarta), Cornelisz and most of his mutineers were hanged. Two of the men were put ashore near present-day Kalbarri and never heard of again. Priceless 17th-century artefacts, silver coins, timbers from the hull and 37 tonnes of stone blocks intended for the portico of a castle in Batavia have been salvaged and are displayed in the WA Museum in Fremantle and Geraldton.

Other famous ships include the *Zuytdorp*, wrecked in 1712 below the towering cliffs near Kalbarri. Pieces of hull, cannons, anchors and some coins have been retrieved, but there has been little sign of the 100 000 guilders that were on board. The *Verguld Draeck* or *Gilt Dragon*, wrecked on a reef 100 km north of Perth, in 1656, was discovered in 1963. Relics such as glass bottles and bronze and pottery utensils offer a fascinating insight into Dutch life 300 years ago. Shipwreck sites are protected; see *Fact File*, p. 212, for relevant contact details.

The South-West

A string of holiday centres south of Perth soon give way to the famous big swells, limestone cliffs and vineyards of the Margaret River district. Curving east, fronting the Southern Ocean, the coastal scenery is of vast inlets, majestic forests and remote beaches.

Middleton Beach, Albany

An hour or two south of Perth, the large centres of Rockingham, Mandurah and Bunbury offer plenty of opportunities for coastal pleasure and adventure with their comprehensive range of facilities and protected Indian Ocean beaches. South-west, Busselton faces the calm waters of Geographe Bay, punctuated by the town's famous jetty.

The 140 km limestone coast lies sandwiched between the cliff-tops and historic lighthouses of Cape Naturaliste and Cape Leeuwin. Regarded as Western Australia's premier touring destination, it is a maze of forest and farmland, intersected by the rolling vineyards of Margaret River. The Leeuwin–Naturaliste National Park protects the coastline, where powerful surfing breaks, stunning unspoilt beaches, granite headlands and a riddle of limestone caves vie for the visitor's attention.

The Southern Ocean coastline is an exhilarating sweep of high cliffs, karri forest, large protected inlets and sharply defined beaches of white sand and vivid blue water. Settlement here is sparse; farmland is interspersed with long lonely swaths of national park, and the population is confined to a couple of major centres, including Denmark and Albany. Fishing, walking, surfing, diving and whale-watching are popular activities across the region.

Yanchep
Muchea
NEERABUP NP
MARMION
MARINE PARK
WANNEROO
SCARBOROUGH
CITY BEACH
TRIGG
COTTESLOE
Rottnest Island
FREMANTLE
PERTH
Mundaring
ARMADALE
Byford
KWINANA
MONADNOCKS
CONSERVATION
RESERVE
ROCKINGHAM
SHOALWATER ISLANDS
MARINE PARK
SERPENTINE
NP
North
Dandalup
Singleton
Mandurah
Pinjarra
Dawesville
Peel
Inlet
Dwellingup
Harvey
Estuary
Lake Clifton
Waroona
LANE
POOLE
Preston Beach
YALGORUP
NATIONAL
PARK
RESERVE
Myalup
Harvey
OCEAN
Binningup Beach
LESCHENAULT
PENINSULA CP
WELLINGTON
NP
Australind
Bunbury
Collie
Boyanup
TUART FOREST
NP
Cape Naturaliste
HMAS Swan
Dunsborough
Geographe
Bay
Capel
Donnybrook
Yallingup
Ngilgi Cave
LEEUWIN–NATURALISTE
NATIONAL PARK
Busselton
Kirup
Mullalyup
Balingup
Gracetown
Cowaramup
Margaret River
Prevelly
Nannup
Bridgetown
LEEUWIN–
NATURALISTE NP
Cape Freycinet
Boranup Forest
BROCKMAN
Manjimup
Hamelin Bay
Karridale
Jewel Cave
SCOTT
NP
GINGILUP
SWAMPS
NATURE RESERVE
Augusta
Cape Leeuwin
Pemberton
Black Point
SHANNON
NP
NR
LAKE MUIR
NR
Mount Barker
PORONGURUP
NP
D'ENTRECASTEAUX
Northcliffe
MOUNT
FRANKLAND
NP
Mt Liptrap
171
NATIONAL PARK
Point D'Entrecasteaux
Sandy Is
Broke Inlet
Cliffy Head
Walpole
Nornalup
Mt Shadforth
Denmark
Wilson
Inlet
WAYCHINICUP NP
Bald Island NR
Two Peoples Bay
Albany
King George Sound
Little Grove
Peaceful Bay
OWINGUP NR
QUARRUM NR
WILLIAM BAY NP
William Bay
WEST CAPE
HOWE NP
West Cape Howe
TORNDIRRUP
NATIONAL PARK
WALPOLE–NORNALUP
NATIONAL PARK

INDIAN

N
0   30 km
Scale

Must see, must do

► Experience the sea life beneath
   Busselton Jetty
► Explore the caves of the
   Limestone Coast
► Catch a wave off Margaret River
► Tour historic lighthouses
► Soak up the historic and natural
   heritage of Albany

Longest jetty
The picturesque Busselton Jetty is, at 2 km,
the longest jetty in Australia. It is a major
dive site, its many pylons and the warm
currents attract myriad forms of sea life.

Surfing
The Margaret River coastline is a renowned
surfing area. Huge swells roll in from the
uninterrupted expanse of the Indian Ocean,
attracting surfers from around the world.

Two capes
Cape Naturaliste and Cape Leeuwin mark either
end of the rough-hewn wedge of land known as
the Limestone Coast. Each cape is marked with
a historic lighthouse, and both are known for
their sea views and whale-watching.

Whales
Whales are frequent visitors in the south-west:
humpbacks migrate along the Indian Ocean
coastline in autumn and spring; southern rights
breed along the Southern Ocean coast from
June to October.

SOUTHERN   OCEAN

Oldest settlement
Albany is Western Australia's oldest settlement.
Soldiers and convicts aboard the *Amity* arrived
in 1826. A full-size replica of the ship sits at
the centre of town.

Albany ☎ (08) 9841 1088; Margaret River ☎ (08) 9758 0166; www.margaretriverwa.com

Fact File

When to go
The region enjoys a Mediterranean climate, with warm to hot summers and mild winters. Summer temperatures are warmer along the Indian Ocean coastline, where the average daily maximum is 29°C as compared to 25°C at Albany. May–Sept are the wettest months; the Southern Ocean coastline is a little drier than the Indian Ocean coastline during this period. For weather updates, contact the Bureau of Meteorology (BOM): 1900 955 366, www.bom.gov.au

Top coastal events
Feb	*Crab Fest* (Mandurah)
Mar	*Down South Festival* (arts, Albany)
Mar–April	*Salomon Masters* (men's surfing, Margaret River)
	SunSmart Classic (women's surfing, Margaret River)
Easter	*Great Southern Wine Festival* (Albany)
May	*Busselton Festival of Triathlon*
Nov	*Ironman Western Australia* (Busselton)
	The Sunday Times Margaret River Wine Festival

Safety
Swimming There are lifesaving clubs in Albany, Bunbury, Denmark, Mandurah and Margaret River. For details of patrols, along with updates on weather and conditions at key beaches, contact Surf Life Saving WA: (08) 9244 1222; www.mybeach.com.au Protected inlet and estuary beaches throughout the south-west offer safe swimming, but always seek local advice. The open surf beaches on both the Indian and Southern Ocean coastlines can be extremely dangerous.

Other water activities The best weather conditions for boating in this area are late summer and early autumn. The waters around Perth are fairly protected by offshore reefs and islands, which reduce the size of the swells. Surfers need to take care along the Margaret River coastline, which is subject to big, powerful waves. There are a range of surfing breaks suitable for different levels of experience; check with locals before heading out. Contact BOM's coastal waters service on 1900 969 903 (southern district) and its marine warnings service on 1300 659 223 (statewide).

Restrictions/regulations
Fishing A recreational licence is required in WA and bag, size and possession limits apply. For further information contact WA Dept of Fisheries: (08) 9841 7766 (Albany); (08) 9752 2152 (Busselton); www.fish.wa.gov.au

Marine reserve The Shoalwater Islands Marine Park protects the islands and surrounding waters off the Rockingham coast. Recreational activities are permitted; check with CALM regarding proposed fishing bans in sanctuary zones: (08) 9368 4399.

Boating For information about state rules and regulations and safety practices, contact the Dept for Planning and Infrastructure: (08) 9216 8999; www.dpi.wa.gov.au/imarine

National parks Visitor fees as well as camping fees apply to some WA national parks. Contact Dept of Conservation and Land Management (CALM): (08) 9334 0333; www.naturebase.net

Shipwrecks Historic shipwrecks and associated relics are protected by law. Recreational diving is permitted on many sites. For further information contact the WA Maritime Museum: (08) 9431 8444; www.mm.wa.gov.au

CLIMATE												BUSSELTON
	J	F	M	A	M	J	J	A	S	O	N	D
Max °C	29	28	26	23	19	17	16	17	18	20	24	27
Min °C	14	14	13	11	9	8	8	8	8	9	11	13
Rain mm	10	11	22	42	118	175	167	117	75	52	24	13
Raindays	3	2	4	8	15	19	22	19	16	13	7	4

CLIMATE												ALBANY
	J	F	M	A	M	J	J	A	S	O	N	D
Max °C	25	25	24	22	19	17	16	16	17	19	21	24
Min °C	14	14	13	12	10	8	8	7	8	9	11	12
Rain mm	27	24	28	63	102	103	124	106	82	78	48	25
Raindays	8	9	11	14	18	19	21	21	18	15	13	10

South from Rockingham

Rockingham, an hour from Perth, is a top windsurfing destination. Offshore, Shoalwater Islands Marine Park protects the colonies of 16 seabird species and superb underwater reefs. Ferry tours operate from September to June, and take in the sea lion colony on Seal Island and the penguin colony and viewing centre on Penguin Island. Swimming, surfing, diving, snorkelling, dolphin-watching tours and dolphin swims are among the attractions.

Mandurah is a major holiday destination with a population of 35 000. The Murray, Serpentine and Harvey rivers meet here, forming the vast inland

Busselton Jetty

waterway of Peel Inlet and Harvey Estuary. The junction was a meeting point for the people of the Wardandi, who travelled here to barter. Today both the estuaries and ocean offer superb sailing, windsurfing, fishing and swimming.

At Yalgorup National Park a chain of 10 lakes borders the coastline, shielded by dunes and patches of forest and heathland. Campgrounds, picnic sites and walking trails cater to visitors. The park's signature attraction is the rock-like structures known as thrombolites that fringe Lake Clifton, in the north. Like the stromatolites of Shark Bay (see *Shark Bay and Outback Coast*, p. 232), these structures are created by algae-like organisms that represent the earliest forms of life on earth.

Bunbury, Busselton, Dunsborough

Bunbury is the regional capital of the south-west and a working port. Golden beaches and good surf attract holiday-makers, as do the wildlife-watching opportunities. Sea-kayaking tours to see whales and dolphins are popular. Visit the Dolphin Discovery Centre for interpretive displays and information on where and how to spot dolphins.

Bottlenose dolphins are frequently spotted in this region

Caves of the cape

The stretch of coast between Cape Naturaliste and Cape Leeuwin is composed of granite dating back 2000 million years and capped by limestone formed just 2 million years ago. Numerous caves and other features pockmark this young and therefore relatively soft and malleable limestone surface. Flowing or seeping water from the surface shapes the caves. Calcium carbonate in the limestone is dissolved by the waters and then re-forms in an array of cave structures including feathery shawls and stalactites. For the original inhabitants of the area, the Wardandi, the caves have a special significance: they provide the passage to the afterlife and are the domain of sea gods. The caves stretch the length of the coast but there is a concentration near the town of Margaret River. CaveWorks is an interpretative centre at Lake Cave; passes for Lake, Mammoth and Jewel caves are available here. Giants and Calgardup caves are administered by CALM (national parks service). Ngilgi Cave, near Yallingup, one of the largest caves, is administered by the visitor information centre at Busselton. See *Margaret River coastline*, p. 223, for more detail.

Busselton, a key agricultural centre and popular holiday spot, lies half an hour further south. Its landmark feature is the town jetty, which stretches 2 km across the shallow blue–green waters of the evocatively named Geographe Bay. Built in 1865, the jetty serviced American whaling ships; later it was extended to take a railway line (now a tourist attraction) for the shipment of timber. Visitors can walk the length of the jetty, or hitch a ride on the jetty's train that trundles back and forth. Beneath the jetty is another world altogether. Around the many pylons, corals, fish, anemones and sponges assemble in an explosion of colour, lured by the warm waters of the Leeuwin Current. Needless to say, the jetty is a popular diving and snorkelling site. Those without such aquatic inclinations can visit the underwater observatory and watch the scenery through windows set 8 m below the surface. The calm waters of Geographe Bay are perfect for windsurfing, sailing and fishing.

The small town of Dunsborough, which lies at the western end of Geographe Bay, has peaceful beaches and opportunities for a range of activities including whale-watching. The diving is good, particularly around the massive, intricate structure of HMAS *Swan*, which was scuttled in 1997.

Limestone Coast

This wild and beautiful coast, from Cape Naturaliste in the north to Cape Leeuwin in the south, faces the full, unfettered force of the Indian Ocean. Large areas are protected within Leeuwin–Naturaliste National Park. Visitors come for the scenery, walking, fishing and surfing. Campgrounds are located in the south of the park.

Contacts

Visitor information

Albany
Proudlove Pde
(08) 9841 1088

Augusta
Blackwood Ave
(08) 9758 0166

Bunbury
Old Railway Station
(08) 9721 7922
www.bunburytourism.org.au

Busselton
38 Peel Tce
(08) 9752 1288
www.downsouth.com.au

Denmark
60 Strickland St
(08) 9848 2055

Mandurah
75 Mandurah Tce
(08) 9550 3999

Margaret River
cnr Bussell Hwy and
Turnbridge Rd
(08) 9757 2911

Rockingham
43 Kent St
(08) 9592 3464

Parks and reserves

Dept of Conservation and Land Management (CALM)
General information on parks and marine reserves
(08) 9334 033
www.naturebase.net

D'Entrecasteaux NP
(08) 9776 1207

Leeuwin–Naturaliste NP
(08) 9756 1101

Shoalwater Islands Marine Park
(08) 9368 4399

Torndirrup NP
(08) 9840 1027

Walpole–Nornalup NP
(08) 9840 1027

William Bay NP
(08) 9840 1027

Yalgorup NP
(08) 9582 933

Other

Cape Leeuwin Lighthouse
(08) 9758 1920

Cape Naturaliste Lighthouse
(08) 9755 3955

CaveWorks
(08) 9757 7411

Surfing the Margaret River coastline

Around Yallingup

This tiny town (population approximately 200) is cradled within national park surrounds. Visit the 1903 Cape Naturaliste Lighthouse (via Dunsborough, see p. 221). From here, take the 3.2 km walking track to explore a clutch of small limestone pinnacles and watch for humpback whales (autumn and spring) from one of the best lookouts along the coast. The beaches of Yallingup are renowned for their fishing and surfing. Between May and June, large schools of salmon move up the coast on their spawning run, offering anglers the chance to snag fish weighing up to 8 kg, while the quality of the surfing breaks at Yallingup and Smiths beaches contribute significantly to the region's reputation as one of the country's top three or four surfing destinations.

Around Margaret River

Margaret River is known the world over as a premier wine-producing region. The first vines were planted in 1967, and the region's 40 wineries now produce about 15 percent of the country's total wine product. The scenery is a patchwork of emerald-green pastures and neatly tended vineyards. There are cellar-door tastings, B&Bs and clusters of interesting shops and galleries. In contrast to this highly domesticated landscape, the adjacent coastline, around 10 km west, is rugged and remote; it is also home to Margaret River's other signature attraction, outstanding surf (see *Margaret River coastline*, opposite).

Cape walk

A 140 km walking track edges the magnificent coastline between Cape Naturaliste and Cape Leeuwin. The walk can be done as a whole or in sections. For further details contact the national parks service, CALM (see *Contacts*, p. 221).

Karri Forests to Hamelin Bay

The Boranup Forest, part of Leeuwin–Naturaliste National Park, has regenerated from the extensive logging that took place between 1890 and 1991. Karri is one of two species that dominate the famous tall forests of Western Australia, the other being jarrah. Karri trees are among the tallest trees in the world, often reaching 90 m in less than 100 years (the trees in this forest reach about 60 m). There are picnic spots along the way, a campground and superb views of the Hamelin Bay coastline from Boranup Lookout.

At the height of the south-west's logging boom, Hamelin Bay was a major port servicing the shipping of huge tonnages of karri and jarrah to the east coast, England and South Africa. The skeleton of the old wharf is all that remains of this activity. Hamelin Bay's exposure to treacherous north-west winds resulted in 11 wrecks. There is now a wreck trail (for experienced or accompanied divers) and the beach is popular with anglers. A 13 km return walk leads south along the coast from Hamelin Bay to Cosy Corner.

Cape Leeuwin

Cape Leeuwin, where the Southern and Indian oceans meet, is reached from the tiny township of Augusta. The cape was named by explorer/navigator Matthew Flinders after the Dutch exploration ship the *Leeuwin* (meaning lioness). The lighthouse was opened in 1896, but only after 16 ships had been wrecked off the treacherous shores. The lighthouse

MARGARET RIVER *coastline*

From Gracetown to Cape Freycinet, the Margaret River coastline is mostly protected within the bounds of Leeuwin–Naturaliste National Park. Stretches of long sandy beaches are intersected by rugged cliffs, which bear the brunt of giant ocean swells. Attractions include magnificent surf, extraordinary scenery and sites of geological and historic interest.

Visitor information
See *Contacts*, p. 221

Meekadaribee Falls

An easy 2 km walk leads from Ellensbrook Homestead to the lovely Meekadaribee waterfall. At the grotto a display outlines a legend of the area's original inhabitants, the Wardandi people.

Ellensbrook Homestead

Built in 1857, this wattle and daub structure (open daily), was the first home of the Bussell family, after whom Busselton was named. It was the hub of a beef and dairy cattle property, which stretched 30 km along the coast.

Surfers Point

Surfers Point, near the mouth of Margaret River, hosts the top international surfing event, the Salomon Masters. Along with the 40 or so other breaks along the limestone coast, it derives its power (waves of 2.5 m are common) from the uninterrupted ocean between the continents of Africa and Australia.

Prevelly

This is the favoured surfing, diving and swimming spot for Margaret River locals. There are extraordinary views of the coastline as you approach the settlement across the Leeuwin–Naturaliste Ridge. As well as famous surfing breaks, there are protected swimming spots suitable for families.

Caves

There are several caves to explore near Margaret River: Giants, Calgardup, Mammoth and Lake caves (see *Caves of the cape*, p. 221). At the mouth of Lake Cave is CaveWorks, an interpretive centre with displays detailing the geology and history of these fascinating structures.

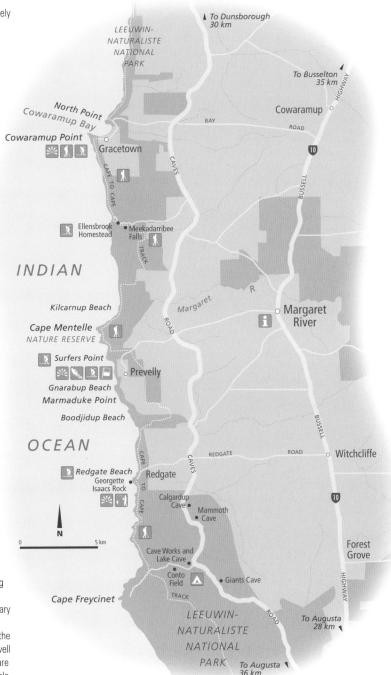

ACCESS, FACILITIES, SAFETY

- Tracks to some of the coastline's more remote surfing and fishing spots are 4WD only
- There are two national park campgrounds with basic facilities within a few kilometres of CaveWorks
- Seek advice before entering caves; for details see *Caves of the cape*, p. 221
- Surfers need to exercise extreme care: choose the break best suited to your level of experience and, if in doubt, seek local advice
- There is patrolled swimming at Prevelly; many of the beaches in the area are subject to large swells, which can create extremely hazardous conditions for swimmers

is open for tours. The stairs are steep but from the top wonderful views of the rugged coastline await. The cape is one of the state's best whale-watching spots.

Walpole to Denmark

The southern coastline between the small fishing and farming towns of Walpole and Denmark is spectacular, a landscape of high cliffs interspersed with wide, open beaches, inlets and estuaries.

The tiny town of Walpole lies embedded within the broad swaths of Walpole–Nornalup National Park, on the shore of a large protected inlet, which is an angler's delight. The national park coastline is protected as a wilderness area, which means access is limited to walkers. The park's inland scenery is of mighty forests and granite hills; a highlight is the Valley of the Giants Tree Top Walk, which leads through the canopy of giant tingle trees. Camping, canoeing, swimming, fishing and scenic driving head the list of park activities.

The century-old timber town of Denmark sits at the foot of Mount Shadforth, overlooking Denmark River and Wilson Inlet. A thick fringe of forest provides a stark contrast to the bright white and blue of the beaches. The surf is great – the top spot is Ocean Beach – while the fishing in the inlet is exceptional, particularly for whiting. The shops and cafes of the town have a friendly and slightly

alternative feel. The outstanding natural setting is best appreciated at nearby William Bay National Park, where attractions include sand dunes, massive wave-smoothed boulders, karri forests and Greens Pool, a sheltered swimming spot, perfect for families.

Above Cape *Leeuwin Lighthouse*
Right Fishing at *Walpole Inlet*

*The whaler chaser
Cheynes IV is a highlight
of Albany's Whale World*

Whales and whaling

Whale World in Albany is a museum devoted to the history of whaling and the industry that saw the establishment of many settlements in southern Australia but which nearly eradicated stocks of a now revered species. The museum is at Frenchman Bay on the site of the former Cheynes Beach Whaling Co. Station. Among the exhibits is the fully restored whale chaser, *Cheynes IV*. At its busiest, the station processed over 850 whales each year, with estimates of the total number caught and processed exceeding 12 000. The centre closed in 1978, as world-wide bans on whaling took effect.

Whale-watchers look for two species of whale in the waters of the south-west: the southern right and the humpback. Southern rights migrate to the south coast of Australia from Antarctica between June and October. They tend to stay in Southern Ocean waters, but they occasionally make forays further north. Humpbacks migrate from Antarctica to the tropical waters of northern Australia, heading north along the east and west coasts of the continent. In Western Australia, they are best seen along the Indian Ocean coastline in autumn as they head north and again in spring as they return south.

Albany

The city of Albany (population 31 000) combines historic charm with natural beauty. The area was settled by soldiers and convicts who arrived aboard the *Amity* in 1826. The town's magnificent harbour, with ideal access to the sea-lanes between Europe and Asia and eastern Australia, became a whaling station and later a coaling depot for steamships. Museums now occupy three historic buildings, and a life-size replica of the *Amity* stands next to one, the Residency Museum.

The town is set against a band of soaring granite hills and overlooks the sparkling blue waters of King George Sound. It is a major holiday centre, with a commensurate range of facilities. The fishing

is excellent, with prolific whiting in the bays. The seascapes and wrecks of the sound are a mecca for divers: top spots include the scuttled wrecks of the massive HMAS *Perth* and the whale chaser, *Cheynes III*; and Michaelmas and Breaksea islands, which guard the entrance to the sound. Swimmers have a range of calm-water and surf beaches to choose from; the town's popular Middleton Beach is patrolled in summer. Whale-watching and whaling history are a big drawcard.

Nearby Torndirrup National Park has some unusual rock formations – The Gap, Natural Bridge and The Blowholes – along with sheer cliffs, beautiful beaches and dunes. There is good walking but no camping or other facilities.

D'Entrecasteaux National Park

This 170 000 ha park preserves rugged cliffs, beaches, sand dunes and pockets of karri. It is largely the domain of 4WD enthusiasts – only a handful of sites are suitable for conventional vehicles. Camping, walking and fishing are the main activities.

Esperance and the Nullarbor

Past Albany, Western Australia's south-east coast offers a range of remarkable natural environments – some of the world's richest plant communities, the stark expanse of the Nullarbor, deserted beaches and scattered offshore islands. Fishing, bushwalking and wildlife-watching here are amply rewarded.

Esperance
Esperance offers abundant opportunities for watersports – kayaking, windsurfing, diving and snorkelling. The long white beaches and rocky coves provide plenty of opportunities for fishing.

Wildflower wonderland
Fitzgerald River NP contains one of the world's richest collections of plant species. More than 1800 species have been recorded, with 62 plants endemic to the park. The spring to late-summer flowering is spectacular.

Stokes NP
The deep inlet, fringed by shady paperbark trees, attracts many waterbirds – 29 species have been recorded in the national park, including shelducks, great egrets and oystercatchers.

Bremer Bay
From July to October southern right whales calve in the calm waters of the bays along this section of coast. The tiny township is noted for its river and beach fishing.

The south-east coast is dramatic and remote. A succession of granite headlands and superlative powdery white-sand beaches face the deep blue waters of the Southern Ocean. Rolling plains and magnificent wildflowers extend into the hinterland. A few tiny towns are scattered along this southern route, and there is the busy town of Esperance, but long tracts of wilderness coast dominate. The soaring coastal cliffs of the Great Australian Bight emerge near Israelite Bay.

Fishing, boating and diving in the region are excellent, but it is the area's often unique flora and fascinating wildlife that deserve special mention. The many islands of the Archipelago of the Recherche, offshore from Esperance, have seabird, seal and sea lion breeding areas. Pods of dolphins swim here, in season southern right whales can be spotted and the birdlife is abundant.

The soils and the climate – increasingly dry as you move east towards the Nullarbor – create a variety of landscapes that support an incredible diversity of flora. Fitzgerald River National Park, classified as a UNESCO World Biosphere Reserve, is particularly noteworthy.

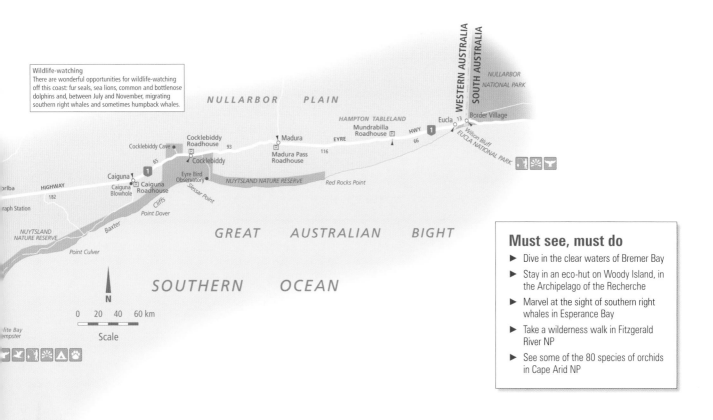

Wildlife-watching
There are wonderful opportunities for wildlife-watching off this coast: fur seals, sea lions, common and bottlenose dolphins and, between July and November, migrating southern right whales and sometimes humpback whales.

Must see, must do

▶ Dive in the clear waters of Bremer Bay

▶ Stay in an eco-hut on Woody Island, in the Archipelago of the Recherche

▶ Marvel at the sight of southern right whales in Esperance Bay

▶ Take a wilderness walk in Fitzgerald River NP

▶ See some of the 80 species of orchids in Cape Arid NP

The ruins of the jetty at Eucla

Fact File

When to go
The region experiences a temperate climate with mild to hot summers and cool, wet winters. July–Oct are the months to watch for whales. Wildflowers bloom all year, but late spring to early summer is the ideal season. For weather updates contact the Bureau of Meteorology (BOM): 1900 955 366, www.bom.gov.au

Top coastal events
Jan	Hopetoun Summer Festival
Feb	Offshore Angling Classic (Esperance)
Sept	Wildflower Show (Esperance)
Oct–Nov	Festival of the Wind (Esperance, even-numbered years)

Safety
Swimming There are potentially dangerous rips at many Southern Ocean beaches, however, there are also calm inlets and bays ideal for swimming. Take special care at isolated beaches. Twilight Cove (Esperance) has regular surf lifesaving patrols on weekends and public holidays Oct–Mar. For details of patrols, along with updates on weather and conditions at key beaches, contact Surf Life Saving WA: (08) 9244 1222; www.mybeach.com.au

Other water activities Many sheltered bays around Esperance provide good conditions for recreational boating. For weather reports contact BOM: 1900 955 363; www.bom.gov.au There is a recorded forecast for coastal marine warnings on 1300 659 223.

Road safety Parts of this region are remote and visitors should be self-sufficient and well prepared. 4WD tracks within national parks require special care. For up-to-date road reports contact Main Roads WA: 1800 013 314; www.mrwa.gov.au

Restrictions/regulations
Fishing A recreational licence is required in WA and bag, size and possession limits apply. For further information contact WA Dept of Fisheries: (08) 9482 7333 (Perth); www.fish.wa.gov.au

Boating For information about state rules and regulations and safety practices, contact Dept for Planning and Infrastructure: (08) 9216 8999; www.dpi.wa.gov.au/imarine

National parks Visitor fees as well as camping fees apply to some WA national parks. Water is limited at national parks in this region and in some cases water must be carried in. Timber is scarce; gas stoves are recommended. Visitors should be self-sufficient. Contact Dept of Conservation and Land Management (CALM): (08) 9334 0333; www.naturebase.net

CLIMATE												ESPERANCE
	J	F	M	A	M	J	J	A	S	O	N	D
Max °C	26	26	25	23	20	18	17	18	19	21	23	25
Min °C	16	16	15	13	11	9	8	9	10	11	13	14
Rain mm	22	27	31	43	76	82	98	84	58	50	36	17
Raindays	6	6	8	11	14	16	17	17	14	12	10	7

Following pages The sublime Lucky Bay, Cape Le Grande National Park Below Great Ocean Drive, near Esperance

Bremer Bay
The coastal hamlet of Bremer Bay, 181 km north-east of Albany, lies at the mouth of the Bremer River and adjacent to the Fitzgerald River National Park. The bay's crystal-clear waters are ideal for swimming and those willing to plunge into the cool depths will find some great diving, with leafy sea dragons, sea lions, dolphins and other marine creatures. For anglers, Australian salmon, trevally, tommy ruff and whiting are typical hauls. A highlight from July to October is the chance to see the southern right whales that come to calve in the calm bays.

Fitzgerald River National Park
Recognised as one of the most diverse botanical regions in the world, the unique Fitzgerald River National Park (240 000 ha) contains an astonishing 1800-plus flowering plant species. This rich flora has created a haven for wildlife, including threatened species such as the rare ground parrot and the marsupial mouse known as a dibbler. There are good walking tracks and the craggy coastline, buffeted by Southern Ocean winds, provides a vantage point for whale-watching. Point Ann and Four Mile Beach are well-known lookouts. There are camping sites, but visitors must bring their own water.

Providing access to the east side of the national park is Hopetoun; lovely protected beaches and some top fishing are on offer in this small but charming seaside village.

Stokes National Park

At Stokes National Park (10 667 ha), 80 km west of Esperance, sand dunes and heathland back the sweeping beaches of Stokes Inlet. The deep, tranquil waters attract shorebirds and waterbirds, such as shelducks, egrets and oystercatchers. Camping, kayaking, bushwalking and birdwatching are popular.

Esperance

The only town of any size along this coast is Esperance, a busy regional centre, 490 km east of Albany, with a population of almost 10 000. The town, named after the French frigate *L'Esperance*, which sought shelter here in 1792, was briefly an access port for the Coolgardie goldfields in the 1890s, but it has seen real growth in the last 50 years as agriculture in the region has boomed. Millions of tonnes of grain and minerals are shipped annually from the port.

Esperance offers plenty of holiday activities. You can windsurf, sail, dive or snorkel around the many offshore islands of the Archipelago of the Recherche, also known as the Bay of Isles; horseride along Cape Le Grand Beach or take a beach safari. The remote coast offers outstanding beach- and rock-fishing and charter boats take anglers out among the islands to catch samson fish, queen snapper and red snapper.

The Great Ocean Drive, a 38 km circuit, takes in the intriguing Pink Lake (at times rendered a vivid pink by algae), lovely Twilight Bay and Picnic Cove, as well as Australia's first wind farm, which harnesses the winds of the Roaring Forties.

Cape Le Grand National Park

Cape Le Grand National Park, 50 km south-east of Esperance by road, is a world of its own, with spectacular coastal scenery and pristine beaches nestled between rugged headlands. A belt of heath sweeps inland. A demanding walk to the top of Frenchmans Peak (262 m), one of a chain of granite peaks, provides stunning views, but there are also less strenuous bushwalking trails. Anglers will find excellent rock-fishing and there is easy access to most park sites, with camping at Lucky Bay and Le Grand Beach. The rich variety of flora supports kangaroos, small native mammals such as honey possums and many bird species.

Cape Arid National Park

Further east, Cape Arid National Park (279 832 ha) embraces banksia woodlands, heaths and semi-arid

Sea lions are prolific on the Archipelago of the Recherche

Archipelago
of the Recherche

Esperance overlooks the Archipelago of the Recherche, 105 coastal islands scattered across the aquamarine waters of the Southern Ocean. Cruises to Woody Island, 14 km offshore, enable visitors to fish, swim, snorkel, camp or stay in safari huts (from September to April). Regular sights are the dolphins cavorting, seals and sea lions sunning themselves on the rocks and even whales surfacing in season. Cormorants nest in the ledges of the steep granite islands, sea eagles soar on the thermals and there are shearwater rookeries.

Contacts

Visitor information

Esperance Dempster St
(08) 9071 4543 or
1300 664 455
www.visitesperance.com

Parks and reserves

**Dept of Conservation and
Land Management (CALM)**
General information on parks
and marine reserves
(08) 9334 033 (Perth)
www.naturebase.net

Cape Arid NP
(08) 9075 0055

Cape Le Grand NP
(08) 9071 3733

Fitzgerald River NP
(08) 9835 5043

Stokes NP
(08) 9071 3733

Activities

Contact visitor information centres (see above) for details of activities, tours and charter services.

eucalypt woodlands. More than 160 bird species, including noisy honeyeaters, flock for the pollen and nectar of the flowering banksias. It is edged by beautiful deserted beaches, with marked trails as well as wilderness walks and camping at several sites. Most of the park is 4WD only, and visitors should take generous supplies of water, especially in summer.

East to the Nullarbor

Continuing east on the Eyre Highway leads past Cocklebiddy, where visitors can access some of the Nullarbor's remarkable network of underground caves. The tiny outpost of Eucla is the last stop before the South Australian border. At Eucla National Park (3340 ha), cloaked in a low blanket of mallee scrub and heathland, there are brilliant views of the coast's dramatic, weather-ravaged limestone cliffs from Wilson Bluff. The Old Overland Telegraph Station, which once provided a link between the east and west of the continent, abandoned in 1929, is slowly disappearing beneath drifting sand dunes.

Shark Bay and Outback Coast

The coastline bordering Western Australia's vast outback is a place of towering rust-red cliffs and isolated beaches. Highlights include World Heritage-listed Shark Bay, the pristine waters of the Ningaloo Reef and a wealth of marine life.

Cape Peron

Western Australia's outback coast is consistently awe-inspiring – impressive in scale, in its often harsh beauty and its ecological diversity. The sun beats down on ravaged cliffs. There are beaches of pale sand or trillions of tiny white shells; offshore lie coral reefs and uninhabited islands. The clear waters of the Indian Ocean shimmer, a startling palette of turquoise and emerald green. National parks and nature and marine reserves protect many of the most precious areas.

The coast is remarkable for its environmental gems, a number of them of world significance. Many visitors come for the area's isolation and the opportunity to see some of the marine world's most fascinating creatures, including rare dugongs and whale sharks – the world's largest fish. Shark Bay is classified as a World Heritage area for its intense natural beauty, the variety and richness of its flora and fauna and its biological and geological importance. At Monkey Mia, wild dolphins skim into the shoreline almost daily to be handfed. Another highlight is the 260 km Ningaloo Reef, one of the country's iconic wilderness areas and another haven for marine wildlife.

Historic towns such as Cossack, and major centres such as Exmouth and Port Hedland, which service the state's industrial behemoths producing iron ore, salt and natural gas, are other fascinating aspects of this remote region.

Parts of this coastline are extremely remote and visitors should ensure they are well prepared. Some roads are 4WD only; in many cases distances between supply stops are significant. In summer, temperatures routinely sit in the low forties.

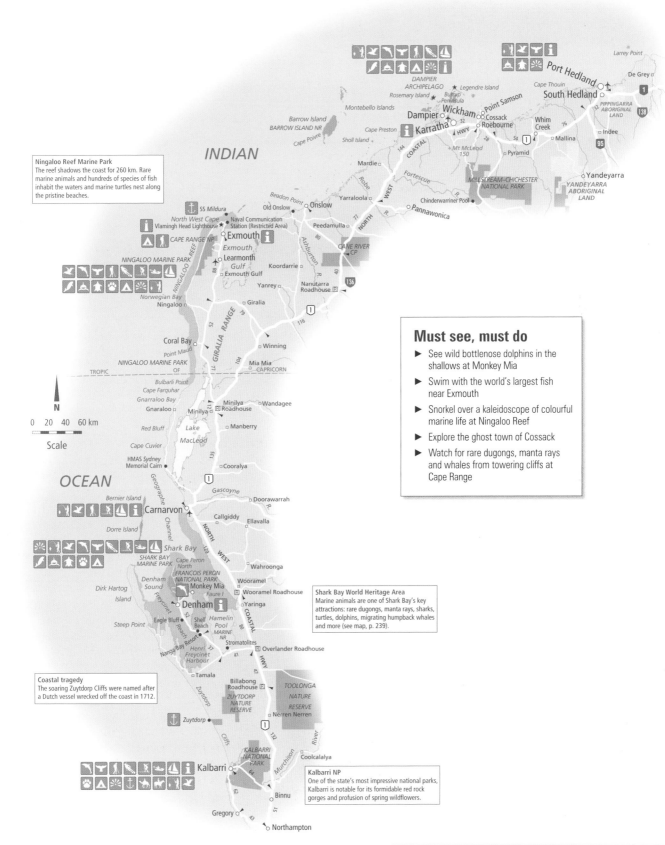

INDIAN

OCEAN

Ningaloo Reef Marine Park
The reef shadows the coast for 260 km. Rare marine animals and hundreds of species of fish inhabit the waters and marine turtles nest along the pristine beaches.

TROPIC OF CAPRICORN

N

0 20 40 60 km
Scale

Coastal tragedy
The soaring Zuytdorp Cliffs were named after a Dutch vessel wrecked off the coast in 1712.

Larrey Point
De Grey
Port Hedland
Cape Thouin
South Hedland
PIPPINGARRA ABORIGINAL LAND
DAMPIER ARCHIPELAGO
★ Legendre Island
Rosemary Island ★
Burrup Peninsula
Montebello Islands
Point Samson
Whim Creek
Indee
Dampier Wickham
Cossack
Karratha Roebourne
Mallina
Barrow Island
BARROW ISLAND NR
Cape Preston
Sholl Island
Mt McLeod 150
Pyramid
YANDEYARRA ABORIGINAL LAND
Yandeyarra
Cape Poivre
Mardie
MILLSTREAM–CHICHESTER NATIONAL PARK
Yarraloola
Chinderwarriner Pool
Beadon Point
Old Onslow Onslow
Pannawonica
SS Mildura
North West Cape
Vlamingh Head Lighthouse ★
Naval Communication Station (Restricted Area)
Peedamulla
CAPE RANGE NP
Exmouth
CANE RIVER CP
Exmouth Gulf
Learmonth
Koordarrie
NINGALOO MARINE PARK
Exmouth Gulf
Yanrey
Nanutarra Roadhouse
Norwegian Bay
Giralia
Ningaloo
GIRALIA RANGE
Winning
Coral Bay
Point Maud
Mia Mia
Wandagee
NINGALOO MARINE PARK
Bulbarli Point
Cape Farquhar
Gnaraloo Bay
Minilya Roadhouse
Gnaraloo Minilya
Manberry
Red Bluff
Lake MacLeod
Cape Cuvier
Cooralya
HMAS Sydney Memorial Cairn
Gascoyne
Doorawarrah
Bernier Island
Carnarvon
Callgiddy
Ellavalla
Dorre Island
SHARK BAY MARINE PARK
Shark Bay
Wahroonga
Cape Peron North
Wooramel
FRANCOIS PERON NATIONAL PARK
Wooramel Roadhouse
Denham Sound
Monkey Mia
Faure I
Yaringa
Dirk Hartog Island
Denham
Eagle Bluff
Shell Beach
Hamelin Pool
MARINE NR
Stromatolites
Steep Point
Nanga Bay Resort
Henri Freycinet Harbour
Freycinet Reach
Tamala
Overlander Roadhouse
Billabong Roadhouse
TOOLONGA NATURE RESERVE
ZUYTDORP NATURE RESERVE
Nerren Nerren
Zuytdorp
Cliffs
KALBARRI NATIONAL PARK
Kalbarri
Coolcalalya
Murchison River
Binnu
Gregory
Northampton

Must see, must do

► See wild bottlenose dolphins in the shallows at Monkey Mia

► Swim with the world's largest fish near Exmouth

► Snorkel over a kaleidoscope of colourful marine life at Ningaloo Reef

► Explore the ghost town of Cossack

► Watch for rare dugongs, manta rays and whales from towering cliffs at Cape Range

Shark Bay World Heritage Area
Marine animals are one of Shark Bay's key attractions: rare dugongs, manta rays, sharks, turtles, dolphins, migrating humpback whales and more (see map, p. 239).

Kalbarri NP
One of the state's most impressive national parks, Kalbarri is notable for its formidable red rock gorges and profusion of spring wildflowers.

Fact File

When to go
Kalbarri in the south has a Mediterranean-type climate with a maximum average temperature of 27°C. Carnarvon is known for its warm winters but it can experience cyclones and floods. Further north, the Pilbara coast is hot and arid, with summer temperatures regularly soaring to 40°C. For weather updates contact the Bureau of Meteorology (BOM): 1900 955 366, www.bom.gov.au If you are planning on wildlife-watching, check the best season: for example, migrating humpback whales (June–Oct), turtle-nesting (Nov–Jan), turtle-hatching (Jan–Feb), whale sharks (Mar–July). Aug–Nov is best for wildflowers.

Top coastal events
Mar   *Sport Fishing Classic* (Kalbarri)
June   *Pilbara Pursuit Jetboat Classic* (Karratha)
Aug   *Carnarvon Festival*
           Game-fishing Classic (Dampier)
           Roebourne Cup and Ball
Oct   *Octoberfest* (Exmouth)
           Gamex Tournament (game fishing, Exmouth)
Nov   *Blessing of the Fleet* (Kalbarri)

Safety
Swimming Always seek local advice before swimming. Sea snakes, stonefish, cone shells and sharks are just some of the dangers in tropical waters (see also *Taking Care*, p. 260). At present no beaches in this region are patrolled. For information regarding patrolled beaches contact Surf Life Saving WA: (08) 9244 1222; www.mybeach.com.au

Other water activities There is excellent diving around Shark Bay, but the town of Denham does not have hire equipment or compressed air; divers are advised to bring all equipment. For weather reports contact BOM: 1900 955 363; www.bom.gov.au There is a recorded forecast for coastal marine warnings on 1300 659 223.

Road safety Some roads in this region are isolated and many are 4WD only. Travellers should carry adequate supplies and be self-sufficient. Seek local advice about road and weather conditions. For up-to-date road reports contact Main Roads WA: 1800 013 314; www.mrwa.gov.au

Restrictions/regulations
Fishing A recreational licence is required in WA and bag, size and possession limits apply. For further information contact WA Dept of Fisheries: (08) 9482 7333 (Perth); (08) 9193 8600 (Broome); www.fish.wa.gov.au

Boating For information about state rules and regulations, safety practices and cyclone contingency plans, contact WA Dept for Planning and Infrastructure: (08) 9216 8999; www.dpi.wa.gov.au/imarine

National parks Visitor fees as well as camping fees apply to some WA national parks. Contact Dept of Conservation and Land Management (CALM): (08) 9334 0333; www.naturebase.net

CLIMATE												KALBARRI
	J	F	M	A	M	J	J	A	S	O	N	D
Max °C	33	34	32	29	26	23	21	22	24	26	28	31
Min °C	20	21	19	16	13	11	10	10	11	12	15	17
Rain mm	5	8	14	20	64	85	75	53	24	16	7	2
Raindays	1	2	2	4	8	11	12	10	7	4	3	1

CLIMATE											PORT	HEDLAND
	J	F	M	A	M	J	J	A	S	O	N	D
Max °C	26	26	25	22	20	17	17	18	20	22	24	25
Min °C	17	17	16	14	11	9	8	8	10	12	14	16
Rain mm	107	109	118	131	116	109	91	61	67	68	72	86
Raindays	9	8	9	9	8	8	7	6	6	7	8	8

Protected marine environments Shark Bay and Ningaloo marine parks have zones specifying permitted activities. For information contact CALM: (08) 9334 0333; www.naturebase.net Further information is also available from regional parks offices and visitor information centres (see *Contacts*, opposite).

Shipwrecks Historic shipwrecks and associated relics are protected. Recreational diving is permitted on many sites. For further information contact WA Maritime Museum: (08) 9431 8444; www.mm.wa.gov.au

Shark Bay has one of the world's largest populations of dugongs

Kalbarri

Kalbarri, 100 km north of Geraldton, is bordered by an imposing coastline of white sand dunes and 100 m high cliffs, extending more than 200 km north. Having gouged its way through 80 km of ancient red and white banded sandstone, here the Murchison River spills into the Indian Ocean. There are many activities available, including top surfing at Kalbarri (some breaks are recommended for seasoned surfers only), beach horserides, camel safaris and a range of tours.

Surrounding the town, the dramatic landscape of Kalbarri National Park (183 004 ha) supports hundreds of bird species as well as an abundance of kangaroos and rock wallabies. For walkers, marked trails of various lengths weave through the park; or visitors can kayak, abseil, swim, surf, snorkel or dive. The fishing is excellent, though the river mouth, reefs and rocky shorelines can be hazardous. More leisurely pursuits include enjoying the 500 or so wildflower species that carpet the park from June to November, or whale- and dolphin-spotting from the cliff-tops.

The rugged coast has had its share of shipwrecks including the *Batavia*, which ran aground on the

Feeding the dolphins at Monkey Mia

Contacts

Visitor information

Carnarvon Robinson St
(08) 9942 1146

Denham 71 Knight Tce
(08) 9948 1253 or
1300 133 733

Exmouth Murat Rd
(08) 9949 1176
www.exmouth-australia.com

Kalbarri Grey St
(08) 9937 1104
www.kalbarriwa.info

Karratha Karratha Rd
(08) 9144 4600

Port Hedland 13 Wedge St
(08) 9173 1711

Shark Bay 71 Knight Tce
Denham
(08) 9948 1253
www.sharkbay.wa.gov.au

Parks and reserves

**Dept of Conservation and
Land Management (CALM)**
General information on parks
and marine reserves
(08) 9334 0333
www.naturebase.net

Cape Range NP
(08) 9949 2808

Kalbarri NP
(08) 9937 1140

Ningaloo Marine Park
(08) 9949 1676

Shark Bay Marine Park
(08) 9948 1208 (Denham)
(08) 9948 1366 (Monkey Mia)

Activities

Contact visitor information
centres (see above) for details
of activities, tours and
charter services.

Houtman Abrolhos Islands, just south of Kalbarri, in 1629 and the *Zuytdorp,* in 1712. For more about shipwrecks see *Shipwreck Coast*, p. 217.

Shark Bay World Heritage Area

World Heritage-listed Shark Bay is one of the world's natural treasures, protected within Shark Bay Marine Park. The park covers 1500 km of coastline and almost 750 000 ha. Seventeen species of mammal and 98 species of reptile and amphibian, along with 320 species of fish and 230 bird species have been recorded in the area (see *Shark Bay – natural wonder*, p. 239).

Aboriginal people knew the bay traditionally as Cartharrugudu, or two bays. When English buccaneer William Dampier tacked into the bay in 1699 he named it Sharks Bay, upon noting the abundant sharks; in fact, huge tiger sharks still frequent these waters, drawn by the plentiful food. Thousands of dugongs, marine turtles, sea snakes, whale sharks and migrating humpback whales swim here. Molluscs, hermit crabs and various invertebrates inhabit the shoreline. The birdlife is equally fascinating and diverse: raptors such as ospreys and sea eagles wheel overhead, there are parrots from the state's south, and over 35 Asian migratory species visit the bay.

Below the bay's surface, 4000 sq km of waving seagrass meadows – the largest in the world and a critical component of the region's extraordinary ecosystem – provide food and sanctuary for marine creatures but particularly for rare dugongs (see *The elusive dugong,* p 236).

Denham and Hamelin Pool

The former pearling port of Denham, Shark Bay's only town, is small but busy, a base for organising 4WD tours, deep-sea fishing charters, kayaking, bike hire, windsurfers and so on. Accommodation here is friendly and laid-back – cottages, caravan parks and a few hotels. There is also accommodation at Nanga.

At Hamelin Pool, about 88 km from Denham, a boardwalk allows closer access to the clusters of strange, rock-like stromatolites that grow in the hypersaline waters. Created by micro-organisms, these 3000-year-old stromatolites are a link with one of the most ancient forms of life on earth. Nearby, the old Telegraph Station, built in 1884, has visitor information and a tearoom.

Monkey Mia

The beach at Monkey Mia, 27 km north-east of Denham, annually attracts more than 100 000 visitors, who come to see the wild dolphins that swim into the crystal-clear shallows almost every day to be handfed by the rangers. Visitors welcome the chance to observe these playful creatures at such close range. Another familiar sight here is the pelicans that scud into the water in search of food.

A sprawling but comparatively low-key resort complex at Monkey Mia includes motel rooms and a caravan park. Plans for an extensive marina were defeated recently in a grassroots campaign to protect this precious area from over-development.

*A diver encounters
a whale shark*

Whale sharks – gentle giants

Every year from March to June the biggest fish in the world cruise into the warm waters around Shark Bay. Whale sharks (*Rhincodon typus*) are usually 4 to 12 m long but can grow to 18 m in length and weigh many tonnes. Yet these massive creatures are placid, harmless filter-feeders. Little is known about them, although they appear to be highly migratory. Whale sharks are protected in Australian waters and swimming with these gentle giants has become a popular pastime during the season.

The elusive dugong

Dugongs are shy, elusive marine mammals that grow to around 3 m in length and weigh up to 400 kg. They are herbivorous, grazing on vast amounts of seagrass, which has earned them the name 'sea cow'. Although they may live to 70 years, dugongs do not start to breed until they are about 10 years old and their slow rate of reproduction has made them vulnerable to extinction. Shark Bay has one of the largest populations of dugongs in the world, with the bay's shallow, warm water and extensive seagrass meadows providing a safe environment for them to graze, breed and raise their young.

Activities in Shark Bay

Sanctuary zones within Shark Bay Marine Park protect specific areas, but recreational and commercial fishing are allowed in the rest of these rich fishing grounds. As well as the thriving fishing industry, fragrant sandalwood has been exported from the Shark Bay area for more than a century and substantial quantities of salt are harvested and exported.

Diving and snorkelling are both highly recommended, revealing a unique combination of tropical and temperate fish, including brilliantly coloured angelfish, lined butterfly fish and wrasse as well as green turtles and dugongs, fascinating corals and sponge communities. In shallow water off Cape Peron lies the wreck of the *Gudron*, sunk in 1901 and known as a top dive site. Tours can be arranged.

Francois Peron National Park

Four kilometres north-east of Denham, Francois Peron National Park, spreading 52 500 ha across the peninsula that juts into Shark Bay, was once a pastoral station. Today the arid shrublands and dry clay pans, or birridas, which define this often forbidding landscape, are an important animal sanctuary. Feral foxes, cats, goats and rabbits are systematically being removed and rare native wildlife re-introduced. Birdlife is prolific with fairy wrens, scrub wrens, finches as well as seabirds – more than 100 bird species live along the coast and in the coastal desert. Magnificent white-breasted sea eagles and ospreys nest on the headlands. Thorny devils are abundant and other lizards and reptiles thrive in the park. In spring and summer, banksias, grevilleas and wildflowers bloom profusely. From the towering red cliffs you can watch for dolphins, sharks, dugongs and manta rays gliding beneath the water's surface. A walking trail takes in the original Peron Homestead and outbuildings. The park has campsites with limited facilities.

Steep Point and Dirk Hartog Island

At the northern end of the Zuytdorp Cliffs, Steep Point is the most westerly landfall on the Australian mainland and renowned as a great land-based fishing spot. Sheer 70 m high cliffs rise from the Indian Ocean swells. The isolated beach faces narrow South Passage and across to Dirk Hartog Island where, in 1616, Dutch mariner Dirk Hartog was the first European known to land in Australia.

Carnarvon

Further north along the North West Coastal Highway, just over 900 km from Perth, lies Carnarvon, the commercial centre for the rich Gascoyne District. Irrigated plantations of tropical fruit (notably bananas), salt harvesting and fishing are the primary industries, though for visitors one of the biggest attractions is the warm winter weather. Visitors can explore the town's heritage precinct or take the quaint tramway that runs almost 2 km out over the ocean on One Mile Jetty, built in 1897. Anglers will find mulloway, mackerel and tuna; blue manna crabs are in season from March to July.

North West Cape and Ningaloo Reef

The sky glows blue almost every day of the year on the state's North West Cape. It is hot in summer and warm the remainder of the year, with no wet season. A warning though – when it does rain,

SHARK BAY – *natural wonder*

Shark Bay World Heritage Area, 830 km north of Perth, covers 2.2 million ha, 70 percent of which is sea. The richness and diversity of its marine life is astonishing. Its pristine waters are home to endangered dugongs, dolphins, whale sharks, spreading fields of seagrass meadows and much more.

Visitor information
See *Contacts*, p. 235

Dirk Hartog Island
This is WA's largest island. It was named after Dutch mariner Dirk Hartog who, in 1616, was the first European known to step ashore on Australian soil.

Francois Peron NP
Originally a sheep station, this property was made a national park in 1990 and is now an important wildlife sanctuary.

Ancient life forms
The still, salt-dense waters at Hamelin Pool have proved the perfect environment for rock-like stromatolites, created by cyano-bacteria, one of the oldest forms of life on earth.

Far west
Steep Point is the most westerly point of the mainland. Access is by 4WD only.

Shell Beach
The sun glints off the tiny white bivalve shells that are packed 10 m deep along this sheltered shoreline, stretching for 60 km.

Monkey Mia
Bottlenose dolphins have been coming here to be handfed since the 1960s.

Wooramel Seagrass Bank
Covering 1030 sq km, the world's largest seagrass meadow is the perfect environment for dugongs.

ADVICE AND WARNINGS

- Strict conservation rules apply at World Heritage-listed Shark Bay; seek local advice or contact the Department of Conservation and Land Management (CALM) (see *Fact File*, p. 234)
- Many areas around Shark Bay are 4WD only
- Fishing restrictions apply in certain areas; check with local authorities and Fisheries WA for full details (see *Fact File*, p. 234)
- Summer weather conditions can be extreme; always carry drinking water and wear a broad-brimmed hat and sensible shoes for walking

it may well be part of a cyclone. Beautiful sandy beaches, crystalline waters and the opportunity to explore the remarkable Ningaloo Reef Marine Park and Cape Range National Park draw visitors to this remote region. The modern town of Exmouth, with a population of about 2500, is the area's largest settlement, founded in 1967 as a support town for a US naval communication station. It is well provided with services, and tours of all types can be arranged – boat cruises, kayaking trips, turtle-watching, scenic flights and 4WD tours, to name a few.

Coral Bay

Coral Bay, with a population of just 120, has direct access to Ningaloo Reef Marine Park and a seemingly endless beach stretching off into the distance. Literally step off the beach and start swimming for some wondrous snorkelling, diving and wildlife-watching. The waters surrounding the bay are in a sanctuary zone.

Swimming in the tropics

Remember that these are tropical waters: sea snakes, stonefish, cone shells and sharks are just some of the dangers. Seek local advice on conditions (see also *Taking Care*, p. 260).

Cape Range wildflowers

Burrup Peninsula – ancient art gallery

The Burrup Peninsula, also known as Murujuga, contains an astonishing 10 000 ancient petroglyphs, or rock engravings. The engravings at this site are among the oldest, most varied and most densely concentrated in the world; they testify to the 30 000-year history of Aboriginal people in the region. Rock engravings, shell middens, shelters and various archaeological sites provide a detailed record of the lifestyle, religion and culture of the area's traditional inhabitants. Tours are available; bookings are through visitor information at Karratha (see *Contacts*, p. 235).

Ningaloo Marine Park

Ningaloo Marine Park contains one of the world's longest fringing reefs, a coral ribbon hugging the coast for 260 km, with coral outcrops as close as 20 m from the shoreline. A shallow, sandy lagoon between the reef and the shore provides ideal snorkelling conditions.

The turquoise waters attract several species of marine turtle, majestic manta rays and around 500 species of fish, including dozens of brightly coloured tropical species. Humpback whales visit the outer reef and Exmouth Gulf from August to October. This is also the only site in the world where whale sharks (see p. 238) appear regularly and close to shore. Snorkelling alongside these massive creatures has become one of the region's signature attractions. Another rare experience is the opportunity to see green, loggerhead and hawksbill turtles nesting and hatching in the dunes from October to January. Swimming, surfing, sea-kayaking and coral-viewing (there are almost 200 species of coral) are other activities.

The Ningaloo area is also known for its superlative reef-fishing and is a mecca for game-fishers, with black and blue marlin, mahi mahi and sailfish (seek local advice about strict sanctuary zones within the park).

Cape Range National Park

Thirty-nine kilometres south of Exmouth is the northern boundary of Cape Range National Park. Remote and rugged, the harsh but spectacular park holds surprising treasures: rocky gorges, deep canyons, a network of hidden caves and a ragged limestone range. Red kangaroos, euros and emus can be sighted and more than 600 flowering plant

species have been identified on the peninsula. The park occupies 50 581 ha and craggy cliffs overlook its 50 km of pristine beaches.

Milyering, the park's visitor centre, offers an excellent introduction to the region. There are marked walking trails and 90 camping bays with limited facilities (you must bring your own water). Most areas are accessible by 2WD vehicles. Rangers advise visitors not to undertake walks in summer when temperatures are intense.

At the tip of the cape, Vlamingh Head Lighthouse, built in 1912 and now fully restored, is a vantage point for panoramic views (check with visitor information for opening times).

The Pilbara

The Pilbara is the industrial heart of the state's north-west. It is hot (summer temperatures sit in the forties), it is isolated and its modern towns, such as Karratha with a population of 10 000, support vast iron-ore mines and offshore gas rigs. Less well known are the Pilbara's wealth of Aboriginal art, the unspoilt coastline and the islands of the Dampier Archipelago.

Dampier, Karratha's port, situated on the craggy Burrup Peninsula, overlooks the 40 or so islands of the Dampier Archipelago. The islands – the nearest is 20 minutes from Dampier's King Bay by boat – attract divers, bushwalkers and bird- and wildlife-watchers. Turtles nest in the dunes, dolphins, dugongs and humpback whales inhabit the waters and birdlife flourishes. Fishing, snorkelling and sightseeing cruises can be arranged. The offshore fishing is famed – sailfish, marlin, mackerel, tuna, barracuda and coral fish (check for protected marine zones). Point Samson is also popular for its fishing and beaches.

Historic towns reveal the Pilbara coast's European history. Roebourne, 14 km from the coast, established in 1866 and the region's oldest existing town, has some fine heritage buildings. Cossack, the first port in the north-west, established in 1863 and for some years a pearling base, was abandoned after the harbour silted up. Nine of its handsome historic buildings have been restored.

Port Hedland

Port Hedland, with a population of 15 000, is one of the world's largest ports in terms of tonnage – it handles $3 billion worth of product annually. Some of the world's longest trains (including one a record-breaking 7.3 km long) snake through the arid country to the port. Vast bulk carrier vessels glide through a narrow harbour entrance adjacent to the main street. This is an industrial town and there are tours of the impressive iron works, port and salt processors. However, there is good fishing (the mangrove-lined coast also invites creek fishing), there are beaches, whale-watching and turtle-nesting in season, and the town is a practical base for exploring the Pilbara's remarkable outback.

From Port Hedland it is 365 km along remote outback roads north-east to Broome.

Above Coral Bay
Inset Pelicans are one of many species that thrive in these unspoilt environs

Broome and Kimberley Coast

The remote Kimberley traces a deeply indented coastline to the Northern Territory border. Offshore lies a necklace of tiny islands, such as the evocatively named Buccaneer and Bonaparte archipelagos.

This is frontier land – a vast, untapped, untrammelled wilderness with a unique coastline. The Indian Ocean's jade-green waters wash onto pristine beaches, and craggy russet-hued cliffs rise against the huge sky. Some stretches are wild – inaccessible by land, virtually impossible to reach by sea. Swampy mangroves flourish along the labyrinthine estuaries of major rivers – like the Drysdale and Prince Regent – as they ease their way into tidal mudflats and pour sluggishly into the ocean. Elsewhere, astonishing tides of 10 m or more surge through narrow channels and coastal gorges, creating thundering whirlpools and 'horizontal waterfalls'.

Visitors can enjoy the sophisticated, resort-type pleasures of Broome, retreat to safari-style tents or eco-lodges in isolated pockets along the coast, or camp. Charter boats explore the reefs, coast and myriad islands; and helicopters and light planes reveal the Kimberley's grandeur and hidden treasures. The region's fishing is guaranteed to satisfy the most ardent angler, the birdwatching is outstanding and the marine life includes migrating whales, sharks, rare dugongs and marine turtles.

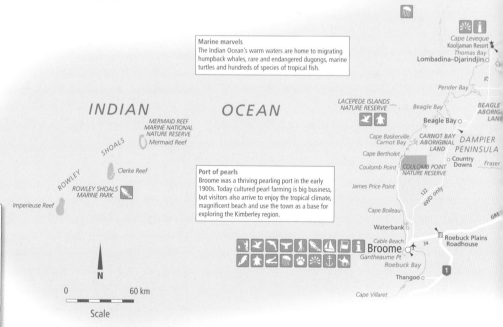

Marine stingers
Dangerous marine stingers inhabit shallow coastal waters in northern WA. Always seek local advice. Swim within enclosures where possible.

Marine marvels
The Indian Ocean's warm waters are home to migrating humpback whales, rare and endangered dugongs, marine turtles and hundreds of species of tropical fish.

Port of pearls
Broome was a thriving pearling port in the early 1900s. Today cultured pearl farming is big business, but visitors also arrive to enjoy the tropical climate, magnificent beach and use the town as a base for exploring the Kimberley region.

INDIAN OCEAN

MERMAID REEF MARINE NATIONAL NATURE RESERVE
Mermaid Reef

SHOALS

Clerke Reef

ROWLEY

ROWLEY SHOALS MARINE PARK

Imperieuse Reef

Cape Leveque
Kooljaman Resort
Thomas Bay
Lombadina–Djarindjin

Pender Bay

LACEPEDE ISLANDS NATURE RESERVE

Beagle Bay

BEAGLE ABORIG LAND

Beagle Bay

Cape Baskerville   CARNOT BAY   DAMPIER
Carnot Bay   ABORIGINAL   PENINSULA
            LAND
Cape Bertholet   Country
Coulomb Point   COULOMB POINT   Downs   Fraser
            NATURE RESERVE
James Price Point

Cape Boileau

Waterbank

Roebuck Plains Roadhouse

Cable Beach   Broome   34
Gantheaume Pt
Roebuck Bay

Thangoo

Cape Villaret

0   60 km

N

Scale

Must see, must do

▶ Go mud-crabbing on the remote Dampier Peninsula

▶ Enjoy Broome's Shinju Matsuri, 'festival of the pearl'

▶ Fly over the spectacular Buccaneer Archipelago, or 'Thousand Islands'

▶ See 120 million-year-old dinosaur footprints at Gantheaume Point

▶ Visit some of the Kimberley's ancient rock-art sites

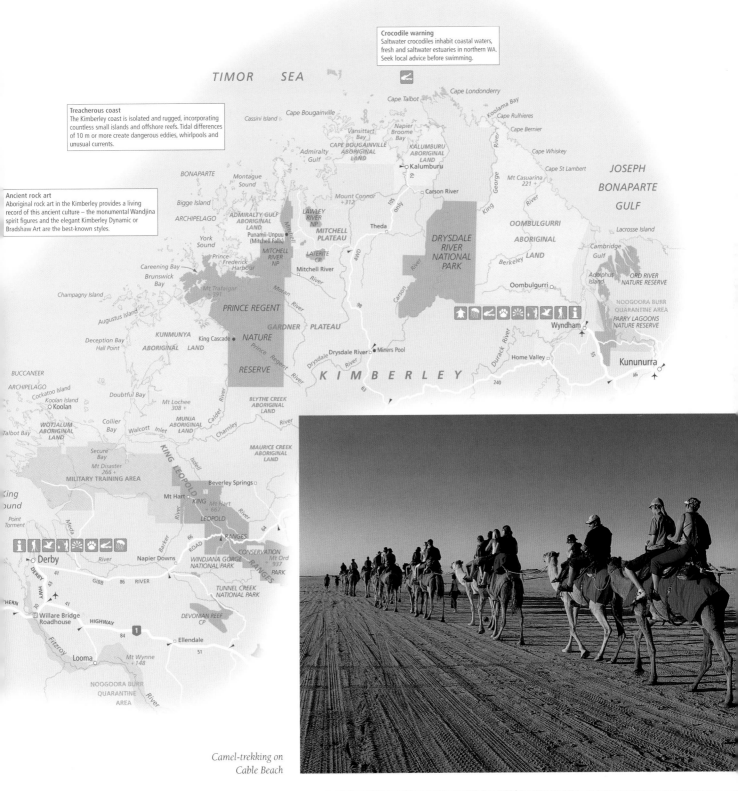

TIMOR SEA

Crocodile warning
Saltwater crocodiles inhabit coastal waters, fresh and saltwater estuaries in northern WA. Seek local advice before swimming.

Cape Londonderry

Cape Talbot

Cape Bougainville

Cassini Island

Koolama Bay
Cape Rulhieres
Cape Bernier

Treacherous coast
The Kimberley coast is isolated and rugged, incorporating countless small islands and offshore reefs. Tidal differences of 10 m or more create dangerous eddies, whirlpools and unusual currents.

Vansittart Bay
Napier Broome Bay

Cape Whiskey

Cape St Lambert

JOSEPH BONAPARTE GULF

BONAPARTE

Montague Sound

Admiralty Gulf

CAPE BOUGAINVILLE ABORIGINAL LAND

KALUMBURU ABORIGINAL LAND
Kalumburu

Mt Casuarina 221 +

Ancient rock art
Aboriginal rock art in the Kimberley provides a living record of this ancient culture – the monumental Wandjina spirit figures and the elegant Kimberley Dynamic or Bradshaw Art are the best-known styles.

Bigge Island

ARCHIPELAGO

ADMIRALTY GULF ABORIGINAL LAND
Punamii-Unpuu (Mitchell Falls)

LAWLEY RIVER NP

MITCHELL PLATEAU

Mount Connor +312

Carson River

George River

King River

OOMBULGURRI ABORIGINAL LAND

Lacrosse Island

York Sound

MITCHELL RIVER NP

Theda

LATERITE CP

Mitchell River

DRYSDALE RIVER NATIONAL PARK

Berkeley River

Cambridge Gulf

Adolphus Island

ORD RIVER NATURE RESERVE

Careening Bay
Brunswick Bay

Prince Frederick Harbour

Mt Trafalgar 391

Moran River

Carson River

Oombulgurri

NOOGOORA BURR QUARANTINE AREA

PARRY LAGOONS NATURE RESERVE

Champagny Island

PRINCE REGENT

Augustus Island

GARDNER PLATEAU

Wyndham

Deception Bay
Hall Point

KUNMUNYA ABORIGINAL LAND

King Cascade

NATURE

RESERVE

Prince Regent River

Drysdale River

Miners Pool

Durack River

Home Valley

Kununurra

BUCCANEER

ARCHIPELAGO

Cockatoo Island

Koolan Island
Koolan

K I M B E R L E Y

240

Doubtful Bay

Mt Lochee 308 +

BLYTHE CREEK ABORIGINAL LAND

Talbot Bay

WOTJALUM ABORIGINAL LAND

Collier Bay

Walcott Inlet

Caldel River

Charnley River

MUNJA ABORIGINAL LAND

MAURICE CREEK ABORIGINAL LAND

King Sound

Point Torment

Secure Bay

Mt Disaster 266 +

MILITARY TRAINING AREA

KING LEOPOLD

Isdell River

Meda River

Derby

Napier Downs

Barker River

Beverley Springs

Mt Hart

KING

Mt Hart + 667

LEOPOLD

RANGES

CONSERVATION

Mt Ord 937

PARK

DERBY HWY

GIBB

86

RIVER

ROAD

WINDJANA GORGE NATIONAL PARK

RANGES

HIGHWAY

84

Willare Bridge Roadhouse

THERN

Ellendale

TUNNEL CREEK NATIONAL PARK

DEVONIAN REEF CP

51

Fitzroy River

Looma

Mt Wynne + 148

NOOGOORA BURR QUARANTINE AREA

River

Camel-trekking on Cable Beach

Fact File

When to go
The Kimberley region experiences a tropical monsoon climate with two main seasons – the Wet and the Dry. Summers (Oct–Mar) are hot and humid, and winters are warm. Almost 90 percent of the heavy annual rainfall occurs Dec–Mar, in short but torrential bursts. Spectacular thunderstorms and dramatic night-time lightning can occur at this time; cyclone activity is also possible. Coastal breezes temper Broome's climate. Winter months are best for exploring, boating and beachcombing. In summer Broome is less crowded, the countryside is greener and the waterfalls are at their peak. For weather updates contact the Bureau of Meteorology (BOM): 1900 955 366; www.bom.gov.au

Top coastal events
Easter	*Dragon Boat Regatta* (Broome)
May	*King Tide Day* (celebrating highest tide in Australia, Derby)
June	*Moonrise Rock Festival* (Derby)
	Mowanjum Festival (indigenous art and culture, Derby)
June–July	*Race Round* (horseracing week, Broome)
Aug–Sept	*Shinju Matsuri Festival* (pearl festival, Broome)
	Opera Under the Stars (Broome)
Sept	*Munumburra Music Festival* (Wyndham)
Nov	*Mango Festival* (Broome)

Safety
Swimming Crocodiles inhabit waters along this coast (see following). Potentially deadly marine stingers (box jellyfish) inhabit shallow coastal waters Oct–April. Seek local advice before swimming; look for and observe warning signs (see also *Taking Care*, p. 260). Broome's Cable Beach is patrolled. For details of patrols, along with updates on weather and conditions at key beaches, contact Surf Life Saving WA: (08) 9244 1222; www.mybeach.com.au

Crocodiles Dangerous saltwater or estuarine crocodiles inhabit the coastline and many tidal rivers, creeks and inland waterways north of the De Grey River (just north of Port Hedland). Be crocodile-wise: observe warning signs, and seek local advice before swimming, fishing or boating.

Other water activities The north coast is hazardous with king tides, whirlpools, islands and reefs. Use proper navigation charts and seek local advice about conditions. Boating self-sufficiency is required due to the area's isolation and limited rescue facilities. Beware of crocodiles and stingers (Oct–April) throughout the region (see *Taking Care*, p. 260). For weather reports contact BOM: 1900 955 363; www.bom.gov.au There is a recorded forecast for coastal marine warnings on 1300 659 223.

Road safety Roads are isolated and many are 4WD only. Travellers should carry adequate supplies and be self-sufficient. Seek local advice about road and weather conditions. For up-to-date road reports contact Main Roads WA: 1800 013 314; www.mrwa.gov.au

Restrictions/regulations
Fishing A recreational licence is required in WA and bag, size and possession limits apply. For further information contact WA Dept of Fisheries: (08) 9482 7333 (Perth); (08) 9193 8600 (Broome); www.fish.wa.gov.au

Boating For information about state rules and regulations, licensing requirements, safety practices and cyclone contingency plans, contact the WA Dept for Planning and Infrastructure: (08) 9216 8999; www.dpi.wa.gov.au/imarine

National parks Visitor fees as well as camping fees apply to some WA national parks. Contact Dept of Conservation and Land Management (CALM): (08) 9334 0333; www.naturebase.net

Marine reserves Rowley Shoals Marine Park protects an area including Mermaid Reef, which is off limits to anglers; some fish and all shellfish within 1.6 km of the reef are protected. For information contact CALM: (08) 9192 1036 (Broome); www.naturebase.net Information is also available from regional parks offices and visitor information centres (see *Contacts*, opposite).

Aboriginal land Some communities offer camping, guided tours and limited supplies, but to visit communities may require a permit. Plan ahead as permits can take several weeks or longer. Contact Dept of Indigenous Affairs: PO Box 7770, Cloisters Sq, Perth; (08) 9235 8000.

Shipwrecks Historic shipwrecks and associated relics are protected by law. Recreational diving is permitted on many sites. For further information contact the WA Maritime Museum: (08) 0431 8444; www.mm.wa.gov.au

CLIMATE												BROOME
	J	F	M	A	M	J	J	A	S	O	N	D
Max °C	33	33	34	34	31	28	28	30	32	33	34	34
Min °C	26	26	25	22	18	15	14	15	18	22	25	26
Rain mm	158	143	101	30	21	23	4	3	1	1	13	77
Raindays	9	9	7	2	2	2	1	0	0	0	1	5

Cable Beach, one of Australia's best

Broome

A unique Australian town, in fact, a unique town full stop, Broome is a quirky blend of outback settlement and seaside resort. It is remote (almost 2400 km north of Perth), clinging to the coastline of the sparsely settled Kimberley, yet its colourful history as a pearling port, its magnificent beach and its balmy tropical climate entice a passing throng of national and international visitors.

Iconic Cable Beach, a 22 km ribbon of white sand, was named in honour of the telegraph cable laid between Broome and Java in 1889, which linked Australia with Asia, Europe and England. In the early 1900s, Broome was the boisterous pearling capital of the world, with more than 300 luggers in port and a non-indigenous population that included Japanese, Chinese, Malays and Europeans. Pearling is still important and lucrative – pearls and pearl by-products from the area have an annual value of around $200 million. The town's multicultural heritage can be seen in the excellent museum, the style of local architecture, the Japanese cemetery (where 900 Japanese graves testify to the perils of pearling) and the annual Shinju Matsuri, 'festival of the pearl'.

Holiday-makers who jet in, and those doing the long haul by road through Australia's vast northern reaches, swim at Cable Beach (except during the stinger season – see *Fact File*, opposite), take sunset camel rides and inspect the restored pearling luggers. At Gantheaume Point (7 km south of town), 120 million-year-old dinosaur footprints are revealed at low tide at the base of the red sandstone cliffs. The rocks also enclose Anastasia's Pool, a small pool built by a former lighthouse keeper for his arthritic wife.

Those interested in learning a little more about the saltwater and freshwater crocodiles that inhabit northern coastal and some inland waterways might visit Broome Crocodile Park, home to more than 4000 crocodiles. Broome Bird Observatory, 25 km east on the shores of Roebuck Bay, is one of the best places to observe some of the 300 or so species of migratory water birds that arrive each year from the Northern Hemisphere.

Cruising the Coast

Cruise ships and light aircraft leave regularly from Broome to explore the Kimberley coastline, with its countless reefs, islands, gulfs, bays and formidable cliff-faces guarding the hinterland.

The drama and beauty of Cape Leveque

Broome to Cape Leveque

A rough, unformed sandy road leads 122 km across the Dampier Peninsula from Broome to Beagle Bay, a tiny town on Aboriginal land with a historic church built by the Pallotine Monks in 1918, and remarkable for its pearl-shell embellished altar. Another 75 km leads to Cape Leveque Lighthouse – its white tower emerging from a mass of greenery and vivid red soil – overlooking King Sound and across to the Buccaneer Archipelago, a maze of almost 1000 islands. The cape's isolated Kooljaman Resort caters to guests with deluxe safari-style tents or palm-frond shelters. Iron-ore deposits at Yampi Sound were among the world's richest, with millions of tonnes of ore extracted from Cockatoo Island, before a get-away-from-it-all resort opened in this remote spot in the tropics.

Contacts

Visitor information

Broome cnr Broome Hwy and Bagot Rd
(08) 9192 2222
www.ebroome.com

Christmas Island
(08) 9164 8382
www.christmas.net.au

Cocos (Keeling) Islands
(08) 9162 6790
www.cocos-tourism.cc

Derby 2 Clarendon St
(08) 9191 1426 or
1800 621 426
www.derbytourism.com.au

Wyndham Kimberley Motors
6 Great Northern Hwy
(08) 9161 1281

Parks and reserves

Dept of Conservation and Land Management (CALM)
General information on parks and marine reserves
(08) 9168 0200 (Broome)
www.naturebase.net

Mitchell River NP
See *CALM* above

Prince Regent Nature Reserve
See *CALM* above

Activities

Contact visitor information centres (see above) for details of activities, tours and charter services.

For scuba divers, a highlight is Rowley Shoals, a chain of coral atolls 280 km west, offering a kaleidoscope of colour with 200 species of coral and an extraordinary variety of tropical fish. Most of the area is within a marine park.

Closer to the coast are the four sandy Lacepede Islands, named by Nicolas Baudin, after Count Lacepede, a politician and naturalist. These islands, now within Lacepede Nature Reserve, are the main Kimberley nesting site for green turtles, which come ashore nightly from October to March. Birdlife here is also prolific.

The water around Cape Leveque and the Buccaneer Archipelago is a milky turquoise–aqua, due to silt moving from King Sound on the massive tides. One of the region's signature attractions is the 'horizontal waterfall' at Talbot Bay, where huge tides cause vast amounts of water to sluice through the opening on each turning tide.

Prince Regent River, which runs dead straight for about 100 km between towering sandstone cliffs, is joined by a mass of tributaries as it flows into the sea. Around 40 km inland, the multi-layered King Cascade waterfall is a favourite destination for visitors. The river is largely within Prince Regent Nature Reserve, a lush wilderness spanning 630 000 ha in the state's highest rainfall region, kept pristine by its sheer inaccessibility. Restricted public access is by boat or plane only. The area has been declared a UNESCO World Biosphere Reserve.

At Careening Bay, visitors can still see the bulbous boab tree carved by Phillip Parker King's carpenter when HMC *Mermaid* was careened here in 1820. The vessel was on the first British survey of the Kimberley coast. Further north, at scenic Prince Frederick Harbour, green vegetation and red cliffs soaring 200 m mark the entrance to the Hunter River. Ships use this harbour as a base for helicopter flights to the impressive Mitchell Falls, 50 km inland.

Rounding the northern coast, other rivers spill into the sea, having carved their way across the Kimberley plateau. King George River emerges into Koolama Bay (12 km upstream are the spectacular 100 m high King George Falls) and the last dramatic gorge is where Berkeley River pours into the sea, just south of Cape St Lambert.

Staircase to the moon

When a full moon and a low tide coincide at Cable Beach (from March to October), the light reflects on the mudflats, creating an optical illusion of stairs to the moon.

Previous pages *The 'floating' landforms of Talbot Bay*
Right *Wandjina rock art*

Kimberley treasure – ancient rock art

Aboriginal art is one of the great treasures of the Kimberley region. The most famous figures depicted in the ancient rock art are the Wandjina. These eerie, staring figures with mouthless faces and other-worldly haloes are said to represent Kaiara spirits, ancient ancestors from the sky and sea who brought rain and fertility. As well as the Wandjina figures there are monumental goannas, crocodiles, tortoises and other creatures. These paintings date back thousands of years, yet older still, it seems, are the Kimberley Dynamic or Bradshaw images. In these, elegant, elongated figures dance and sway, wearing tassels, skirts and exotic headdresses; in some, stylised bird and animal motifs appear. Caves on rugged Bigge Island in the Bonaparte Archipelago feature some exceptional rock art, depicting sailing ships and figures smoking pipes, reflecting the arrival of Europeans. These images were painted by the Wunambal people.

The crystal-clear waters of the Cocos Islands

Offshore islands

Off the Western Australian coastline, lying in the brilliant tropical seas of the Indian Ocean, are two of Australia's most remote island outposts. Christmas Island, an Australian territory since 1958, is 1500 km off the state's north-west coast. It nurtures a culturally diverse population of around 1500, which is drawn from Australia and a number of Asian nations. A national park protects two-thirds of the island and a range of unique wildlife, while the surrounding waters are a haven for more than 600 species of fish.

The Cocos (Keeling) Islands are a group of 27 islands, around 700 km south-west of Christmas Island, and are Australia's furthest western territory.

Around 450 residents are Cocos Malay; the remaining 150 are mainland Australians on work contracts. The islands, which are a series of coral cays, boast a stunning, unspoilt natural environment of pockets of jungle, coconut palms, white-sand beaches and wildlife-filled water.

Both Christmas Island and the Cocos have a small but growing tourism industry, with visitors attracted by adventure- and nature-based activities including diving, sailing and fishing along with the chance to experience a tropical environment with none of the commercial trappings. Regular flights to both places leave from Perth.

Derby to Wyndham

Derby, tucked into the base of King Sound, is reached from Broome by road along the Great Northern and Derby highways. In the 1880s, the town flourished as a port after gold was discovered inland at Halls Creek, but today the small township, with its roomy, boab tree-lined streets, is a base for exploring the outback Kimberley. Keen anglers will find good jetty and creek fishing and, during the dry season (May to September), some sensational fishing in isolated spots such as Walcott Inlet (huge barramundi, queenfish, cod, immense trevally and more). Remember, though, that the Kimberley

coast and tidal rivers and creeks are all saltwater crocodile territory and the waters can be extremely dangerous (see *Fact File*, p. 242).

Wyndham, a small town located on the muddy tidal waters of Cambridge Gulf, stands at the confluence of the King, Pentecost, Durack, Forest and Ord rivers. The town services a huge live cattle export industry. For those passing through, fishing, 4WD adventures, bushwalking and birdwatching are the main drawcards. It is worth the short detour to the Five Rivers Lookout, at the top of the Bastion Range, for the panoramic view. The roads in this area are remote – be prepared.

Fishing in the Kimberley

The fishing around the region is first-class. There is jetty, creek and rock-fishing in Broome, with the creeks flowing into Roebuck Bay carrying fork-tailed catfish, the much-prized barramundi, mangrove jack and more. For game fishers, there are rich pickings in the offshore waters – one of the world's most prolific sailfish grounds lies just 20 km or so from Broome. Reef fish are plentiful off the coast, but remember that there are also plenty of sharks. Charter boats cater to dedicated and amateur anglers.

Northern Territory
tropical frontier

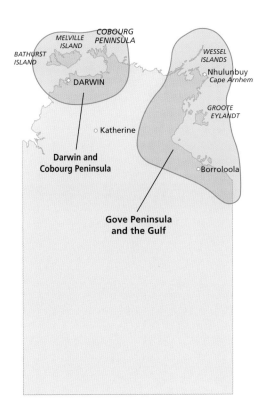

MELVILLE ISLAND
COBOURG PENINSULA
BATHURST ISLAND
DARWIN
WESSEL ISLANDS
Nhulunbuy
Cape Arnhem
GROOTE EYLANDT
Katherine
Darwin and Cobourg Peninsula
Borroloola
Gove Peninsula and the Gulf

Northern Territory's Regions

Darwin and Cobourg Peninsula

Darwin looks towards Asia across the Timor Sea. The city is lively around the docks and along its north coast, where there are white sands, huge tides and brilliant sunsets. The Aboriginal Tiwi Islands and Cobourg Peninsula, north and north-east respectively, attract anglers, cultural tourists and nature lovers. The region boasts many beautiful beaches — wavering ribbons of sand bordering tropical green–blue seas — but these are sandwiched between swollen tidal rivers, vast flood plains replete with wildlife, primordial swamps, mudflats and tangled forests of mangroves. *See p. 250*

Gove Peninsula and the Gulf

Gove, part of Arnhem Land, is the preserve of the Yolngu. Despite the presence of a large mining operation, the beaches are pristine. The Gulf estuaries branch into lily-clotted billabongs and sport fringes of giant paperbark. Contingents of 4WD adventurers tour the region in the footsteps of famous explorers. Crocodiles, sharks and marine stingers keep swimmers out of the water, but nothing will keep the anglers away: the Northern Territory, with its fertile offshore waters and barramundi-packed tidal rivers, is an internationally famous fishing destination. Non-fishing tourists take cruises, dive, travel remote 4WD-only tracks, walk, watch the wildlife, camp and soak up the scenery. *See p. 256*

The Northern Territory coastline shares similarities with parts of the coastline of neighbouring states, but overall it is unique. Absent are the scenes of sunbakers and lifeguards on golden sands and bodysurfers dodging the breaks. This is a wild, remote and difficult-to-access territory; a place visited for its untouched scenery, ecological riches and unparalleled fishing opportunities. It is an adventure coast, where danger and excitement go hand-in-hand.

The Northern Territory coast stretches 5437 km from Western Australia in the west to Queensland in the east. It fronts the Timor Sea, the Arafura Sea and the Gulf of Carpentaria. Most of its 887 islands, including Melville Island, the second largest in Australia after Tasmania, are Aboriginal land, as indeed is the greater part of the mainland coastline.

The best time to visit is during the Dry, which runs from April to October. Many areas are extremely remote. Sites on Aboriginal land may require permits. Book well ahead and plan carefully.

Opposite A storm brews across the Top End's tropical waters
Left Brilliant starfish are a feature of the Darwin Coast

☎ (08) 8936 2499; www.tourismtopend.com.au

Darwin and Cobourg Peninsula

Facing the tropical waters of the Timor and Arafura seas, at the northern limits of the continent, this is a genuine frontier coastline: wild, remote, sparsely populated and ripe with opportunities for adventure.

The red–gold cliffs of Cobourg Peninsula

The beauty of Darwin lies in its tropical wilderness. The twice-rebuilt city (the result of World War II and then Cyclone Tracy in 1974), with its population of 90 000, crouches amid a tangle of mangroves, red-hued headlands, and beaches washed by huge 7 m tides. It is heavily reliant on its waterfront for trade and supplies. It faces Indonesia across the Timor Sea and is closer to the cities of Asia than it is to Australia's population centres in the south-east of the continent. The water has its share of tropical menaces (crocodiles, stingers), but is much prized for its superlative views and sunsets, and wildlife-watching and fishing opportunities.

East of Darwin to the Van Diemen Gulf are flood plains formed by the seasonal overflow of a succession of mighty tropical rivers. Access is difficult and during the Wet almost impossible, but adventurous anglers and nature lovers keep returning. Further east still is Arnhem Land, one of the country's most remote and least traversed regions. Access is strictly limited, however, visitors can sample the region's beauty and cultural heritage by visiting Cobourg Peninsula in the north-east.

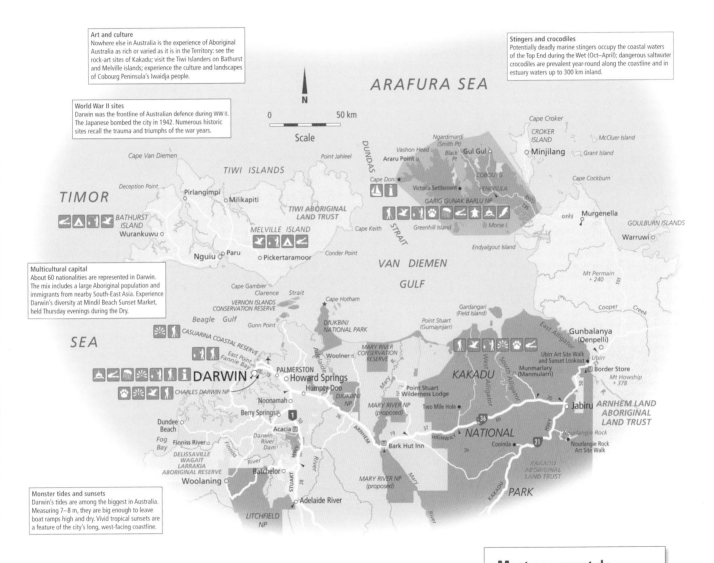

Art and culture
Nowhere else in Australia is the experience of Aboriginal Australia as rich or varied as it is in the Territory: see the rock-art sites of Kakadu; visit the Tiwi Islanders on Bathurst and Melville islands; experience the culture and landscapes of Cobourg Peninsula's Iwaidja people.

World War II sites
Darwin was the frontline of Australian defence during WW II. The Japanese bombed the city in 1942. Numerous historic sites recall the trauma and triumphs of the war years.

Stingers and crocodiles
Potentially deadly marine stingers occupy the coastal waters of the Top End during the Wet (Oct–April); dangerous saltwater crocodiles are prevalent year-round along the coastline and in estuary waters up to 300 km inland.

Multicultural capital
About 60 nationalities are represented in Darwin. The mix includes a large Aboriginal population and immigrants from nearby South-East Asia. Experience Darwin's diversity at Mindil Beach Sunset Market, held Thursday evenings during the Dry.

Monster tides and sunsets
Darwin's tides are among the biggest in Australia. Measuring 7–8 m, they are big enough to leave boat ramps high and dry. Vivid tropical sunsets are a feature of the city's long, west-facing coastline.

ARAFURA SEA

N

0   50 km
Scale

TIMOR

SEA

TIWI ISLANDS

Cape Van Diemen

Deception Point

Pirlangimpi
Milikapiti

TIWI ABORIGINAL LAND TRUST

BATHURST ISLAND
Wurankuwu

MELVILLE ISLAND

Nguiu
Paru
Pickertaramoor

Cape Gambier
Clarence Strait

Point Jahleel

Cape Keith

Conder Point

VAN DIEMEN

GULF

DUNDAS

STRAIT

Vashon Head
Araru Point
Cape Don

Ngardimardi (Smith Pt)
Black Pt
Gul Gul
Victoria Settlement

COBOURG
PENINSULA
GARIG GUNAK BARLU NP

Greenhill Island

Cape Croker
CROKER ISLAND
Minjilang

McCluer Island
Grant Island

Cape Cockburn

Morse I.
Endyalgout Island

Murgenella
only

GOULBURN ISLANDS
Warruwi

Mt Permain + 240

Cooper Creek

VERNON ISLANDS CONSERVATION RESERVE

Beagle Gulf
Gunn Point

Cape Hotham

DJUKBINJ NATIONAL PARK

MARY RIVER CONSERVATION RESERVE

Gardangari (Field Island)

Point Stuart (Gurnaynjarr)

East Alligator

Gunbalanya (Oenpelli)

Ubirr Art Site Walk and Sunset Lookout
Ubirr
Border Store

Mt Howship + 378

CASUARINA COASTAL RESERVE

East Point
Fannie Bay

DARWIN

CHARLES DARWIN NP

PALMERSTON
Howard Springs
Humpty Doo
Noonamah

DJUKBINJ NP

Woolner

Point Stuart Wilderness Lodge

MARY RIVER NP (proposed)

Two Mile Hole

KAKADU

Munmarlary (Manmularri)

West Alligator
South Alligator

Jabiru

ARNHEM LAND ABORIGINAL LAND TRUST

Nourlangie Rock
Nourlangie Rock Art Site Walk

Dundee Beach
Fog Bay

Finniss River

Berry Springs
Acacia

Darwin River Dam

Batchelor
Woolaning

DELISSAVILLE WAGAIT LARRAKIA ABORIGINAL RESERVE

Finniss   River

STUART

ARNHEM

Bark Hut Inn

Mary

HIGHWAY

Cooinda

KAKADU

NATIONAL

PARK

KAKADU ABORIGINAL LAND TRUST

LITCHFIELD NP

Adelaide River

MARY RIVER NP (proposed)

Mary River

☎ (08) 8936 2499; www.tourismtopend.com.au

Must see, must do

► Feast on Asian delicacies at Mindil Beach Sunset Market

► Visit a crocodile park

► Take in the views at East Point

► Fish the pristine waters around Cobourg Peninsula

► Learn about the art and culture of the Tiwi Islanders

Fact File

When to go
The Territory's Top End is subject to a Wet/Dry tropical weather pattern. The dry season runs Apr—Oct, give or take a few weeks: temperatures sit fairly constantly in the thirties, but humidity and rainfall are low. During the Wet, the region experiences torrential rain and high humidity; roads flood frequently, and a 4WD vehicle is required to travel outside built-up areas. For further information contact the Bureau of Meteorology (BOM): 1900 926 124; www.bom.gov.au

Top coastal events
July *Darwin Rodeo and Country Music Festival*
July—Aug *Darwin to Ambon Yacht Race*
Sept *Festival of Darwin (arts, culture)*

Safety
Swimming Not a recommended activity anywhere along this coastline or in coastal estuaries: crocodiles are common year-round and marine stingers (box jellyfish) are prevalent during the Wet.

Boating Weather information is vital around this coastline since meteorological conditions can change dramatically and can also affect tidal information. Strong south-easterly winds can occur during the Dry, causing hazardous conditions for boaters. North-west monsoon winds during the Wet are often strong enough for gale warnings to be issued. For weather information and warnings contact BOM: 1300 659 214 (coastal waters); 1300 659 211

(cyclone warnings); www.bom.gov.au Darwin has some of Australia's biggest tides – up to 7 or 8 m; this means boats moored at ramps can be left high and dry. For tidal information, along with general marine safety information and boating regulations/requirements, contact the Dept of Infrastructure, Planning and Environment (DIPE): (08) 8999 5511; www.ipe.nt.gov.au General information is also available at the tourism site: www.fishingtheterritory.com.au

Road travel Some roads in this region are isolated and some are 4WD only; roads may be closed to traffic during the Wet. Travellers should carry adequate supplies and be self-sufficient. Seek local advice about road and weather conditions. For up-to-date road reports and information on closures contact DIPE: 1800 246 199; www.ipe.nt.gov.au

Restrictions/regulations
Fishing Licences are not required for recreational fishing in the NT, but regulations are in place to ensure the quality of recreational fishing is maintained. Worth noting are the restrictions that apply to the highly sought after barramundi: a bag limit of five and a minimum length of 55 cm. For further information contact NT Fisheries within the Dept of Business, Industry and Resource Development: (08) 8999 2144; www.fisheries.nt.gov.au Information is also available at the tourism site: www.fishingtheterritory.com.au

Garig Gunak Barlu NP Visitors to this park on the Cobourg Peninsula must apply for and purchase a permit. Apply well in advance by contacting Cobourg

CLIMATE												DARWIN
	J	F	M	A	M	J	J	A	S	O	N	D
Max °C	32	31	32	33	32	31	30	31	32	33	33	33
Min °C	25	25	24	24	22	20	19	21	23	25	25	25
Rain mm	406	349	311	97	21	1	1	7	19	74	143	232
Raindays	21	20	19	9	2	0	1	2	7	12	16

Peninsula Sanctuary and Marine Park Board: PO Box 469, Palmerston, NT 0831; (08) 8999 4814 (phone); (08) 8999 4524 (fax). Permits to the park allow drivers to traverse Arnhem Land, however, vehicles must travel straight through without stopping (a trip of five to six hours). For other travel to Arnhem Land contact the Northern Land Council: (08) 8920 5100; www.nlc.org.au

Kakadu NP Entry and camping fees apply; roads may be closed during the Wet.

Tiwi Islands Visitors must travel to the islands as part of an organised tour. For further details contact Tourism Top End: (08) 8936 2499; www.tourismtopend.com.au Camping anglers are permitted to stop overnight at six designated areas on Bathurst and Melville islands (three each); for information and permits contact the Amateur Fishermen's Association of the Northern Territory: (08) 8945 6455; www.afant.com.au

Darwin Wharf

Darwin
Darwin is built on a small peninsula that juts out into one of the finest harbours in northern Australia. The suburbs stretch away along a coastal strip of yellow beaches and sandstone cliffs, to the north and east. Beyond are reserves protecting this fascinating coastal landscape in a near-pristine condition.

Wharf and Esplanade
Darwin's massive wharf complex, at the foot of the CBD, has been revamped over the last two decades. Major shipping activity in Port Darwin now interacts with a vibrant restaurant and retail trade. Points of interest include the Australian Pearling Exhibition, where displays chart the history and growth of the lucrative pearling industry in northern Australia, and the Deckchair Cinema, where, during the Dry, patrons watch movies under a tropical sky as the sun sets across the water.

Around the corner, facing the water on the city's south-west side, is the Esplanade, fronted by the green expanse of Bicentennial Park. Here, extensive walking trails lead to lookout points with stunning views and a series of memorial sites, many commemorating events of World War II.

Saltwater crocodile

Saltwater crocodile facts

The saltwater or estuarine crocodile (*Crocodylus porosus*) is one of Australia's most feared animals – and with good reason: attacks on humans are frequent and often fatal. The adult male can reach 7 m in length, but averages 5 m.

The species is found throughout South-East Asia and northern Australia. Despite its large numbers in northern Australia, the species is listed as threatened; Australia, with its strong protection laws, represents the species' best chance of survival.

'Salties', as they are known, reside mostly in the tidal estuaries of the northern rivers but can be found hundreds of kilometres out to sea or, indeed, a couple of hundred kilometres upstream, lurking in freshwater billabongs and swamps.

Female crocodiles lay 50 eggs, which take 90 days to incubate. The sex of the hatchlings is determined by the incubation temperature. There is a less than 1 percent chance that all of the eggs will reach adulthood.

Despite their bad press, saltwater crocodiles are quiet, private creatures: they generally stay out of sight and underwater, unless hungry or threatened. To view in safety, visit Darwin Crocodile Farm or Crocodylus Park, both in the vicinity of Darwin.

Contacts

Visitor information

Darwin (Top End including Tiwi Islands)
cnr Mitchell and Knuckey sts
(08) 8936 2499 or
1300 138 886
www.tourismtopend.com.au

Parks and reserves

Charles Darwin NP
(08) 8947 2305

Garig Gunak Barlu NP
Permits and bookings
(08) 8999 4814
Black Point Ranger Station
(08) 8979 0244

Kakadu NP
(08) 8938 1121
www.deh.gov.au/parks/kakadu

Activities

Contact visitor information centres (see above) for details of activities, tours and charter services.

Wander past Old Admiralty House (1879) and Lyons Cottage (1925) where there is a museum with exhibits on the history of Darwin. At the northern end of the Esplanade, at Doctors Gully, is Aquascene, a very popular Darwin attraction: every day at high tide, hundreds of fish swim to shore to be fed by hand – operators instruct visitors on how to feed the fish and identify the many species.

Charles Darwin National Park

This 48 sq km reserve lies just 5 km from the centre of Darwin. It protects an area of wetland set within a maze of inlets, islands and bays, laced with 36 different species of mangrove. Shell middens testify to occupation by the area's original inhabitants, the Larrakia, while bunkers and storage units recall the World War II years, when Darwin was on the frontline of Australia's defence against the Japanese. There are walking and cycling trails, a lookout across the wetlands to the city, and picnic facilities; the park closes at 7 pm and camping is not permitted.

Fannie Bay

Fannie Bay arcs north–south along the western front of suburban Darwin. At the southern end is Cullen Bay Marina, the departure point for harbour cruises and ferries and a pleasant waterfront dining and retail precinct. The magnificent 42 ha Darwin Botanic Gardens, with its 1500-strong collection of tropical plant species, runs parallel to the coastline.

Mindil Beach, a 2 km ribbon of white sand, is where Darwinians come to fish, walk and watch the spectacular northern sunsets. It is also the site of one of Australia's most famous outdoor markets, the Mindil Beach Sunset Market. Here, every Thursday evening from late April to the end of October, thousands of people turn up to buy arts and crafts from the Top End and neighbouring Asia, indulge in New Age therapies and sample food from around the world.

At East Point Recreation Reserve, at the northern end of Fannie Bay, locals and visitors swim year-round in Lake Alexander. A short stretch of parkland, complete with bicycle trail, separates the lake from a seaside cove, beautiful to look at but not for swimming, particularly during the Wet when the marine stingers arrive. East Point is the site of the East Point Military Museum, which is housed in an old coastal battery, and recalls the grim days of World War II when, in 1942, 200 Japanese aircraft bombed Darwin, killing more than 200 people. The views here of the city and surrounding coastline are sensational.

Unfurling from the northern limit of suburban Darwin, the peaceful Casuarina Coastal Reserve features long white beaches, dunes, mangroves and monsoon vine thickets; explore via the foreshore bicycle and walking track.

Tiwi Islands

Sunset at Mindil Beach

Neighbouring Bathurst and Melville islands, also known as the Tiwi Islands, are the traditional home of the Tiwi people. Although part of the Northern Territory (they lie to the immediate north of Darwin), the islands, with a combined population of 3000, have their own land council and strong local government. The islands' economic mainstays are plantation timber, aquaculture, arts and crafts, and sustainable tourism. One- and two-day tours depart, by air, from Darwin. Visitors are able to explore the local environment – a tropical feast of rainforest, waterfalls and rugged coastline – learn something of Tiwi history and culture, and purchase art and craft objects including trademark batik and silk-screened clothing. The islands are a popular destination for self-sufficient anglers. Six beaches on Melville and Bathurst islands (three on each) have been designated for angler camping. Permits are essential and can be obtained from the Amateur Fishermen's Association of the Northern Territory (see *Fact File*, p. 252).

Arnhem Land

Arnhem Land occupies a huge swath of the Top End and is under the custodianship of several Aboriginal groups. The World Heritage-listed Kakadu National Park is open to all. The park takes in a sizeable chunk of the Van Diemen Gulf coastline, a sweep of flood plains and mighty river estuaries, teeming with birds and fish and myriad plant species. The easiest way to experience this

Darwin fishing

Some of the best blue-water fishing in Australia is available straight out of Darwin. You can fish from the shore or wharves of the city, take a dinghy and explore the coastal estuaries, mangroves and sandbars, with barramundi always the prize catch (watch for crocodiles), or join a charter to fish the fertile offshore waters for game and reef fish.

Left *Cobourg Peninsula*
Inset *Mangroves proliferate
along the Top End coastline*

otherwise difficult-to-access coastal landscape is on a cruise along the East Alligator River, departing from Border Store. The park has superb adventure opportunities for campers, walkers, anglers and nature lovers.

The rest of Arnhem Land, that is, most of it, spreads east from the rugged Arnhem Land plateau, which runs north to south for 500 km. Barely 15 000 people, mostly traditional owners, inhabit this near-pristine wilderness. Only a few places are open to general tourism. These include the Gove Peninsula (see *Gove Peninsula and the Gulf*, p. 256) and the Cobourg Peninsula (see below).

Cobourg Peninsula

Some 570 km north-east of Darwin (by road), the Cobourg Peninsula and its surrounding waters are protected by the 4500 sq km Garig Gunak Barlu National Park. The name is from the language of the four Iwaidja clan groups that share custodianship of the area: garig is a local language name; gunak means land; barlu means water. The park preserves a landscape of sandy beaches, dunes, red–gold cliffs, rainforest, lagoons, swamps, coral reefs and a rich marine life that includes dugongs and six species of marine turtles. Humans have occupied the peninsula for over 40 000 years, and the landscape is marked with sites of rich cultural and spiritual significance. Indonesian islanders traded with the Iwaidja for centuries. In the 1830s the British attempted to establish an outpost here; the ruins of

Victoria Settlement, accessible by boat or guided tour, are all that remain of their 11-year tenure.

Visitors come to Cobourg Peninsula for the extraordinary fishing opportunities in pristine waters and for the genuine adventure experience this undisturbed paradise offers. Access is strictly controlled. All visitors must apply for a permit (see *Fact File*, p. 252). Road access is 4WD only; drivers must apply for a permit well ahead of travelling as there are limits on the number of cars allowed to traverse Arnhem Land at any one time, and roads may close for ceremonial reasons; travellers also arrive by air and boat. Campsites are located at Black Point (BYO everything), where there is also a ranger station and general store; an upmarket eco-lodge is located at Cape Don.

People and art
of Arnhem Land

Arnhem Land was occupied by a dozen or so clans or language groups for at least 40 000 and possibly as many as 60 000 years prior to European settlement. The extraordinary rock art of the region is the most startling legacy of this long tenure. Around 5000 rock-art sites have been identified, the richest collection in the world. The coastal clans were among only a few groups in Australia to have contact with the outside world, which occurred through trade with fishermen from Sulawesi. The Europeans failed to penetrate the vast, remote reaches of Arnhem Land, although their comings and goings were recorded on the walls of the rock shelters. The land was declared an Aboriginal reserve in 1931 and today remains the preserve of Aboriginal groups. The rock art is best seen at a number of sites within Kakadu National Park (see *Contacts*, p. 253).

Gove Peninsula and the Gulf

This remote coastline traverses the eastern reaches of Arnhem Land and wide plains and rivers of the Gulf of Carpentaria. Sparsely populated and barely serviced, it is the terrain of 4WD adventurers, anglers and those interested in indigenous culture.

Gove Peninsula

The Aboriginal territory of Arnhem Land stretches from the border with Kakadu to the Territory's east coast, covering around 100 000 sq km of land. The Gove Peninsula, on the east coast, traditional home of the Yolngu, is the most accessible of the Arnhem communities. Its main town, Nhulunbuy, services a substantial mining industry, but locals extend a warm welcome to visitors who come for some of the best gamefishing in Australia, great diving, wildlife-watching and the opportunity to experience the rich Yolngu culture.

The coastline sweeps south to the state border, dipping into the remote heart of the Gulf Country – a place of vast, river-laced plains. The coast, a tangle of mangroves, swamps and overflowing waterways, is virtually inaccessible to all but the intrepid anglers who float their craft along the rivers, from base camps upstream, in the quest for that prized game fish, barramundi.

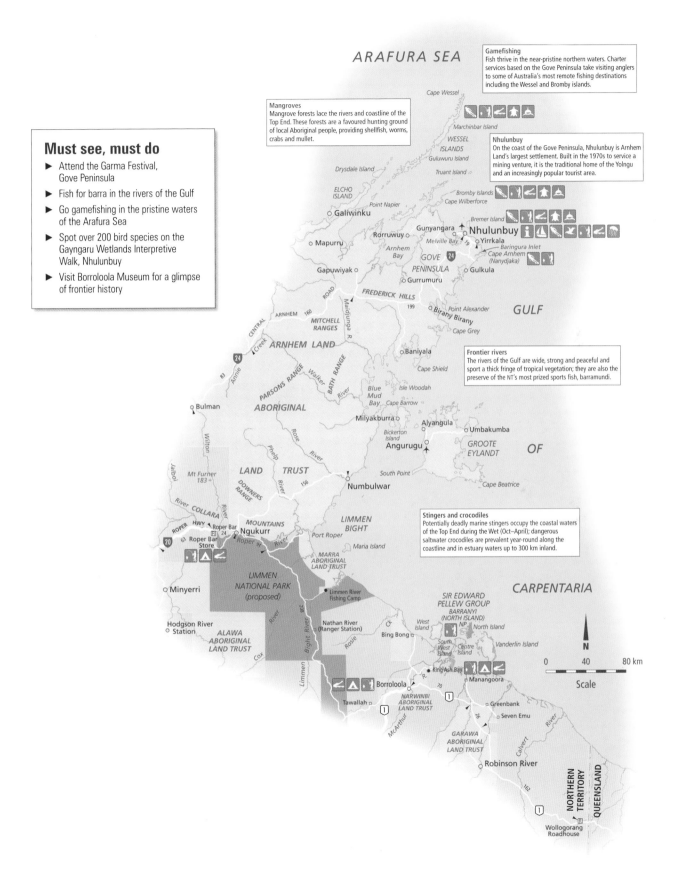

Must see, must do

► Attend the Garma Festival, Gove Peninsula

► Fish for barra in the rivers of the Gulf

► Go gamefishing in the pristine waters of the Arafura Sea

► Spot over 200 bird species on the Gayngaru Wetlands Interpretive Walk, Nhulunbuy

► Visit Borroloola Museum for a glimpse of frontier history

ARAFURA SEA

Gamefishing
Fish thrive in the near-pristine northern waters. Charter services based on the Gove Peninsula take visiting anglers to some of Australia's most remote fishing destinations including the Wessel and Bromby islands.

Mangroves
Mangrove forests lace the rivers and coastline of the Top End. These forests are a favoured hunting ground of local Aboriginal people, providing shellfish, worms, crabs and mullet.

Nhulunbuy
On the coast of the Gove Peninsula, Nhulunbuy is Arnhem Land's largest settlement. Built in the 1970s to service a mining venture, it is the traditional home of the Yolngu and an increasingly popular tourist area.

Frontier rivers
The rivers of the Gulf are wide, strong and peaceful and sport a thick fringe of tropical vegetation; they are also the preserve of the NT's most prized sports fish, barramundi.

Stingers and crocodiles
Potentially deadly marine stingers occupy the coastal waters of the Top End during the Wet (Oct–April); dangerous saltwater crocodiles are prevalent year-round along the coastline and in estuary waters up to 300 km inland.

CARPENTARIA

Cape Wessel

Marchinbar Island

WESSEL ISLANDS

Guluwuru Island

Drysdale Island

Truant Island

ELCHO ISLAND

Point Napier

Galiwinku

Mapurru

Rorruwuy

Gunyangara

Bromby Islands
Cape Wilberforce

Bremer Island

Nhulunbuy
Yirrkala

Melville Bay

Arnhem Bay

GOVE PENINSULA

Baringura Inlet
Cape Arnhem
(Nanydjaka)

Gapuwiyak

Gulkula

Gurrumuru

FREDERICK HILLS

Point Alexander

Birany Birany

GULF

Cape Grey

ARNHEM LAND

MITCHELL RANGES

Maidjunga R.

199

160

ROAD

CENTRAL ARNHEM

Baniyala

Cape Shield

Bulman

PARSONS RANGE

BATH RANGE

Walker River

Isle Woodah

Blue Mud Bay

Cape Barrow

ABORIGINAL

Milyakburra

Alyangula

Umbakumba

83

Annie Creek

Wilton

Rose River

Bickerton Island

Angurugu

GROOTE EYLANDT

OF

LAND

TRUST

Phelp River

156

South Point

Cape Beatrice

Mt Furner 183

DOWNERS RANGE

Numbulwar

River COLLARA

Jalboi

Roper Bar

Roper Bar Store

Ngukurr

MOUNTAINS

Roper 91 River

LIMMEN BIGHT

Port Roper

Maria Island

MARRA ABORIGINAL LAND TRUST

Minyerri

LIMMEN NATIONAL PARK (proposed)

Limmen River Fishing Camp

SIR EDWARD PELLEW GROUP

BARRANYI (NORTH ISLAND) NP

North Island

CARPENTARIA

Hodgson River Station

ALAWA ABORIGINAL LAND TRUST

Cox River

Limmen Bight River

Nathan River (Ranger Station)

Rosie River

Bing Bong

West Island

South West Island

Centre Island

Vanderlin Island

Borroloola

Tawallah

NARWINBI ABORIGINAL LAND TRUST

King Ash Bay

Manangoora

0   40   80 km

Scale

N

McArthur River

GARAWA ABORIGINAL LAND TRUST

Greenbank

Seven Emu

River

Robinson River

Calvert River

162

NORTHERN TERRITORY

QUEENSLAND

Wollogorang Roadhouse

Fact File

When to go
The territory's Top End is subject to a Wet/Dry tropical weather pattern. The Dry, by far the preferred touring season, runs Apr–Nov, give or take a few weeks: temperatures sit in the thirties but humidity and rainfall are low. During the Wet, the region experiences torrential rain and high humidity; roads flood frequently, and a 4WD vehicle is required to travel outside built-up areas. For further information contact the Bureau of Meteorology (BOM): 1900 926 124; www.bom.gov.au

Top coastal events
Easter *Borroloola Fishing Classic*
August *Garma Festival* (indigenous culture, Gove Peninsula)

Safety
Swimming Not a recommended activity anywhere along this coastline or in coastal estuaries: crocodiles are common year-round and marine stingers (box jellyfish) are prevalent during the Wet.

Diving As above. Team up with an experienced charter service – this area is not a place to dive independently.

Boating Strong south-easterly winds can occur during the Dry, causing hazardous conditions for boaters. North-west monsoon winds during the Wet are often strong enough for gale warnings to be issued. Boaters

need to be aware of the high risk of cyclones during this season. For weather information and warnings contact BOM: 1300 659 214 (coastal waters); 1300 659 211 (cyclone warnings); www.bom.gov.au For tidal information, along with general marine safety information and boating regulations, contact the Dept of Infrastructure, Planning and Environment (DIPE): (08) 8999 5511; www.ipe.nt.gov.au

Road travel Most roads in this region are isolated and suitable only for 4WD vehicles; roads may be closed to traffic during the Wet. Travel across traditional Aboriginal land may require a permit (see *Restrictions/regulations*, below). Travellers should carry adequate supplies and be self-sufficient. Seek local advice about road and weather conditions. For up-to-date road reports and information on closures contact DIPE: 1800 246 199; www.ipe.nt.gov.au

Restrictions/regulations
Fishing Licences are not required for recreational fishing in the NT but a range of regulations are in place to ensure the quality of recreational fishing is maintained. Worth noting are the restrictions that apply to the highly sought after barramundi: a bag limit of five and a minimum length of 55 cm. For further information contact NT Fisheries within the Dept of Business, Industry and Resource Development: (08) 8999 2144; www.fisheries.nt.gov.au Information

CLIMATE											NHULUNBUY	
	J	F	M	A	M	J	J	A	S	O	N	D
Max °C	32	32	31	31	31	29	29	29	30	31	32	32
Min °C	25	25	25	24	23	21	20	20	21	23	25	26
Rain mm	251	239	244	255	75	20	15	4	3	7	25	194
Raindays	16	16	16	13	9	5	5	2	1	1	2	10

on fishing is also available at the tourism site: www.fishingtheterritory.com.au Crocodiles pose a threat to both land-based and boat anglers; for safety tips see *Taking Care*, p. 260.

Arnhem Land Visitors must purchase a permit to travel across Arnhem Land. Apply to the Northern Land Council well in advance of travelling: (08) 8920 5100; www.nlc.org.au Communities may close roads at short notice for funerals and other ceremonies. Visitors are not permitted to travel by road to the communities along the northern coastline (travel by air).

Gove Peninsula Permits are not required to visit the town of Nhulunbuy, but they are required for travel to surrounding areas, including the beaches. There is a permit office in town; contact the Dhimurru Land Management Aboriginal Corporation: (08) 8987 3992.

Gove Peninsula

The vast plains of the Gulf coastline

The Gove Peninsula is the traditional land of the Yolngu. The Yolngu comprise 13 clan groups who speak Yolngu Matha, the Aboriginal language that covers the area roughly from Blue Mud Bay in the south and Wessel Islands in the north. The main township, Nhulunbuy, population 4000, was built in the early 1970s to service Nabalco's bauxite mining and alumina processing venture.

During the Dry, visitors can travel along the Central Arnhem Road to reach the peninsula. The trip takes about 12 hours from Katherine along a

Left *Lilies clog some rivers of the Territory*
Inset *Flatback turtles are one of the Top End's many reptile species*

Contacts

Visitor information

Borroloola and the Gulf
www.grtpa.com.au

Darwin (Gove Peninsula)
cnr Mitchell and Knuckey sts
(08) 8936 2499 or
1300 138 886
www.tourismtopend.com.au

Katherine (The Gulf)
cnr Lindsay St and Katherine Tce
(08) 8972 2650
www.krta.com.au

Nhulunbuy and Gove Peninsula
(08) 8987 1985
www.ealta.org

Activities

Contact visitor information centres (see above) for details of activities, tours and charter services.

4WD track (apply for a permit from the Northern Land Council, see *Fact File,* opposite); flights are also available. There is a range of accommodation in Nhulunbuy. Visitors wishing to access the recreational reserves around Nhulunbuy, including the beaches, must apply locally for a permit (see *Fact File,* opposite).

Fishing tops the list of activities on the peninsula (see *Fishing the east coast,* right). There are two beautiful beaches near Nhulunbuy and many others around the peninsula; the Gove Yacht Club, which welcomes visitors, looks out over tranquil Melville Bay. Local charters run diving tours to the surrounding islands and reefs; waiting to be explored are complex coral gardens, drop-offs and an amazingly rich and complex marine life population that includes turtles, sharks, stingrays and colourful reef fish. There is good snorkelling – and fishing – at Baringura and Nanydjak (Cape Arnhem). The Gayngaru Wetlands Interpretive Walk in Nhulunbuy explores a lagoon wetland, which extends 7 km along the coastline and is home to over 200 species of birds. The settlement of Yirrkala, about 15 km south-east of Nhulunbuy, has an outstanding collection of bark paintings. The Garma Festival, a major cultural event, takes place each year at Gulkula, 30 km south-west of Yirrkala.

The Gulf

Flat plains and swollen rivers are the landscape features here, along with mangrove forests and paperbark swamps, clumps of pandanus and billabongs bobbing with waterlilies. A handful of small settlements are linked by an unsealed (4WD) road. The Gulf's coastal geography of myriad inlets clogged with vegetation confounded explorers Ludwig Leichhardt and Burke and Wills and remains virtually inaccessible today – except by boat.

Roper Bar, a sealed section of road across the Roper River, separates the fresh water upstream from the brackish water downstream. The river is over 100 m wide at this point and flanked by paperbarks. About 3 km from the crossing is Roper Bar Store, where you can buy fuel and supplies, camp and organise fishing trips along the river.

Borroloola, 453 km south, sits alongside the McArthur River. The town, settled in 1885, is on Narwinbi Aboriginal Land, but permits are not required. It is known for its excellent barramundi fishing; the Borroloola Fishing Classic, held each Easter, fills the small town to bursting point. There is a range of accommodation and a couple of fishing tour operators; popular are tours to the offshore waters of the Sir Edward Pellew Group, incorporating Barranyi National Park, about 15 km from the McArthur River estuary. Make time to visit Borroloola Museum, housed in the 1886 police station.

Fishing the east coast

The rich waters of the Gove region rate among the best light-to-medium sportfishing areas of Australia. Spanish mackerel, coral trout, sailfish and marlin abound. Key offshore spots include the Wessel Islands, Bromby Islands and Bremer Island.

The rivers of the Gulf are mostly fished near the coast, with anglers taking advantage of the option of fresh- and saltwater fishing, depending on the season. The target fish is barramundi, Australia's premier native sport fish. Barramundi can weigh up to 50 kg, although they average 6 kg.

Taking Care

safety and environment

For all its superlative beauty, the Australian coastline is environmentally fragile and can be dangerous. But by being aware and implementing some precautionary practices, beachgoers can help protect their surroundings and themselves.

Personal Safety

Sun and Heat Exposure

Over-exposure to the sun is dangerous but can be avoided by taking the following precautions.

- Always use an umbrella, shade or tent for a day at the beach.
- Apply sunscreen (30+) every two hours. A high factor sunscreen will provide 96 percent protection against harmful UV rays but should be used in conjunction with shade and adequate clothing.
- Wear a shady hat and sunglasses; check the sunglasses when purchasing to ensure they comply with Australian standards.
- Wear suitable clothing: between swims, put on a long-sleeved top or shirt; dress children in protective bathing suits – many have long sleeves.

Extreme heat is a fact of life in many areas of Australia. If you intend to travel to a hot area of the continent, plan your trip to coincide with the cooler months (April to November). In hot conditions, try to avoid the outdoors between 11 am and 3 pm, and drink plenty of water.

Swimming

Australia has 10 000 beaches and only a tiny fraction of these are patrolled. Patrolled beaches are common in the suburbs of cities and around major holiday towns. Rural beaches will generally have patrols on weekends and public holidays. For details contact the relevant surf lifesaving association (see *Useful Numbers*, p. 267). Observe the following tips.

- Swim between the flags. The yellow and red flags mark the safe areas to swim. Look back to the beach regularly to check that you are still between the flags.
- Whenever possible, swim at beaches patrolled by lifesavers.
- Read and obey all warning signs.
- If unsure about conditions, check with a lifesaver. In an unpatrolled area, seek local advice.
- Never swim alone.
- Always supervise children when they are in the water. Explain to children the difference between swimming in the ocean and in a pool.
- Never run or dive into water, even if you have checked the depth.

How to identify **rips**

A rip is a strong current running out to sea from a surf beach. It can carry you out very quickly. A rip is created when water from broken waves flows back to the sea in channels between sandbanks. Rips can be extremely powerful and even strong swimmers find it hard to swim against them. If you are caught in a rip, swim across it, not against it. Try and determine the shortest distance to a safe area, and swim to that area, keeping parallel to the shore. Swim into shore only when you are clear of the rip.

If you are not a strong swimmer, remember the three Rs: relax, raise your arm, wait to be rescued. To identify a rip, look for the following:

- water discoloured by sand
- foam on the water's surface beyond the beach area
- waves breaking further out (usually on either side of the rip)
- debris floating out to sea
- an area of rippled water amid calm water.

- Do not swim for half an hour after eating.
- Do not swim under the influence of drugs or alcohol.
- If you get into trouble, stay calm: relax, raise your arm for help and float on your back.

Above *Supervising children on the beach*
Opposite *Surf lifesavers, Bondi Beach*

Boating

Regulations dealing with boating safety vary from state to state. Contact the relevant authority (see *Useful Numbers*, p. 267) for information on registration, required safety equipment and boat operator licensing; these authorities can also provide tidal charts, updated weather forecasts, information on the location of boat ramps and a copy of international boating rules.

Make sure you use a vessel that suits the conditions. Small craft should not be used in rough water. Spend enough time in calm conditions to familiarise yourself with your boat's capabilities before venturing into rough and/or open water. Shallow, seemingly protected waters – estuaries, bays, large lakes – can become extremely choppy in windy conditions. Offshore boating demands a larger boat, more experience and a greater level of preparedness to cope with the risks involved.

Entrances between estuaries and the ocean – known as bars – are notoriously hazardous for boats. Anglers in boats under 4 m should only attempt bar crossings in calm conditions; boats of 5 or 6 m are a realistic offshore size. Check weather conditions ahead of going out – local radio, the Bureau of Meteorology and state boating organisations have up-to-date information (see *Useful Numbers*, p. 267). Observe the following basic boat-safety tips.

- Check your vessel's equipment and fittings before every journey.
- Make sure you are aware of the relevant state's minimum safety equipment requirements.

- Make sure your engine is serviced regularly.
- A marine radio is an essential safety item. An Emergency Position Indicator Radio Beacon (EPIRB) is also a good idea; this device costs just a few hundred dollars and can be activated in the case of distress – the signal is then relayed to search and rescue authorities.
- Make sure you have sufficient supplies of food and water and extra in case of an emergency.
- Stow all gear securely.
- Remember that it is always colder on the water and the sun is stronger; carry extra waterproof gear and sunscreen.
- Take a first-aid kit.
- Always tell someone reliable where you are going and when you expect to be back.

Rock-fishing

Rock-fishing can be hazardous, and anglers need to take some basic steps to ensure their own safety.

- Be aware of swell sizes, changing tides and weather conditions. Avoid fishing in places that become cut-off when the tide rises.
- Before fishing, watch the sea for about 20 minutes to get a sense of the size of the waves.
- Plan an escape route in case you fall in. If you do fall in, swim away from the rocks and look for a safe place to swim ashore or float until help arrives.
- Wear suitable footwear.
- Fish in the presence of other anglers.
- Seek local advice about dangerous areas.

Surfing

The best surf is often found at remote and unpatrolled areas; in these instances surfers are responsible for their own safety. Avoid putting yourself and others at risk by observing the following tips.

- If you are inexperienced, take lessons.
- Always surf with someone else.
- Only surf if you can swim 200 m through turbulent water without tiring.
- Check conditions thoroughly before entering the water: listen to weather reports, talk to locals and watch the water carefully for rips and currents.
- Pick out a landmark – a tree or headland – and use it to maintain your position.
- Avoid collisions by paddling clear of the take-off area.

Children surfing at Port Elliot, South Australia

- Practise courtesy to your fellow surfers to avoid scuffles over territory.
- Avoid areas where local surfers are known to be aggressive.

Diving

Scuba diving is a highly regulated activity in Australia. A strict rating system applies, based on the experience of the individual diver, which is determined by the number of diving hours he or she has accrued. Reputable operators adhere to this system and will not take inexperienced divers to inappropriate sites. The following are a few key points to remember.

- Only scuba dive if you have completed an accredited course.
- No matter what your level, if you are entering unfamiliar waters always dive with a local diver.
- Before diving, ensure you have the correct equipment for the conditions. Seek expert advice if you are diving in an area you are unfamiliar with.
- Check that all your equipment is in good working order before every dive.
- Make sure your wetsuit is suitable for the conditions.
- Check the weather forecast and also assess the weather and the dive site before entering the water.
- When diving from a boat, it is always best to dive with a buddy. Fly a dive flag and make sure someone stays to mind the boat.
- Have contact details and emergency numbers available and have a plan in case of an emergency.

There are numerous safety and personal health issues associated with diving. For details contact the member-based organisation, Divers Alert Network (DAN), listed under *Useful Numbers*, p. 267.

Dangerous Creatures

The Australian coastline is home to a variety of dangerous and even deadly creatures. Swimmers, surfers and divers should check conditions with locals before entering the water. This is particularly so in remote areas or places where there are no beach patrols.

Marine stingers (box jellyfish) There are two species of dangerous marine stingers found in Australia's tropical waters north from Agnes Water in Queensland to Exmouth in Western Australia. The highly venomous chironex and the less common irukandji are usually found in coastal waters from October to May. Many popular beaches in northern Queensland have a stinger resistant enclosure for swimmers. It is not safe to swim at other places. Observe signs and heed local warnings. In case of a sting, seek immediate medical aid. Douse the sting in vinegar. Ice packs can be applied to relieve pain but do not rub. CPR may be required – a severe attack can slow down or stop breathing or cause heart failure.

Sharks Sharks are unpredictable and little is known about why they occasionally attack humans. There are dangerous sharks in many of Australia's coastal waters. Many species will attack without killing, but the larger, faster species, notably tiger sharks and white sharks, are proven killers. Take precautions to avoid possible shark attack by swimming in patrolled areas, swimming with others, avoiding discoloured water and leaving the water before sunset.

Above Overseas visitors take diving lessons on the Great Barrier Reef Below Marine stinger warning notice, Queensland

The dangerous saltwater crocodile

Sea snakes There are around 21 species of sea snakes (marine reptiles) in Australia's tropical waters. Some species have a powerful venom that is dangerous to humans. Sea snakes can usually be recognised by their paddle-like tail. They can be inquisitive and aggressive if handled or trodden on, so stay well away from them. Anti-venom is available. Seek medical advice immediately if bitten.

Stonefish Stonefish are found in the tropics, usually around shallow coral and rocks or camouflaged in mud and sand. The brownish–green fish has 13 venomous dorsal spines, which can cause a painful sting when pressure is applied. The venom can be lethal. Avoid contact by wearing sturdy sandshoes around the water; it is best not to turn rocks or pick up coral. Seek medical advice immediately if stung.

Blue-ringed octopus These small creatures, about the size of a golf ball when fully grown, are common on shallow coral reefs and in rock pools around Australia. They are pale brown to yellow in colour, but electric blue rings light up when the octopus is threatened. The beak can bite through a wet suit; although the bite might be painless, the highly toxic venom can cause paralysis. Definitely do not touch. There is no known antidote. Seek medical advice immediately if bitten.

Crocodiles Two varieties are found in northern Australia: man-eating saltwater (estuarine) crocodiles and the less dangerous freshwater species. Saltwater crocodiles are found in tidal estuaries but can travel to freshwater areas, sometimes as far as 300 km upstream, as well as up to 100 km out to sea. Freshwater crocodiles are much smaller, with a long narrow snout, but they can be aggressive if mating or protecting their young. They are found in tropical rivers. Both varieties are well camouflaged. Be crocodile-wise:

- heed local warning signs
- take special care in tidal estuaries
- avoid swimming, paddling or camping near water in crocodile-infested areas
- anglers should avoid wading into rivers or leaning out of boats in crocodile-prone areas.

Remote Driving

Many areas described in this book are remote and good planning is needed to ensure a safe trip. Different areas present different hazards: the northern tropical regions, for example, are subject to monsoon conditions during the Wet (October/November to April), at which time roads flood. When planning a journey to a remote spot, consider the following.

- Are all the roads sealed? If not, will a 4WD vehicle be required?
- Do long distances separate places where supplies, including petrol, are available?
- Will it be necessary to carry extra water?
- Are roads likely to close? If this is a possibility, do you know how and where to get information on closures?
- Is there accommodation available en route? If not, are there places to camp?
- Will a communications device be needed? Services are improving, but mobile-phone coverage of remote areas is still poor. A satellite phone could be a good idea. For emergency use, carry an EPIRB (see *Boating*, p. 262).

- Are you covered in the event of a breakdown? What are the limits of your coverage? Motoring organisations in each state provide emergency roadside assistance for a small yearly fee (check where assistance is available). Join the organisation in your state (RACV, NRMA, etc) and enjoy reciprocal membership rights across the country.

Bushwalking

Around Australia there are sensational coastal walking routes, some of which are known the world over, such as the walks across Freycinet Peninsula in Tasmania and Wilsons Promontory in Victoria. These popular walks take in very remote areas. Avoid danger by following a few simple rules.

- If walking in a national park or other reserve, seek advice from park staff and advise them of your route.
- Advise a friend or relative of your itinerary.
- Walk with other people or join a tour.
- In very remote areas, carry an EPIRB (see *Boating*, p. 262) – remember that in remote areas a mobile phone is unlikely to work.
- Carry good wet- and cold-weather gear. Even at the height of summer, coastal conditions can change dramatically.
- Find out about facilities available at campsites en route. Are water and wood supplied? Are fires allowed? Are there showers and toilets? Are bookings necessary?

Conservation and Special Areas

Coastal Care

Australia's coastal waters are amazingly diverse: they contain thousands of species of fish, hundreds of species of coral and a plethora of rare and unique marine ecosystems. The country's 10 000 or so beaches, many of them remote and unspoilt, provide endless opportunities for escape and leisure. It would be a mistake to take it all for granted. Industry, forestry, shipping, fishing, population expansion and, yes, tourism, place enormous pressure on what is essentially a very fragile environment. Caring for the coast is a shared responsibility. Every effort towards conservation, no matter how small, makes a difference. There are many ways of helping ensure the coast remains a place we can all enjoy for many years to come.

Above Coastal walking *requires care and planning*
Below Turtles *are one of Australia's endangered marine species*

First **aid**

If you are planning to spend a lot of time around water, first-aid training will be indispensable. Hundreds of lives, many of them children's, are saved each year by the administration of basic first aid. It is also advisable to carry a first-aid kit. Basic kits that cover most minor accidents are widely available at places like camping stores. Specialty kits, designed for particular environments and/or types of travel, are best purchased through St John Ambulance Australia (see *Useful Contacts*, p. 267), which also offers first-aid training.

- Dispose of fats and oils carefully. If you tip them down the sink, they end up in the ocean.
- Clean up after your dog; dog droppings on the beach are a major problem; droppings on the street wash into our oceans (thousands of tonnes a year).

Shipwreck heritage

Around 6500 shipwrecks lie strewn in Australia's coastal waters. The Commonwealth's Historic Shipwreck Act of 1976 protects historic wrecks and associated relics in coastal waters, while complementary state and territory legislation provide protection for wrecks in rivers, harbours and bays. All wrecks more than 75 years old are automatically protected, and many more recent wrecks are covered by special declaration. Divers can use many wreck sites for recreational purposes but must not damage or remove any part of the wreck. In a small number of cases, wrecks lie protected within a no-entry zone; in these cases divers must apply for a special permit. Contact the Commonwealth Department of the Environment and Heritage (see *Useful Numbers*, opposite); its website provides links to the various state departments.

- Place cigarette butts in a bin. Left on the beach or on the street, they can be washed out to sea.
- If camping, do not use soaps and detergents in creeks or rivers.
- When camping or at the beach, take all your own litter away and pick up litter left by other people.
- Avoid taking glass bottles to the beach; they are an environmental and safety hazard.
- Stick to tracks when walking and driving. Crossing sand dunes either on foot or in your car can damage the dunes and the surrounding fragile vegetation.
- Do not remove sea life from beaches, rocks or, if diving, underwater.
- Do not park you car on the beach or drive on the beach unless there are signs stating explicitly that these activities are allowed.
- Be aware of fishing regulations set down by the states and territories. These regulations apply to size and number of fish, types of equipment and often specify bans on catching certain species or fishing at particular times of the year (see *Fact File* in each region).
- When fishing, limit your catch: only keep what you can eat – release the rest.
- If you use a boat with an engine, make sure it is well-serviced and not leaking oil.
- Choose an operator, charter-boat service or tour-guide service with a stated commitment to protecting the environment. If in doubt, ask.

Marine Parks and Reserves

Australia has a large number of reserves protecting coastal areas; many are overseen by the relevant state or territory and a handful are the responsibility of the Commonwealth. The reserves range from tiny conservation zones protecting activity in a single bay, beach or estuary (such as regulations governing whale-watching in Hervey Bay) to vast marine parks such as those protecting the Great Australian Bight and the Great Barrier Reef. In most cases, normal recreational activities are permitted. However, there may be specific restrictions in some zones relating to certain types of fishing equipment or protecting threatened or rare species. In large areas like the Great Barrier Reef, the regulations are complex and vary from zone to zone (detailed GBR charts are available, or seek local advice from authorities). In a small number of places around Australia, fishing is banned; in others, there are laws limiting access to the waterfront. (There is specific information in the *Fact File* section of each region within this book.) Signage, particularly in major tourist areas, often indicates what you can and cannot do. The national park authorities in each state usually have jurisdiction over these areas (see *Useful Numbers*, opposite).

Snorkellers and divers are encouraged to protect coral reefs

National Parks

National parks protect extensive coastal areas around Australia. Each state and territory administers its own parks; a handful of parks are administered by the federal body, Parks Australia. In some states, permits are required to visit parks; these can be purchased at park gates or regional park offices. Many national parks allow camping (fees often apply). In a number of popular places campsites are available by ballot, or by booking well in advance. There are a few regulations that apply universally to national parks around Australia.

- Firearms and pets are not allowed.
- All flora and fauna and cultural and heritage sites are protected; items are not to be disturbed or removed.
- Visitors must stay on walking and vehicle tracks.
- Fires should only be lit as directed, most often in fireplaces provided. In some cases, open fires are not permitted at all.
- If the park allows firewood to be collected, use only fallen, dead timber for this purpose.

Aboriginal Land

Aboriginal land is privately owned land, and Aboriginal communities, like other landowners, can grant or refuse permission to people wanting to enter their land. Potential visitors must apply to the relevant authority for a permit. More popular tourist areas, such as Cobourg Peninsula in the Northern Territory (see *Darwin and Cobourg Peninsula*, p. 250) have a streamlined application system; in other areas, permits can take much longer. Allow adequate time before a trip to make sure you have the permits required. Where travel to Aboriginal land is described in this book, details of how to apply for a permit are set out in the *Fact File* of the relevant region. Transit permits are available to people wanting to travel along public roads that traverse Aboriginal land. Private roads on Aboriginal land may close at short notice for ceremonies and other local events. Visitors are asked to respect the wishes of the local community in regard to activities such as fishing, camping, walking and visiting special sites.

Useful Numbers

Emergency
Police, ambulance and fire dial 000
Mobile users dial 112

First aid
St John Ambulance
1300 360 455

Swimmer safety
Surf Life Saving Queensland
(07) 3846 8000
www.lifesaving.org.au

Surf Life Saving New South Wales
(02) 9984 7188
www.surflifesaving.com.au

Surf Life Saving Victoria
(03) 9534 8201
www.surflifesaver.com.au

Surf Life Saving Tasmania
(03) 6272 7788
www.slst.asn.au

Surf Life Saving South Australia
(08) 8354 6900
www.surfrescue.com.au

Surf Life Saving Western Australia
(08) 9244 1222
www.mybeach.com.au

Marine safety
Maritime Safety Queensland
(07) 3253 4500
www.transport.qld.gov.au

New South Wales Waterways Authority
(02) 9563 8556
www.waterways.nsw.gov.au

Marine Safety Victoria
(03) 9655 3399
www.marinesafety.vic.gov.au

Marine and Safety Tasmania
(03) 6233 8801
www.mast.tas.gov.au

Transport South Australia
1300 360 067
www.transportsa.gov.au

Department for Planning and Infrastructure, Western Australia
(08) 9216 8000
www.dpi.wa.gov.au

Department of Infrastructure, Planning and Environment (NT)
(08) 8999 5511
www.ipe.nt.gov.au

Bureau of Meteorology
Directory of all services
1900 926 113
www.bom.gov.au

Marine forecasts Australia-wide
1900 955 370

Australian three-month seasonal outlook
1900 926 162

Safe surfing
www.coastalwatch.com.au

Safe diving
Divers Alert Network (DAN)
(03) 9886 9166
www.danseap.org

Sun protection
SunSmart (Cancer Council)
www.sunsmart.com.au

Historic shipwrecks
Department of the Environment and Heritage (Commonwealth)
(02) 6274 2116
www.deh.gov.au/heritage/shipwrecks

Parks and marine reserves
Queensland Parks and Wildlife Service
(07) 3227 8185
www.epa.qld.gov.au

New South Wales National Parks and Wildlife Service
1300 361 967
www.nationalparks.nsw.gov.au

Parks Victoria
13 1963
www.parkweb.vic.gov.au

Tasmania Parks and Wildlife Service
1300 135 513
www.parks.tas.gov.au

Department for Environment and Heritage, South Australia
(08) 8124 4700
www.environment.sa.gov.au

Department of Conservation and Land Management, Western Australia
(08) 9334 0333
www.naturebase.net

Parks and Wildlife Commission of the Northern Territory
(08) 8999 5511
www.nt.gov.au/ipe/pwcnt

Index

The first section of this index (see below) is a listing of places; it includes towns, visitor attractions, water features and landforms, and national parks and other reserves. The second section of the index (see p. 276) lists activities, such as surfing and fishing, and special coastal attractions, such as beaches and whales.

The following abbreviations and contractions are used in the index:

JBT	– Jervis Bay Territory	SA	– South Australia
NSW	– New South Wales	Tas	– Tasmania
NT	– Northern Territory	Vic	– Victoria
Qld	– Queensland	WA	– Western Australia

Places

Activities and attractions

*Activities and coastal sites and attractions, such as beaches, birds, lighthouses and shipwrecks, appear in **bold** in the index below. For a summary of Australia's best coastal features, activities and attractions, go to Best of the Coast, pp. 1–29*

Acknowledgements

EXECUTIVE EDITORS
Astrid Browne, Explore Australia Publishing
Averil Moffat, Australian Geographic

SERIES EDITORS
Margaret Barca
Ingrid Ohlsson

PROJECT EDITOR
Ingrid Ohlsson

DESIGN
Peter Dyson, P.A.G.E. Pty Ltd

LAYOUT
P.A.G.E. Pty Ltd

CARTOGRAPHY
Will Pringle, Australian Geographic

ADDITIONAL CARTOGRAPHY
Chris Crook, Country Cartographics
Paul de Leur, Explore Australia Publishing

PICTURE RESEARCH
Chrissie Goldrick, Australian Geographic

ADDITIONAL PICTURE RESEARCH
Rachel Pitts, Explore Australia Publishing

COPY EDITOR
Kate Daniel

PROOFREADER
Nina Paine

INDEX
Fay Donlevy

PRE-PRESS
Digital Imaging Group Pty Ltd

RESEARCH AND PHOTOGRAPHIC ASSISTANCE
The publisher would like to thank the following organisations for their assistance with research and/or the provision of photographs:

Bureau of Meteorology
Lord Howe Island Visitor Centre
South Australian Tourism Commission
Tourism New South Wales
Tourism Queensland
Tourism Tasmania
Tourism Victoria

PHOTOGRAPHY CREDITS

COVER
Ningaloo Reef *Andrew Gregory*

BACK COVER
(top to bottom)
Cape Peron *Andrew Gregory*
Snorkelling, Cocos (Keeling) Islands *Don Fuchs (Australian Geographic)*
Seals, Sir Joseph Banks Group of Islands *Peter Aitchison (Australian Geographic)*

ENDPAPERS & COVER FLAPS
The Coorong *Nick Rains*
Leeuwin–Naturaliste National Park *Brett Dennis (Lochman Transparencies)*

HALF-TITLE PAGE & TITLE PAGE
Coastline near Broome *Andrew Gregory*
North Stradbroke Island *Andrew Gregory*

CONTENTS
(first page, top to bottom)
Byron Bay *Andrew Gregory*
Humpback whale, Hervey Bay *Tourism Queensland*
Snorkelling, Great Barrier Reef *Nick Rains*

(second page, clockwise from top left)
Port Campbell National Park *John Meier*
Surfer near Perth *Mike Langford (Auscape)*
Hatchling turtles off the Darwin coast *Jiri Lochman (Australian Geographic)*

(third page, top to bottom)
Cape Byron Lighthouse *Tourism New South Wales*
Fishing off Lord Howe Island *Grahame McConnell (Australian Geographic)*
Netting the catch, Fleurieu Peninsula *Christo Reid*

EDGE OF PARADISE
Nullarbor Plain *Ted Mead*

BEST OF THE COAST
Page 1 TQ; 2 JM; 3 JF (Ausc); Dick Smith (Aus Geo); 5 JF (Ausc); 6–7 NR (Aus Geo); 8 DF (Aus Geo); 9 DF (Aus Geo); 10 BB (Aus Geo); 11 Ern Mainka; 12 JL (Aus Geo); 13 Jon Poyner; 14 Mark Simmons (Oceanwide Images); 15 Bill Boyle (Oceanwide Images); 16–17 Stuart Hutchison; 18 JM; 19 Rachel Pitts; 20 DF (Aus Geo); 21 Mark Spencer (Aus Geo); 22 DF (Aus Geo); 23 TQ; 24 PA (Aus Geo); 25 DF (Aus Geo); 26 Steve Ryan; 27 Mike Langford (Ausc); 28 DF (Aus Geo); 29 George Apostolidis (TT); 30–1 AG.

QUEENSLAND
Page 32 JF (Ausc); 33 TQ; 34 TQ; 36 TQ; 37 Geoff Taylor; 38 (top) DF, (bottom) AG; 40 (top) DF, (bottom) TQ; 42 JF (Ausc); 44 TQ; 45 AG; 46 JF (Ausc); 47 TQ; 48 TQ, (inset) PA (Aus Geo); 50 JM; 52 MM (Aus Geo); 53 TQ; 54 TQ; 55 TQ; 56–7 AG; 58 BB (Aus Geo), (inset) Kevin Deacon (Aus Geo); 60 NR; 61 DF; 62 TQ; 64 MM (Aus Geo); 65 (main and inset) TQ; 66 (top) TQ; (bottom) MM (Aus Geo); 67 AG; 68 DF; 70 MM (Aus Geo); 71 TQ; 72 DF; 73 (top) MM (Aus Geo), (bottom) TQ; 74–5 JF (Ausc); 76 BB (Aus Geo); 77 (top) Murray Spence (Aus Geo), (bottom) TQ.

NEW SOUTH WALES
Page 78 AG; 79 TNSW; 80 AG; 82 Phillip Hayson; 83 AG (EAP); 84 JF (Ausc); 86–7 JM; 88 Phillip Hayson; 89 (top) Esther Beaton (Aus Geo), (bottom) AG; 90 DF; 92 EAP; 93 DF; 94 (top & bottom) Mitch Reardon (Aus Geo); 95 (top) DF, (bottom) JM; 96 DF; 98 Peter McNeill; 100 Barry Ashenhurst (Ausc); 101 TNSW; 102 Peter McNeill; 103 TNSW; 104 DF; 105 (top) Jon Poyner, (bottom) DF; 106 Grahame McConnell (Aus Geo); 108 Mike Langford (Aus Geo); 109 Grahame McConnell (Aus Geo), (inset) Mike Langford (Aus Geo); 110–11 Ian Hutton; 112 TNSW; 114 JB (EAP); 115 Ken Stepnell (EAP), (inset) Peter McNeill (Aus Geo); 116 (top) AG, (bottom) DF; 117 AG; 118 DF.

VICTORIA
Page 120 Jonathon Barter; 121 NR (EAP); 123 Gary Lewis (EAP); 124 BB; 125 BB; 126 (top & bottom) ML (Aus Geo); 127 TV, (inset) ML (Aus Geo); 128 JLR (Ausc); 129 BB; 131 Paul Sinclair; 132 Paul Sinclair; 133 (top) Gary Lewis (EAP), (bottom) TV; 134–5 Peter Jarver; 136 AG; 139 DF (Aus Geo);

140 DF (Aus Geo); 141 DF (Aus Geo); 142 Rory McGuinness (Aus Geo); 143 AG; (inset) Rory McGuinness (Aus Geo); 145 JM; 146 Ken Stepnell (EAP), (inset) ML (Aus Geo); 147 Steve Ryan; 148 JB; 149 (top & bottom) ML (Aus Geo); 150–1 Steve Ryan; 152 TV; 154 JM; 155 JM.

TASMANIA
Page 156 DF (Aus Geo); 157 Kevin Deacon; 158 JS; 160 TT; 161 EAP; 162 Dick Smith (Aus Geo); 163 John de la Roche (TT); 164 Rob Blaker; 166 Bruce Miller (Aus Geo); 167 George Apostolidis (TT); 168 George Apostolidis (TT); 170–1 Grant Dixon; 172 Esther Beaton (Aus Geo); 173 DF (Aus Geo); 174 BB (Aus Geo); 176 Rob Walls (Aus Geo); 177 JS; 178 JS.

SOUTH AUSTRALIA
Page 180 CR; 181 PA (Aus Geo); 182 JM; 184 SATC; 185 JM; 186 & 187 SATC; 189 Melinda Berge (Aus Geo); 190 CR; 191 Alex Steffe (LT); 192 SATC; 193 Stewart Roper (LT), (inset) SATC; 194 (top & bottom) Rachel Pitts; 196 BB (Aus Geo); 198 NR (EAP); 199 ML (Aus Geo), (inset) SATC; 200 CR; 202 & 203 SATC; 204–5 AG; 206 Ted Mead, (inset) BD (LT).

WESTERN AUSTRALIA
Page 208 BD (LT); 209 DF (Aus Geo); 210 BBE (LT); 212 LS (LT); 213 Dick Bielby (LT); 214 AG; 216 AG; 217 JL (LT); 218 BBE (LT); 220 AG; 221 Paul Raffaele (Aus Geo); 222 BD (LT); 224 (top) Heidi Marfurt (EAP), (bottom) AG; 225 BBE (LT); 226 AG; 228 LS (LT); 229 Gary Bell (Ausc); 230–1 JM; 232 AG; 234 Ben & Lyn Cropp (Ausc); 235 Paul Raffaele (Aus Geo); 236 Mark Spencer (Ausc); 238 AG; 239 BBE (LT), (inset) Paul Raffaele (Aus Geo); 241 AG; 242 AG; 243 Dick Smith (Aus Geo); 244–5 JF (Ausc); 246 BB; 247 DF (Aus Geo).

NORTHERN TERRITORY
Page 248 DH (Aus Geo); 249 DH (Aus Geo); 250 DH (Aus Geo); 252 AG; 253 DH (Aus Geo); 254 AG; 255 Barry Skipsey (Aus Geo), (inset) DH (Aus Geo); 256 AG; 258 Murray Spence (Aus Geo); 259 DH (Aus Geo), (inset) JL (Aus Geo).

TAKING CARE
Page 260 Robbie Newman (Aus Geo); 261 (top) Warren Field (Aus Geo), (bottom) BB (Aus Geo); 262 SATC; 263 (top & bottom) MM (Aus Geo); 264 TQ; 265 (top) Simon Carter (Aus Geo), (bottom) JL (Aus Geo); 266 MM (Aus Geo).

ABBREVIATIONS

AG	Andrew Gregory
Ausc	Auscape International
Aus Geo	Australian Geographic
BB	Bill Bachman
BBE	Bill Belson
BD	Brett Dennis
CR	Christo Reid
DF	Don Fuchs
DH	David Hancock
EAP	Explore Australia Publishing
JB	J. P. & E. S. Baker
JF	Jean-Paul Ferrero
JL	Jiri Lochman
JM	John Meier
JLR	Jean-Marc La Roque
JS	Joe Shemesh
LS	Len Stewart
LT	Lochman Transparencies
ML	Mike Leonard
MM	Mike McCoy
NR	Nick Rains Photography
PA	Peter Aitchison
SATC	South Australian Tourism Commission
TNSW	Tourism New South Wales
TQ	Tourism Queensland
TT	Tourism Tasmania
TV	Tourism Victoria